Inside System Storage:
Volume III

Tony Pearson

Inside System Storage: Volume III

Tony Pearson

Foreword by Carlos Pratt

Dedication

To my fellow bloggers, whose differences of opinion and diversity of thought made my time spent in the blogosphere truly exciting

To my friends and family, especially those who follow my blog in an effort to figure out what I do for a living

To my coworkers at IBM, many of whom helped me research topics, and provided insight and ideas for writing my blog

Contents

Foreword

When Tony told me of his second book, I was quite surprised since I thought he was jumping too fast on an update of his first excellent book, *Inside System Storage Volume 1*.

Surprise, SURPRISE!! Much better than an update, it was an EXCELLENT compilation of exchanges of opinion and some controversy, mainly through his blog.

On his second book he reminded us in many ways how quickly companies can disappear when he mentions that we all would remember where we were when we learned that STK was bought by SUN. Well today I have friends that have changed companies **twice:** STK→SUN→Oracle. Anyone remember where you were when it was announced that Oracle was buying SUN? I do …

Not long ago, while doing a quick social visit to Tony's office, he mentioned to me he was writing a third book and I immediately asked him to share with me his draft. Once again my friend surprised me when, instead of a draft, he handed me the practically final version of the book.

If you are one of the few people who read forewords, let me tell you that you will not be disappointed. Tony gives continuity to his *Volume II* and goes through his blog history and on his already known style, OPENLY publishes all points of view, even if that view is a reply on his blog that directly attacks him. This last shows one of the qualities that I admire on Tony: he has nothing to hide, so he doesn't care what types of comments he gets, and he knows that in the end he wins.

Ever since I met Tony around thirteen years ago I have identified him as a storage professional with brilliant points of view on storage and in many ways a storage visionary. As a simple example, let me just say that he was one of the first storage bloggers in the world.

I hope that reading this blog-history book, third on his collection, helps the reader not only to enjoy the reading, but also to see how storage has evolved not only for IBM but for the rest of the digital storage industry from the view of a person that has lived much of its evolution.

Carlos Pratt

IBM Storage Performance

October 1, 2011

Introduction

This blog-based book, or "blook", comprises the postings from *Inside System Storage*, a blog discussing computer storage concepts in general and IBM System Storage™ products in particular. It picks up where Volume II left off: the blog posts are presented in chronological order, from May 2008 to March 2009. Each month is its own chapter, and I provide an introduction of what was going on for each month.

Feedback from my first book was appreciation for the *behind-the-scenes* insight into the workings of IBM. Early in my career, one of my coworkers lent me his copy of Tracy Kidder's non-fiction book *Soul of a New Machine*, which tracked a team of hardware and software engineers at Data General over the course of a year as they built a new computer system. My coworker claimed he personally knew Tom West, one of the engineers in the book. That book provided me a glimpse into the world of IT hardware and software development.

Encouraged by this feedback, I provided even more *behind-the-scenes* in my second book. One IBM executive told me Volume II could serve as a textbook example of the types of unhealthy work environments described by Robert Sutton in his book *The No Asshole Rule*. I had not read that book until after Volume II was published. Six months later, New Line Cinema and Warner Bros. Studios would release the movie *Horrible Bosses*. Coincidence?

In this book, I dial it back at bit, focusing instead on the technical. Through these books, I hope that I can help the future generation of storage administrators, engineers, and sales and marketing personnel deal with their challenges, both technical and managerial.

I have always enjoyed telling stories as a way to build relationships, explain complicated concepts, and pass on knowledge and wisdom. As with any good story, there are four essential elements: setting, characters, conflict, and resolution.

Setting

I started working for IBM in June 1986 as a storage software engineer on DFSMS for z/OS, the storage management component of the mainframe operating system. I worked my way up to lead architect and spent a lot of time traveling to visit clients. I have been known throughout IBM for my

"Tony stories" and "Trip Reports" in which I would pass on my observations and insights.

After the Y2K scare subsided, I was asked to be the lead architect for what is now called IBM Tivoli Storage Productivity Center. This was started in IBM's Systems and Technology Group (hardware division) but was transferred to IBM's Software Group, replacing me and many others with Tivoli personnel.

My mainframe background allowed me to join the "Linux on System z" team, and I led a group of testers to qualify all of our disk and tape products for this new operating system, and pursue a variety of Linux-related projects.

In 2003, I switched over to IBM Marketing, promoting a variety of new products, including IBM's SAN Volume Controller, Tivoli Storage Productivity Center, and SAN File System.

By January 2006, I was named chief marketing strategist for the IBM System Storage product line. Here's a subset of what I accomplished for IBM in my short time on the job:

- Coordinated a Quantified Customer Value (QCV) study of over 1500 companies.

- Based on the survey results, developed a powerful "System Storage" strategy that was based on helping clients address IT challenges, rather than organized around existing product categories.

- Coordinated 18 customer focus groups in USA, Europe, and Asia to make sure the strategy resonated in different languages and different cultures.

- Traveled the world "socializing" this new strategy with IBM sales reps, IBM Business Partners and clients.

- Adopted new forms of Social Media, producing not just a successful blog, but also the first historic IBM product launch in the virtual world known as "Second Life".

- Won the "Best Recognized Brand" Impact award for IBM System Storage products from Liquid Brand Marketing agency. Twice.

I started blogging on September 1, 2006 to promote IBM's 50th anniversary of disk systems. Of the thousands of blogs written by IBMers, most are private inside the IBM firewall accessible to other IBM employees only. Mine is public, outside the firewall, accessible to all: clients, prospects, IBM Business Partners, and yes, even our competitors.

A year later, I was ranked one of the top 10 storage bloggers by *Network World* magazine. Unfortunately, we had just gotten a new VP of Marketing who felt social media was not a viable activity and pressured me to leave her department. I lucked out, as there was an opening in the IBM Executive Briefing Center in Tucson, AZ that welcomed me to transfer over.

My new manager allowed me to continue blogging, and by 2009 I was ranked third most influential IBM blogger on IBM DeveloperWorks.

Characters

It might also help to understand the key players in the IT Storage marketplace. At the time of this writing, there are estimated over 40 storage system vendors. IBM, Hewlett-Packard (HP), EMC, Hitachi Data Systems (HDS), Dell, Network Appliance (NetApp), and Sun Microsystems make up the "top seven" that account for over 70 percent of the revenues. Some of the key bloggers in this book are:

- My arch nemesis Barry Burke (*BarryB, Storage Anarchist),* Mark Twomey (*StorageZilla),* and Chuck Hollis (*ChuckH)* from EMC
- Hu Yoshida and Claus Mikkelsen from HDS
- Barry Whyte (*BarryW),* Tom Rauchut, Carlos Pratt, and Alan Lepofsky from IBM
- Val Bercovici (*ValB)* and Kostadis Roussos from NetApp
- Jeff Savit and Taylor Allis from Sun Microsystems
- Marc Farley from 3PAR
- Mark Peters and Steve Duplessie from Enterprise Strategy Group
- John Toigo, an independent consultant
- Stephen Foskett, an independent blogger
- Robin Harris, blogger at StorageMojo

Conflict

Most in the blogosphere agree that the comments are often more interesting than the blog post itself. Not all blogs allow for comments, but mine does. This makes the blog more interactive. Much of the "conflict" in this book is buried in the comments.

The new VP of Marketing for IBM System Storage was "classically trained" in marketing 20 years ago, and had very strong opinions on how to do it properly. Some of her ideas will appear in this book. She commissioned my replacement to come up with a new set of themes, under the moniker of "Information Infrastructure". I gave the original set, "Virtualization, Availability, Management, Performance" (VAMP), the nickname "Vampire" themes, and I facetiously countered with my own "SCARY" set with Security, Compliance, Availability and Retention. I couldn't think of any words that started with the letter "Y". It was October of 2007 and Halloween was in the air.

In addition to this shake-up in management, IBM was promoting its new strategy, and had just made two major acquisitions that affected storage. The first, XIV, had developed an innovative disk system, and the second, Diligent, had developed an innovative virtual tape system with data deduplication capability. This book spans the year after these two acquisitions, the development and promotion of this new IBM strategy, and my new job as a Senior Consultant at the Tucson Executive Briefing Center.

Resolution

To my surprise, the SCARY themes I proposed were accepted, but rearranged to spell CARS to make it easier for salespeople to remember.

However, we were instructed that when presenting these four themes, we needed to do them in ASRC order. The marketing person in charge of Availability wanted to be first, and the person in charge of Compliance wanted to be last. Why? Psychologists agree that when people are presented with a list, they tend to remember the first and last items more than the ones in the middle.

The graphics on the cover of this book were created by professional graphics designers to represent each "critical success factor":
- Availability – A heartbeat monitor (red)
- Security – A padlock (green)
- Retention – A magnifying glass inspecting the Rosetta Stone (blue)
- Compliance – A gavel from a legal courtroom (purple)

Even though I am not in marketing anymore, the new VP of Marketing for IBM System Storage finds my blogs a valuable contribution to their overall efforts to promote IBM's solutions and offerings.

Blogging has been deeply rewarding. I have been asked to write articles for magazines, participate in press conferences and magazine interviews, and be part of Q&A panels and webinars. Regardless of which department I work for, using my blog to provide value to my fellow IBM teammates, IBM Business Partners, and our clients has been a good career move.

About this Book

You can order additional copies of this book, and all the other books in my series, directly from my publisher LULU, online at:

> http://www.lulu.com/spotlight/990_tony

In this book, I try to provide additional insight and observations. These are designated with a photo or graphical icon introducing side commentary. Each post starts with a heading including the date, title, and post number. All posts are numbered 293 to 422.

External links that appeared in my blog are shown in [brackets]. If I reference another post contained in this book, I designate that by post number [#nnn]. If you would like to follow the links, go to the original post on the *Inside System Storage* blog, which can be found at:

> https://www.ibm.com/developerworks/mydeveloperworks/blogs/InsideSystemStorage/

If that is too much typing for you, try the short URL:

> http://ibm.co/brAeZ0 (last character is a zero)

More information on the IBM System Storage offerings can be found at:

> www.ibm.com/storage

Blog postings and comments have been edited for content and formatting. All fonts were converted to 10-point Book Antiqua. I have tried to set the highlighting, bold, underline, and italics to match the posts as they appeared on the web page. Royalty-free graphics purchased from Shutterstock that appear in this book were converted to horizontal alignment with square wrapping style and reduced in size as appropriate.

Comments related to the blog post are included where relevant, with personal emails redacted. When I comment as the author, I will list this as either "Response" or "Addition". Comments from others may or may not reflect the views and opinions of the companies they work for.

I personally designed the front and back cover art using the open source GNU Image Manipulation Program (GIMP) graphics editing tool. The graphics were used as part of the "Information Infrastructure" marketing campaign introduced during the time span of this book.

There is a "Reference" section in the back, including the following:

- Blog Roll
- IBM Social Computing Guidelines
- Glossary of Acronyms and Terms (GOAT)
- Units of Storage

It was fellow IBMer Mike Stanek who suggested that I develop a glossary of acronyms and terms, and I give him credit for coining the term "GOAT". This GOAT serves as a quick reference guide for acronyms and other key phrases.

I hope you enjoy this book.

Acknowledgements

I would like to thank my editor, Susan Pollard, for reviewing, editing and formatting this book. I would like to thank my colleagues, Jack Arnold, Curtis Neal, Harley Puckett, and Scott Venuti for their technical reviews, emotional support and assistance. I would like to also thank the EBC support staff: Kris Keller, Kristy Knight, Lee Olguin, and Shelly Jost. Finally I would like to thank my manager, Bill Terry, for allowing me to continue blogging.

2008

May

The two busiest times at the Tucson Executive Briefing Center are April/May and October/November. This is probably due to the fact that IBM's sales commission plans are based on the first and second half of each calendar year. With recent acquisitions of XIV and Diligent, there were a lot of companies coming to Tucson for a storage briefing.

2008 May 1 — Management Complexity Factor for Media and Entertainment Industry (293)

Continuing this week's theme on "best of breed", some questions arise: How is this calculated or determined? How is one storage solution "better" than another? Which attributes weigh more heavily in the decision?

Some attributes are directly measurable, like storage performance. For this, gather up a list of all the storage products you are interested in, go to the [Storage Performance Council website], determine whether SPC-1 or SPC-2 more closely matches your application workload, and then choose the best product from the benchmarks, discarding any vendors that don't bother to have benchmarks posted. The new SPC-2 benchmark was created, in part, to address new workloads for the Media and Entertainment industry. (For a comparison of the two, see my post [SPC benchmarks for Disk System Performance].)

However, other attributes, like "easy to manage", are not as straightforward to measure. One client compared the complexity of different solutions by counting the number of cables involved to connect the various parts of each solution. Only external cables were considered. All of the cables inside an IBM System Storage DS8000 would not be counted. By this measure, a single IBM System z10 EC mainframe connected to a single IBM DS8000 disk system over a few FICON cables would therefore be "less complicated" than a thousand x86 servers connected via FCP SAN switches to dozens of disk systems.

I thought of this when fellow IBM blogger Alan Lepofsky posted [Lenovo x300 versus Macbook Air commercial], pointing to this YouTube video:

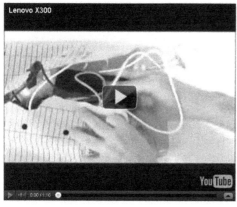

[YouTube video: Lenovo x300 vs. MacBook Air]

But counting cables only handles the hardware part of the interconnections. You have to also consider the interconnections between the software, between users, and between IT administrators. It is not always obvious where those connections are and how to count them into consideration.

This month, IBM introduced the first "Management Complexity Factor" (MCF) for the Media and Entertainment industry. IBM MCF, a result of IBM's acquisition of NovusCG, and is an essential part of "Storage Optimization Services" being offered by IBM. Here is an excerpt from the [IBM Press Release]:

> "'Media companies are facing a double-edged sword with the exponential rise in digital media storage needs, coupled with concerns about optimizing storage to be more efficient,' said Steve Canepa, vice president of Media and Entertainment, IBM. 'By quickly and cost-effectively analyzing the interconnected IT and storage environments that increasingly comprise media operations, MCF for Media helps our clients identify opportunities for improvement and align their IT and business strategies.'"

Since 1995, IBM has invested more than $18 billion on public acquisitions, making it the most acquisitive company in the technology industry based on volume of transactions.

IBM has a strong global focus on the media and entertainment industry across all of its services and products, serving all the major industry segments -- entertainment, publishing, information providers, media networks, and advertising.

For more information on IBM, please visit [www.ibm.com/media].

technorati tags: SPC, storage, performance, benchmarks, SPC-1, SPC-2, complexity, Steve Canepa, IBM, MCF, acquisitions

Comment: by Barry Burke (EMC), the Storage Anarchist

Oh, come on, Tony.

You can't seriously suggest that SPC-1 and SPC-2 are the only two possible workloads in the world.

If they were, then why is the SPC spending so much time creating SPC-3? Truth be told, we'll have to get to probably SPC-10 before there's any chance that the SPC covers any significant subset of real-world workloads.

And even then, it's extremely doubtful that any of them will represent the workloads that today's DMX handles on a daily basis. But that's not the point of your post, so we'll save that for another day.

TTFN!

 A lot of people enjoy my analogies. In the following post, I compare Sun Microsystems' "Open Storage" project with re-heating frozen dinners from Simply Dinners. Even my friends at Sun felt the analogy worked well. It was to kick off my week-long theme related to "Do It Yourself" projects spanning May 5 to 8.

2008 May 5 — Simply Dinners and Open Storage from Sun (294)

Happy [Cinco De Mayo] everyone!

I had a great weekend, participating in this year's ["World Laughter Day"] yesterday, and preparing for tonight's festivities found me pulling out the various packages from "Simply Dinners" from my freezer.

A Tucson-based company, [Simply Dinners] offers an alternative to restaurant eating. My sister went there, assembled a set of freezer-proof plastic bags containing all the right ingredients based on specific recipes, and gave them to me for my birthday, and they have been sitting in my freezer ever since... until last weekend.

My sister was careful to choose items that fit my [Paleolithic Diet] that my nutritionist has me on. However, I was skeptical that any plastic bag full of frozen groceries would be any better than anything I could assemble on my own. I did, after all, attend "chef school" and do know how to cook well. Each package was intended to be a "dinner for two" but, since I am single, was two meals each for me.

So, I decided to try them out, which would also give me more room in my freezer for incoming items, and they came out very well. The outside of each plastic bag was a label that explained all the steps required to heat the food. Partially-cooked vegetables were wrapped in foil, and went in for the last 10 minutes of cooking the meat. The process was straightforward, and the meals were delicious, but nothing I could not have done on my own with a recipe and a trip to the grocery store.

The question is whether someone with little or no skills could achieve similar or acceptable results. I have friends who are limited to assembling sandwiches from luncheon meats and cheese slices, as anything involving heat other than simply boiling water is beyond their skills.

What does this have to do with storage? Blogger Taylor Allis from Sun Microsystems has a few posts [Sun is on to something - Open Storage] and [An Easier Storage Platform - OpenSolaris] that explain Sun's recent press release [Sun Microsystems Extends World's First Open Storage Platform with New Services and Tools in OpenSolaris Operating System].

The key difference between "cooking for yourself" and "building your own storage" is that you aren't building storage for just yourself. Unless you are a one-person SMB company, you are building storage that all of your employees and managers count on to do their jobs, and by extension your customers and stockholders count on.

Of course I had to read responses from others before jumping in with my thoughts. Dave Raffo from Storage Soup writes [Sun going down in storage], feeling this is yet another indication that Sun has lost their mind, recounting previous events that support that theory. EMC blogger Mark Twomey in his StorageZilla posts [When Open Isn't] felt a little bit guilty kicking a competitor when down. EMC blogger Chuck Hollis questions the reasons people might be tempted to even try this in his post [Do-it-Yourself Storage]. Here's an excerpt:

> "Vendor Lock-In?
>
> I really, really struggle with this concept, I do. Here's why:
>
> Anything I use and get comfortable with -- well, I'm 'locked in' to a certain degree. If I use a lot of storage software X; well, I'm sort locked in, aren't I? Or, if I put my servers-as-storage on a three-year lease, I'm kind of locked in, aren't I?"
>
> > (For EMC, vendor lock-in is great when customers are using and comfortable with EMC products, and awful when they use and are comfortable with storage from someone else. But nobody who is "comfortable" with what they have ever complains about "vendor lock-in," do they? It's the ones who are growing uncomfortable and feel trapped in changing. How involved a company's use of EMC's proprietary interfaces is can greatly determine the obstacles

in switching to a different vendor. Of course, if you count yourself as someone growing uncomfortable with your existing storage vendor, IBM can help you fix that problem, but that is a subject for another post.)

Worried about "vendor lock-in"? Try "admin lock-in", where you must keep a storage admin around because he or she was the one that put your storage together. I've seen several companies held hostage by their system admins for home-grown scripts that serve as "duct tape for the enterprise". The other issue is whether you have storage admins who have the necessary hardware and software engineering skills to put suitable storage together. There are some very smart storage admins I know who could, and others that would have a difficult time with this.

No doubt this is promising for the home office. I myself have taken several PCs that were running older versions of Windows but were not powerful enough to upgrade to Windows Vista, wiped them clean, loaded Linux, and configured them from everything from simple browser workstations to full LAMP application server configurations. While this might sound easy, I am a professional hardware and software engineer with Linux skills. I have no doubt that someone with sufficient engineering and Solaris skills could put together a storage system for home use.

One area where Sun definitely benefits from this "Open Storage" approach is to develop Solaris skills. I have no personal experience with OpenSolaris, but assume that if you learn it, you would be able to switch over to full Solaris quite easily. Today, most people have Windows, Linux and/or MacOS skills coming into the workforce, and this could be Sun's way of getting new fresh faces who understand Solaris commands to replace retiring "baby boomers". The lack of Solaris-knowledgeable admins is perhaps one reason why companies are switching to IBM AIX, Linux or Windows in their data center.

Certainly, IBM's strategic choice to support Linux has been a great success. People learn Linux on their home systems, and at school, and are able to carry those skills to Linux running on everything from the smallest IBM blade server to IBM's biggest mainframe.

The videos on Sun for the "recipes" on how to put together various "storage configurations in ten minutes" appear simpler than last summer's "How to hack an Apple iPhone to switch away from AT&T" procedures.

⌀technorati tags: Cinco De Mayo, World Laughter Day, Simply Dinners, Paleolithic, diet, Taylor Allis, OpenSolaris, Solaris, open storage, Dave Raffo, Mark Twomey, Chuck Hollis, EMC, Sun, Linux, Windows, MacOS, mainframe, blade, recipes, hack, Apple, iPhone, AT&T

Comment from Taylor Allis (Sun Microsystems)

Our Open Storage announcement drummed up interest in the industry - and for good reason...

 There is nothing worse than government hypocrisy. The same government that mandates that private corporations be required to keep and protect all their emails, to make them available for eDiscovery, failed to do so itself.

2008 May 6 — Washington Gets e-Discovery Wakeup Call (295)

Continuing my week's theme on how bad things can get following the "Do-it-Yourself" plan, I start with James Rogers' piece in *Byte and Switch*, titled [Washington Gets E-Discovery Wakeup Call]. Here's an excerpt:

> "A court filing today reveals there may be gaps in the backup tapes the White House IT shop used to store email. It appears that messages from the crucial early stages of the Iraq War, between March 1 and May 22, 2003, can't be found on tape. So, far from exonerating the White House staffers, the latest turn of events casts an even harsher light on their email policies.

> Things are not exactly perfect elsewhere in the federal government, either. A recent [report from the Government Accountability Office (GAO)] identified glaring holes in agencies' antiquated email preservation techniques. Case in point: printing out emails and storing them in physical files."

You might think that laws requiring email archives are fairly recent. For corporations, they began with laws like Sarbanes-Oxley that the second President Bush signed into law back in 2002. However, it appears that laws for US Presidents to keep their emails were in force since 1993, back when the *first* President Clinton was in office.

> (We might as all get used to saying this in case we have Hilary as our "second" President Clinton next January!)

In *Ars Technica*, Timothy B. Lee wrote [An elephant never forgets? George W. Bush's lost e-mails]. Here's an excerpt:

> "The Federal Record Act requires the head of each federal agency to ensure that documents related to that agency's official business

be preserved for federal archives. The Watergate-era Presidential Records Act augmented the FRA framework by specifically requiring the president to preserve documents related to the performance of his official duties. A [1993 court decision] held that these laws applied to electronic records, including e-mails, which means that the president has an obligation to ensure that the e-mails of senior executive branch officials are preserved.

In 1994, the Clinton administration reacted to the previous year's court decision by rolling out an automated e-mail-archiving system to work with the Lotus-Notes-based e-mail software that was in use at the time. The system automatically categorized e-mails based on the requirements of the FRA and PRA, and it included safeguards to ensure that e-mails were not deliberately or unintentionally altered or deleted.

When the Bush administration took office, it decided to replace the Lotus Notes-based e-mail system used under the Clinton Administration with Microsoft Outlook and Exchange. The transition broke compatibility with the old archiving system and the White House IT shop did not immediately have a new one to put in its place.

Instead, the White House has instituted a comically primitive system called 'journaling,' in which (to quote from a [recent Congressional report]), 'a White House staffer or contractor would collect from a 'journal' e-mail folder in the Microsoft Exchange system copies of e-mails sent and received by White House employees.' These would be manually named and saved as 'PST' files on White House servers.

One of the more vocal critics of the White House's e-mail-retention policies is Steven McDevitt, who was a senior official in the White House IT shop from September 2002 until he left in disgust in October 2006. He points out what would be obvious to anyone with IT experience: the system wasn't especially reliable or tamper-proof."

So we have White House staffers manually creating PST files, and other government agencies printing out their emails and storing them in file cabinets. When I first started at IBM in 1986, before Notes or Exchange existed, we used PROFS on VM on the mainframe, and some of my colleagues printed out their emails and filed them in cabinets. I can understand how government employees, who might have grown up using mainframe systems like PROFS, might have just continued the practice when they switched to Personal Computers.

Perhaps the new incoming White House staffs hired by George W. Bush were more familiar with Outlook and Exchange and, rather than learning to use IBM Lotus Notes and Domino, found it easier just to switch over. I am not going to debate the pros and cons of "Lotus Notes/Domino" versus "Microsoft Outlook/Exchange" as IBM has automated email archiving systems that work great for both of these, as well as for Novell GroupWise. So, taking the benefit of the doubt, when President Bush took over, he tossed out the previous administration's staff and brought in his own people, and let them choose the office productivity tools they were most comfortable with. Fair enough; happens every time a new President takes office. No big surprise there.

However, doing this without a clear plan on how to continue to comply with the email archive laws already on the books, and that it continues to be bad **several years later**, is appalling. I can understand why businesses are upset in deploying mandated archiving solutions when their own government doesn't have similar automation in place.

technorati tags: James Rogers, Washington, White House, Iraq War, Sarbanes-Oxley, George W. Bush, incompetence, Timothy B. Lee, Steven McDevitt, elephant, Federal Record Act, email, e-mail, archive, IBM, Lotus, Notes, Domino, Microsoft, Outlook, Exchange, Novell, GroupWise

The "blog fights" I have had over the years against EMC blogger Barry Burke (the Storage Anarchist) are now legendary in the blogosphere, earning him the title of my "arch-nemesis"!

2008 May 7 — The Pot and the Kettle (296)

While HDS blogger Hu Yoshida and IBM blogger Barry Whyte make a [great case for why you should buy IBM SAN Volume Controller], my favorite arch-nemesis and fellow blogger BarryB on his Storage Anarchist blog feels the SVC is "blue spray paint".

BarryB's latest round of red-meat rhetoric is his amusing post [This is like déjà vu all over again], titled after a [quote from Yogi Berra]. BarryB pokes fun at Andy Monshaw's comments in Chris Preimesberger's eWeek article [IBM's Big Storage Picture], and my post earlier this week about Sun's "Open Storage" initiative [Simply Dinners and Open Storage from Sun #294], as if the two were somehow connected.

He feels I was unfair to accuse EMC of "proprietary interfaces" without spelling out what I was referring to. Here are just two, along with the whines we hear from customers that relate to them.

EMC PowerPath multipathing driver

Typical whine: *"I just paid a gazillion dollars to renew my annual EMC PowerPath license, so you will have to come back in 12 months with your SVC proposal. I just can't see explaining to my boss that an SVC eliminates the need for EMC PowerPath, throwing away all the good money we just spent on it, or to explain that EMC chooses not to support SVC as one of PowerPath's many supported devices."*

EMC SRDF command line interface

Typical whine: *"My storage admins have written tons of scripts that all invoke EMC SRDF command line interfaces to manage my disk mirroring environment, and I would hate for them to re-write this to use IBM's (also proprietary) command line interfaces instead."*

Certainly BarryB is correct that IBM still has a few remaining "proprietary" items of its own. IBM has been in business over 80 years, but it was only the last 10-15 years that IBM made a strategic shift away from proprietary and over to open standards and interfaces. The transformation to "openness" is not yet complete, but we have made great progress. Take these examples:

- The System z mainframe - IBM had opened the interfaces so that both Amdahl and Fujitsu made compatible machines. Unlike Apple which forbids cloning of this nature, IBM is now the single source for mainframes because the other two competitors could not keep up with IBM's progress and advancements in technology.

  (**Update:** Due to legal reasons, the statements referring to Hercules and other S/390 emulators have been removed.)

- The z/OS operating system - While it is possible to run Linux on the mainframe, most people associate the z/OS operating system with the mainframe. This was opened up with UNIX System Services to satisfy requests from various governments. It is now a full-fledged UNIX operating system, recognized by the [Open Group] that certifies it as such.

- As BarryB alludes, the unique interfaces for disk attachment to System z known as Count-Key-Data (CKD) was published so that both EMC and HDS can offer disk systems to compete with IBM's high-end disk offerings. Linux on System z supports standard Fibre Channel, allowing you to attach an IBM SVC and anyone's storage. Both z/OS and Linux on System z support NAS storage, so IBM N series, NetApp, even EMC Celerra could be used in that case.

- The System i itself is still proprietary, but recently IBM announced that it will now support standard block size (512 bytes) instead of the awkward 528 byte blocks that only IBM and EMC support today.

That means that any storage vendor will be able to sell disk to the System i environment.

- Advanced copy services, like FlashCopy and Metro Mirror, are as proprietary as the similar offerings from EMC and HDS, with the exception that IBM has licensed them to both EMC and HDS. Thanks to cross-licensing, you can do [FlashCopy on EMC] equipment. Getting all the storage vendors to agree to open standards for these copy services is still work in progress under [SNIA], but at least people who have coded z/OS JCL batch jobs that invoke FlashCopy utilities can work the same between IBM and EMC equipment.

So for those out there who thought that my comment about EMC's proprietary interfaces in any way implied that IBM did not have any of its own, the proverbial ["pot calling the kettle black"] so to speak, I apologize.

BarryB shows off his [PhotoShop skills] with the graphic below. I take it as a compliment to be compared to an All-American icon of business success.

TonyP and Monopoly's Mr. Pennybags

Separated at Birth?

However, BarryB meant it as a reference back to a long time ago when IBM was a monopoly of the IT industry, which, according to [IBM's History], ended in 1973. In other words, IBM stopped being a monopoly before EMC ever existed as a company, and long before I started working for IBM myself.

The anti-trust lawsuit that BarryB mentions happened in 1969, which forced IBM to separate some of the software from its hardware offerings, and prevented IBM from making various acquisitions for years to follow, forcing IBM instead into technology partnerships. I'm glad that's all behind us now!

⌑**technorati tags:** HDS, Hu Yoshida, IBM, Barry Whyte, SVC, BarryB, Storage Anarchist, blue, spray paint, red-meat rhetoric, Yogi Berra, Andy Monshaw, Chris Preimesberger, eWeek, Open storage, Sun, proprietary interfaces, mainframe, z/OS, UNIX, Open Group, CKD, NAS, NetApp, Photoshop

Comment: by Barry Burke (EMC), the Storage Anarchist
Thanks. You've made my point much better than I did myself.

And glad you like the photo - hauntingly similar, huh?

PowerPath, by the way, isn't replaced by SVC. At least, not until the SVC can:

- Load balance across multiple host HBAs, each ideally targeted at different paths to the target storage for maximum availability -- and dynamically balancing the workload based on the actual real-time performance of each path.

- Transparently redirect I/O's should one path or HBA fail or become overloaded.

- Encrypt/decrypt all the data for one or more LUNS -- on the fly, and irrespective of which HBA port/path (separately licensed feature built into the latest version of PowerPath).

(Maybe SVC already does all these things -- if so, I'm sure BarryW will chime in soon to correct me).

As to SRDF -- moving from one proprietary CLI to another is indeed undesirable.

But moving from SRDF to IBM's equivalents also requires sacrificing utility, recoverability and function. Who wants to get locked in to a solution that does less and doesn't scale as large?

And for total transparency, I note that only the blade-server version of the "i" support 512-byte FC interfaces. The workhorse models of the family still rely on 520/528 byte blocks... Is that going to change any time soon?

Comment from Mekbar Kalanlar (Turkey)

Thanks everything ;)

Comment from Barry Whyte (IBM)

As if by magic, a Barry appeared...

So SDD does load balance, failover and all the usual things you would expect from a multi-path driver. It doesn't do encryption, as that would need the same specific hardware/software support in all the devices SDD supports. Must also place some overhead on the host CPU and storage systems. I believe encryption was only recently added to PP and costs even more.

So quite often the entire SVC system, hardware, licenses etc. can be deployed by customers for less than they were paying for their PowerPath licenses, and the SVC license is a one off payment!

Comment from AO
BarryW, you should know by now that there is no free lunch. Your claim about "one off payment" does not fly.

Comment: by Barry Burke (EMC), the Storage Anarchist
PowerPath's encryption option uses the host CPU to do the actual encryption, and doesn't depend upon the hardware in the storage (although it is tightly integrated so that local and remote replicas are accessible by hosts in a Dev or DR scenario).

And I wasn't aware that with SDD I could have two HBAs in a host connected to two separate SVC nodes, each of which are connected to different front-end ports on the storage accessing the same LUN. I had thought that you could only balance through a single SVC node... Interesting.

Must be a bear to keep synchronized -- is there a Redbook that explains the interaction between SDD and the SVC nodes to ensure that data isn't corrupted or lost in the event of a path or node failure?

Comment from Barry Whyte (IBM)
At any one time, a given I/O will be sent down a given path. SDD will load balance work across available preferred paths. SVC will provide guaranteed in-order processing of any I/O. Quite simple really.

In the event of a path or node failure, either SVC would never see the I/O, or the host would never see completion (as per any storage system) - so the host would re-try and all is well. Standard behavior.

AO -- not sure what you mean, capacity license is one off -- maintenance and service another matter.

Comment from AO
True BarryW, but the same would apply to the PowerPath license as well. The SVC license is just like any other SW license, what makes it the fantastic and unique "one off payment" compared to other SW licenses?

Comment from Barry Whyte (IBM)
Is it not the case that PowerPath is an annual license?

Comment from AO
The basic licensing model for PowerPath is an initial licensing fee plus maintenance over the desired time period. Maintenance could then be renewed as with other SW packages. I am sure there are other licensing

schemes available negotiated on quantity etc. but an annual license is not the standard model.

Comment from Jay Maynard (Hercules Developer) aka "Tron Guy"

"Since IBM published the interfaces, some clever x86-server vendors tried to sell IBM-compatible systems based on the [Hercules] emulator, but were closed down because they were unwilling to pay IBM for the z/OS operating system."

Either there are vendors out there that I hadn't heard of (always possible), or else Tony's getting things rather badly wrong: neither of the two vendors I do know about was selling anything based on Hercules.

I'll also note that there are plenty of portions of the z/system architecture that are less than completely documented, or in some cases not at all.
-- Jay

Response from Tony Pearson (IBM)
Jay, it looks like I got things "badly wrong". The two commercial vendors had developed their own S/390 emulation software. However, anyone using Hercules to run TPF, z/OS, z/VM, or z/VSE has to license the latter from IBM.

Here is one story related to one of the commercial vendors:

http://www.itjungle.com/big/big032007-story01.html

Comment from Roger Bowler (Creator of the Hercules ESA/390 Emulator)
Tony, one more thing that's badly wrong is your statement that these vendors were, "unwilling to pay IBM for the z/OS operating system". Neither of the vendors concerned has shown themselves to be in any way unwilling to pay IBM. In fact one of the vendors (PSI) is currently taking legal action to force IBM to accept license fees to permit z/OS to run on the PSI platform, while IBM is adopting the anti-competitive position that they will not license z/OS on any non-IBM platform.

Here's the story:

http://www.tech-news.com/another/ap200704b.html

If you wanted to illustrate IBM's openness, you could hardly have chosen a worse example. IBM's "strategic shift away from proprietary" looks like it's gone into reverse gear as far as the z/OS world is concerned.
--Roger Bowler

Response from Tony Pearson (IBM)

Roger, I was not aware of the on-going litigation. I have removed the statements with an update above.

-- Tony

One night in college, a local bar owner announced "*last call*" and gave everyone a choice, leave now or stay for another three hours. A few of us stayed. He locked the doors with a chain and padlock, as he could not legally be "open for business" after 1:00 am. We didn't feel locked-in, as we were having a good time.

2008 May 8 — More Exploration into Vendor Lock-In (297)

My theme this week was to focus on "Do-it-Yourself" solutions, such as the "open storage" concept presented by Sun Microsystems, but it has morphed into a discussion on vendor lock-in. Both deserve a bit of further exploration.

There were several reasons offered on why someone might pursue a "Do-it-Yourself" course of action.

Building up skills

In my post [Simply Dinners and Open Storage], I suggested that building a server-as-storage solution based on Sun's OpenSolaris operating system could serve to learn more about [OpenSolaris], and by extension, the Solaris operating system. Like Linux, OpenSolaris is open source and has distributions that run on a variety of chipsets, from Sun's own SPARC, to commodity x86 and x86-64 hardware. And as I mentioned in my post [Getting off the island], a version of OpenSolaris was even shown to run successfully on the IBM System z mainframe.

"Learning by Doing" is a strong part of the [Constructivism] movement in education. One Laptop Per Child [OLPC] uses this approach. IBM volunteers in Tucson and 40 other sites [help young students build robots] constructed from [Lego Mindstorms] building blocks. Edward De Bono uses the term [operacy] to refer to the "skills of doing", preferred over just "knowing" facts and figures.

However, I feel OpenSolaris is late to the game. Linux, Windows and MacOS are all well-established x86-based operating systems that most home office/small office users would be familiar with, and OpenSolaris is positioning itself as "the fourth choice".

Familiarity

In my post [Washington Gets e-Discovery Wakeup Call #295], I suggested that the primary motivation for the White House to switch from Lotus Notes over to Microsoft Outlook was familiarity with Microsoft's offerings. Unfortunately, that also meant abandoning a fully-operational automated email archive system for a manual do-it-yourself approach copying PST files from journal folders.

Familiarity also explains why other government employees might print out their emails and archive them on paper in filing cabinets. They are familiar with this process; it allows them to treat email in the same manner as they have treated paper documents in the past.

Cost, Control, and Unique Requirements

The last category of reasons can often result if what you want is smaller or bigger than what is available commercially. There are minimum entry-points for many vendors. If you want something so small that it is not profitable, you may end up doing it yourself. On the other end of the scale, both Yahoo and Google ended up building their data centers with a do-it-yourself approach, because no commercial solutions were available at the time. (IBM now offers [iDataPlex], so that has changed!)

While you could hire a vendor to build a customized solution to meet your unique requirements, it might turn out to be less costly to do-it-yourself. This might also provide some added control over the technologies and components employed. However, as EMC blogger Chuck Hollis correctly pointed out for [Do-it-yourself storage], your solution may not be less costly than existing off-the-shelf solutions from existing storage vendors when you factor in scalability and support costs.

Of course, this all assumes that storage admins building the do-it-yourself storage have enough spare time to do so. When was the last time your storage admins had spare time of any kind? Will your storage admins provide the 24x7 support you could get from established storage vendors? Will they be able to fix the problem fast enough to keep your business running?

From this, I would gather that if you have storage admins more familiar with Solaris than Linux, Windows or MacOS, and select commodity x86 servers from IBM, Sun, HP, or Dell, they could build a solution that has less vendor lock-in than something off-the-shelf from Sun. Let's explore the fears of vendor lock-in further.

The storage vendor goes out of business

Sun has not been doing so well, so perhaps "open storage" was a way to warn existing Sun storage customers that building your own may be the next alternative. The New York Times title of their article says it all: ["Sun Microsystems Posts Loss and Plans to Reduce Jobs"]. Sun is a big company, so I don't expect them to close their doors entirely this year, but certainly fear of being locked-in to any storage vendor's solution gets worse if you fear the vendor might go out of business.

The storage vendor will get acquired by a vendor you don't like

We've seen this before. You don't like vendor A, so you buy kit from vendor B, only to have vendor A acquire vendor B after your purchase. Surprise!

The storage vendor will not support new applications, operating systems, or other new equipment

Here the fear is that the decisions you make today might prevent you from choices you want to make in the future. You might want to upgrade to the latest level of your operating system, but your storage vendor doesn't support it yet. Or maybe you want to upgrade your SAN to a faster bandwidth speed, like 8 Gbps, but your storage vendor doesn't support it yet. Or perhaps that change would require re-writing lots of scripts using the existing command line interfaces (CLI). Or perhaps your admins would require training for the new configuration.

The storage vendor will raise prices or charge you more than you expect on follow-on upgrades

For most monolithic storage arrays, adding additional disk capacity means buying it from the same vendor as the controller. I heard of one company recently who tried to order entry-level disk expansion drawer, at a lower price, solely to move the individual disk drives into a higher-end disk system. Guess what? It didn't work. Most storage vendors would not support such mixed configurations.

If you are going to purchase additional storage capacity to an existing disk system, it should cost no more than the capacity price rate of your original purchase. IBM offers upgrades at the going market rate, but not all competitors are this nice. Some take advantage of the vendor lock-in, charging more for upgrades and pocketing the difference as profit.

Vendor lock-in represents the obstacles in switching vendors in the event the vendor goes out of business, fails to support new software or hardware in the data center, or charges more than you are comfortable with. These obstacles can make it difficult to switch storage vendors, upgrade your applications, or meet other business obligations. IBM SAN Volume Controller and TotalStorage Productivity Center can help reduce or eliminate many of these concerns. IBM Global Services can help you, as much or as little, as you want in this transformation. Here are the four levels of the do-it-yourself continuum:

Let me figure it out myself	Tell me what to do	Help me do it	Do it for me
This is the self-service approach. Go to our website, download an [IBM Redbook], figure out what you need, and order the parts to do-it-yourself.	IBM Global Business Services can help understand your business requirements and tell you what you need to meet them.	IBM Global Technology Services can help design, assemble and deploy a solution, working with your staff to ensure skill and knowledge transfer.	IBM Managed Storage Services can manage your storage, on-site at your location, or at an IBM facility. IBM provides a variety of cloud computing and managed hosting services.

So, if you are currently a Sun server or storage customer concerned about these latest Sun announcements, give IBM a call, we'll help you switch over!

⌐technorati tags: do-it-yourself, OpenSolaris, Solaris, Sun, Linux, SPARC, Yahoo, Google, iDataPlex, x86, x86-64, x64, mainframe, EMC, Chuck Hollis, HP, Dell, SAN, monolithic, disk, storage, system, arrays, open storage, NYT, New York Times, vendor lock-in, IBM, Global Services, GBS, GTS, SVC, TotalStorage, Productivity Center, Managed Storage Services, cloud computing

2008 May 9 — Traveling Next Two Weeks (298)

I'll be traveling the next two weeks.

IBM Systems & Technology Group - Technical Conference

**12 - 15 May, 2008
Los Angeles, CA**

The week of May 11-15, I'll be in Los Angeles, California for the [IBM Systems & Technology Group Technical Conference]. I'll be presenting two topics:

- Understanding Web 2.0 and Digital Archive workloads

- IBM storage strategy - information infrastructure for the new enterprise data center

The week after that, May 18-19, I'll be in Orlando, Florida for [IBM Pulse 2008] conference, which combines Tivoli and Maximo conferences of years past. I'll be co-presenting two topics:

- Data Protection Strategies, with Greg Tevis

- Making your disk storage more flexible and efficient, with Dave Merbach

If you're at either and want to meet up, let me know (either by comment, or click on the ✉email-Tony-Pearson button down in the right panel).

technorati tags: IBM, STC08, TivoliPulse08, pulse08, ibmpulse, Los Angeles, Orlando, Greg Tevis, Dave Merbach, Tivoli, Maximo

Comment from Paul
Hi, it's just in USA? What about Germany?

Regards, Paul

This conference was in Los Angeles, so it was easy enough for me and two other colleagues from the Tucson EBC, Jack Arnold and Glenn Hechler, to take a road trip in a single car. You really get to know a lot about someone spending so much time together!

2008 May 12 — STC 2008 Day 1 (299)

This week I'm in Los Angeles for the Systems Technology Conference (STC '08). We has over 1900 IT professionals attending, of which 1200 IBMers from North America, Latin America, and Asia Pacific regions, as well as another 350 IBM Business Partners. The rest, including me, are worldwide or from other areas.

Enterprise Systems

Last January, IBM reorganized its team to be more client-focused. Instead of focused on products, we are now client-centric, and have teams to cover our large enterprise systems through direct sales force, business systems for sales through our channel business partners, and industry systems for specific areas like deep computing, digital surveillance and retail systems solutions.

In addition to 788 sessions to attend these next four days, we had a few main tent sessions. My third line (my boss' boss' boss) David Gelardi presented Enterprise Systems. This is the group I am in.

Business Systems

Akemi Watanabe presented for Business Systems. Her native language is Japanese, so to do an entire talk in English was quite impressive. Her focus is on SMB accounts, those customers with less than 1000 employees that are looking for easy-to-use solutions. She mentioned IBM's new [Blue Business Platform] which includes Lotus Foundation Start, an Application Integration Toolkit, and the Global Application Marketplace.

Part of this process is the merger of System p and System i into "POWER" systems, and then offering both midrange and enterprise versions of these that run AIX, i5/OS and Linux on POWER. It turns out that only 9 percent of our System i customers are only on this platform. Another 87 percent have Windows, so it makes sense to offer i5/OS on BladeCenter, to consolidate Windows servers from HP, Dell, or Sun over to IBM.

Meanwhile, IBM's strategy to support Linux has proven successful. 25 percent of x86 servers now run Linux. IBM has 600 full-time developers for Linux, over 500 of which contributed to the latest 2.6 kernel development. Our ["chiphopper"] program has successfully ported over 900 applications. There are now over 6500 applications that run on Linux applications, on our strategic alliances with Red Hat (RHEL) and Novell (SUSE) distributions of Linux.

Her recommendation to SMB reps: learn POWER systems, BladeCenter, and Linux. I agree!

Industry Systems

Mary Coucher presented Industry systems. In addition to the game chips for the Sony PlayStation, Nintendo Wii, and Microsoft Xbox-360, this segment focuses on Digital Video Surveillance (DVS), Retail Solutions, Healthcare and Life sciences (HCLS), OEM and embedded solutions, and Deep computing. She mentioned our recently announced iDataPlex solution.

IBM is focused on "real-world-aware" applications, which includes traffic, crime, surveillance, fraud, and RFID enablement. These are streams of data that happen real-time, that need to be dealt with now, not later.

Most people know that IBM built a large portion of the top 500 supercomputers, but a few may not realize that IBM also has delivered solutions to the top 100 green companies. IBM success is explained in more detail in this [Press Release].

The group split up to four different platform meetings: Storage, Modular, Power, and Mainframe. Barry Rudolph presented for the Storage platform. He talked about the explosion in information, business opportunities, risk and cost management. IBM has shifted from being product-focused, to the stack of servers and storage, to our latest focus on solutions across the infrastructure. He mentioned our DARPA win for [PERCS] which stands for productive, easy-to-use, reliable computing system.

Exciting times at IBM!

⌐**technorati tags:** STC08, IBM, North America, Latin America, Asia Pacific, David Gelardi, enterprise systems, Akemi Watanabe, Mary Coucher, HCLS, real-world aware, OEM, deep computing, DVS, RHEL, SUSE, HP, Sun, Dell, Storage, Modular, Power, Mainframe, Barry Rudolph, DARPA, PERCS

2008 May 13 — STC 2008 Day 2 (300)

This is the second day of our Systems Technology Conference (STC08) in Los Angeles, California. We have over 700 break-out sessions, packed in 16 times slots across 47 rooms.

IBM Strategy - the New Enterprise Data Center (NEDC)

In February, IBM launched its corporate-wide strategy for the "new enterprise data center", which I discussed already in my post [Is your data center ready for the future?]

My session was the first in the morning, at 8:30am, but managed to pack the room full of people. A few look like they just rolled in from Brocade's special get-together at Casey's Irish Pub the night before. I presented how IBM's storage strategy for the information infrastructure fits into the greater corporate-wide themes. To liven things up, I gave out copies of my book [Inside System Storage: Volume I] to those who asked or answered the toughest questions.

Data Deduplication and IBM Tivoli Storage Manager (TSM)

IBM's Toby Marek compared and contrasted the various data deduplication technologies and products available, and how to deploy them as the repository for TSM workloads. She is a software engineer for our TSM software product, and gave a fair comparison between IBM System Storage N series Advanced Single Instance Storage (A-SIS), IBM Diligent, and other solutions out in the marketplace. If you are going to combine technologies, it is best to dedupe first, then compress, and finally encrypt the data. She also explained that the many clever ways that TSM does data reduction at the client side greatly reduces the bandwidth traffic over the LAN, as well as reducing disk and tape resources for storage. This includes progressive "incremental forever" backup for file selection, incremental backups for databases, and adaptive sub-file backup. Because of these data reduction techniques, you may not get as much benefit as deduplication vendors claim.

The Business Value of Energy Efficiency Data Centers

Scott Barielle did a great job presenting the issues related to the Green IT data center. He is part of IBM "STG Lab Services" team that does energy efficiency studies for customers. It is not unusual for his team to find potential savings of up to 80 percent of the Watts consumed in a client's data center.

IBM has done a lot to make its products more energy efficient. For example, in the United States, most data centers are supplied three-phase 480V AC current, but this is often stepped down to 208V or 110V with power distribution units (PDUs). IBM's equipment allows for direct connection to this 480V, eliminating the step-down loss. This is available for the IBM System z mainframe, the IBM System Storage DS8000disk system, and larger full-frame models of our POWER-based servers, and will probably be rolled out to some of our other offerings later this year. The end result saves 8 to 14 percent in energy costs.

(Last October, IBM's Randy Malik made a similar case in his presentation: [High Voltage Distributions].)

Scott had some interesting statistics. Typical US data centers only spend about 9 percent of their IT budget on power and cooling costs. The majority of clients that engage IBM for an energy efficiency study are not trying to reduce their operational expenditures (OPEX), but have run out, or close to running out, of total kW rating of their current facility, and have been turned down by their upper management to spend the average $20 million USD needed to build a new one. The cost of electricity in the USA has risen very slowly over the past 35 years, and is more tied to the fluctuations of Natural Gas than it is to Oil prices.

(A recent article in the Dallas News confirmed this: ["As electricity rates go up, natural gas' high prices, deregulation blamed"].)

Cognos v8 - Delivering Operational Business Intelligence (BI) on Mainframe

Mike Biere, author of the book [Business Intelligence for the Enterprise], presented Cognos v8 and how it is being deployed for the IBM System z mainframe. Typically, customers do their BI processing on distributed systems, but 70 percent of the world's business data is on mainframes, so it makes sense to do your BI there as well. Cognos v8 runs on Linux for System z, connecting to z/OS via [HiperSockets].

There are a variety of other BI applications on the mainframe already, including DataQuant, Alphablox, IBI WebFocus, and SAS Enterprise Business Intelligence. In addition to accessing traditional online transaction processing (OLTP) repositories like DB2, IMS, and VSAM, using the [IBM WebSphere Classic Federation Server], Cognos v8 can also read Lotus databases.

Business Intelligence is traditionally a query, reporting, and online analytics process (OLAP) for the top 10 to 15 percent of the company, mostly executives and analysts, for activities like business planning, budgeting, and forecasting. Cognos PowerPlay stores numerical data in an [OLAP cube] for faster processing. OLAP cubes are typically constructed with a batch cycle, using either "Extract, Transfer, Load" [ETL] or "Change Data Capture" [CDC], which plays to the strength of IBM System z mainframe batch processing capabilities. If you are not familiar with OLAP, Nigel Pendse has an article [What is OLAP?] for background information.

Over the past five years, BI has been more and more deployed for the rest of the company, knowledge workers tasked with doing day-to-day operations. This phenomenon is being called "Operational" Business Intelligence.

For more on this, see the IBM Systems Magazine article [Upgrade Your Mainframe with Operational Business Intelligence].

IBM GPFS - Fundamentals and What's New

Glen Corneau, who is on the IBM Advanced Technical Support team for AIX and System p, presented the IBM General Parallel File System (GPFS), which is available for AIX, Linux-x86 and Linux on POWER. Unfortunately, many of the questions were related to Scale-out File Services (SoFS), which my colleague Glenn Hechler was presenting in another room during this same time slot.

GPFS is now in its 11th release since its introduction in 1997. All of the IBM supercomputers on the [Top 500 list] use GPFS. The largest deployment of GPFS is 2241 nodes. A GPFS environment can support up to 256 file systems, each file system can have up to 2 billion files across 2 PB of storage. GPFS supports "Direct I/O" making it a great candidate for Oracle RAC deployments. Oracle 10g automatically detects if it is using GPFS, and sets the appropriate DIO bits in the stream to take advantage of GPFS features.

Glen also covered the many new features of GPFS, such as the ability to place data on different tiers of storage with policies to move to lower tiers of storage or delete after a certain time period, all concepts we call Information Lifecycle Management. GPFS also supports access across multiple locations and offers a variety of choices for disaster recovery (DR) data replication.

Perhaps the only problem with conferences like this is that it can be an overwhelming ["fire hose"] of information!

⊘technorati tags: IBM, STC08, new enterprise data center, storage, strategy, deduplication, TSM, Diligent, A-SIS, Green IT, Toby Marek, Scott Barielle, , Brocade, High Voltage, PDU, DS8000, disk, systems, mainframe, POWER, Randy Malik, OPEX, Natural Gas, Electricity, BI, Cognos, OLAP, GPFS, Glen Corneau, AIX, Top500, Disaster Recovery

2008 May 14 — STC 2008 Day 3 (301)

Continuing this week in Los Angeles, I went to some interesting sessions today at the Systems Technical Conference (STC08).

System Storage Productivity Center (SSPC) - Install and Configuration

Dominic Pruitt, an IT specialist in our IBM Advanced Technical Support team, presented SSPC and how to install and configure it. For those confused about the difference between TotalStorage Productivity Center and System Storage Productivity Center, the former is pure software that you install on a Windows or Linux server, and the latter is an IBM server, pre-installed with Windows 2003, TotalStorage Productivity Center software, TPCTOOL command line interface, DB2 Universal Database, the DS8000 Element Manager, SVC GUI and CIMOM, and [PuTTY] rLogin/SSH/Telnet terminal application software.

SSPC speeds up the deployment of TotalStorage Productivity Center. The [SSPC Planning Worksheet] captures all of the pieces of information you need to activate the machine. On March 8, IBM simplified the [procedure to change the SSPC host name].

Of course, the problem with having a server pre-installed with a lot of software is that there is always someone that wants to customize it further. For those who just want to manage their DS8000 disk systems, for example, it is possible to uninstall the SVC GUI, CIMOM and PuTTY, and re-install them later when you change your mind. As a general rule, it is not wise to mix CIMOMs on the same machine, as it might cause conflicts with TCP ports or Java level requirements, so if you want a different CIMOM than SVC, uninstall the SVC CIMOM first. For those who have SVC, the SSPC replaces the SVC Master Console, so you can safely turn off the SVC CIMOM on your existing SVC Master Consoles.

The base level is TotalStorage Productivity Center "Basic Edition", but you can upgrade the Productivity Center for Disk, Data and Fabric components with license keys. You can also run Productivity Center for Replication, but IBM recommends adding processor and memory to do this (IBM offers this as an orderable option). Whether you have the TotalStorage software or SSPC hardware, Productivity Center has a cool role-to-groups mapping feature. You can create user groups, either on the Windows server, the Active Directory, or other LDAP, and then map which roles should be assigned to users in each group.

Since Productivity Center manages a variety of different disk systems, it has made an attempt to standardize some terminology. The term "storage pool" refers to an extent pool on the DS8000 or a managed disk group on the SAN Volume Controller. Since the DS8000 can support both mainframe CKD volumes and LUNs for distributed systems, the term "volume" refers to a CKD volume or LUN, and "disk" refers to the hard disk drive (HDD).

To help people learn Productivity Center, IBM offers single-day "remote workshops" that use Windows Remote Desktop to allow participants to install, customize and use the software with no travel required.

IBM Integrated Approach to Archiving

Dan Marshall, IBM global program manager for storage and data services on our Global Technology Services team, presented IBM's corporate-wide integration to support archive across systems, software, and services. One attendee asked me why I was there, given that "archive" is one of my areas of subject matter expertise that I present often at the Tucson Executive Briefing Center. I find it useful to watch others present the material, even material that I helped to develop, to see a different slant or spin on each talking point.

Archive is one area that brings all parts of IBM together: systems, software and services. Dan provided a look at archive from the services angle, providing an objective unbiased view of the different software and systems available to solve specific challenges.

Encryption Key Manager (EKM) Design and Implementation

Jeff Ziehm, IBM tape technical sales specialist, presented IBM's EKM software, how it works in a tape environment, and how to deploy it in various environments. Since IBM is all about being open and non-proprietary, the EKM software runs on Java on a variety of IBM and non-IBM operating systems. IBM offers "key tool" command line interface (CLI) for the LTO-4 and TS1120 tape systems and "iKeyMan" graphical user interface (GUI) for theTS1120. Since it runs on Java, IBM Business Partners and technical support personnel often just [download and install EKM] onto their own laptops to learn how to use it.

Virtual Tape Update

We had three presenters at this one. First, Jeff Mulliken, formerly from Diligent and now a full IBM employee, presented the current ProtecTIER software with the HyperFactor technology. Then Abbe Woodcock, IBM tape systems, compared Diligent with IBM's TS7520 and just-announced TS7530 virtual tape libraries. Finally Randy Fleenor, IBM tape sales leader, presented IBM's strategy going forward in tape virtualization.

Let's start with Diligent. The ProtecTIER software runs on any x86-64 server with at least four cores and the correct Emulex host bus adapter (HBA) cards. Using Red Hat Enterprise Linux (RHEL) as a base, the ProtecTIER software performs its deduplication entirely in-line at an "ingest rate" of 400-450 MB/sec. This is all possible using 4GB memory-resident "dictionary table" that can map up to 1 PB of back end physical storage, which could represent as much as 25PB of "nominal" storage. The server is then point-to-point or SAN-attached to Fibre Channel disk systems.

As we learned yesterday from Toby Marek's session, there are four ways to perform deduplication:

- Full-file comparisons. Store only one copy of identical files.

- Fixed-chunk comparisons. Files are carved up into fixed-size chunks, and each chunk is compared or hashed to existing chunks to eliminate duplicates.

- Variable-chunk comparisons. Variable-length chunks are hashed or diffed to eliminate duplicate data.

- Content-aware comparisons. If you knew data was in PowerPoint format, for example, you could compare text, photos or charts against other existing PowerPoint files to eliminate duplicates.

IBM System Storage N series Advanced Single Instance Storage (A-SIS) uses fixed-chunk method, and Diligent uses variable-chunk comparisons. Diligent does this using "data profiling". For example, let's say most of my photographs are pictures of people, buildings, landscapes, flowers, and IT equipment. When I back these up, the Diligent server "profiles" each and determines if any existing data have a similar profile that might have at least 50 percent similar content. Diligent than reads in the data that is mostly likely similar, does a byte-for-byte ["diff" comparison], and creates variable-length chunks that are either identical or unique to sections of the existing data. The unique data is compressed with LZH and written to disk, and the sequential series of pointer segments representing the ingested file is written in a separate section on disk.

That Diligent can represent profiles for 1PB of data in as little as 4GB memory-resident dictionary is incredible. By comparison, 10TB data would require 10 million entries on a content-aware solution, and 1.25 billion entries for one based on hash-codes.

Abbe Woodcock presented the TS7530 tape system that IBM announced on Tuesday. It has some advantages over the current Diligent offering:

- Hardware-based compression (TS7520 and Diligent use software-based compression)

- 1200 MB/sec (faster ingest rate than Diligent)
- 1.7PB of SATA disk (more disk capacity than Diligent)
- Support for i5/OS (Diligent's emulation of ATL P3000 with DLT7000 tapes not supported on IBM's POWER systems running i5/OS)
- Ability to attach a real tape library
- NDMP backup to tape
- iSCSI attachment
- tape "shredding" (virtual equivalent of degaussing a physical tape to erase all previously stored data)

Randy Fleenor wrapped up the session telling us IBM's strategy going forward with all of the virtual tape systems technologies. Until then, IBM is working on "recipes" or "bundles", putting Diligent software with specific models of IBM System x servers and IBM System Storage DS4000 disk systems to avoid the "do-it-yourself" problems of its current software-only packaging.

Understanding Web 2.0 and Digital Archive Workloads

I got to present this in the last time slot of the day, just before everyone headed off to the [Westin Bonaventure hotel] for our big fancy barbecue dinner. Like my previous session on IBM Strategy, this session was more oriented toward a sales audience, but both garnered a huge turn-out and were well-received by the technical attendees.

This session was requested because these new applications and workloads are driving IBM to acquire small start-ups like XIV, deploy Scale-out File Services (SoFS), and develop the innovative iDataPlex server rack.

The session was fun because it was a mix of explanation of the characteristics of Web 2.0 services, my own experience as a blogger and user of Google Docs, Flickr, Second Life and TiVo, and an exploration in how database and digital archives will impact the growth in computing and storage requirements.

I'll expand on some of these topics in later blog posts.

⊘**technorati tags:** IBM, SSPC, System Storage, TotalStorage, Productivity Center, Windows 2003, Linux, TPCTOOL, DB2, DS8000, SVC, GUI, CLI, CIMOM, PuTTY, SSH, Java, LDAP, CKD, Volume, LUN, HDD, workshops, Dominic Pruitt, Dan Marshall, Global Technology Services, GTS, archive, Jeff Ziehm, EKM, keytool, iKeyMan, LTO-4, TS1120, VTL, Diligent, ProtecTIER, HyperFactor, Jeff Mulliken, Abbe Woodcock, Randy Fleenor, TS7520, TS7530, x86-64, RHEL, deduplication, A-SIS, diff, LZH, compression, i5/OS, DLT7000, P3000, NDMP, iSCSI, shredding, DS4000, Westin Bonaventure,

Web2.0, digital archive, XIV, SOFS, iDataPlex, Google Docs, Second Life, Flickr, TiVo

2008 May 15 — STC 2008 Day 4 (302)

I'm glad this is the final day of the IBM Systems Technical Conference (STC08) here in Los Angeles. While I enjoyed the conference, one quickly reaches saturation point with all the information presented.

XIV Architecture Overview

Before this conference, many of the attendees didn't understand IBM's strategy, didn't understand Web 2.0 and Digital archive workloads, and didn't understand why IBM acquired XIV to offer "yet another disk system that serves LUNs to distributed server platforms." Brian Sherman changed all that!

Brian Sherman, IBM Advanced Technical Support (ATS), is part of the exclusive dedicated XIV technical team to install these boxes at client locations, so he is very knowledgeable with the technical aspects of the architecture. He presented what the current XIV-branded model that clients can purchase now in select countries, and what the IBM-branded model will change when available worldwide.

Those who missed my earlier series on XIV can find them here:

- [IBM acquires XIV #229]
- [Entering a New Era in IT information #230]
- [EMC Electrocutes the Elephant #231]
- [Spreading Out the Re-replication Process #232]
- [More Questions about XIV Architecture #233]
- [Cleaning up the Circus Gold #234]

Beyond this, Brian gave additional information on how thin provisioning, storage pools, disk mirroring, consistency groups, management consoles, and microcode updates are implemented.

N series and VMware Deep Dive

Norm Bogard, IBM Advanced Technical Support, presented why the IBM N series makes such great disk storage for VMware deployments. This was clearly labeled as a "deep dive", so anyone who got lost in all of the acronyms could not blame Norm for misrepresentation.

IBM has been doing server virtualization for over 40 years, so it makes sense that it happens to be the number one reseller of VMware offerings. VMware ESX server is a hypervisor that runs on x86 host, and provides an emulation layer for "guest Operating Systems". Each guest can have one or more virtual disks, which are represented by VMware as VMDK files. VMware ESX server accepts read/write requests from the guests and forwards them on to physical storage. Many of VMware's most exciting features require storage to be external to the host machine. [VMotion] allows guests to move from one host to another, [Distributed Resource Scheduler (DRS)] allows a set of hosts to load-balance the guests across the hosts, and [High Availability (HA)] allows the guests on a failed host to be resurrected on a surviving host. All of these require external disk storage.

ESX server allows up to 256 LUNs, attached via FCP and/or iSCSI, and up to 32 NFS mount points. Across LUNs, ESX server uses VMFS file system, which is a clustered file system like IBM GPFS that allows multiple hosts to access the same LUNs. ESX server has its own built-in native multipathing driver, and even provides FCP-iSCSI and iSCSI multipathing. In other words, you can have a LUN on an IBM System Storage N series that is attached over both FCP and iSCSI, so if the SAN switch or HBA fails, ESX server can fail over to the iSCSI connection.

ESX server can use NFS protocol to access the VMDK files instead. While the default is only 8 NFS mount points, you can increase this to 32 mount points. NAS can take advantage of Link Aggregate Control Protocol [LACP] groups, what some call "trunking" or "EtherChannel". This is the ability to consolidate multiple streams onto fewer inter-switch Ethernet links, similar to what happens on SAN switches. For the IBM N series, IBM recommends a "fixed" path policy, rather than "most recently used".

IBM recommends disabling Snapshot schedules, and setting the Snap reserve to 0 percent. Why? A snapshot of an ESX server datastore has the VMDK files of many guests, all of which would have had to quiesce or stop to make the data "crash consistent" for the Snapshot of the datastore to even make any sense. So, if you want to take Snapshots, it should be something you coordinate with the ESX server and its guest OS images, and not scheduled by the N series itself.

If you are running NFS protocol to N series, you can turn off the "access time" updates. In normal file systems, when you read a file, it updates the "access time" in the file directory. This can be useful if you are looking for files that haven't been read in a while, such as software that migrates infrequently accessed files to tape. Assuming you are not doing that on your N series, you might as well turn off this feature and reduce the unnecessary write activity to the IBM N series box.

ESX server can also support "thin provisioning" on the IBM N series. There is a checkbox for "space reserved". Checked means "thick provisioning" and unchecked means "thin provisioning". If you decide to use "thin provisioning" with VMware, you should consider setting AutoSize to automatically increase your datastore when needed, and to auto-delete-snap your oldest snapshots first.

The key advantage of using NFS rather than FCP or iSCSI is that it eliminates the use of the VMFS file system. IBM N series has the WAFL file system instead, and so you don't have to worry about VMFS partition alignment issue. Most VMDK are misaligned, so the performance is sub-optimal. If you can align each VMDK to a 32KB or 64KB boundary (depending on guest OS), then you can get better performance. WAFL does this for you automatically, but VMFS does not. For Windows guests, use "Windows PE" to configure correctly-aligned disks. For UNIX or Linux guests, use "fdisk" utility.

What Industry Analysts are saying about IBM

Vic Peltz gave a presentation highlighting the accolades from securities analysts, IT analysts, and news agencies about IBM and IBM storage products. For example, analysts like that IBM offers many of the exciting new technologies their clients are demanding, like "thin provisioning", RAID-6 double-drive protection, SATA, and Solid State Drive (SSD) drive technology. Analysts also like that IBM is open to non-IBM heterogeneous environments. Whereas EMC Celerra gateways support only EMC disk, IBM N series gateways and IBM SAN Volume Controller support a mix of IBM and non-IBM equipment.

Analysts also like IBM's "data-center-wide" approach to issues like security and "Green IT". Rather than focusing on these issues with individual point solutions, IBM attacks these challenges with a complete "end-to-end" solution approach. A typical 25,000 square foot data center consumes $2.6 million dollars USD in power and cooling today, and IBM has proven technologies to reduce this cost by half. IBM's DS8000 on average consume 26.5 to 27.8 percent less electricity than a comparable EMC DMX-4 disk system. IBM's tape systems consume less energy than comparable Sun or HP models.

IBM iDataPlex product technical presentation

Vallard Benincosa, IBM Technical Sales Specialist, presented the recently-announced [IBM System x iDataPlex]. This is designed for our clients that have thousands of x86 servers, that buy servers "racks at a time", to support Web 2.0 and digital archive workloads. The iDataPlex is designed for efficient power and cooling, rapid scalability, and usable server density.

iDataPlex is such a radical design departure that it might be difficult to describe in words. Most racks take up two floor tiles, each tile is 2 foot by 2 foot square. In that space, a traditional rack would have servers that were 19 inches wide slide in horizontally, with flashing lights and hot-swappable disks in the front, and all the power supply, fans, and networking connections in the back. Even with IBM BladeCenter, you have chassis in these racks, and then servers slide in vertically in the front, and all of the power supply, fan, and networking connections in the back. To access these racks, you have to be able to open the door on both the front and back. And the cooling has to go through at least 26.5 inches from the front of the equipment to the back.

iDataPlex turns the rack sideways. Instead of two feet wide, and four feet deep, it is four feet wide, and two feet deep. This gives you two 19 inch columns to slide equipment into, and the air only has to travel 15 inches from front to back. Less distance makes cooling more efficient.

Next, iDataPlex makes the only thing in the back the power cord, controlled by an intelligent power distribution unit (iPDU) so you can turn the power off without having to physically pull the plug. Everything else is serviced from the front door. This means that the back door can now be an optional "Rear Door Heat Exchanger" [RDHX] that is filled with running water to make cooling the rack extremely efficient. Water from a cooler distribution unit (CDU) can power about three to four RDHX doors.

Let's say you wanted to compare traditional racks with iDataPlex for 84 servers. You can put 42 "1U" servers in two racks each, each rack requires 10 kVA (kilo-volt-amps) so you give it two 8.6 kVA feeds each, that is four feeds, and at $1500-2000 dollars USD per month, will cost you $6000-8000. The iDataPlex you can fit 84 servers in one 20 kVA rack, with only three 8.6 kVA feeds, saving you $1500-2000 USD per month.

Fans are also improved. Fan efficiency is based on their diameter, so small fans in 1U servers aren't as effective as iDataPlex's 2U fans, saving about 12-49W per server. Whereas typical 1U server racks spend 10-20 percent of their energy on the fans, the iDataPlex spends only about 1 percent, saving 8 to 36 kWh per year per rack.

Each 2U chassis snaps into a single power supply and a bank of 2U fans. A "Y" power cord allows you to have one cord for two power supplies. A chassis can hold either two small server "flexnodes" or one big "flexnode". An iDataPlex rack can hold up to 84 small servers or 42 big servers. Since each "Y" cord can power up to four "flexnode" servers, you greatly reduce the number of PDU sockets taken, leaving some sockets available for traditional 1U switches.

The small "flexnode" server can have one 3.5 inch HDD or two 2.5 inch HDD, either SAS or SATA, and the big "flexnode" can have twice these. If you need more storage, there is a 2U chassis that holds five 3.5 inch HDD or eight 2.5 inch HDD. These are all "simple-swappable" (servers must be powered down to pull out the drives). For hot-swappable drives, there is a 3U chassis with twelve 3.5 inch SAS or SATA drives.

The small "flexnode" server has one [PCI Express] slot, the big servers have two. These could be used for [Myrinet] clustering. With only 25W power, the PCI Express slots cannot support graphics cards.

The iDataPlex is managed using the "Extreme Cluster Administration Toolkit" [XCAT]. This is an open source project under Eclipse that IBM contributes to.

Finally was the concept of "pitch". This is the distance from the center of one "cold aisle" to the next "cold aisle". On typical data centers, a pitch is 9 to 11 tiles. With the iDataPlex it is only three tiles when using the RDHX doors or six tiles without. Most data centers run out of power and cooling before they run out of floor space, so having denser equipment doesn't help if it doesn't also use less electricity. Since the iDataPlex uses 40 percent less power and cooling, you can pack more racks per square foot of an existing data center floor with the existing power and cooling available. That is what IBM calls "usable density"!

What Did You Say? Effective Questioning and Listening Techniques

Maria L. Anderson, IBM Human Resources Learning, gave this "professional development" talk. I deal with different clients every week, so I fully understand that there is a mix of art and science in crafting the right questions and listening to the responses. The focus was on how to ask better questions and improve the understanding and communication during consultative engagements. This involves the appropriate mix of closed and open-ended questions, exchanging or prefacing as needed. This was a good overview of the ERIC technique (Explore, Refine, Influence, and Confirm).

Well, that wraps up my week here in Los Angeles. Special thanks to my two colleagues, Jack Arnold and Glenn Hechler, both from the Tucson Executive Briefing Center, who helped me prepare and review my presentations!

⬭**technorati tags:** IBM, STC08, XIV, Web2.0, ATS, N series, VMware, host, guest, VMDK, VMFS, WAFL, VMotion, DRS, HA, FCP, iSCSI, NFS, NAS, Multipathing, SAN, HBA, failover, datastore, LACP, EtherChannel, LUN, Windows PE, fdisk, Linux, UNIX, Brian Sherman, Norm Bogard, Vic Peltz, RAID-6, SATA, SSD, Green IT, DS8000, EMC, DMX-4, Vallard Benincosa, iDataPlex, PDU, iPDU, CDU, RDHX, Maria Anderson, HR learning, ERIC

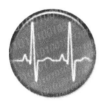 Before IBM's acquisition of MRO Software, Tivoli and Maximo held separate conferences. This year, a combined conference was born. Since both Tivoli and Maximo are focused on availability, the "pulse" symbol from the "Information Infrastructure" themes was reused. I was there for this inaugural event!

2008 May 18 — Pulse 2008 Day 1 (303)

It seems like I just get out of one conference and am already into another. This week I am at Pulse 2008, which combines the best of IBM Tivoli and Maximo into one conference. Like many conferences, this one starts on Sunday and ends on Thursday.

We're at the Swan and Dolphin hotels at [Walt Disney World] in Orlando, Florida. I've been to several conferences in Orlando, but this is my first time at the Swan and Dolphin. (When I walked into the main lobby, I had a bout of "déjà vu". IBM LotusSphere was here last year, and they had a complete replica made in SecondLife!)

If you haven't been to Walt Disney World resorts, whether for a conference or vacation, there are two things you need to know:

1. Nothing is within a short "walking distance"; you need to take a bus or boat to get anywhere.

2. Despite this, you will be doing a lot of walking, so wear comfortable shoes!

Pulse encouraged everyone to blog and take pictures to post onto Flickr, and here are a few from Sunday:

(1) Lou and Elizabeth from [Syclo], an IBM Business Partner

(2) Greg Tevis explains FilesX, recently acquired by IBM

(3) Kevin and Diana from [Odin Technologies] that manage RFID tags

Photos are below – you can see all of this set on my Flickr page [Pulse 08 - Day 1].

technorati tags: IBM, ibmpulse, Pulse08, Walt Disney Resort, Swan, Dolphin, Flickr, photos, Syclo, Birlasoft, Odin Technologies, Eaton, Powerware, Lotus Greenhouse, Tivoli, SWAT, Maximo

2008 May 19 — Pulse 2008 Day 2 Main Tent (304)

I attended the main tent sessions on Day 2 (Monday). The focus was on Visibility, Control, and Automation.

Steve Mills

Steve Mills, IBM senior VP and Group Executive of the IBM Software Group, presented some insightful statistics from the IBM Global Technology Outlook study, some recent IBM wins, and other nuggets of IT trivia:

- In 2001, there were about 60 million transistors per human being. By 2010, this is estimated to increase to one billion per human.

- In 2005, there were about 1.3 billion RFID tags, by 2010 this is estimated to grow to over 30 billion.

- IBM helped the City of Stockholm, Sweden reduce traffic congestion 20-25 percent using computer technology.

- Only about 25 percent data is original; the remaining 75% is replicated.

- In 2007, there were approximately 281 Exabytes (EB), expected to increase to 1800 EB by the year 2011.

- 70 percent of unstructured data is user-created content, but 85 percent of this will be managed by enterprises.

- Only 20 percent of data is subject to compliance rules and standards, and about 30 percent subject to security applications.

- Human error is the primary reason for breaches, with 34 percent of organizations experiencing a major breach in 2006.

- 10 percent of IT budget is energy costs (power and cooling), and this could rise to 50 percent in the next decade.

- 30 to 60 percent of energy is wasted. During the next 5 years, people will spend as much on energy as they will on new hardware purchases.

Al Zollar

Al Zollar is the General Manager of IBM Tivoli. He discussed the 20-some recent software acquisitions, including Encentuate and FilesX, earlier this year.

"The time has come to fully industrialize operations."
- Al Zollar

What did Al mean by "industrialize"? This is the closed-loop approach of continuous improvement, including design, delivery, and management.

Al used several examples from other industries:

- Henry Ford used standardized parts and process automation. Assembly of an automobile went from 12 hours by master craftsmen to delivering a new model T every 23 seconds off an assembly line.

- Power generation was developed by Thomas Edison. A satellite picture showed the extent of the [Blackout of 2003 in Northeast US and Canada]. The time for "smart grid" has arrived, making sensors and meters more intelligent. This allows non-essential IP-enabled appliances in our homes or offices to be turned off to reduce energy consumption.

- [McCarran International Airport] integrated the management of 13,000 assets with IBM Tivoli Maximo Enterprise Asset Management (EAM) software, and was able to increase revenues through more accurate charge-back.

Unlike traditional Enterprise Resource Planning (ERP) applications, EAM offers the deep management of four areas: production equipment, facilities, transportation, and IT.

When compared to these other industries, management of IT is in its infancy. The expansion of [Web 2.0] and Service-Oriented Architecture [SOA] is driving this need. What people need is a "new enterprise data center" that IBM Tivoli software can help you manage across operational boundaries. IBM can integrate through open standards with management software from Cisco, Sun, Oracle, Microsoft, CA, HP, BMC Software, Alcatel Lucent, and SAP. Together with our ecosystems of technology partners, IBM is meeting these challenges.

IBM clients have achieved return on investment by getting better control of their environment. This week there are client experience presentations Sandia National Labs, Spirit AeroSystems, Bank of America, and BT Converged communication services.

Live Demo

Chris O'Connor used some of his staff as "actors" to show an incredible live demo of various Tivoli and Maximo products for the mythical launch of "Project Vitalize", the new online web store for a new "Aero Z bike" from the mythical VCA Bike and Motorcycle Company.

Shoel Perelman played the role of "CIO". The CIO locked down all spending and asked the IT staff to make the shift from bricks-and-mortar to web sales of this new product in 15 months. While the company and situation were mythical, all the products that were part of the live demo are readily available. The CIO had three goals:

1. **Visibility**

    What do we have? Where is it? What's connected to what? Traditionally, these would be answered from lists in spreadsheets. The CIO had a goal to deploy IBM Tivoli Application Dependence Discover Manager (TADDM) which, with an easy to understand view, discovered all hardware and software and how each piece serves the business applications.

2. **Control**

    Each of the teams has processes and needed them consistent and repeatable, tightly linked together. Time is often wasted on the phone coordinating IT changes. For this, the CIO had a goal to deploy Tivoli Change and Configuration Management Database (CCMDB) for "strict change control". The process dashboard is accessible for all teams, to see how all projects are progressing. There is also a Compliance dashboard, which identifies all changes by role, clearly spelling out who can do what.

3. **Automation**

There is a lot of computerized machinery, including manufacturing assets and robotics. The CIO set a goal to "do more with existing people", and needed to automate key processes. Sales rep wanted to add a new distributor to key web portal. This was all done through their "service catalog". When they needed to deploy a new application, they were able to find servers with available capacity and adjust using automatic provisioning. Thanks to IBM, the IT staff no longer gets paged at 3 o'clock in the morning, and fewer days are spent in the "war room". They now have confidence that the launch will be successful.

Ritika Gunnar played the role of "Operations manager". She highlighted five areas:

1. "Service viewer" dashboard with green/yellow/red indicators for all of their edge, application, and database servers. This allows her to get more accurate data 4-5 times faster.

2. Tivoli Enterprise Portal eliminates bouncing around various products.

3. Tivoli Common Reporting for CPU utilization of all systems helps find excess capacity using IBM Tivoli Monitor.

4. On average, 85 percent of problems are caused by IT changes to the environment. IBM can help find dependencies so that changes in one area do not impact other areas unexpectedly.

5. Process Automation will show changes that have been completed, are in progress, or are overdue. She can see all steps in a task or change request. A "workflow" automates all the key steps that need to be taken.

Laura Knapp played the role of "Facilities manager". She wanted to see all processes that apply to her work using a role-based process dashboard. The advantage of using IBM is that it changes work habits, reduces overtime by 42 percent, and improves morale. The IT staff now works as team, collaborates more, and gets jobs done faster with fewer mistakes. Employees are online, accessing, monitoring, and managing data quicker -- in days, not weeks.

IBM Tivoli Enterprise Console (TEP) served as a common vehicle. She was able to pull up floor plan online, displaying all of the managed assets and mapped features. With the temperature overlay from Maximo Spatial, she was able to review hot spots on data center floor. Heat can cause servers to fail or shut down.

Power utilization chart at peak loads can now anticipate, predict and watch power consumption, and were able to justify replacement with newer, more energy-efficient equipment.

The CIO got back on stage and explained the great success of their launch. They use Webstore usage tracking, security tools tracking all new registrations, and tracking server and storage load. It now only takes hours, not weeks, to add new business partners and distributors. Tivoli Service Quality Assurance tools track all orders placed, processed, and shipped. Faster responsiveness is a competitive advantage. Their IT department is no longer seen as a stodgy group, but as a world class organization.

The live demo showed how IBM can help clients with rapid decision making, speed and accuracy of change processes, and automation to take actions quickly. The result is a strong return on investment (ROI).

Liz Smith

Liz Smith, IBM General Manager of Infrastructure Services, presented the results of an IBM survey to CEOs and CIOs asking questions like: What is the next big impact? Where are you investing? What will new data centers look like?

The five key traits they found for companies of the future:

1. Hungry for change
2. Innovative beyond customer imagination
3. Globally integrated
4. Disruptive by nature
5. Genuine, not just generous

The IT infrastructure must be secure, reliable, and flexible. Taking care of the environment is a corporate responsibility, not just a way to reduce costs.

The five entry points for IBM Service Management are: Integrate, Industrialize, Discover, Monitor, and Protect. IBM Service management and compliance are critical for the Globally Integrated Enterprise, with repeatable, scalable, and consistent processes that enable change to an automated workflow. This reduces errors, risks, and costs, and improves productivity. IBM has talent, assets and experience to help any client get there.

Lance Armstrong

Lance lives in Austin, TX, where IBM Tivoli is headquartered, so this made a good choice as a keynote speaker. He is best known for winning seven "Tour de France" bicycle races in a row, but he gave an inspirational talk about how he survived cancer.

In 1996, Lance was diagnosed with cancer. Surprisingly, he said it was the greatest thing that happened to him, and gave him new perspective on his life, family, and the sport of bicycling. Back then, there wasn't a WebMD, Google, or other Web 2.0 social networking sites for Lance to better understand what he was going through, learn more about treatment options, or find others going through the same ordeal.

After his treatment, he was considered "damaged goods" by many of the leading European bicycle teams. So, he joined the US Postal Service team, not known for their wins, but often invited to sell TV rights to American audiences. Collaborating with his coaches and other members of his team, he revolutionized the bicycling sport, analyzed everything about the race, and built up morale. He won the first "yellow jersey" in 1999, and did so each year for a total of seven wins.

Lance formed the [Livestrong foundation] to help other cancer survivors. Nike came to him and proposed donating 5 million "rubber bracelets" colored yellow to match his seven yellow jerseys, with the name "Livestrong" embossed on them, that his foundation could then sell for one dollar apiece to raise funds. What some thought was a silly idea at first has started a movement. At the 2004 Olympics, many athletes from all nations and religious backgrounds wore these yellow bracelets to show solidarity with this cause. To date, the foundation has sold over 72 million yellow bracelets, and these have served to provide a symbol, a brand, and a color identity to his cause.

He explained that doctors have a standard speech to cancer survivors. As a patient, you can go out this doorway and never tell anyone, keep the situation private. Or you can go out this other doorway and tell everybody your story. Lance chose the latter, and he felt it was the best decision he ever made. He wrote a book titled [It's Not About the Bike: My Journey Back to Life].

His call to action for the audience: find out what can you do to make a difference. A million non-governmental organizations [NGO] have started in the past 10 years. Don't just give cash; also give your time and passion.

Lots of things to think about!

technorati tags: IBM, Steve Mills, Al Zollar, Henry Ford, Thomas Edison, Chris O'Connor, Shoel Perelman, Laura Knapp, Ritika Gunnar, Lance Armstrong, Livestrong, bracelets, yellow jersey, Tour de France, cancer survivor

2008 May 19 — Pulse 2008 Day 2 Breakout Sessions (305)

Continuing my summary of Pulse 2008, the premiere service management conference focusing on IBM Tivoli solutions, I attended and presented breakout sessions on Monday afternoon.

Tivoli Storage "State-of-the-Subgroup" update

Kelly Beavers, IBM director of Tivoli Storage, presented the first breakout for all of the Tivoli Storage subgroup. Tivoli has several subgroups, but Tivoli Storage leads with revenues and profits over all the others. Tivoli storage has top performing business partner channel of any subgroup in IBM's Software Group division. IBM is the world's #1 provider of storage (hardware, software, and services), so this came to no surprise to most of the audience.

Looking at just the Storage Software segment, it is estimated that customers will spend $3.5 billion US dollars more in the year 2011 than they did last year in 2007. IBM is #2 or #3 in each of the four major categories: Data Protection, Replication, Infrastructure management, and Resource management. In each category, IBM has growing market share, often taking away share from the established leaders.

There was a lot of excitement over the FilesX acquisition. I am still trying to learn more about this, but what I have gathered so far is:

- Like turning a "knob", you can adjust the level of backup protection from traditional discrete scheduled backups, to more frequent snapshots, to continuous data protection (CDP). In the past, you often used separate products or features to do these three.

- It can perform "instantaneous restore" by performing a virtual mount of the backup copy. This gives the appearance that there store is complete.

48   May 2008

This year marks the 15th anniversary of IBM Tivoli Storage Manager (TSM), with over 20,000 customers. Also, this year marks the 6th year for IBM SAN Volume Controller, having sold over 12,000 SVC engines to over 4,000 customers.

Data Protection Strategies

Greg Tevis, IBM software architect for Tivoli Technical Strategy, and I presented this overview of data protection. We covered three key areas:

1. Protecting against unethical tampering with Non-erasable, Non-rewriteable (NENR) storage solutions

2. Protecting against unauthorized access with encryption on disk and tape

3. Protecting against unexpected loss or corruption with the seven "Business Continuity" tiers

There was so much interest in the first two topics that we only had about 9 minutes left to cover the third! Fortunately, Business Continuity will be covered in more detail throughout the week.

Business-Driven Storage

Henk de Ruiter from ABN AMRO bank presented his success story implementing Information Lifecycle Management (ILM) across his various data centers using IBM systems, software, and services.

Making your Disk Systems more Efficient and Flexible

I did not come up with the titles of these presentations. The team that did specifically chose to focus on the "business value" rather than the "products and services" being presented. In this session, Dave Merbach, IBM software architect, and I presented how SAN Volume Controller (SVC), TotalStorage Productivity Center, System Storage Productivity Center, Tivoli Provisioning Manager, and Tivoli Storage Process Manager work to make your disk storage more efficient and flexible.

technorati tags: IBM, Kelly Beavers, ibmpulse, Pulse08, Tivoli, Greg Tevis, FilesX, data protection, CDP, TSM, SVC, ILM, Henk de Ruiter, ABN AMRO, David Merbach, TotalStorage, Productivity Center, TPM, Storage Process Manager, NENR, WORM, tape, disk, systems

For many, IBM's choice of Guadalajara seemed odd. Knowing that the journalists would probably ask, we found several mentions of the area being referred to as the "Silicon Valley of Mexico". We updated the "Wikipedia" page for Guadalajara to mention this, printed it out with the phrase highlighted in yellow, and provided to the journalists at this event. This made it look like Guadalajara was the best and most obvious choice for IBM's new briefing center.

2008 May 20 — Global Archive Solutions Center launches in Guadalajara Mexico! (306)

Today was a special day! IBM launched the world's first "Global Archive Solutions Center" in Guadalajara, Mexico. We had a formal "ribbon cutting", shown here were the following dignitaries (from left to right):

- Eugenio Godard, IBM Guadalajara site level executive

- Andy Monshaw, IBM General Manager of IBM System Storage

- Cindy Grossman, IBM VP of Tape and Archive solutions

- Luis Guillermo Martinez Mora, Secretary of economic development for the state of Jalisco, Mexico

- José Décurnex, IBM General Manager for the country of Mexico

In the morning, we had a series of speeches from Cindy Grossman, Andy Monshaw, Eugenio Godard, and Federico Lepe (technology advisor for the governor for the state of Jalisco, Mexico).

While the hordes of press journalists, analysts, and clients were taking the lab tour, we took a snap of the front entrance. The day was packed with activity.

- After the lab tour, IBMers Clod Barrera and Craig Butler presented to the analysts.

- Cindy Grossman explained why IBM created a solutions center specific to archive solutions, and why we chose Guadalajara for its location.

- I presented the pains and challenges companies are facing, and why they should partner with IBM for archive solutions to address those requirements.

Harley Puckett and I split the group. Harley is my colleague at the IBM Tucson Executive Briefing Center and was the focal point for the various

aspects of launching for the past eight months. He presented and moderated the presentations and demos to a collection of prospective clients.

That's me on the left, with Harley on the right. I moderated a series of speakers to press and analysts. These included:

- Mark LaBelle, Spectrum Health server and storage manager, and Steve Lawrence, Spectrum Health image solutions architect, presented their success story using IBM Grid Medical Archive Solution (GMAS). [Spectrum Health] manages seven hospitals and 130 service locations in Michigan, USA.

- Mark Uren, ABSA technical architect, presented their success story working with IBM in deploying their Information Lifecycle Management (ILM) which includes Enterprise Content Management and archiving. Mark flew in all the way from Johannesburg, South Africa. [ABSA] is the financial services subsidiary of Barclay's serving the African continent.

- Jeffrey Beallor, president of [Global Data Vaulting], presented his success story as both a client and IBM Business Partner, offering backup and archiving solutions through "Software as a Service" (SaaS) business model. Global Data Vaulting has its data centers in Canada, but provides services to clients worldwide.

We had a Q&A panel with the company representatives from Spectrum Health, ABSA, and Global Data Vaulting, followed by a Q&A panel with the collection of IBM executives to take questions from the press and analysts. Special thanks to Cyntia, Daniela, Carlos, Raul, and Salvador for their help in making this a successful event!

(All three photos on this blog post taken by Mauricio, a professional photographer IBM hired for this event.)

technorati tags: IBM, Andy Monshaw, Cindy Grossman, GASC, Global Archive, Solutions Center, Guadalajara, Jalisco, Mexico, Clod Barrera, Spectrum Health, ABSA, Global Data Vaulting, ILM, SaaS, GMAS

 Most IBM announcements happen on Tuesday, so when I recap these, I start with, "Well, it's Tuesday again..." This has now become a signature phrase for my blog. Rather than repeat information in Press Releases, I try to provide my own perspective.

2008 May 27 — Announcement Recap May 2008 (307)

Well, it's Tuesday again, and we had several announcements this month, so here is a quick recap. We had some things announce May 13, and then some more announcements today, but since I was busy with conferences, I will combine them into one post for the entire month of May 2008.

This time, I thought I would go "audio" with a recording from Charlie Andrews, IBM director of product marketing for IBM System Storage:

 Listen to IBM's Charlie Andrews discuss new storage announcements (right click to "save as" an MP3 file, or use player below)

If you are unable to listen, you can read the details for each here:

- [IBM System Storage TS7530 virtual tape library (VTL)]
- [N series]

Also today IBM announced special 5-packs for LTO-4 and DDS-6 tape cartridge media. Here is the [Press Release].

Comment from Boris (Russia)

I like IBM Virtualization Engine TS7530. Very fast restore time!

 This post opened a "can of worms." I learned not to mention or compare stock prices of competitors. As Mark Twain said, "…there are liars, damned liars, and statisticians!" My suggestion that IBM's rise in stock price, in comparison to EMC's declining stock price, implied some major market shift, was attacked nine ways from Sunday.

2008 May 29 — Part of the Profit Stream (308)

I'm glad to be back home in Tucson for a few weeks. All of these conferences kept me from reading up with what was going on in the blogosphere.

A few of us at IBM found it odd that EMC would announce their new Geographically Dispersed Disaster Restart (GDDR) the week BEFORE their "EMC World" conference. Why not announce all of the stuff all at once instead at the conference? Were they worried that the admission that "Maui" software is still many months away would cause that much of a negative stigma? The decision probably went something like this:

> EMCer #1: GDDR is finally ready. Should we announce now, or wait ONE week to make it part of the things we announce at EMC World?

> EMCer #2: We are not announcing much at EMC World and what people really want us to talk about -- Maui -- we aren't delivering for a while. Why can't people understand we are company of hardware engineers, not software programmers! So, better not be associated with that quagmire at all.

> EMCer #1: Yes, boss, I see your point. We'll announce this week then.

My fellow blogger and intellectual sparring partner, Barry Burke, on his *Storage Anarchist* blog, posted ["Are you wasting money on your mainframe DR solution?"] to bring up the GDDR announcement. The key difference is that IBM GDPS works with IBM, EMC, and HDS equipment, being the fair-and-balanced folks that IBM clients have come to expect, but it appears EMC

GDDR works only with EMC equipment. Because GDDR does less, it also costs less. I can accept that. You get what you pay for. Of course, IBM does have a variety of protection levels, and one probably will meet your budget and your business continuity needs.

To correct Barry's misperception, companies that buy IBM mainframe servers do have a choice. They can purchase their operating system from IBM, get their Linux or OpenSolaris from someone else like Red Hat or Novell, or build their own OS distribution from readily available open source. And unlike other servers that might require at least one OS partition from the vendor, IBM mainframes can run 100 percent Linux. GDPS supports a mix of OS data. z/OS and Linux data can all be managed by GDPS. Companies that own mainframes know this. I can forgive the misperception from Barry, as EMC is focused on distributed servers instead, and many in their company may not have much exposure to mainframe technology, or have ever spoken to mainframe customers.

But what almost had me fall out of my chair was this little nugget from his post:

> "If you're an IBM mainframe customer, you are - by definition – IBM's profit stream."

Honestly, is there anyone out there that does not realize that IBM is a for-profit corporation? In contrast, Barry would like his readers to believe that EMC is selling GDDR at cost, and that EMC is a non-profit organization. While IBM has been delivering actual solutions that our clients want, EMC continues to rumor that someday they might get around to offering something worthwhile. In the last six months, the shareholders have interpreted both strategies for what they really are, and the stock prices reflect that:

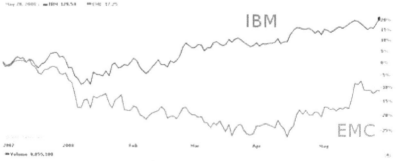

(courtesy of [finance.yahoo.com])

(**Disclosure:** I own IBM stock. I do not own EMC stock. Stock price comparisons by Yahoo were based on publicly reported information. The colors blue and red to represent IBM and EMC, respectively, were selected by Yahoo graph-making facility. The color red does not necessarily imply EMC is losing money or having financial troubles.)

Of course, I for one would love to help Barry's dream of EMC non-profitability come true. If anyone has any suggestions how we can help EMC approach this goal, please post a comment below.

⊘**technorati tags:** IBM, GDPS, EMC, GDDR, Maui, EMC World, HDS, Yahoo Finance, stock price, non-profit, strategy, shareholders

Comment from Marc Wambeke, Huizingen / Harelbeke, Belgium

Please explain this statement: "GDPS does not require z/OS to run at either primary, secondary, or tertiary locations." It might be just a confusion on terminology but I thought GDPS always involved z/OS?

Comment from Barry Burke (EMC), the Storage Anarchist

Whether intentional or not, methinks you may have insulted the intelligence of your readership (again).

Those seeking a more factual perspective of GDDR vs. GDPS and EMC vs. IBM stock performance might want to follow the link to my blog...

Comment from AO

All corporations try to be profitable; I do not think anyone doubts that. TonyP, the stock chart graph is really an all-time low. You are of course biased but do you seriously believe that anyone would buy your argument about the shareholders interpretations? Basic math tells you that the graph will look very different depending on the chosen time span. I believe you should avoid these kind of statements if you want to be taken seriously by customers.

Response from Tony Pearson (IBM)

Marc, My apologies. I was thinking one thing but wrote another. GDPS was originally for z/OS data only, but has been extended to support other data, including Linux data. That did not come across as I wrote above, so I will update to say:

"GDPS supports a mix of OS data. z/OS and Linux data can all be managed by GDPS."

-- Tony

Response from Tony Pearson (IBM)

AO, Fair enough. I was trying to point out that both IBM and EMC are (at this time anyways) for-profit companies, and both corporations profit from the recent resurgence in interest in mainframe technologies. I chose six months because that was when IBM started sharing its views on the new z10 EC mainframe, but provided an active link to Yahoo Finance so that people could generate their own comparisons.
-- Tony

Comment from Barry Burke (EMC), the Storage Anarchist

For the record, EMC's GDDR also supports multiple host operating systems in addition to z/OS -- including virtually all non-IBM server platforms -- with cross-platform consistency, as is often required for mission-critical BC/DR.

In this context, GDDR does more, and costs less, than GDPS.

Addition from Tony Pearson (IBM)

I feel a bit vindicated. The New York Times Freakonomics blog uses a similar Wal-Mart versus Target stock price comparison using the same blue and red color scheme:

> http://freakonomics.blogs.nytimes.com/2008/05/29/are-wal-marts-products-normal/

-- Tony

Comment from Steve Todd (EMC)

Hi Tony,

You quoted: "Why can't people understand we are company of hardware engineers, not software programmers!"

I understand the attempt at humor and can read this comment as such but I would like to respond with two important facts:

1. EMC engineers (in my organization at least) are predominantly software developers.

2. We call ourselves "software engineers" as opposed to "programmers". There's a big difference.

All the best,
Steve

Response from Tony Pearson (IBM)

Steve, Yes, I was poking fun. Plenty of "tongue in cheek", as intended. Software engineering is more difficult than hardware engineering. True for everybody.
-- Tony

Response from Tony Pearson (IBM)

Sorry, Barry, but GDPS also supports a variety of other platforms, including: AIX, Solaris, HP-UX, Linux on POWER, Linux on x86-64, VMware, Windows AS, Windows 2003, and the new Windows 2008. This is all done through the GDPS/DCM component (Distributed Cluster Manager), which includes both server and storage failover automation.
-- Tony

Comment from Chuck

Hi Tony,

The link to Barry Burke's blog is amazing. While everyone is entitled to their own opinion, the misinformation at his site is astounding. Does he work for EMC or is he really that misinformed?

Response from Tony Pearson (IBM)

Chuck, Yes, Barry Burke is a real person who works for EMC.
-- Tony

 Several people thought that I coined the term "bleg", the process of publicly begging for information or assistance in your blog. Actually, I borrowed this term from the Freakonomics blog.

2008 May 30 — Eleven Answers about Deduplication from IBM (309)

Continuing my catch-up on past posts, Jon Toigo on his *DrunkenData* blog, posted a ["bleg"] for information about deduplication. The responses come from the "who's who" of the storage industry, so I will provide IBM's view. (Jon, as always, you have my permission to post this on your blog!)

1. **Please provide the name of your company and the de-dupe product(s) you sell. Please summarize what you think are the key values and differentiators of your wares.**

   IBM offers two different forms of deduplication. The first is IBM System Storage N series disk system with Advanced Single Instance Storage (A-SIS), and the second is IBM Diligent ProtecTIER software. Larry Freeman from NetApp already explains A-SIS in the [comments on Jon's post], so I will focus on the Diligent offering in this post. The key differentiators for Diligent are:

   o Data agnostic. Diligent does not require content-awareness, format-awareness, nor identification of backup software used to send the data. No special client or agent software is required on servers sending data to an IBM Diligent deployment.

   o Inline processing. Diligent does not require temporarily storing data on back-end disk to post-process later.

   o Scalability. Up to 1PB of back-end disk managed with an in-memory dictionary.

   o Data Integrity. All data is diff-compared for full 100 percent integrity. No data is accidentally discarded based on assumptions about the rarity of hash collisions.

2. **InfoPro has said that de-dupe is the number one technology that companies are seeking today — well ahead of even server or storage virtualization. Is there any appeal beyond squeezing more undifferentiated data into the storage junk drawer?**

   Diligent is focused on backup workloads, which has the best opportunity for deduplication benefits. The two main benefits are:

   o Keeping more backup data available online for fast recovery.

   o Mirroring the backup data to another remote location for added protection. With inline processing, only the deduplicated data is sent to the back-end disk, and this greatly reduces the amount of data sent over the wire to the remote location.

3. **Every vendor seems to have its own secret sauce de-dupe algorithm and implementation. One, Diligent Technologies (just acquired by IBM), claims that theirs is best because it collapses two functions — de-dupe then ingest — into one inline function, achieving great throughput in the process. What should be the gating factors in selecting the right de-dupe technology?**

As with any storage offering, the three gating factors are typically:

- o   Will this meet my current business requirements?

- o   Will this meet my future requirements for the next 3-5 years that I plan to use this solution?

- o   What is the Total Cost of Ownership (TCO) for the next 3-5 years?

Assuming you already have backup software operational in your existing environment, it is possible to determine the necessary ingest rate: how many "Terabytes per Hour" (TB/h) must be received, processed and stored from the backup software during the backup window. IBM intends to document its performance test results of specific software/hardware combinations to provide guidance to clients' purchases and planning decisions.

For post-process deployments, such as the IBM N series A-SIS feature, the "ingest rate" during the backup only has to receive and store the data, and the rest of the 24-hour period can be spent doing the post-processing to find duplicates. This might be fine now, but as your data grows, you might find your backup window growing, and that leaves less time for post-processing to catch up. IBM Diligent does the processing inline, so is unaffected by an expansion of the backup window.

IBM Diligent can scale up to 1PB of back-end data, and the ingest rate does not suffer as more data is managed.

As for TCO, post-process solutions must have additional back-end storage to temporarily hold the data until the duplicates can be found. With IBM Diligent's inline methodology, only deduplicated data is stored, so less disk space is required for the same workloads.

4. **Despite the nuances, it seems that all block level de-dupe technology does the same thing: removes bit string patterns and substitutes a stub. Is this technically accurate or does your product do things differently?**

IBM Diligent emulates a tape library, so the incoming data appears as files to be written sequentially to tape. A file is a string of bytes. Unlike block-level algorithms that divide files up into fixed chunks,

IBM Diligent performs diff-comparisons of incoming data with existing data and identifies ranges of bytes that duplicate what already is stored on the back-end disk. The file is then a sequence of "extents" representing either unique data or existing data. The file is represented as a sequence of pointers to these extents. An extent can vary from 2KB to 16MB in size.

5. **De-dupe is changing data. To return data to its original state (pre-de-dupe) seems to require access to the original algorithm plus stubs/pointers to bit patterns that have been removed to deflate data. If I am correct in this assumption, please explain how data recovery is accomplished if there is a disaster. Do I need to backup your wares and store them off site, or do I need another copy of your appliance or software at a recovery center?**

For IBM Diligent, all of the data needed to reconstitute the data is stored on back-end disks. Assuming that all of your back-end disks are available after the disaster, either the original or mirrored copy, then you only need the IBM Diligent software to make sense of the bytes written to reconstitute the data. If the data was written by backup software, you would also need compatible backup software to recover the original data.

6. **De-dupe changes data. Is there any possibility that this will get me into trouble with the regulators or legal eagles when I respond to a subpoena or discovery request? Does de-dupe conflict with the non-repudiation requirements of certain laws?**

I am not a lawyer, and certainly there are aspects of [non-repudiation] that may or may not apply to specific cases.

What I can say is that storage is expected to return back a "bit-perfect" copy of the data that was written. There are laws against changing the format. For example, an original document was in Microsoft Word format, but is converted and saved instead as an Adobe PDF file. In many conversions, it would be difficult to recreate the bit-perfect copy. Certainly, it would be difficult to recreate the bit-perfect MS Word format from a PDF file. Laws in France and Germany specifically require that the original bit-perfect format be kept.

Based on that, IBM Diligent is able to return a bit-perfect copy of what was written, same as if it were written to regular disk or tape storage, because all data is diff-compared byte-for-byte with existing data.

In contrast, other solutions based on hash codes have collisions that result in presenting a completely different set of data on retrieval. If the data you are trying to store happens to have the same hash code calculation as completely different data already stored on a solution, then it might just discard the new data as "duplicate". The chance for collisions might be rare, but could be enough to put doubt in the minds of a jury. For this reason, IBM N series A-SIS, that does perform hash code calculations, will do a full byte-for-byte comparison of data to ensure that data is indeed a duplicate of an existing block stored.

7. **Some say that de-dupe obviates the need for encryption. What do you think?**

   I disagree. I've been to enough [Black Hat] conferences to know that it would be possible to read the data off the back-end disk, using a variety of forensic tools, and piece together strings of personal information such as names, social security numbers, or bank account codes.

   Currently, IBM provides encryption on real tape (both TS1120 and LTO-4 generation drives) and is working with open industry standards bodies and disk drive module suppliers to bring similar technology to disk-based storage systems. Until then, clients concerned about encryption should consider OS-based or application-based encryption from the backup software. IBM Tivoli Storage Manager (TSM), for example, can encrypt the data before sending it to the IBM Diligent offering, but this might reduce the number of duplicates found if different encryption keys are used.

8. **Some say that de-duped data is inappropriate for tape backup, that data should be re-inflated prior to write to tape. Yet, one vendor is planning to enable an "NDMP-like" tape backup around his de-dupe system at the request of his customers. Is this smart?**

   Re-constituting the data back to the original format on tape allows the original backup software to interpret the tape data directly to recover individual files. For example, IBM TSM software can write its primary backup copies to an IBM Diligent offering onsite, and have a "copy pool" on physical tape stored at a remote location. The physical tapes can be used for recovery without any IBM Diligent software in the event of a disaster. If the IBM Diligent back-end disk images are lost, corrupted, or destroyed, IBM TSM software can point to the "copy pool" and be fully operational. Individual files or servers could be restored from just a few of these tapes.

   An NDMP-like tape backup of a deduplicated back-end disk would require that all the tapes are intact, available, and fully restored to new back-end disk before the deduplication software could do anything. If a single cartridge from this set was unreadable or misplaced, it might impact the access to many TBs of data, or render the entire system unusable.

In the case of a 1PB of back-end disk for IBM Diligent, you would have to recover over a thousand tapes back to disk before you could recover any individual data from your backup software. Even with dozens of tape drives in parallel, it could take you several days for the complete process. This represents a longer "Recovery Time Objective" (RTO) than most people are willing to accept.

9. **Some vendors are claiming de-dupe is "green" — do you see it as such?**

Certainly, "deduplicated disk" is greener than "non-deduplicated" disk, but I have argued in past posts, supported by analyst reports, that it is not as green as storing the same data on "non-deduplicated" physical tape.

10. **De-dupe and VTL seem to be joined at the hip in a lot of vendor discussions: Use de-dupe to store a lot of archival data on line in less space for fast retrieval in the event of the accidental loss of files or data sets on primary storage. Are there other applications for de-duplication besides compressing data in a nearline storage repository?**

Deduplication can be applied to primary data, as in the case of the IBM System Storage N series A-SIS. As Larry suggests, MS Exchange and SharePoint could be good use cases that represent the possible savings for squeezing out duplicates. On the mainframe, many master-in/master-out tape applications could also benefit from deduplication.

I do not believe that deduplication products will run efficiently with "update in place" applications -- that is, high levels of random writes for non-appending updates. OLTP and Database workloads would not benefit from deduplication.

11. **Just suggested by a reader: What do you see as the advantages/disadvantages of software based deduplication vs. hardware (chip-based) deduplication? Will this be a differentiating feature in the future... especially now that Hifn is pushing their Compression/DeDupe card to OEMs?**

In general, new technologies are introduced on software first, and then, as implementations mature, get hardware-based to improve performance. The same was true for RAID, compression, encryption, etc. The Hifn card does "hash code" calculations that do not benefit the current IBM Diligent implementation. Currently, IBM Diligent performs LZH compression through software, but certainly IBM could provide hardware-based compression with an integrated hardware/software offering in the future. Since IBM Diligent's inline process is so efficient, the bottleneck in performance is often the speed of the back-end disk. IBM Diligent can get improved "ingest rate" using FC instead of SATA disk.

Sorry, Jon, that it took so long to get back to you on this, but since IBM had just acquired Diligent when you posted, it took me a while to investigate and research all the answers.

⊘**technorati tags:** IBM, Diligent, Jon Toigo, DrunkenData, bleg, deduplication, A-SIS, NetApp, ProtecTIER, inline, post-process, back-end, disk, data integrity, hash, collision, ingest rate, VTL, non-repudiation, extent, bit-perfect, Microsoft Word, Adobe PDF, diff, Black Hat, encryption, compression, Hifn, FC, SATA

Comment from Jenny (BackupReview.Info)

On the subject of file backup, sharing, and storage…

Online backup is becoming common these days. It is estimated that 70-75% of all PC's will be connected to online backup services within the next decade.

Thousands of online backup companies exist, from one guy operating in his apartment to fortune 500 companies.

Choosing the best online backup company will be very confusing and difficult. One website I find very helpful in making a decision to pick an online backup company is:

http://www.BackupReview.info

This site lists more than 400 online backup companies in its directory and ranks the top 25 on a monthly basis.

Comment from the Islami Isimler

Thousands of online backup companies exist, from one guy operating in his apartment to fortune 500 companies.

Comment from the Open Systems Guy

Methinks it's time for you to start screening your comments for spam Tony ;)

Response from Tony Pearson (IBM)

OSG, Thanks. We have people scanning for these, but some are more difficult to spot than others! I'll let the BackupReview stay as it is relevant in this case.

Comment from BartD

Tony, I liked the way you answered precisely to the questions, as opposed to others who simply cut and paste marketing material. In my opinion, the most useful place for deduplication is in the backup software. This approach will permit a richer set of features, for example integrating the ExaGrid scheme of deduplicate only the older backup versions, or allowing the storage administrator to choose whether to deduplicate the tape copies.
- BartD

Addition from Tony Pearson (IBM)

Trackback to IBM Eye

http://www.ibmeye.com/what-makes-diligent-different/

June

During the summer, temperatures in Tucson exceed 100 degrees Fahrenheit, so few clients come to visit. This gives the EBC team time to catch up on our blogging, researching, and updating presentation materials.

It is only appropriate, then, that this is the month I have a heated exchange with Jeff Savit, a blogger from Sun Microsystems, on the topic of server virtualization. Having worked over 15 years in z/OS and Linux on System z mainframes, I think I know a thing or two on this subject.

 Developing software is incredibly difficult – so much so that one famous programmer estimated that more people have been outside Earth's atmosphere than have written good programming code. I liked the analogy of bees in this post.

2008 Jun 05 — Software Programmers as Bees (310)

A faithful reader of this blog, Tom, sent me a link to Orson Scott Card's article titled [PROGRAMMERS AS BEES (or, how to kill a software company)]. "Is there any truth in this?" Tom asked. Having worked both sides of this fence as I approach my 22 year anniversary at IBM, I guess I can venture some opinions on this piece. Let's start with this excerpt:

> "The environment that nurtures creative programmers kills management and marketing types -- and vice versa."

By this, he means "kills" in the UNIX sense, I imagine, and not the "Grand Theft Auto" sense. Different people solve problems differently. Some programmers have the luxury that they can often focus on a single platform, single chipset, single OS, and so on, but Marketing types are trying to come up with messaging that appeals to a broad audience, from people with business backgrounds to others with more technical backgrounds, and that can be more challenging. For programmers, "creative" is an adjective; for marketers, it's a noun.

> "Programming is the Great Game. It consumes you, body and soul. When you're caught up in it, nothing else matters."

True. As a storage consultant, I find myself writing code a lot, from small programs, scripts, and even HTML code for this blog. When you are in your zone, working on something, you can easily lose track of time.

> "Here's the secret that every successful software company is based on: You can domesticate programmers the way beekeepers tame bees. You can't exactly communicate with them, but you can get them to swarm in one place and when they're not looking, you can carry off the honey. You keep these bees from stinging by paying them money. More money than they know what to do with. But that's less than you might think."

I have never tamed bees, but many of my friends who are still programmers are motivated by factors other than maximizing their income, such as: friendly co-workers, job security, casual attire, and interesting challenges. A few make more than they know what to do with; the rest have ~~girlfriends~~ *"significant others"* who solve that problem for them.

> "One way or another, marketers get control. But... control of what? Instead of finding assembly lines of productive workers, they quickly discover that their product is produced by utterly unpredictable, uncooperative, disobedient, and worst of all, unattractive people who resist all attempts at management."

False. Either marketing had control in the first place (à la Apple, Inc.) or they never had. "Control of what?" is the key phrase here.

> "The shock is greater for the coder, though. He suddenly finds that alien creatures control his life. Meetings, Schedules, Reports. And now someone demands that he PLAN all his programming and then stick to the plan, never improving, never tweaking, and never, never touching some other team's code."

True. But if you don't like surprises, perhaps software engineering is not the right career path for you.

> "The hive has been ruined. The best coders leave. And the marketers, comfortable now because they're surrounded by power neckties and they have things under control, are baffled that each new iteration of their software loses market share as the code bloats and the bugs proliferate. Got to get some better packaging. Yeah, that's it."

This one depends. I've seen teams survive and manage, with junior programmers stepping up to backfill leadership roles, and other times, projects are scrapped, or started anew elsewhere. As for marketers, it doesn't take much to get one baffled, does it?

Thanks for the link, Tom!

Response from Tom Rauchut (IBM)

Tony,

Good review of the article, and nice points you raise in your analysis. I also have two perspectives of this article. One from the technical programmer point-of-view and one from the Manager point-of-view.

I agree with several aspects of this article, particularly the pieces that talk about the communications between the managers (and project managers) and the technical folks. I like the reference to the fact that you can't communicate with the programmers, but you can get them to swarm in one place (hopefully). Agree with that from both perspectives!

I also find the point that the code is never done to be very true. Until somebody steps in and "steals the honey" it's subject to endless refinement whether it really needs it or not.

Good read and an enjoyable little article that hits close to home for many of us.
-- TomR

Addition from Tony Pearson (IBM)

I got some surprising reactions to this one. One felt I trivialized programmers and glorified marketers. Not all programmers have the luxury to limit themselves to a single OS, and I agree with that. Certainly Orson's article was written from the programmer's view, and I tried to answer it from a viewpoint of having done both roles.

Also changed "girlfriends" to "significant others" to be more politically correct.

June is also the month I get asked for career advice, as many college graduates enter the workforce, either as interns or full time employees. The marketplace for IT jobs is hot, but not everyone is cut out to be in IT.

2008 Jun 06 — Summer Jobs and the Singularity (311)

Yesterday's post [Software Programmers as Bees] was not meant as "career advice", but certainly I got some interesting email as if it were. Orson Scott Card was poking fun at the culture clash between software programmers and management/marketers, and I gave my perspective, having worked both types of jobs.

This is June. Many students are graduating from high school or college and looking for jobs. Some of these might be jobs just for the summer to make some spending money, and others might be jobs like internships to explore different career paths. I found both programming and marketing are rewarding and interesting work, but each person is different.

There are a variety of ways to find out what your personality traits are, and then focus on those jobs or career paths that are best for those strengths. Here is an online [Typology Test] based on the work of psychologists Carl Jung and Isabel Myers-Briggs. The result is a four-letter score that represents 16 possible personalities. For example, mine is "ENTP", which stands for "Extroverted, Intuitive, Thinking, Perceiving". You can find out other famous people that match your personality type. For ENTP, I am lumped together with fellow master inventor Thomas Edison, fellow author Lewis Carroll (Alice in Wonderland), Cooking great Julia Child, Comedians George Carlin and Rodney Dangerfield (I get no respect!), movie director Alfred Hitchcock, and actor Tom Hanks.

USA Today had an article ["CEOs value lessons from teen jobs"] which offers some career advice from successful business people. Of course, what worked for them may not work for you, all based on different personality types. Here is an excerpt of the advice I thought the most useful:

- "If you are committed, you will be successful." (Unfortunately, the reverse is also true: if you are successful, you will be asked to move to a different job.)
- "Tackle offbeat jobs. Challenge conventional wisdom within reason. Come into contact with people from all walks of life."
- "Show an interest; demonstrate you want to be on the job."
- "Never limit yourself. Look beyond to what needs to be done, or should be done. Then do it. Stretch. Go beyond what others expect."
- "Find a job that forces you to work effectively with people. No matter what you end up doing, dealing with others will be critical."
- "Bring your best to the table every day. Learn professional responsibility and how to handle difficult situations."
- "Listen carefully to what customers want."

Before IBM, I ran my own business. If you are thinking, "Maybe I will start my own business instead," you might want to see this advice from Venture

Capitalist [Guy Kawasaki on Innovation]. While running your own business has advantages, like avoiding issues "working for the man," it has some disadvantages as well. It is certainly not as easy as some people make it seem to be.

Of course, things are a lot different nowadays than they were when these CEOs were teenagers. And the pace of change does not seem to be slowing down any, either. Here is a presentation on [SlideShare.net] that helps bring to focus the realities of globalization:

But in the future, you will not just be competing with other smart people around the globe. This brings me to "the Singularity". The Institute of Electrical and Electronics Engineers, Inc. (IEEE) has [The Singularity - A Special Report], a whole issue of Spectrum Online devoted to this. Nick Carr offers his thoughts on this on his Rough Type blog in his post [What we talk about when we talk about singularity].

Whether you are a student looking for a job or a seasoned professional willing to share some career advice, enter a comment below.

technorati tags: career advice, Carl Jung, Myers-Briggs, ENTP, USA Today, Thomas Edison, Guy Kawasaki, venture capitalist, Shift Happens, IEEE, Spectrum, Nick Carr, Rough Type, engineers

Comment from John Smyth

Thanks for the information.

Comment from Aksam Gunesi

Thank you…

 This post was meant to help Jon Toigo, an independent consultant, understand IBM's press release for the System z10 mainframe. I was a chief architect for DFSMS on z/OS and worked on the "Linux on z" team, so was able to bring my 15 years' experience on mainframe to bear on this topic.

2008 Jun 11 — Yes, Jon, there is a mainframe that can help replace 1500 x86 servers (312)

After my response to Jon Toigo on *Drunken Data* with my post [Eleven answers about Deduplication #309], Jon followed up with a request to validate the numbers quoted in the February 26 Press Release [IBM launches New System z10 Mainframe], particularly the estimate that a single mainframe can handle to the workload of 1500 x86 servers, in his post [A Bit More Blegging]. The timing is perfect in that IBM launched [the next wave of Project Big Green] today. To avoid sounding like an [editorial from the New York Sun], I checked the facts and spoke to the person in IBM who did all the calculations. Jon, as always, you have my permission to publish this on your site if you want.

> (I cannot take credit for coining the new term "bleg". I saw this term first used over on the [Freakonomics Blog]. If you have not yet read the book *Freakonomics*, I highly recommend it! The authors' blog is excellent as well.)

For this comparison, it is important to figure out how much workload a mainframe can support, how much an x86 can support, and then divide one from the other. Sounds simple enough, right? And what workload should you choose? IBM chose a business-oriented "data-intensive" workload using Oracle database.

> (If you wanted instead a scientific "compute-intensive" workload, consider an [IBM supercomputer] instead, the most recent of which clocked in over 1 quadrillion floating point operations per second, or PetaFLOP.)

IBM compares the following two systems:

Sun Fire X2100 M2, model 1220 server (2-way)

> IBM did not pick a wimpy machine to compare against. The model 1220 is the fastest in the series, with a 2.8 GHz x86-64 dual-core AMD Opteron processor, capable of running various levels of Solaris, Linux, or Windows. In our case, we will use Oracle workloads running on Red Hat Enterprise Linux. All of the technical specifications are available at the [Sun Microsystems Sun Fire X1200]

website. I am sure that there are comparable models from HP, Dell or even IBM that could have been used for this comparison.

IBM z10 Enterprise Class mainframe model E64 (64-way)

This machine can run a variety of operating systems also, including Red Hat Enterprise Linux (RHEL). The E64 has four "multiple processor modules" called "processor books" for a total of 77 processing units: 64 central processors, 11 system assist processors (SAP) and 2 spares. That's right, spare processors: in case any others go bad, IBM has got your back. You can designate a central processor in a variety of flavors. For running z/VM and Linux operating systems, the central processors can be put into "Integrated Facility for Linux" (IFL) mode. On *IT Jungle*, Timothy Patrick Morgan explains the z10 EC in his article [IBM Launches 64-Way z10 Enterprise Class Mainframe Behemoth]. For more information on the z10 EC, see the 110-page [Technical Introduction], or read the specifications on the [IBM z10 EC] website.

Moving Oracle workloads from x86 over to mainframe is quite common since [IBM and Cisco joined forces to meet Linux On Mainframe demand]. For more information on consolidating x86 servers running Oracle over to a mainframe, read the [Quick Reference], IBM Redbook titled ["Using Oracle Solutions on Linux for System z"], or this [presentation by Jim Elliott, IBM System z Specialist].

In a shop full of x86 servers, there are production servers, test and development servers, quality assurance servers, standby idle servers for high availability, and so on. On average, these are only 10 percent utilized. For example, consider the following mix of servers:

- 125 Production machines running 70 percent busy
- 125 Backup machines running idle ready for active failover in case a production machine fails
- 1250 machines for test, development and quality assurance, running at 5 percent average utilization

While [some might question, dispute or challenge this ten percent] estimate, it matches the logic used to justify VMware, XEN, Virtual Iron or other virtualization technologies. Running 10 to 20 "virtual servers" on a single physical x86 machine assumes a similar 5-10 percent utilization rate.

Note: The following paragraphs have been revised per comments received.

Now the math. Jon, I want to make it clear I was not involved in writing the press release nor assisted with these math calculations. *Please, don't shoot the messenger!* Remember this cartoon where two scientists in white lab coats are writing math calculations on a chalkboard, and in the middle there is "and then a miracle happens..." to continue the rest of the calculations?

In this case, the miracle is the number that compares one server hardware platform to another. I am not going to bore people with details like the number of concurrent processor threads or the differences between L1 and L3 cache. IBM used sophisticated tools and third party involvement that I am not allowed to talk about, and I have discussed this post with lawyers representing ~~four~~ (now five) different organizations already, so for the purposes of illustration and explanation only, I have reverse-engineered a new z10-to-Opteron conversion factor as 6.866 z10 EC MIPS per GHz of dual-core AMD Opteron for I/O-intensive workloads running only 10 percent average CPU utilization. Business applications that perform a lot of I/O don't use their CPU as much as other workloads. For compute-intensive or memory-intensive workloads, the conversion factor may be quite different, like 200 MIPS per GHz, as Jeff Savit from Sun Microsystems points out in the comments below.

Keep in mind that each processor is different, and we now have Intel, AMD, SPARC, PA-RISC, and POWER (and others); 32-bit versus 64-bit; dual-core and quad-core; and different co-processor chip sets to worry about. AMD Opteron processors come in different speeds, but we are comparing against the 2.8GHz, so 1500 times 6.866 times 2.8 is 28,337. Since these would be running as Linux guests under z/VM, we add an additional 7 percent overhead or 2,019 MIPS. We then subtract 15 percent for "smoothing", which is what happens when you consolidate workloads that have different peaks and valleys in workload, or 4,326 MIPS. The end is that we need a machine to do 26,530 MIPS. Thanks to advances in "Hypervisor" technological synergy between the z/VM operating system and the underlying z10 EC hardware, the mainframe can easily run 90 percent utilized when aggregating multiple workloads, so a 29,477 MIPS machine running at 90 percent utilization can handle these 26,530 MIPS.

N-way machines, from a little 2-way Sun Fire X2100 to the mighty 64-way z10 EC mainframe, are called "Symmetric Multiprocessors". All of the processors or cores are in play, but sometimes they have to take turns, to wait for exclusive access on a shared resource such as cache or the bus. When your car is stopped at a red light, you are waiting for your turn to use the shared "intersection". As a result, you don't get linear improvement, but rather you get diminishing returns. This is known generically as the "SMP effect", and IBM documents this as [Large System Performance Reference]. While a 1-way z10 EC can handle 920 MIPS, the 64-way can only handle 30,657 MIPS. The 29,477 MIPS needed for the Sun x2100 workload can be handled by a 61-way, giving you three extra processors to handle unexpected peaks in workload.

But are 1500 Linux guest images *architecturally* possible? A long time ago, David Boyes of [*Sine Nomine Associates*] ran 41,400 Linux guest images on a single mainframe using his [Test Plan Charlie], and IBM internally was able to get 98,000 images, and in both cases these were on machines less powerful than the z10 EC. Neither of these tests ran I/O intensive workloads, but extreme limits are always worth testing. The 1500-to-1 reduction in IBM's press release is edge-of-the-envelope as well, so in production environments, several hundred guest images are probably more realistic, and still offer significant TCO savings.

The z10 EC can handle up to 60 LPARs, and each LPAR can run z/VM which acts much like VMware in allowing multiple Linux guests per z/VM instance. For 1500 Linux guests, you could have 25 guests each on 60 z/VM LPARs, or 250 guests on each of six z/VM LPARs, or 750 guests on two LPARs. With z/VM 5.3, each LPAR can support up to 256GB of memory and 32 processors, so you need at least two LPAR to use all 64 engines. Also, there are good reasons to have different guests under different z/VM LPARs, such as separating development/test from production workloads. If you had to re-IPL a specific z/VM LPAR, it could be done without impacting the workloads on other LPARs.

To access storage, IBM offers N-port ID Virtualization (NPIV). Without NPIV, two Linux guest images could not access the same LUN through the same FCP port because this would confuse the Host Bus Adapter (HBA), which IBM calls "FICON Express" cards. For example, Linux guest 1 asks to read LUN 587 block 32 and this is sent out a specific port, to a switch, to a disk system. Meanwhile, Linux guest 2 asks to read LUN 587 block 49. The data comes back to the z10 EC with the data, gives it to the correct z/VM LPAR, but then what? How does z/VM know which of the many Linux guests to give the data to? Both touched the same LUN, so it is unclear which made the request. To solve this, NPIV assigns a virtual "World Wide Port Name" (WWPN), up to 256 of them per physical port, so you can have up to 256 Linux guests sharing the same physical HBA port to access the same LUN. If you had 250 guests on each of six z/VM LPARs, and each LPAR had its own set of HBA ports, then all 1500 guests could access the same LUN.

Yes, the z10 EC machines support Sysplex. The concept is confusing, but "Sysplex" in IBM terminology just means that you can have LPARs either on the same machine or on separate mainframes, all sharing the same time source, whether this be a "Sysplex Timer" or by using the "Server Time Protocol" (STP). The z10 EC can have STP over 6 Gbps InfiniBand over distance. If you wanted to have all 1500 Linux guests time stamp data identically, all six z/VM LPARs need access to the shared time source. This can help in a re-do or roll-back situation for Oracle databases to complete or back-out "Units of Work" transactions. This time stamp is also used to form consistency groups in "z/OS Global Mirror", formerly called "XRC" for Extended Remote Distance Copy. Currently, the "timestamp" on I/O applies only to z/OS and Linux and no other operating systems. (The time stamp is done through the CKD driver on Linux, and contributed back to the open source community so that it is available from both Novell SUSE and Red Hat distributions.) To have XRC have consistency between z/OS and Linux, the Linux guests would need to access native CKD volumes, rather than VM Minidisks or FCP-oriented LUNs.

> (**Note:** This is different from "Parallel Sysplex" which refers to having up to 32 z/OS images sharing a common "Coupling Facility" which acts as shared memory for applications. z/VM and Linux do not participate in "Parallel Sysplex".)

As for the price, mainframes list for as little as "six figures" to as much as several million dollars, but I have no idea how much this particular model would cost. And, of course, this is just the hardware cost. I could not find the math for the $667 per server replacement you mentioned, so don't have details on that. You would need to purchase z/VM licenses, and possibly support contracts for Linux on System z to be fully comparable to all of the software license and support costs of the VMware, Solaris, Linux, and/or Windows licenses you run on the x86 machines.

This is where a lot of the savings come from, as a lot of software is licensed "per processor" or "per core", and so software on 64 mainframe processors can be substantially less expensive than 1500 processors or 3000 cores. IBM does "eat its own cooking" in this case. IBM is consolidating 3900 one-application-each rack-mounted servers onto 30 mainframes, for a ratio of 130-to-1 and getting amazingly reduced TCO. The savings are in the following areas:

- Hardware infrastructure. It's not just servers, but racks, PDUs, etc. It turns out it is less expensive to incrementally add more CPU and storage to an existing mainframe than to add or replace older rack-em-and-stack-em with newer models of the same.

- Cables. Virtual servers can talk to each other in the same machine virtually, such as HiperSockets, eliminating many cables. NPIV allows many guests to share expensive cables to external devices.

- Networking ports. Both LAN and SAN networking gear can be greatly reduced because fewer ports are needed.

- Administration. We have universities that can offer a guest image for every student without having a major impact to the sys-admins, as the students can do much of their administration remotely, without having physical access to the machinery. Companies using mainframe to host hundreds of virtual guests find reductions too!

- Connectivity. Consolidating distributed servers in many locations to a mainframe in one location allows you to reduce connections to the outside world. Instead of sixteen OC3 lines for sixteen different data centers, you could have one big OC48 line instead to a single data center.

- Software licenses. Licenses based on servers, cores or CPUs are reduced when you consolidate to the mainframe.

- Floor space. Generally, floor space is not in short supply in the USA, but in other areas it can be an issue.

- Power and Cooling. IBM has experienced significant reduction in power consumption and cooling requirements in its own consolidation efforts.

All of the components of DFSMS (including DFP, DFHSM, DFDSS and DFRMM) were merged into a single product -- "DFSMS for z/OS" -- which is now an included element in the base z/OS operating system. As a result of these, customers typically have 80 to 90 percent utilization on their mainframe disk. For the 1500 Linux guests, however, most of the DFSMS features of z/OS do not apply. These functions were not "ported over" to z/VM nor Linux on any platform.

> **Note:** DFSMS can backup or dump Linux on System z partitions or volumes. See this [Appendix C. HOWTO backup Linux data through z/OS] for details.

Instead, the DFSMS concepts have been re-implemented into a new product called "Scale-out File Services" (SoFS) which would provide NAS interfaces to a blended disk-and-tape environment. The SOFS disk can be kept at 90 percent utilization because policies can place data, move data, and even expire files, just like DFSMS does for z/OS data sets. SOFS supports standard NAS protocols such as CIFS, NFS, FTP, and HTTP, and these could be access from the 1500 Linux guests over an Ethernet Network Interface Card (NIC), which IBM calls an "OSA Express" card.

Lastly, IBM z10 EC is not emulating x86 or x86-64 interfaces for any of these workloads. No doubt IBM and AMD could collaborate together to come up with an AMD Opteron emulator for the S/390 chipset and load Windows 2003 right on top of it, but that would just result in all kinds of emulation overhead. Instead, Linux on System z guests can run comparable workloads. There are many Linux applications that are functionally equivalent or the same as their Windows counterparts. If you run Oracle on Windows, you could run Oracle on Linux. If you run MS Exchange on Windows, you could run Bynari on Linux and let all of your Outlook Express users not even know their Exchange server had been moved! Linux guest images can be application servers, web servers, database servers, network infrastructure servers, file servers, firewall, DNS, and so on. For nearly any business workload you can assign to an x86 server in a data center, there is likely an option for Linux on System z.

Hope this answers all of your questions, Jon. These were estimates based on basic assumptions. This is not to imply that IBM z10 EC and VMware are the only technologies that help in this area; you can certainly find virtualization on other systems and through other software. I have asked IBM to make public the "TCO framework" that sheds more light on this. As they say, "Your mileage may vary."

For more on this series, check out the following posts:

- [Seven Words #315]
- [Virtualization, Carpools and Marathons #316]
- [Summer Reading for the z10 EC #317]

If in your travels, Jon, you run into someone interested to see how IBM could help consolidate rack-mounted servers over to a z10 EC mainframe, have them ask IBM for a "Scorpion study". That is the name of the assessment that evaluates a specific client situation, and can then recommend a more accurate estimate configuration.

⊘**technorati tags**: Jon Toigo, DrunkenData, bleg, IBM, z10, EC, E64, mainframe, x86, AMD, Opteron, Sun, Fire, X2100, petaFLOP, Freakonomics, Red Hat, RHEL, IFL, VMware, Jim Elliott, Xen, Virtual Iron, Solaris, Linux, Windows, Project Big Green, InfiniBand, STP, Sysplex, Scorpion study, MS Exchange, Bynari, Oracle

Comment from Jon Toigo (DrunkenData)

Thanks for the response, Tony. I am waiting for the dust to settle between you and Jeff over at Sun. I will echo here what I just wrote over on his blog.

1. I was a might sore when a qualified guy like Jeff suggested I was all wet for quoting IBM's press release and conversations with IBM techs.

2. I appreciate it when a knowledgeable guy gets in the middle and submits a view that does not attack me, but rather questions facts in an intelligent way.

3. I really appreciate it when Tony P. jumps in and answers my blegs, as you have so thoughtfully done, in a timely way.

I was (and still am) inclined to believe that I am going to get more resiliency, performance and a better price if I am gung ho about virtualizing a bunch of x86 machines and use a mainframe LPAR rather than a tinkertoy hypervisor approach. That is my mainframe bias showing through. From what I've learned from x86 engineers and from my own testing in my labs, VMware is a wonderful piece of technology from the standpoint of its respect for x86 extents. However, not only the hypervisor, but also the applications must respect the underlying extent code for everything to be shiny. Many apps don't, which seems to put a burden on VMware to catch all the crazy calls and prevent them from destabilizing the stack. That is a technically non-trivial task and one that seems to account for the many abends we have had in our labs and the poor record of crash recovery failover, even when both VM servers are in the same subnet.

After reading your post and Jeff's, there is still some confusion about the number (and type) of machines we can virtualize, both on a VMware server and in a z10 LPAR. You and I agree that we are limited to 16-20 VMs in a virtual x86 server but Jeff says it is two to three times that many. Jeff's initial objection to IBM claims was that z didn't provide sufficient LPARs to host 1500 VMs.

Also, some of the services I was counting on to deliver resiliency (e.g. multiple processors with failover) were not, in Jeff's view, part of the configuration priced to come up with the "1500 VMs at $600-odd per" calculation proffered by Big Blue.

Thirdly, I argued in my Mainframe Exec piece that you were going to realize greater resource efficiency -- especially storage efficiency -- behind the z because of its superior management paradigm (SMS and HSM). Distributed computing just doesn't have these tools, or a common standard (de facto or de jure) for storage attachment and management that approximates mainframe DASD rules. As a result, the storage vendors duke it out at the expense of the consumer in terms of common management and ultimately efficiency.

Jeff said these tools had not been ported to z/OS, or that if they had (I need to go check my notes on this), they were not part of the suite of tools that would be available for use in a z/VM environment (which you must use in order to support LPARs).

These three issues seem pretty key to me. And frankly I remain a tad confused.

Comment from Jeff Savit (Sun Microsystems)

I'm sorry you didn't take the opportunity to challenge my blog, cited as, "some might question, dispute, or challenge this ten percent." That would have been a good time to expose errors, if they exist, in my refutation of IBM claims.

(1) You say WLM and IRD make it possible to run mainframes at 90% utilization. This is impossible.

(2) David Boyes' Test Plan Charlie ran no workload other than booting OS images.

(3) You cannot use Sysplex for coordinating times or recovery with z/VM or z/Linux.

(4) Actual cost per IFL is $125,000, not $100,000, and that doesn't count the cost for RAM.

You are right in suggesting that you would have to add up actual software and hardware costs of both platforms for a fair comparison.

Your figures disagree with the IBM press announcement, [http://www-03.ibm.com/press/us/en/pressrelease/23592.wss] which used to have a footnote number 3 with the math, which now has been removed.

In your analysis, a 64-CPU z10 E64 would be needed. That costs about $26 million US dollars, excluding RAM, disks, and software licenses. That is over 14 times more expensive than 1,500 x2100s (the Sun price includes the RAM and pre-installed OS). If the CPUs are configured as IFLs, then they cost $125,000 each, totaling $8 million dollars. With the minimum RAM configuration of 160GB, it still costs 5.38 times as much as the x2100s.

I will address several other points of contention in my blog. If the x86 servers are managed for higher utilization, far fewer will be needed, and the price difference will be even higher.

Response from Tony Pearson (IBM)

Jeff, you bring up some good points, and so I have made updates to my post. I had not seen your post when it first came out.

(1) Workload Manager (WLM) relates to managing workloads within a single image, and Intelligent Resource Director (IRD) relates to managing workloads across LPARs. These are both beyond the scope of this post, so I will just change this to "Hypervisor" technology to relate to the combination of the System z hardware that supports LPAR in combination with z/VM technology that supports individual guests.

---

(2) I have clarified the discussion of "Test Plan Charlie" to indicate that tens of thousands of guests are indeed possible, but a more realistic amount is several hundred to a few thousand images.

(3) Sorry to confuse "sysplex timer" with "parallel sysplex". I have clarified the paragraph to explain the difference. Yes, Linux does I/O timestamps same as z/OS, and yes both Linux and z/OS data can be in the same consistency group for XRC (z/OS Global Mirror) purposes. I led the team that tested this way back when.

(4) Because single z10 EC processors are so powerful, IBM offers sub-capacity pricing, but that is beyond the scope of this post. I will rephrase to say "six figures" instead.

Additional savings are achieved from reduced software licenses, reduced power consumption, reduced administration. We have clients who have reduced their total cost of ownership migrating workloads from x86 onto System z.

I was unable to locate any press releases discussing "760 cores" with 26 IFL engines, but perhaps this was a z9 calculation, or perhaps an actual client case study.

The "3rd footnote" you mentioned was removed at the request of the trademark holder to eliminate "implied endorsement". I have updated my post to remove references to the same.

I am not suggesting that IBM is working on reverse-engineering the AMD processor to develop an emulator. Any such emulator would only happen if IBM and AMD collaborated together for that purpose.

I agree it is possible to configure application workloads on x86 hardware to run full capacity, but using VMware or migrating to a mainframe just makes reaching 90 percent utilization substantially easier. If the x86 servers are managed, then your "administration costs" will probably increase to achieve "server utilization" improvements. In general, I find the "x86 system admin" staff do not have enough spare time for this added effort.
-- Tony

Addition from Tony Pearson (IBM)

More comments on DrunkenData here:

http://www.drunkendata.com/?p=1759

Comment from Jeff Savit (Sun Microsystems)

Tony, I wasn't going to post again on your blog -- I have quite a conversation going on my blog already :-) -- but saw my name mentioned several times, and considered that sufficient inducement.

It is only technically correct to say that David Boyes' Test Plan Charlie didn't run "I/O intensive workloads", because it ran no workload at all. One cannot use this to extrapolate any behavior under load. David and I have known one another for years (I'm working with him and his colleagues on a project right now and have news to blog on shortly when I'm finished with this distraction) so I am completely familiar with this story. The size of the machine wasn't the sole issue either, as it was also a test of architectural limits. Quite a few of these have been removed in the move from S/390 and VM/ESA to System z and z/VM, though there's still a lot of work to be done to handle truly large systems. For example, even z/VM 5.3 supports only 256GB, which would rule out a single z/VM instance supporting the 1,500 database servers which enjoyed 1.5TB of RAM as originally described.

It's certainly possible to have hundreds or even a few thousand logged on users. Large CMS shops did that 15 years ago. Lots of us did that. But counting users without regard to cost and service level is inappropriate, as IBM's Walt Doherty taught me (and I blogged on).

Barton Robinson, another person I've known for years (we've presented together at conferences like SHARE and SHARE Europe), is probably the best known VM (and z/Linux) performance expert in the world. Nobody considering z/Linux should try to do it without his products; they're that good and essential. He came up with the rule of thumb that 4 MHz of Intel is roughly equivalent to 1 MIPS of mainframe. Everybody understands that this is just a crude estimate: MIPS are highly variable on a given z based on workload (RR instructions give much higher MIPS rates than SS, for example) or even level of multiprogramming. Intel and AMD models vary dramatically in how much work is done per clock cycle, the above quote was several years ago for a single core CPU, and on and on. Useful for doing rough back of the envelope sizing, but you could NEVER call this accurate. To put 4 digits of precision ("6.866" – that's a "rough equivalency"?) with this rough rule of thumb is nonsense, and gives the impression of scientific accuracy that doesn't exist. The ratios could be wildly different.

I suppose it's fair for me to mention that your claim that, "Moving workloads from x86 over to mainframe is quite common," is hardly proven by citing a two year old press release.

I'm sorry you couldn't find the other material I referred to (760 x86 cores and 26 z10 IFLs). IBM has altered the web pages I referred to and removed content. Nothing I can help with.

To your closing points: I never suggested that IBM was trying to reverse engineer AMD processors. I think that was a misconception on Jon's point, reading "emulate AMD" where "provide equivalent capacity" was intended. The distributed marketplace has completely changed, and now virtualization is everywhere. You no longer need a mainframe to do it.

Response from Tony Pearson (IBM)

Jeff,

Apparently you did not see the rest of my posts on this series. Here they are:

- Seven Words [#315]
- Virtualization, Carpools and Marathons [#316]
- Summer Reading for System z10 EC [#317]

I think you are shooting the messenger. I did not write the press release being discussed, but rather am just explaining how it was written and how the marketing claims were developed.

WLM and IRD: Perhaps I should have said, "On z/OS, WLM and IRD help achieve 90 percent utilization, but on z/VM, other advanced hypervisor technology, representing synergy between the software and the z10 EC hardware, also allow you to achieve 90 percent utilization."

It seems false to assume that since z/VM and Solaris are different than z/OS that this implies that neither can also achieve 90 percent utilization. My Honda Civic gets over 35 MPG, does that mean that someone else's Ford or Chevy could not achieve 35 MPG because they are not made by Honda, or share common parts?

1500 servers with 1GB RAM each does not equal 1.5TB of RAM. A majority of the contents on each server is OS, and often the same files are duplicated across all of these, and don't come into play. 256GB on z/VM is plenty for less than 10 percent utilized mix of production, test and development servers being virtualized. And that is 256GB per z/VM; you can have up to 60 LPARs. Speaking to my colleagues, they felt that 4 z/VM LPARs would be sufficient to handle this mixed 10 percent average workload.

Barton's sizing was probably for compute-intensive workloads, and mine is for I/O-intensive workloads. I agree that for compute-intensive workloads, like math calculations, that supercomputers based on single core and dual core processors can provide a better deal.

And since you brought up Marist College, the kind folks over there are running over 700 images under z/VM for their 600 plus students, and managing it all with just two people. This is where the savings happen. Your focus on hardware only shows you are missing the Total-Cost-of-Ownership picture.

I agree that virtualization is everywhere; IBM offers it on every server we sell. You will see in my other posts mentioned in this series that the point is that consolidating servers on any platform is often more cost-effective than running 10 percent utilized with only a single application on a single machine. It just happens that the mainframe can often consolidate more I/O intensive business-oriented workloads on a single machine better than alternative server choices.

-- Tony

Comment from Jeff Savit (Sun Microsystems)

Tony,

I'm disappointed in the response I read. Barton's sizing was not for compute intensive workloads. You're just making that up. It's a well-known rule of thumb with his name on it, and for any workload. How do I know? Because he's expressed this to me directly, and it's been referred to numerous times. See for example

> http://www2.marist.edu/htbin/wlvtype?LINUX-VM.62939

where he says (October 2006):

> "I've seen the number four presented by an IBMer as 'Barton's number'. After doing some measurements, 1 MIP is about 4 Mhz. This means that for the workloads I measured, a 1 Ghz processor using 25% of the CPU would use about 60 MIPS. When converting a windows workload to Linux on "z", it was more like 5. For the z9, it is also closer to 5. This is very easily measured with the proper tools. You can do a before and after, capture the data for a month and analyze it to death. Your number will still be about 4...."

That's a quote. As Casey Stengel said, "You could look it up."

So: It's not for compute intensive workloads. It's a rough rule of thumb that you misquoted and made look more accurate than it was, to grossly underestimate the number of z10 CPUs needed. You're also not the messenger explaining the IBM press release, because that was never part of their "justification", either before or after they modified the page. Just 'fess up that you made a mistake misquoting Barton's numbers, vastly over-estimating z CPU power.

You also get the memory part wrong. You describe "1500 Linux guest images". That means 1500 copies of the operating system, despite the fact that means 1500 copies in RAM. That's how virtual machines work: you boot up an OS in each one. Technically speaking there is a way to share a small percentage of that, but it's tricky, requires systems programmer magic, and only provides a small payback, but I don't want to get into a tech discussion about NSS and read/only segments and their limitations. Linux isn't CMS, which was designed for this environment, and does this much better. This compares poorly to VMware, which identifies identical virtual machine memory contents and de-dupes them automatically, or Solaris Containers, where a duplicate copy of a binary is never loaded in the first place. Under z/VM the memory is the sum of the virtual machines memory sizes. 1500 virtual machines of 1GB each will have an aggregate of 1.5TB. That's not counting the shadow page tables needed which will enlarge it further. Memory contents can be paged out to disk when not in use, but even lightly loaded guests touch many pages. The 10% utilization is also irrelevant, because this is a shortage of RAM, not CPU. In fact, low CPU utilization is a sign of a thrashing workload caused by insufficient RAM.

Funny you mention Marist. I know the people over there very well, professionally and socially. They're great folks. I know them for many years. One of the system programmers was an officer of the local VM user group when I was its president. I have been to the campus and logged onto the VM system there; I may go there in about two weeks for the next user group meeting. So, let me explain this to you: the equipment is largely donated or subsidized by a large nearby computer manufacturer in Poughkeepsie just up route 9. The 700 images are student labs that are largely not logged on, so they have little performance impact. Each guest is managed by the student, so in reality they have 600+ administrators, not 2. Student time is cheap or free. The service level objectives are appropriate for students, not mission critical applications. This is not the TCO model of the real world, which doesn't have subsidized kit and student labs.

I'm glad you concede that other technologies besides z/OS can permit high utilization. It's also good that you acknowledge that virtualization is everywhere.

Did I leave anything out? How nice for you that you have other blog pages, but the responses I've read here do not provide an incentive to seek them out. I think we're done.

-- Jeff

Response from Tony Pearson (IBM)

Jeff, I guess we will just have to agree to disagree, as I don't think I can convince you that I did not write the original press release, and you cannot convince me that the mainframe is not a great product that can reduce total cost of ownership, as IBM itself is reducing its costs in this manner.

I never quote Mr. Barton, but it is nice to know that others have thought about MIPS-to-GHz conversion factors as well.

Since IBM is able to swap in and swap out to disk, and many Linux guests can share OS disk images, the result is that you get to enjoy the high-performance use of disk cache for much of this.

If you can show a TCO case where consolidating 1500 servers onto a single Sun SPARC-based high-end system is less expensive than an IBM z10 EC, then show it. You mention you have no idea about the price of IBM high-end storage (which I can accept fully, by the way), but Sun sells StorageTek tape, and resells HDS USP arrays, so you can at least use Sun gear for those comparisons. Please include the costs of cables, network switches, PDUs, racks, software licenses, power, and cooling costs to make it a fair comparison as IBM has done.

My argument has been that if you are replacing 1500 older, underutilized 1-way and 2-way rack-mounted servers running a single application each, you might be better off with an IBM z10 EC mainframe, both in tangible costs and intangible benefits of flexibility and simplicity, than replacing with newer rack-mounted servers.

Your efforts to convince everyone that virtualization and consolidation of servers are impractical or cost-prohibitive do not seem to match the results IBM has helped our clients achieve.

Enjoy your 4th of July weekend!

2008 Jun 12 — IBM WebCast - Storage for SAP environments (313)

 IBM is hosting a webcast about storage for SAP Environments. Learn how integrated IBM infrastructure solutions, specifically customized for your SAP environments, can help lower your business costs, increases productivity in SAP development and test tasks, and improve resource utilization. This will include discussion of archive solutions with WebDAV, ArchiveLink and DR550; IBM Business Intelligence (BI) Accelerator; IBM support for SAP [Adaptive Computing]; and performance benchmark results. The session is intended for SAP and storage administrators, IT directors and managers.

Here are the details:

- **Date:** Wednesday, June 18, 2008
- **Time:** 11:00am EDT (8:00am for those of us in Arizona or California)
- **Registration:** Register at the On24 website: [http://event.on24.com/clients/ibm/110218/storage]

The session is targeted to run for 60 minutes.

 Back in the 1991, I helped two Netherland banks, ABN and AMRO, merge their data centers, forming ABN AMRO. Later in 2004, while on the "ILM Assessments Team" for STG Lab Services, I would present to ABN AMRO how IBM could help them adopt best practices. The result was that IBM won a $1.5 Billion services contract over 10 years to help them design and implement an ILM solution.

2008 Jun 13 — Seven Tiers of Storage at ABN AMRO (314)

Two weeks ago, I mentioned in my post [Pulse 2008 - Day 2 Breakout sessions] that Henk de Ruiter from ABN AMRO bank presented his success story implementing Information Lifecycle Management (ILM) across his various data centers. I am no stranger to ABN AMRO, having helped "ABN" and "Amro" banks merge their mainframe data in 1991. Henk has agreed to let me share with my readers more of this success story here on my blog:

Back in December 2005, Henk and his colleagues had come to visit the IBM Tucson Executive Briefing Center (EBC) to hear about IBM products and services. At the time, I was part of our "STG Lab Services" team that performed ILM assessments at client locations. I explained to ABN AMRO that the ILM methodology does not require an all-IBM solution, and that ILM could even provide benefits with their current mix of storage, software and service providers. The ABN AMRO team liked what I had to say, and my team was commissioned to perform ILM assessments at three of their data centers:

- Amsterdam (Netherlands)
- Sao Paulo (Brazil)
- Chicago, IL (USA)

Each data center had its own management, its own decision making, and its own set of issues, so we structured each ILM assessment independently. When we presented our results, we showed what each data center could do better with their existing mixed bag of storage, software, and service providers, and also showed how much better their life would be with IBM storage, software, and services. They agreed to give IBM a chance to prove it, and so a new "Global Storage Study" was launched to take the recommendations from our three ILM studies and flesh out the details to make a globally-integrated enterprise work for them. Once completed, it was renamed the "Global Storage Solution" (GSS).

Henk summarized the above with, "I am glad to see Tony Pearson in the audience, who was instrumental to making this all happen." As with many client testimonials, he presented a few charts on what ABN AMRO is today, the 12th largest bank worldwide, 8th largest in Europe. They operate in 53 countries and manage over one trillion euros in assets.

They have over 20 data centers with about 7 PB of disk and over 20 PB of tape, both growing at 50 to 70 percent CAGR. About 2/3 of their operations are now outsourced to IBM Global Services; the remaining 1/3 is non-IBM equipment managed by a different service provider.

ABN AMRO deployed IBM TotalStorage Productivity Center, various IBM System Storage DS family disk systems, SAN Volume Controller (SVC), Tivoli Storage Manager (TSM), Tivoli Provisioning Manager (TPM), and several other products. Armed with these products, they performed the following:

- **Clean Up.** IBM uses the term "rationalization" to relate to the assignment of business value, to avoid confusion with the term "classification" which many in IT relate to identifying ownership, read, and write authorization levels. Often, in the initial phases of an ILM deployment, a portion of the data is determined to be eligible for cleanup, either to be moved to a lower-cost tier or deleted immediately. ABN AMRO and IBM set a goal to identify at least 20 percent of their data for cleanup.

- **New tiers.** Rather than traditional "storage tiers" which are often just Tier 1 for Fibre Channel disk and Tier 2 for SATA disk, ABN AMRO and IBM came up with seven "information infrastructure tiers" that incorporate service levels, availability, and protection status. They are:

    1. High-performance, highly-available disk with remote replication

    2. High-performance, highly-available disk (no remote replication)

    3. Mid-performance, high-capacity disk with remote replication

    4. Mid-performance, high-capacity disk (no remote replication)

5. Non-erasable, Non-rewriteable (NENR) storage employing a blended disk and tape solution.

6. Enterprise Virtual Tape Library with remote replication and back-end physical tape

7. Mid-performance physical tape

These tiers are applied equally across their mainframe and distributed platforms. All of the tiers are priced per "primary GB", so any additional capacity required for replication or point-in-time copies, either local or remote, are all folded into the base price. ABN AMRO felt a mission-critical application on Windows or UNIX deserves the same Tier 1 service level as a mission-critical mainframe application. Exactly!

- **Deployed storage virtualization for disk and tape.** This involved the SAN Volume Controller and IBM TS7000 series library.

- **Implemented workflow automation.** The key product here is IBM Tivoli Provisioning Manager.

- **Started an investigation for HSM on distributed.** This would be policy-based space management to migrate less frequently accessed data to the TSM pool for Windows or UNIX data.

While the deployment is not yet complete, ABN AMRO feels they have already recognized business value:

- Reduced cost by identifying data that should be stored on lower tiers

- Simplified management, consolidated across all operating systems (mainframe, UNIX, Windows)

- Increased utilization of existing storage resources

- Reduced manual effort through policy-based automation, which can lead to fewer human errors and faster adaptability to new business opportunities

- Standardized backup and other operational procedures

Henk and the rest of ABN AMRO are quite pleased with the progress so far, although recent developments in terms of the takeover of ABN AMRO by a consortium of banks means that the model is only implemented so far in Europe. Further rollout depends on the storage strategy of the new owners. Nonetheless, I am glad that I was able to work with Henk, Jason, Barbara, Steve, Tom, Dennis, Craig and others to be part of this from the beginning and be able to see it rollout successfully over the years.

For more about what was presented at Pulse 2008 conference, see the videos of the keynote speakers at [IBM Pulse - YouTube channel]!

 Not everyone goes back to read comments on earlier blog posts, so to benefit all readers, I created these next three posts as an update to blog post #312 regarding the IBM System z10 mainframe. Today, nearly all new customers who buy an IBM mainframe do so to run many Linux guest images.

2008 Jun 23 — Seven Words (315)

I am saddened to learn that one of my favorite comedians, [George Carlin], passed away yesterday. He was famous for a skit about "seven words" you could not say on Television. A few of those came to mind in the response I got from my post [Yes, Jon, There is a mainframe that can help replace 1500 x86 servers (312)] , which attempted to provide an answer to a simple question about the IBM System z10 Enterprise Class (EC) mainframe.

> **Jon**: So, where is the 1500 number coming from?
> **Tony**: I'll investigate and get back to you.

My post tried to explain how IBM estimated that number. However, my fellow blogger from Sun, Jeff Savit, posted on his blog [No, there isn't a Santa Claus] in response.

> (If Sun's shareholders are expecting anything other than a [lump of coal] under the tree this year, they should probably read Sun's press release about their last [financial results].)

A few others contacted me about this also, from a bunch of rather different angles, from reverse-engineering emulation of other company's chipsets to my use of internal codenames. (There are now MORE than seven words I can't type in this blog!) Jon is just trying to gather information, but his [head hurts] from all of this debate.

This week I will try to clarify some of the confusion.

2008 Jun 25 — Virtualization, Carpools and Marathons (316)

Continuing this week's theme on the z10 EC mainframe being able to perform the workload of hundreds or thousands of small 2-way x86 servers, I offer a simple analogy.

One car, one driver

If you wonder why so many companies subscribe to the notion that you should only run a single application per server, blame Sun, who I think helped promote this idea. Not to be out-done, Microsoft, HP, and Dell think that it is a great idea too. Imagine the convenience for operators to be able to switch off a single machine and impact only a single application. Imagine how much this simplifies new application development, knowing that you are the only workload on a set of dedicated resources.

This is analogous to a single car, single driver, where the car helps get the person from "point A" to "point B" and the single driver represents the driver and sole passenger of the vehicle. If this were a single driver on an energy-efficient motorcycle or scooter, than would be reasonable, but people often drive alone much bigger vehicles -- what Jeff Savit would call "over-provisioning". Chips have increased in processing power much faster than individual applications have increased their requirements, so as a result, you have over-provisioning.

Carpooling - one bus, one driver, and many other passengers riding along

This is how z/OS operates. Yes, you could have up to 60 LPARs that you could individually turn on and off, but where z/OS gets most of its advantages is that you can run many applications in a single OS instance, through the use of "Address Spaces" which act as application containers. Of course, it is more difficult to write for this environment, because you have to be a good z/OS citizen, share resources nicely, and be WLM-compliant to allow your application to be swapped out for others.

While you get efficiencies with this approach, when you bring the OS down, all the apps on that OS image have to stop with it. For those who have "Parallel Sysplex", that is not an issue. For example, let's say you have three mainframes, each running several LPARs of z/OS, and your various z/OS images all are able to process incoming transactions for a common shared DB2 database. Thanks to DB2 sharing technology, you could take down an individual LPAR or z/OS image, and not disrupt transaction processing, because the IP spreader just sends them to the remaining LPARs. A "Coupling Facility" allows for smooth operations if any of the OS images are lost from an unexpected disaster or disruption.

Needless to say, IBM does not give each z/OS developer his or her own mainframe. Instead, we get to run z/OS guest images under z/VM. It was even possible to emulate the next generation S/390 chipset to allow us to test software on hardware that hasn't been created yet. With HiperSockets, we can have virtual TCP/IP LAN connections between images, have virtual coupling facilities, virtual disk and virtual tape, and so on. It made development and test that much more efficient, which is why z/OS is recognized as one of the most rock-solid bullet-proof operating systems in existence.

The negatives of carpooling or taking the bus apply here as well. I have been on buses that have stopped working, and 50 people are stranded. And you don't need more than two people to make the logistics of most carpools complicated. This feeds the fear that has people wanting to have separate manageable units (one-car-one-driver) rather than putting all of their eggs into one basket, having to schedule outages together, and so on.

> (**Disclaimer:** From 1986 to 2001 I helped the development of z/OS and Linux on System z. Most of my 17 patents are from that time of my career!)

Bicycle races and Marathons

The third computing model is the Supercomputer. Here we take a lot of one-way and two-way machines, and lash them together to form an incredible machine able to perform mathematical computations faster than any mainframe. The supercomputer that IBM built for Los Alamos National Laboratory just clocked in at 1,000,000,000,000,000 floating point operations per second. This is not a single operating system, but rather each machine runs its own OS, is given its primary objective, and tries to get it done. *NetworkWorld* has a nice article on this titled: [IBM, Los Alamos smash petaFLOP barrier, triple supercomputer speed record]. If every person in the world was armed with a handheld calculator and performed one calculation per second, it would take us 46 years collectively to do everything this supercomputer can do in one day.

I originally thought of bicycle races as an analogy for this, but having listened to Lance Armstrong at the [IBM Pulse 2008 #304] conference, I learned that biking is a team sport, and I wanted something that had the "every-man-for-himself" approach to computing. So, I changed this to marathons.

The marathon was named after a fabled Greek soldier was sent as messenger from the [Battle of Marathon to the City of Athens], a distance that is now standardized to 26 miles and 385 yards, or 42.195 kilometers for my readers outside the United States.

If you were given the task to get thousands of people from "point A" to "point B" 26-plus miles away, would you chose thousands of cars, each with a lone driver? Conferences with a lot of people in a few hotels use shuttle buses instead. A few drivers, a few buses, and you can get thousands of people from a few places to a few places. But the workloads that are sent to supercomputers have a single end point, so a dispatcher node gives a message to each "Greek soldier" compute node, and has them run it on their own. Some make it, some don't, but for a supercomputer that is OK. When the message is delivered, the calculation for that little piece is done, and the compute node gives it another message to process. All of the computations are assembled to come up with the final result. Applications must be coded very specially to be able to handle this approach, but for the ones that are, amazing things happen.

So, how does "server virtualization" come into play?

Logical Partitions

IBM has had Logical Partitions for quite some time. A logical partition, or LPAR, can run its own OS image, and can be turned on and off without impacting other LPARs. LPARs can have dedicated resources or shared resources with other LPARs. The IBM z10 EC can have up to 60 LPARs. System p and System i, now merged into the new "POWER Systems" product line, also support LPARs in this manner. Depending on the size of your LPAR, this could be for a single OS and application, or a single OS with lots of applications.

Address Spaces/Application Containers

This is the bus approach. You have a single OS, and that is shared by a set of application containers. z/OS does this with address spaces, all running under a single z/OS image, and for x86there are products like [Parallels Virtuozzo Containers] that can run hundreds of Windows instances under a single Windows OS image, or a hundred Linux images under a single Linux OS image. However, you cannot mix and match Windows with Linux, just as all the address spaces on z/OS all have to be coded for the same z/OS level on the LPAR they run in.

Virtual Guests

The term "guests" was chosen to model this after the way hotels are organized. Each guest has a room with its own lockable entrance and privacy, but a shared lobby, and in some countries, shared bathrooms on every hall. This approach is used by z/VM, VMware and others. The z/VM operating system can handle any S/390-chip operating system guest, so you could have a mix of z/OS, TPF, z/VSE, Linux and OpenSolaris, and even other z/VM levels running as guests. Many z/VM developers run in this "second level" mode to develop new versions of the z/VM operating system!

As part of the One Laptop Per Child [OLPC] development team (yes, I am a member of their open source community, and now have developer keys to provide contributions), I have been experimenting with Linux KVM. This was [folded into the base Linux 2.6.20 kernel] and available to run Linux and Windows guest images. This is a nice write-up on [Wikipedia].

The key advantage of this approach is that you are back to one-car-one-driver simplistic mode of thinking. Each guest can be turned on and off without impacting other applications. Each guest has its own OS image, so you can mix different OS on the same server hardware. You can have your own customized kernel modules, levels of Java, etc. Externally, it looks like you are running dozens of applications on a single server, but internally; each application thinks it is the only one running on its own OS. This gives you a simpler coding model to base your test and development on.

Jeff is correct that running less than 10 percent utilization average across your servers is a crying shame, and that it could be managed in a manner that raises the utilization of the servers so that fewer are needed. Just as people could carpool, or could take the bus to work, it just doesn't happen, and data centers are full of single-application servers.

VMware has an architectural limit of 128 guests per machine, and IBM is able to reach this with its beefiest System x3850 M2 servers, but most of the x86 machines from HP, Dell, and Sun are less powerful, and only run a dozen or so guests. In all cases, fewer servers mean that it is simpler to manage, so hosting more applications per server is always the goal in mind.

VMware can soak up 30 to 40 percent of the cycles, meaning the most you can get from a VMware-based solution is 60 to 70 percent CPU utilization (which is still much better than the typical 5 to 10 percent average utilization we see today!); z/VM has been finely tuned to incur as little as 7 percent overhead, so IBM can achieve up to 93 percent utilization.

Jeff argues that since many of the z/OS technologies that allow customers to get over 90 percent utilization don't apply to Linux guests under z/VM, thus all of the numbers are wrong. My point is that there are two ways to achieve 90 percent utilization on the mainframe: one is through z/OS running many applications on a single LPAR (the application container approach), and the other through z/VM supporting many Linux OS images, each with one (or a few) applications (the virtual guest approach).

I am still gathering more research on this topic, so I will try to have it ready later this week.

⊘**technorati tags**: IBM, z10, EC, mainframe, Jeff Savit, Sun, Microsoft, HP, Dell, car, driver, bus, carpool, marathon, z/OS, LPAR, z/VM, guest, address space, application containers, ibmpulse, pulse2008, VMware, x3850

Comment from Oto Kiralam

I am reading your article and I like it very much. Thanks for you to teach me something.

2008 Jun 27 — Summer Reading for z10 EC server virtualization (317)

Wrapping up this week's theme on why the System z10 EC mainframe can replace so many older, smaller, underutilized x86 boxes. This was all started to help fellow bloggers Jon Toigo of *DrunkenData* and Jeff Savit from *Sun Microsystems* understand our IBM press release that we put out last February on this machine with my post [Yes, Jon, there is a mainframe that can help replace 1500 x86 servers] and my follow up post ["Virtualization, Carpools and Marathons"]. The computations were based on running 1500 unique workloads as Linux guests under z/VM, and not running them as z/OS applications.

My colleagues in IBM Poughkeepsie recommended these books to provide more insight and in-depth understanding. Looks like some interesting summer reading. I put in quotes the sections I excerpted from the synopses I found for each.

[In Search of Clusters] by Gregory F. Pfister

"From Microsoft to IBM, Compaq to Sun to DEC, virtually every large computer company now uses clustering as a key strategy for high-availability, high-performance computing. This book tells you why -- and how. It cuts through the marketing hype and techno-religious wars surrounding parallel processing, delivering the practical information you need to purchase, market, plan or design servers and other high-performance computing systems.

- Microsoft Cluster Services ('Wolfpack')
- IBM Parallel Sysplex and SP systems
- DEC OpenVMS Cluster and Memory Channel
- Tandem Server Net and Himalaya
- Intel Virtual Interface Architecture
- Symmetric Multiprocessors (SMPs) and NUMA systems"

Fellow IBM author Gregory Pfister worked in IBM Austin as a Senior Technical Staff Member focused on parallel processing issues, but I never met him in person. He points out that workloads fall into regions called *parallel hell, parallel nirvana,* and *parallel purgatory.* Careful examination of machine designs and benchmark definitions will show that the "industry standard benchmarks" fall largely in *parallel nirvana* and *parallel purgatory.* Large UNIX machines tend to be designed for these benchmarks and so are particularly well suited to *parallel purgatory.* Clusters of distributed systems do very well in *parallel nirvana.* The mainframe resides in *parallel hell* as do its primary workloads. The current confusion is where virtualization takes workloads, since there are no good benchmarks for it.

[Guerilla Capacity Planning] by Neil J. Gunther

"In these days of shortened fiscal horizons and contracted time-to-market schedules, traditional approaches to capacity planning are often seen by management as tending to inflate their production schedules. Rather than giving up in the face of this kind of relentless pressure to get things done faster, Guerrilla Capacity Planning facilitates rapid forecasting of capacity requirements based on the opportunistic use of whatever performance data and tools are available in such a way that management insight is expanded but their schedules are not."

Neil Gunther points out that vendor claims of near-linear scaling are not to be trusted and shows a method to "de-rate" scaling claims. His suggested scaling values for database servers is closer IBM's LSPR-like scaling model than TPC-C or SPEC scaling. I had mentioned that, "While a 1-way z10 EC can handle 920 MIPS, the 64-way can only handle 30,657 MIPS," in my post, but still people felt I was using "linear scaling". Linear scaling would mean that if a 1Ghz single-core AMD Opteron can do four (4) MIPS, and an one-way z10 EC can do 920 MIPS, than one might assume that 1GHz dual-core AMD could do eight (8) MIPS, and the largest 64-way z10 EC can theoretically do 64 x 920 = 58,880 MIPS. The reality is closer to 6.866 and 30,657 MIPS, respectively.

This was never an IBM-vs.-Sun debate. One could easily make the same argument that a large Sun or HP system could replace a bunch of small 2-way x86 servers from Dell. Both types of servers have their place and purpose, and IBM sells both to meet the different needs of our clients. The savings are in total cost of ownership, reducing power and cooling costs, floor space, software licenses, administration costs, and outages.

I hope we covered enough information so that Jeff can go back about talking about Sun products, and I can go back to talk about IBM storage products.

⊘**technorati tags**: IBM, z10, EC, Jon Toigo, DrunkenData, Jeff Savit, Sun, Gregory Pfister, Austin, Neil Gunther, MIPS, LSPR, SPEC, TPC-C, mainframe, scalability, UNIX, Linux, z/OS, HP, Dell

July

I am often travelling in July, either on vacation to escape the Tucson heat or for business. I have been to Japan many times, but on this trip I got to meet one of my biggest fans of my blog! I had never been to India, so the week I spent in Mumbai was also exciting.

IBM encourages all employees to "give back" our time and talents to the charities, the local community, and the world at large. I became actively involved with the One Laptop Per Child (OLPC) to help young students in other countries.

2008 Jul 02 — Sending my baby off to school (318)

With pride and joy, I shipped my baby off today. My "baby" in this case was an [XS School Server] that I built and configured with software as a platform to develop an [Educational Blogging System] for [Proyecto Ceibal] who are the "One Laptop Per Child" group in Uruguay [OLPC Uruguay].

> (Earlier this year, I build a test XS School Server that was used to help and support [OLPC Nepal] by working with their local NGO team [OLE Nepal]. I wrote about this back in February in my post [Understanding the LAMP platform for Web 2.0 workloads].)

Based on this success, and perhaps because I am also fluent in Spanish, I was asked to help with Proyecto Ceibal, the team for OLPC Uruguay. Normally the XS school server resides at the school location itself, so that even if the internet connection is disrupted or limited, the school kids can continue to access each other and the web cache content until internet connection is resumed. However, with a diverse development team with people in United States, Uruguay, and India, we first looked to Linux hosting providers that would agree to provide free or low-cost monthly access. We ~~spent~~ (make that "wasted") the month of May investigating. Most that I talked to were not interested in having a customized Linux kernel on non-standard hardware on their shop floor and wanted instead to offer their own standard Linux build on existing standard servers, managed by their own system administrators, or were not interested in providing it for free. Since the XS-163 kernel is customized for the x86 architecture, it is one of those exceptions

---

where we could not host it on an IBM POWER or mainframe as a virtual guest.

This got picked up as an [idea] for the Google's [Summer of Code] and we are mentoring Tarun, a 19-year-old student, to act as lead software developer. However, summer was fast approaching, and we wanted this ready for the next semester. In June, our project leader, Greg, came up with a new plan: build a machine and have it connected at an internet service provider that would cover the cost of bandwidth, and be willing to accept this with remote administration. We found a volunteer organization to cover this -- Thank you Glen and Vicki!

We found a location, so the request to me sounded simple enough: put together a PC from commodity parts that meet the requirements of the customized Linux kernel, the latest release being called [XS-163]. The server would have two disk drives, three Ethernet ports, and 2GB of memory; it would be installed with the customized XS-163 software, SSHD for remote administration, Apache web server, PostgreSQL database, and PHP programming language. Of course, the team wanted this for as little cost as possible, and for me to document the process so that it could be repeated elsewhere. Some stretch goals included having a dual-boot with Debian 4.0 Etch Linux for development/test purposes, an alternative database such as MySQL for testing, a backup procedure, and a Recover-DVD in case something goes wrong.

Some interesting things happened:

1. The XS-163 is shipped as an ISO file representing a LiveCD bootable Linux that will wipe your system clean and lay down the exact customized software for a one-drive, three-Ethernet-port server. Since it is based on Red Hat's Fedora 7 Linux base, I found it helpful to install that instead, and experiment moving sections of code over. This is similar to geneticists extracting the DNA from the cell of a pit bull and putting it into the cell for a poodle. I would not recommend this for anyone not familiar with Linux.

    I also experimented with modifying the pre-built XS-163 CD image by cracking open the squashFS, hacking the contents, and then putting it back together and burning a new CD. This provided some interesting insight, but in the end was able to do it all from the standard XS-163 image.

2. Once I figured out the appropriate "scaffolding" required, I managed to proceed quickly, with running versions of XS-163, plain vanilla Fedora 7, and Debian 4, in a multi-boot configuration.

3. The BIOS "raid" capability was really more like BIOS-assisted RAID for Windows operating system drivers. This "fake raid" wasn't supported by Linux, so I used Linux's built-in "software raid" instead, which allowed some partitions to be raid-mirrored, and other partitions to be un-mirrored. Why not mirror everything? With two160GB SATA drives, you have three choices:

    o   No RAID, for a total space of 320GB

    o   RAID everything, for a total space of 160GB

    o   Tiered information infrastructure, use RAID for some partitions, but not all.

The last approach made sense, as a lot of the data is cache web page images, and is easily retrievable from the internet. This also allowed the system to have some "scratch space" for downloading large files and so on. For example, 90GB mirrored that contained the OS images, settings and critical applications, and 70GB on each drive for scratch and web cache, results in a total of 230GB of disk space, which is 43 percent improvement over an all-RAID solution.

4. While [Linux LVM2] provides software-based "storage virtualization" similar to the hardware-based IBM System Storage SAN Volume Controller (SVC), it was a bad idea putting different "root" directories of my many OS images on there. With Linux, as with most operating systems, it expects things to be in the same place where it last shutdown, but in a multi-boot environment, you might boot the first OS, move things around, and then when you try to boot second OS, it doesn't work anymore, or corrupts what it does find, or hangs with a "kernel panic". In the end, I decided to use RAID non-LVM partitions for the root directories, and only use LVM2 for data that is not needed at boot time.

5. While they are both Linux, Debian and Fedora were different enough to cause me headaches. Settings were different, parameters were different, file directories were different. Not quite as religious as MacOS-versus-Windows, but you get the picture.

6. During this time, the facility was out getting a domain name, IP address, subnet mask and so on, so I tested with my internal 192.168.x.y and figured I would change this to whatever it should be the day I shipped the unit. (I'll find out next week if that was the right approach!)

7. Afraid that something might go wrong while I am in Tokyo, Japan next week (July 7-11), or Mumbai, India the following week (July 14-

18), I added a Secure Shell [SSH] daemon that runs automatically at boot time. This involves putting the public key on the server, and each remote admin has their own private key on their own client machine. I know all about public/private key pairs, as IBM is a leader in encryption technology, and was the first to deliver built-in encryption with the IBM System Storage TS1120 tape drive.

8. To have users have access to all their files from any OS image required that I either (a) have identical copies everywhere, or (b) have a shared partition. The latter turned out to be the best choice, with an LVM2 logical·volume for "/home" directory that is shared among all of the OS images. As we develop the application, we might find other directories that make sense to share as well.

9. For developing across platforms, I wanted the Ethernet devices (eth0, eth1, and so on) match the actual ports they are supposed to be connected to in a static IP configuration. Most people use DHCP so it doesn't matter, but the XS software requires this, so it did. For example, "eth0" as the 1 Gbps port to the WAN, and "eth1/eth2" as the two 10/100 Mbps PCI NIC cards to other servers. Naming the internet interfaces to specific hardware ports was different on Fedora and Debian, but I got it working.

10. While it was a stretch goal to develop a backup method, one that could perform Bare Machine Recovery from media burned by the DVD, it turned out I needed to do this anyways just to prevent me from losing my work in case things went wrong. I used an external USB drive to develop the process, and got everything to fit onto a single 4GB DVD. Using IBM Tivoli Storage Manager (TSM) for this seemed overkill, and [Mondo Rescue] didn't handle LVM2+RAID as well as I wanted, so I chose [partimage] instead, which backs up each primary partition, mirrored partition, or LVM2 logical volume, keeping all the time stamps, ownerships, and symbolic links intact. It has the ability to chop up the output into fixed sized pieces, which is helpful if you are going to burn them on 700MB CDs or 4.7GB DVDs. In my case, my FAT32-formatted external USB disk drive can't handle files bigger than 2GB, so this feature was helpful for that as well. I standardized to 660 GiB [about 692GB] per piece, since that met all criteria.

> (The mainframe equivalent is DFSMShsm or DFSMSdss DUMP, which by the way can be used with Linux for System z DASD CKD partitions. See this helpful [HOWTO back up your Linux partitions and volumes through z/OS] guide.)

11. The folks at [SysRescCD] saved the day. The standard "SysRescueCD" assigned eth0, eth1, and eth2 differently than the three base OS images, but the nice folks in France that write SysRescCD created a customized [kernel parameter that allowed the assignments to be fixed per MAC address] in support of this project. With this in place, I was able to make a live Boot-CD that brings up SSH, with all the users, passwords, and Ethernet devices to match the hardware. Installed this LiveCD as the "Rescue Image" on the hard disk itself, and also made a Recovery-DVD that boots up just like the Boot-CD, but contains the 4GB of backup files.

    For testing, I used Linux's built-in Kernel-based Virtual Machine [KVM] which works like VMware, but is open source and included into the 2.6.20 kernels that I am using. IBM is the leading reseller of VMware and has been doing server virtualization for the past 40 years, so I am comfortable with the technology. The XS-163 platform with Apache and PostgreSQL servers as a platform for [Moodle], an open source class management system, and the combination is memory-intensive enough that I did not want to incur the overheads running production this manner, but it was great for testing!

With all this in place, it is designed to not need a Linux system admin or XS-163/Moodle expert at the facility. Instead, all we need is someone to insert the Boot-CD or Recover-DVD and reboot the system if needed.

Just before packing up the unit for shipment, I changed the IP addresses to the values they need at the destination facility, updated the [GRUB boot loader] default, and made a final backup which burned the Recover-DVD. Hopefully, it works by just turning on the unit,[headless], without any keyboard, monitor or configuration required. Fingers crossed!

So, thanks to the rest of my team: Greg, Glen, Vicki, Tarun, Marcel, Pablo and Said. I am very excited to be part of this, and look forward to seeing this become something remarkable!

⊘technorati tags: XS School Server, Proyecto, Ceibal, OLPC, Uruguay, OLE, Nepal, LAMP, Web2.0, Google, Summer of Code, SSH, sshd, Apache, PostgreSQL, PHP, Red Hat, Fedora, Debian, Linux, Ethernet, BIOS, RAID, fakeraid, LiveCD, Boot-CD, Recover-DVD, DFSMS, DFSMShsm, DFSMSdss, DUMP, mainframe, LVM2, SVC, TSM, GRUB, Mondo Rescue, partimage, SysRescCD, KVM, GRUB

Comment from Bruno Cornec (Hyper-Linux)

I'm curious to know why MondoRescue you mentioned in your mail didn't work for you. Any log that you would have kept and that could help me helping you?

Response from Tony Pearson (IBM)

Bruno, I believe the problem was that we were using multi-boot and RAID1 + LVM2 on a dual SATA-drive configuration, and this apparently confused the MondoRescue utility. I tried a variety of things, burnt many DVD coasters, and in the end went with SysRescCD instead. So far it has saved as, as we were hacked, and I was able to perform a recovery remotely of the affected system. We used MondoRescue successfully with the folks in Nepal for a standard single-boot configuration.

-- Tony

Back in 1992, our Lab Director, Lynn Yates, insisted that every IBMer that went to the SHARE conference in Atlanta had to submit a "trip report". Mine was 24 pages long. Everyone else's was just half a page each. These days, I use my blog for this purpose.

2008 Jul 03 — Off to Japan and India (319)

Well, the weather here has turned awful, so I better turn off my computer to avoid lightning-strike damage.

For those looking for something to do to enjoy the "4th of July" US Independence day holiday tomorrow, there is the [Team America: Sing-a-long] at Tucson's Loft Cinema at 6pm, you can still see the fireworks after the show is over. I did this last year and it was a lot of fun.

Also, you can check out the IBM Wimbledon build on Second Life. Here's the SLURL: [http://slurl.com/secondlife/IBM%207/133/180/23]. Several IBMers will be "in world" at this virtual location on 4th of July. For all of my readers looking to check out Second Life, see what IBM can do, or talk to people who are familiar with this technology, here's your chance.

As for me, I'll be spending my "long weekend" in an airplane. Here's my travel schedule.

- July 7-11: Tokyo, Japan - business meetings with IBM sales reps
- July 13-18: Mumbai, India - business meetings with IBM business partners
- July 24-27: San Diego, California - [Comic-Con] and [Octagon Global Recruiting] -- my thanks to ABC, the producers of the TV show "LOST", and the [Dharma Initiative] for the invitation!

If you will be at any of these locations on any of these dates and want to meet up, please let me know. You can click on the "send e-mail to Tony Pearson" button on the right panel of my blog.

> (I was hoping that while I was in Asia, I could stop over and visit the schools I helped in Nepal and my friends at the Open Learning Exchange [OLE Nepal] as part of the One Laptop Per Child [OLPC Nepal] program, but I did not get all my ducks lined up for this with the appropriate travel approvals, visas and logistics. My apologies to Bryan, Sulochan and the rest of the team. Perhaps next year!)

Enjoy your weekend!

technorati tags: IBM, Tokyo, Japan, Mumbai, India, Wimbledon, SecondLife, OLE Nepal, OLPC, ABC, LOST, Dharma Initiative, Octagon Global Recruiting

Comment from Mark Twomey (EMC)

You're going to Comic-Con?
Awesome! :)

Response from Tony Pearson (IBM)

Mark, That's right. There are still some tickets left for Thursday and Friday.
-- Tony

2008 Jul 07 — Lessons Learned from IBM Project Big Green (320)

Well, I'm in Tokyo, Japan, and even though the [G8 Summit] is over in Sapporo, we could notice the heightened security here in Tokyo.

Companies here in Japan are very concerned about rising energy costs. Over on *The Raised Floor* blog, Will Runyon's post [Lessons Learned] points to David Metcalfe's article on GreenerComputing.com titled [Lessons Learned from IBM's Big Green Initiative]. Here are select excerpts:

1. **Exploit IT's information management role**

"... firms don't have the detailed electricity consumption data they need to implement energy efficiency initiatives. What they have is an energy bill for a facility."

A common adage is that, *"You can't manage what you don't measure."* IBM has beefed up the ability to measure and monitor electricity usage, not just IBM servers and storage, but also non-IBM IT equipment and facilities infrastructure like UPS, HVAC, lighting and security alarm systems.

2. **Hitch Green IT to data center refurbishment projects**

"Energy savings alone don't constitute a business case to overhaul an existing data center, undertake a refurbishment project or build a new Green Data Centre."

Either CIOs don't have the measurements of electricity to perform an ROI or cost/benefit analysis, or the facilities folks that sense improvements are possible may not see the big picture compared to other business investments. Instead, IBM seeks to incorporate IT energy efficiency best practices into existing business plans for data center improvements.

3. **Tackle corporate energy efficiency and emissions**

"... a strategy discussion and corporate carbon diagnostic are the start point to stimulate demand. Not a cold sell on Green IT."

Project Big Green is more than just an IT project. IBM's Global Business Services consultants have transformed it into a Carbon Management Strategy encompassing employees, information, property, the supply chain, customers and products. For companies that are looking at reducing their carbon footprint overall, this approach makes a lot of sense.

4. **Differentiate offerings by industry and country**

"The inability to get more power into urban data centers has driven demand for energy efficiency by banks, telcos and outsourcers."

Different countries, and different industries, have different priorities. Europe, and in particular the UK, focuses on carbon emissions as much as energy costs due to mandatory emissions caps. For data centers in the largest cities, an increase in electrical supply may not be available, or be too expensive, and the time it takes to build a new data center elsewhere, typically 12-18 months, may not be soon enough to handle current business growth rates. Energy efficiency projects can help buy them some time.

5. **Plan for slow customer adoption**

> "IBM is developing the market for IT energy efficiency and carbon management services. And it's very much an early stage market today."

IBM is frequently on the forefront of new technologies and emerging markets, so it is no surprise that we are used to dealing with slow customer adoption. The combination of high energy costs, tightening regulations and stakeholder pressure will drive the market. Larger companies and government organizations that have the means to make these necessary changes will probably lead the adoption curve.

6. **Prepare for investment barriers to IT energy efficiency**

> "With the low hanging fruit picked, IBM has found that there is an unwillingness to spend money on planting a new orchard."

IBM has helped IT clients with quick fixes offering rapid payback such as adjusting data center temperature and humidity to reduce energy consumption. But in the current economic environment, persuading firms to install variable speed fans with a 6-year payback is much tougher. Again, this is a matter of CIOs and other upper level management balancing financial investment decisions with some foresight and vision for the future.

Project Big Green launched back in May 2007, and last month IBM renewed its commitment with Project Big Green 2.0, continuing to enhance product and service offerings in support for this much needed area. And while the leaders in the G8 Summit will discuss a variety of topics, three top "green" issues on their agenda include rising energy costs, global climate change and controlling carbon emissions.

technorati tags: IBM, Tokyo, Japan, G8, Summit, 2008, Raised Floor, Greener Computing, David Metcalfe, ROI, rising energy costs, global, climate change, carbon emissions

2008 Jul 09 — Alan Lepofsky joining SocialText (321)

I was surprised to learn today that [Alan Lepofsky will be joining SocialText] as their Director of Marketing. Last January, IBM and SocialText [announced a partnership] between their Wiki product and IBM Lotus Connections.

Alan was a leader in blogging about IBM Lotus technologies and was very helpful to me over the past few years in deploying new Lotus technologies at the IBM Tucson Executive Briefing Center. The Lotus team taught me how to use Second Life, using the LotusSphere 2007 build to demonstrate the various possibilities that we used to run IBM System Storage events last year.

Alan, I wish you the best of luck on your exciting new position!

⊘**technorati tags**: IBM, Alan Lepofsky, Lotus, Connections, SocialText, Wiki, LotusSphere, SecondLife

2008 Jul 10 — Goldilocks and the Three Bears (322)

At the table in the kitchen, there were three bowls of porridge. Goldilocks was hungry. She tasted the porridge from the first bowl.

"This porridge is too hot!" she exclaimed.

So, she tasted the porridge from the second bowl.

"This porridge is too cold," she said

So, she tasted the last bowl of porridge.

"Ahhh, this porridge is just right," she said happily and she ate it all up.

-- [Goldilocks and the Three Bears]
illustration by Arthur Rackham from [*English Fairy Tales*, by Flora Annie Steel]

Continuing my week in Tokyo, Japan, I was going to title this post "Chunks, Extents and Grains", but decided instead to use the fairy tale above.

Fellow blogger BarryB from EMC, on his *The Storage Anarchist* blog, once again shows off his [PhotoShop talents], in his post [the laurel and hardy of thin provisioning]. This time, BarryB depicts fellow blogger and IBM master inventor, Barry Whyte, as Stan Laurel and fellow blogger Hu Yoshida from HDS as Oliver Hardy.

At stake is the comparison in various implementations of *thin provisioning* among the major storage vendors. On the "thick end", Hu presents his case for 42MB chunks on his post [When is Thin Provisioning Too Thin]. On the "thin end", IBMer BarryW presents the "fine-grained" details of Space-efficient Volumes (SEV), made available with the IBM System Storage SAN Volume Controller (SVC) v4.3, in his series of posts:

- [SVC 4.3.0 - Space-Efficient (thin provisioning), Mirroring and much more]
- [SVC 4.3.0 - SEV and SEFC in detail]
- [Morcombe and Wise]

BarryB paints both implementations as "extremes" in inefficiency. Some excerpts from his post:

"... Hitachi's 'chubby' provisioning is probably more performance efficient with external storage than is the SVC's 'thin' approach. But it is still horribly inefficient in context of capacity utilization.

... the 'thin extent' size used by Symmetrix Virtual Provisioning is both larger than the largest that SVC uses, and (significantly) smaller than what Hitachi uses.

'Free' may be the most expensive solution you can buy...

Before you rush off to put a bunch of SVCs running (free) SEV in front of your storage arrays, you might want to consider the performance implications of that choice. Likewise, for Hitachi's DP, you probably want to understand the impact on capacity utilization that DP will have. DP isn't free, and it isn't very space efficient, either."

BarryB would like you to think that since EMC has chosen an "extent" size between 257KB and 41MB it must therefore be the optimal setting, not too hot, and not too cold. As I mentioned last January in my post [Does Size Really Matter for Performance?], EMC engineers had not yet decided what that extent size should be, and BarryB is noticeably vague on the current value. According to this [VMware whitepaper], the thin extent size is currently 768 KB in size. Future versions of the EMC Enginuity operating environment may change the thin extent size.

(I am sure the EMC engineers are smarter and more decisive than BarryB would lead us to believe!)

BarryB is correct that any thin provisioning implementation is not "free", even though IBM's implementation is offered at no additional charge. Some writes may be slowed down waiting for additional storage to be allocated to satisfy the request, and some amount of storage must be set aside to hold the metadata directory to point to all these chunks, extents or grains. For the convenience of not having to dynamically expand LUNs manually as more space is needed, you will pay both a performance and capacity "price".

However, as they say, the [proof of the pudding is in the eating], or perhaps I should say *porridge* in this case. Given that the DMX4 is slower than both HDS USP-V and IBM SVC, you won't see EMC publishing industry-standard [SPC benchmarks] using their "thin extent" implementation anytime soon. IBM allows a choice of grain size, from 32KB to 256KB, in an elegant design that keeps the metadata directory less than 0.1 to 0.5 percent overhead. I would be surprised if EMC can make a case to be more efficient than that! The performance tests are still being run, but what I have seen so far, people will be very pleased with the minimal impact from IBM SEV, an acceptable trade-off for improved utilization and reduced out-of-space conditions.

So if you are a client waiting for your EMC equipment to be fully depreciated so you can replace it for faster equipment from IBM or HDS, you can at least improve its performance and capacity utilization today by virtualizing it with IBM SAN Volume Controller.

technorati tags: Goldilocks, Three Bears, IBM, Tokyo, Japan, EMC, BarryB, PhotoShop, Barry Whyte, HDS, Hu Yoshida, USP-V, SVC, SEV, Stan Laurel, Oliver Hardy, Symmetrix, DMX4, metadata, directory, SPC, benchmarks

This would be my first time to India. I am one of the co-founders of the Tucson Laughter Club based on Hasya Yoga started by Dr. Madan Kataria from Mumbai, India. Mumbai is also called "Bollywood" and I was able to watch a movie in an authentic theater. At a dinner with executives from IBM India, I asked one of them why India had so many beautiful women. He laughed and was too embarrassed to answer.

2008 Jul 11 — From Tokyo to Mumbai (323)

Thirteen months ago, fellow IBM blogger Bob Sutor suggested the potential for avatars to [move from one virtual world to another]. I thought this was far, far in the future myself, but this week, IBM and Linden Labs, the makers of Second Life, successfully teleported an avatar from SecondLife over to OpenSim. Here is the [Press Release].

Linden Labs has this [FAQ] for the interoperability announcement. The [Wall Street Journal] and [Financial Times] discuss the significance and importance of this major development.

If you are thinking there is no business value here, consider that Cisco has this incredible [11-minute demonstration video] that has presenters in one city on the stage at another city.

Well, my job is done here in Tokyo, and my team is off next to Mumbai, India. This of course will take the bulk of tomorrow in airplanes and airports, and not be as easy as teleporting in the metaverse!

technorati tags: IBM, Bob Sutor, Linden Labs, Second Life, secondlife, OpenSim, Cisco, Tokyo, Japan, Mumbai, India, metaverse, teleport, avatar

 Prior to working for IBM, I worked at McDonald's. Not flipping burgers, but working in the central office that managed seven local restaurants in the Tucson area. I did data entry and computer programming for the accounting department. I make it a point to eat at least once at a McDonald's in every country I visit.

2008 Jul 14 — Taking a Tuk-Tuk to McDonald's (324)

We have successfully arrived to Mumbai, India. Since this is my first time in India, I decided to check out the town by going to the local McDonald's® restaurant. As a former software engineer of McDonald's, I love the food, and try to visit a McDonald's in every country I visit. Wikipedia calls our transportation an [Auto Rickshaw], but the locals called it  a "tuk-tuk". This is not my first time in one; they have them in Thailand and Mexico as well.

We had the hotel identify the address of the closest McDonald's to our hotel.

From past experience I know that tuk-tuk drivers will suggest alternatives, in an effort to earn a larger fare, or to redirect to a preferred location where the

driver might get special kick-backs. Our driver was no different.

The traffic was treacherous, the roads were in roughshod condition, and sad looking stray dogs digging through piles of rubbish were everywhere. The local "Daily News and Analysis" newspaper this week estimates that there are over 70,000 stray dogs in Mumbai alone. What to do with all of these strays is a

matter of controversy. In preparation for the Olympic Games, China has asked its restaurants to [take "dog" off their menus]. Having lived in one of the poorest countries, and one of the richest, nothing surprises me anymore.

My IBM colleague, Curtis Neal, decided to join me for this adventure. Finally, after about 20 minutes, our driver parks the tuk-tuk. He told us the restaurant is only about three blocks away by foot, he would allow us to treat him to lunch, and then he will take us back to the hotel. While we appreciated his fantastic imagination, we told him we just wanted to be taken one-way to the restaurant, to drop us off at the front door, and we would find another tuk-tuk for the return.

After a bit of argument, we settled on being left only one block away, and we would walk the rest. While we could not see exactly where the restaurant was when we got out, he at least pointed us in the right direction.

The problem was that we approached the restaurant from behind, and came up to its equivalent of a "drive thru" window, ordered our food, and then went to the second window to pick up our order. We were eating on the street. It was not until I decided to take this photo of the restaurant, that we discovered there was an entire seating area upstairs, and around the corner the main entrance!

There were plenty of tuk-tuks picking up and dropping people off, so we have no idea why our previous driver was unwilling to take us the entire distance.

Cows are sacred here in India, so there are no beef-based hamburgers to choose from. My choices for sandwiches were:

- [McChicken]®
- Fish Filet
- Veggie burger, made from brown rice
- Salad burger, basically a [BLT] without the bacon

Since my nutritionist asked me to avoid carbs and fried foods, I chose the McChicken with cheese combo meal with fries and a Coke.

Getting back was also a challenge. While we had no problem haling a tuk-tuk, we had no idea the address of our hotel, and our driver had no idea where it was. We ended up driving around the city until we found a different hotel, asked them if they knew where it was, and then eventually getting to our hotel. This is something I should have planned for in advance, getting a card with the hotel details on it before leaving.

While it might seem like a simple trip, Curtis and I probably learned more about India this way than spending a week inside the comforts of our hotel.

⌐technorati tags: IBM, Mumbai, India, McDonald's, China, stray dogs, restaurant, menu, Olympics, McChicken, Coke, tuk-tuk, auto rickshaw

Comment from Steve Todd (EMC)

Tony, I'm enjoying your "travel around the world" blogging but I'm having a hard time processing your "I have a nutritionist" with "I eat at McDonalds" statements! ;>) Steve

Response from Tony Pearson (IBM)

Steve, it was meant as a bit of humor, doing opposite of what my nutritionist, Jennifer Higgins, would advise, while I am out of town. (She would oppose the bun; at home I usually ask for my burgers to be wrapped in lettuce instead.)

This is not to imply that McDonald's food is not nutritious. The nutritional details about each item on the menu can be found here:

> http://www.mcdonalds.com/usa/eat/nutrition_info.html

-- Tony

Comment from Jack:

"Having lived in one of the poorest countries, and one of the richest, nothing surprises me anymore." These Lines from your blog are with respect to which country?

Please Google the below links for classification on poverty:

- http://en.wikipedia.org/wiki/Economy_of_India
- http://en.wikipedia.org/wiki/Official_languages_of_India

Response from Tony Pearson (IBM)

Jack, I grew up in Bolivia, which is generally ranked among the bottom half of the countries based on GDP per capita (PPP). It currently has a PPP of $2900 according to Wikipedia:

> http://en.wikipedia.org/wiki/Economy_of_Bolivia

I now live in the USA, with a PPP of $48,000. Second only to Switzerland. See:

> http://en.wikipedia.org/wiki/Economy_of_USA

India falls somewhere in between, with a PPP of $4,543.
-- Tony

 This post introduced a new dilemma. One of the comments asked about the DS5000 which we had not yet announced. I had to consult with IBM Legal on how to respond.

2008 Jul 15 — 2008 Announcements for July 15 (325)

Well, it's Tuesday, and so it is "announcement day" again! Actually, for me it is Wednesday morning here in Mumbai, India, but since I was "press embargoed" until 4pm EDT in talking about these enhancements, I had to wait until Wednesday morning here to talk about them.

World's Fastest 1TB tape drive

IBM announced its new enterprise [TS1130 tape drive] and corresponding [TS3500 tape library support]. This one has a funny back-story. Last week while we were preparing the Press Release, we debated on whether we should compare the 1TB per cartridge capacity as double that of Sun's Enterprise T10000 (500GB), or LTO-4 (800GB). The problem changed when Sun announced on Monday they too had a 1TB tape drive, so now instead of saying that we had the "World's <u>First</u> 1TB tape drive", we quickly changed

this to the "World's <u>Fastest</u> 1TB tape drive" instead. At 160MB/sec top speed, IBM's TS1130 is 33 percent faster than Sun's latest announcement. Sun was rather vague when they will actually ship their new units, so IBM may still end up being first to deliver as well.

Here is an IBM podcast to hear more about it:

Listen to IBM's Charlie Andrews describe the new IBM TS1130 1 TB tape drive]

While EMC and other disk-only vendors have stopped claiming that "tape is dead", these recent announcements from IBM and Sun indicate that indeed tape is alive and well. IBM is able to borrow technologies from disk, such as the Giant Magnetoresistance (GMR) head over to its tape offerings, which means much of the R&D for disk applies to tape, keeping both forms of storage well invested. Tape continues to be the "greenest" storage option, more energy efficient than disk, optical, film, microfiche and even paper.

Improved Reporting

On the LTO front, IBM enhanced the reporting capabilities of its [TS3310] midrange tape library. This includes identifying the resource utilization of the drives, reporting on media integrity, and improved diagnostics to support library-managed encryption.

IBM System Storage DR550

As a blended disk-and-tape solution, the [IBM System Storage DR550] easily replaces the EMC Centera to meet compliance storage requirements. IBM announced that we have greatly expanded its scalability, being able to support both 1TB <u>disk</u> drives, as well as being able to attach to either IBM or Sun's 1TB <u>tape</u> drives.

Massive Array of Idle Disks (MAID)

IBM now offers a "Sleep Mode" in the firmware of the [IBM System Storage DCS9550], which is often called "Massive Array of Idle Disks" (MAID) or spin-down capability. This can reduce the amount of power consumed during idle times.

That's a lot of exciting stuff. I'm off to breakfast now.

⊘**technorati tags**: IBM, TS1130, TS3500, tape, systems, 1TB, drive, library, LTO, LTO-4, TS3310, Charlie Andrews, DR550, MAID, DCS9550, Sleep Mode, Sun, EMC

Comment from Tmasteen

When can we expect some announcements/docs about the DS5000?

Response from Tony Pearson (IBM)

Tmasteen, Sorry, I can't talk about unannounced products.
-- Tony

Comment from Nils Aatland

Nominal TS1130 read/write performance is 160 MB/sec (uncompressed) if you use long tape (JB). What about read/write performance with standard length tape (JA)? I've checked TS1130 Data Sheet, I cannot find anything about this. For me it seems that capacity is 640 GB (JA assumed), but what about performance?

Response from Tony Pearson (IBM)

Nils, I spoke to Randy Fleenor, who is my contact in Tape world, who confirmed that the 160MB/sec native data rate applies to any of the supported tape cartridge capacities.

Also, the TS1130 can write or append TS1120-format tapes, but in this case you get slower performance. The TS1130 is not emulating a TS1120, but rather making the cartridge format compatible so that it can be read back in a TS1120 drive.
-- Tony

Comment from Nils Aatland

Hi,

I'm confused, I've got the following information from IBM Norway

New IBM 3592 E06 Enterprise Tape Drive (Jaguar 3)

- Third generation 3592 Enterprise Tape Drive
    - same form factor as Jag1/2; plug compatible with existing 3592 models
- For use with all existing 3592 media types (JB, JX, JA, JR, JJ, JW)
- Jag3 Cartridge Capacity:
    - 1 TB cartridge capacity with JB/JX media
    - 640 GB capacity with JA/JW media;
    - 128 GB with JJ/JR media
- Jag3 Data rate:
    - 160 MB/s data rate with JB/JX media
    - 140 MB/s with JA/JW/JJ/JR media
- Can read and write 3592 E05 (Jag2) format
    - 150 MB/s with JB/JX media; 140 MB/s with JA/JW/JJ/JR media (vs. 100 MB/s native data rate for Jag2)
    - same cartridge capacities as Jag2 (700 GB for JB/JX; 500 GB for JA/JW)
    - Jag3 can reformat Jag2 media to Jag3, and Jag3 media to Jag2
- Can read 3592 J1A (Jag1) format (write not supported)
- Supports System Managed, Library Managed and Application Managed Encryption
- Available for 3584, 3494, C20, 3577 tape library install, as well as rack install
    - supporting both high-end (3592 J70 and C06 CU attach) as well as open systems attachment

- Dual-port 4GB Fibre Channel interface
- Can upgrade existing 3592 E05 tape drives to Jag3 (3592 EU6)
  - but will not include the new Jag3 drive Ethernet port
- CU-attach will not support Jag 1/2/3 drive intermix, and all CU-attached 3592 E06 drives must be encryption-enabled

Regards
Nils

Comment from Russell Schneider (Jeskell, an IBM Business Partner)

Tony, Hello! Is there any good benchmark data available on TS1130 vs. LTO-4? I have a large user trying to make that decision for a massive TSM implementation at this time. Thanks!

Response from Tony Pearson (IBM)

Russell, it depends on the TSM server platform. For TSM on z/OS, TS1130 is the better choice, offering both ESCON and FICON attachment. For all other platforms, the tradeoffs favor LTO-4. TS1130 is faster (160MB/sec) and higher capacity (1TB per cartridge) than LTO-4 (120MB/sec and 800GB cartridges), but if you don't need all the other additional features of the TS1130, the LTO-4 can be more cost-effective solution.
-- Tony

2008 Jul 16 -- Rock the Vote - 2008 Best Product Awards (326)

Network Products Guide has two of my favorite IBM products up for "Best Product of 2008" awards.

IBM System Storage SAN Volume Controller is up for:

- "Best Storage"
- "Best Virtualization"

IBM System z10 Enterprise Class mainframe server is up for:

- "Best Cryptography"
- "Best Data Center Management"
- "Best Server Solution"
- "Best Virtualization"

If you'd like to put in your vote, go to their virtual [Voting Booth].

Rather than pay for a tour of the city, I hopped in a taxi to go see a Ballywood movie. The taxi driver offered to wait for me in his cab outside in the heat for the three hours so that he could take me back to the hotel. Instead, I invited him to see the movie with me, thus promoting him from "driver" to "cultural consultant".

2008 Jul 17 — Brain Rules for Presenters (327)

I had the afternoon free, so I went to see a "Bollywood" movie filmed here on location in Mumbai, India titled "Jaane Tu Ya Jaane Na" which I was told roughly translates to "I know you, but I really don't know you." Here is [the official website], [picture galleries], [film reviews], and a [plot synopsis (spoiler alert, gives away all the surprises and the totally predictable ending)].

I was warned that this musical would be nearly three hours long, that the singing and dialogue would be in Hindi language, and there would be no English subtitles. I don't speak Hindi, and would not be able to understand a single word the actors said.

How bad could it be?

Despite the fact that there were nearly 20 members in the cast, the story jumps back and forth in both place and time, with some dream sequences thrown in for cinematic effect, I was able to understand quite a bit. I thoroughly enjoyed this movie! Perhaps it's a sign of a good movie that you can understand most of it purely from the visual aspects.

The same can be said for presentations that you give in foreign countries. Both in Japan and India, I had plenty of visuals to complement the text on the page, and the words that I spoke. Shawn over at [Anecdote] blog points to this great presentation by Garr Reynolds, author of [Presentation Zen]. The slide deck below has some key takeaways and quotes from Dr. John Medina's latest book "Brain Rules" that apply to presentations.

As the world becomes more globally integrated, communicating visually will be an important skill to develop.

technorati tags: IBM, Mumbai, India, Bollywood, Hindi, Japan, Garr Reynolds, John Medina, Brain Rules

Comment from Marc Farley (3PAR)

Tony, Good to see you are getting a little free time while you're there. I was wondering if you were working on a song and dance act to go along with your presentations?

Bloggers from EMC and NetApp often fling poo at each other, and the only take-away from this is that EMC doesn't understand NetApp products, and sometimes NetApp doesn't' understand EMC products. I felt it would be good to step in and point this out to everyone. (Note: If you like the graphic, you can buy a tee-shirt over at Café Press.)

2008 Jul 18 — The Murals in Restaurants (328)

"The murals in restaurants are on par with the food in museums."
--- Peter De Vries

The quote above applies to blogs as well. Those about competitive products of which the blogger has little to no hands-on experience tend to be terribly misleading or technically inaccurate. We saw this last month as Sun Microsystems' Jeff Savit tried to discuss the IBM System z10 EC mainframe.

This time, it comes from EMC bloggers discussing NetApp equipment, and by association, IBM System Storage N series gear. I was going to comment on the ridiculous posts by fellow bloggers from EMC about SnapLock compliance feature on the NetApp, but my buddies at NetApp had already done this for me, saving me the trouble.

From EMC:

- [NetApp's Compliance Isn't Compliant], by Scott Waterhouse
- [NetApp SnapLock badly Broken] , by Mark Twomey (StorageZilla)
- [Got Rabies?], by Mark Twomey (StorageZilla)

From NetApp:

- [Responsibility vs. Hysteria], by Val Borcovici
- [NetApp SnapLock Continues Working], by Kostadis Roussos

The hysterical nature of writing from EMC, and the calm responses from NetApp, speak volumes about the cultures of both companies.

The key point is that none of the "Non-erasable, Non-Rewriteable" (NENR) storage out there are certified as compliant by any government agency on the planet. Governments just aren't in the business of certifying such things. The best you can get is a third-party consultant, such as [Cohasset Associates], to help make decisions that are best for each particular situation.

In addition to SnapLock on N series, IBM offers the [IBM System Storage DR550], WORM tape and optical systems, all of which have been deemed compliant to the U.S. Securities and Exchange Commission [SEC 17a-4] federal regulations by Cohasset Associates. For medical patient records and images like X-rays, IBM offers the Grid Medical Archive Solution [GMAS] designed to meet the requirements of the U.S. Health Insurance Portability and Accountability Act [HIPAA]. For other government or industry regulations, consult with your legal counsel.

⊘**technorati tags**: IBM, EMC, NetApp, N series, SnapLock, compliance, compliant, NENR, WORM, DR550, SEC, 17a-4, GMAS, HIPAA, tape, optical, disk, systems, Cohasset Associates, z10, EC, mainframe, Sun

Comment from Val Bercovici (NetApp)

Love the De Vries quote Tony!

Comment from Mark Twomey (EMC), aka StorageZilla

> "Those about competitive products of which the blogger has little to no hands-on experience tend to be terribly misleading or technically inaccurate."

Well if that's true doesn't that go for you too since all IBM is doing is shipping someone else's box?

I had a FAS in the old lab (I don't now since the job changed), what have you done from the plane seat recently?

Comment from Val Bercovici (NetApp)

Zilla, clearly you never touched that old FAS in the lab. Otherwise you'd be working here at NetApp like everyone else at EMC who experiences how cool and simple networked storage can be :)

Response from Tony Pearson (IBM)

Mark, IBM does work on the N series in Tucson, and we have them in our Tucson Executive Briefing Center where we demo the units to our clients. IBM won design awards for the facial plates that are unique from the NetApp FAS appliances.

-- Tony

Comment from Mark Twomey (EMC), aka StorageZilla

Val: We all know you think you're selling the glory of god in a box but it looked and smelt like just another NAS box to me. I'll admit at the time it was much easier to set up than Celerra but that ain't true anymore, boss.

Tony: Was that sarcasm or are you telling me the only value you add to that banana is a bruise?

Love the box while you can but having worked for Moshe I know what he thinks of NetApp because he wasn't afraid of using expletives when he told us what he thought of NetApp. The EMC way is to kill all internal competitors, so the moment you spot a NAS Interface module for Nextra (If there wasn't one in development already) you'll be able to claim a lot more than some nice face plates as your own.

Comment from Val Bercovici (NetApp)

Ah Zilla, ignorance like yours about our products is music to my ears. It's always easier to compete against a misinformed opponent.

As to Moshe's motives for joining IBM, well let's just say he has a BIG target in his sights - and it's not NetApp. I'd be looking over your shoulder for all the ghosts of EMC's glorious past now on the XIV payroll if I were you.

Not only do they know how to compete against all the dirty tactics they pioneered, but they also know where all the EMC skeletons are still buried :)

Response from Tony Pearson (IBM)

Mark, no, not sarcasm, just pointing out the falsehood of your premise that just because N series are manufactured elsewhere that a person like me from Tucson can't have hands-on knowledge to discuss it in my blog. We do a lot of testing of products here in Tucson, since we are also a software lab, and have both N series and NetApp gear to work with.

You also imply that IBM is merely a reseller of NetApp equipment, but IBM and NetApp have an OEM agreement instead, so you are wrong on that as well.
-- Tony

 As a result of my many mentions to the TV show LOST on my blog, I received an email from "Octagon Global Recruiting". This was all a social media campaign to get more bloggers to discuss the show. I took seven challenging "Dharma Initiative" tests online. Based on my results, the producers from ABC invited me to attend Comic-Con in person to apply for a role as an extra on the TV show. I was not selected, but had a great time!

2008 Jul 23 — Comic-Con Day 1 (329)

Having survived my two weeks in Asia, I am now taking a vacation, to attend the [Comic-Con 2008] convention in San Diego, California.

technorati tags: Comic-Con

2008 Jul 29 — Everything but the SAN switch itself (330)

Once again it's Tuesday, which means IBM announcement day!

Today IBM announced [two new DS3400 SAN Express Models]. These two new models will replace the IBM System Storage DS3400 SAN Express Kit model 41U and 42U to be withdrawn from marketing today. The DS3000 series of scalable, flexible, and affordable storage solutions support IBM System x, System p, and BladeCenter servers.

Two new IBM System Storage DS3400 SAN Express Kits are being introduced that provide the parts needed to setup and configure a SAN with the exception of a SAN switch that can be ordered separately. The IBM System Storage DS3400 SAN Express Kits contain Emulex EZPilot software that enables automated installation and configuration of the SAN components. IBM System Storage DS3400 SAN Express Kits models 41S and 42S and Emulex EZPilot software work in conjunction with the IBM TotalStorage SAN16B-2 Express Model Switch which comes with eight ports and eight 4 Gbps SFPs. The EZPilot software can support configurations with either one or two SAN16B-2 switches.

The 41S is a single-controller model DS3400 with two HBA cards and four cables. The 42S is the dual-controller model with two HBA cards and eight cables.

technorati tags: IBM, DS3400, SAN, Express, models, System x, System p, BladeCenter, disk, storage, systems, single-controller, dual-controller, 41S, 42S, Emulex, EZPilot

August

We had several exciting announcements this month on August 12, but the VP of Marketing decided to experiment with "going dark", not putting out any press releases or blog posts until the official launch of the "Information Infrastructure" initiative on September 8. This made for some awkward situations on the blogosphere. Not surprisingly, the handful of executives and marketeers who thought this failed experiment was a good idea no longer work in IBM System Storage.

2008 Aug 11 — Charging per Watt not per Square Foot (331)

Fellow blogger Robin Harris over on *Storage Mojo* has a great post titled [Power-play, power work] where he points to Christian Belady's post [Changing Data Center Behavior Based on Chargeback Metrics]. The focus is on metrics. The average data center is 10 to 15 years old, and the metrics used to chargeback IT expenses were often based on square footage.

The focus on square footage resulted in higher density. This reminds me of the classic IBM commercial ["The Heist"] where Gil panics that the roomful of servers are missing, and Ned explains that it was all consolidated onto a single IBM server.

I suspect few people picked up on the fact that the acronym for ["new enterprise data center"] spells "Ned", our donut-eating hero in these series of videos.

The two main points in [Belady's presentation] were:

- Costs in the data center are proportional to power usage rather than space.
- Power efficiency is more of a behavior problem than it is a technology problem.

This is definitely a step in the right direction. Both servers and storage systems consume a large portion of the energy on the data center floor. IBM Tivoli Usage and Accounting Manager can include energy consumption as part of the chargeback calculations.

⊙**technorati tags**: Robin Harris, StorageMojo, chargeback, IBM, server, storage, Gil, Ned, The Heist, Christian Belady, Microsoft, TUAM

Comment from Anon

Have you seen The Storage Anarchist's post on XIV?

Response from Tony Pearson (IBM)

Anon, Yes, anyone getting news about IBM products and services from EMC employees is about as bad as basing your views of Microsoft Vista operating system from Apple television ads. My blog about that here: [#332 below]
-- Tony

Comment from Anon

Thanks, but the links do seem to go to real IBM web pages. So why is there so much silence about it?

Response from Tony Pearson (IBM)

Anon, I've been so busy talking to excited clients that I haven't had time to blog. I'll get around to it later when things start to slow down a bit.

-- Tony

 In an effort to make an inside joke about how stupid I felt the "going dark" experiment was, I found a comic that combined "dark" and "experiment" with a reference to the Dark Knight from the Batman movie franchise, and Microsoft's failed Mohave experiment.

2008 Aug 13 — Deceptively Delicious (332)

I really enjoy web comic *Geek and Poke*, a recent example is titled [Microsoft's New Approach].

The comic combines the recent popularity in cookbooks to help parents get their children to eat more vegetables, such as Jessica Seinfeld's [Deceptively Delicious: Simple Secrets to Get Your Kids Eating Good Food], with the popularity of the latest Batman movie, [The Dark Knight]. To be

fair, I have not reviewed the recipe book, but certainly being the wife of comedian Jerry Seinfeld and mother of his children sufficiently qualifies her to write such a book. I did have the pleasure to see this movie at an IMAX movie theater in Hartford, CT a few weeks ago. I highly recommend it. (See also my friend Pam's awesome [review of this movie]). Some have argued the movie franchise has "gone dark" from the previous Batman movies and may not be appropriate for children. Hiding vegetables in meals may not be the right thing for children either.

In the comic, the young boy sees right through it, using the word "mojave" as the new slang for "deceive". In Arizona, Mojave refers to both the [desert in the northern part of the state], and the [Native American tribe] that live there. But in this case, it refers to Microsoft's deceptive [Mojave Experiment].

Unlike IBM that repeatedly delivers unique and innovative new products to the marketplace, Microsoft pulls the old ["bait and switch"] routine. In a series of hidden camera interviews, Microsoft asks skeptical people who have never used Microsoft Vista operating system their opinions. As expected, all express concerns of problems they have heard about Microsoft's new OS, from friends, colleagues or Apple television advertisements. On a scale of 0 (won't touch it) to 10 (can't wait to have it), the average skeptic rated Vista with a paltry 4.4 score.

The Microsoft interviewers then show them the new "Microsoft Mojave" Operating System, and ask these same skeptics for their opinions, of which many (35 out of 140 by one account) express they like it, find this new OS useful and intuitive. The interviewers then explain that this Mojave OS was nothing more than the existing Vista OS already in the marketplace. The average rating for Mojave OS was a significantly higher 8.5 score. Just like hiding spinach in a meal to get your kids to eat it. They tricked you, and you said you liked it!

On *ZDnet*, Adrian Kingsley-Hughes takes Microsoft to task in his post [The "Mojave Experiment"] Just an exercise in guided clicking or does it highlight some of the problems with Windows Vista] and his follow-up post [Dissecting Microsoft's Mojave Experiment]. His conclusion: He considers the marketing experiment cleverly devious, but the outcome of the experiment is vacuous.

Perhaps the key take-away is whom should prospective customers listen to when evaluating a new product. Microsoft is reasonable in feeling that customers should not base their opinions about Vista solely on lopsided Apple television commercials. Apple, Inc. is one of Microsoft's primary competitors. I feel, however, that if you have friends or colleagues who have shared with you their hands-on experiences, that indeed should have much higher weighting.

Nothing, of course, beats personal experience. If you want to try out one of IBM's latest products for yourself, please contact your local IBM Business Partner or IBM sales representative.

⊘**technorati tags**: IBM, Geek and Poke, Jessica Seinfeld, Jerry Seinfeld, Deceptively Delicious, The Dark Knight, IMAX, Batman, Mojave, Desert,

Native American, tribe, Microsoft, Vista, Mojave Experiment, hidden camera, interview, ZDnet, Adrian Kingsley-Hughes, Apple

Addition from Tony Pearson (IBM)

Paul Levinson has a review of Dark Knight here:

> http://paullevinson.blogspot.com/2008/07/dark-knight-transcends.html

2008 Aug 14 — IBM Global CEO Study 2008 on IBM TV (333)

IBM TV has an interesting 8-minute video which includes highlights of the recent IBM Global CEO study. Worth a look!

For those who prefer a deeper look, you can [download the study], or [listen to the podcast].

◌**technorati tags**: IBM, Global CEO Study, IBM TV

Comment from Prent

Seems pretty content-free. Are you sure you posted the right video? All I saw was people at a boring conference milling around. On top of terrible music.

Response from Tony Pearson (IBM)

Prent,
Yes, it's the correct video. It is just a highlights video, feel free to download the full study if you want more details.

-- Tony

2008 Aug 19 — Storage Symposium 2008 in Montpelier France (334)

If you missed the [IBM System Storage and Storage Networking Symposium] in San Diego, California last month (like I did because I was in Japan and India), here is your chance to attend the one next month in Europe, September 8-11, in beautiful [Montpellier, France]. Several of my colleagues from the IBM Tucson Executive Briefing Center are scheduled to speak at this event.

And maybe, perhaps, some IBM executives, will have something important to say next month also! Stay tuned!

For a list of other IBM events this year, see the [2008 schedule].

technorati tags: IBM, storage, symposium, events, San Diego, California, Japan, India, Europe, Montpellier, France

David Gelardi is my third-line manager, and is the IBM Vice President in charge of all the executive briefing centers, benchmark centers, and design centers for IBM's Systems and Technology Group.

2008 Aug 27 — Big Iron anything but rusty at IBM (335)

I am glad not everyone is on vacation in August!

Brian Womack from Investor's Business Daily interviewed IBM vice president David Gelardi in the article [Big Iron Anything But Rusty For Mainframe Pioneer IBM]. Here are some excerpts:

"IBM says revenue for its mainframe business rose 32% in the second quarter compared with a year earlier, easily outpacing overall sales growth of 13%. A big driver was February's launch of IBM's next-generation mainframe line, the z10, and its first big upgrade since 2004. IBM spent about $1.5 billion on the new line.

With their power and size, mainframes have some unique advantages over (distributed) servers. Many companies cobble together many servers, powered by industry standard chips made by Intel (INTC) and Advanced Micro Devices, (AMD) to do jobs that were once the province of mainframes. IBM, too, sells such servers.

IBD: Can you tell me more about this business?

Gelardi: Traditionally, the mainframe was the back-office powerhouse for batch and transactional processing -- sort of the thing behind banks, the thing behind retailers, the thing behind insurance companies.

It's the thing that, if you screw this up, you just gave your whole business away. The new thing, which is really sort of the second driver of growth, is the introduction of Linux (an open-source operating system popular with some servers) on the mainframe. Z-Linux (IBM's Linux mainframe software) is where we have been able to drive substantially new workloads to the mainframe.

IBD: Why is the mainframe business important to IBM?

Gelardi: It's a very differentiated product environment where we feel very confident that we can say to a client, look, we built this thing from the casters all the way up; the software stack, all the way up. We've built into this a level of performance and scalability and efficiency. We're very, very confident that we can resolve any issue (for customers).

Let me give you an example. If I take (1,500 Intel) servers . . . and put them on a single mainframe, I'll have no performance problems whatsoever. But I'm taking all of that workload that was on 1,500 separate servers and consolidating them on one mainframe. While it may be a million-dollar machine and up, it's actually cheaper than those 1,500 servers.

IBD: What are some big drivers for your clients today?

Gelardi: Energy. If you look at a workload on a previous generation mainframe, z9, for the equivalent performance on a z10, I'm going to use 15% less energy for the same amount of performance.

Look at the (physical data-center space) in the industry. The question used to be, 'How much space do you want?' The question now is, 'How much energy are you going to consume?' It's more efficient to manage the workloads inside the larger (mainframe).

IBD: So, you're saying that using a mainframe addresses these modern problems better than servers?

Gelardi: Correct.

IBD: Is it hard to convince people of that?

Gelardi: It's a legitimate question for clients who never had a mainframe. There are a few. (In those cases) it will probably be more complicated (to convince them).

However, a year or so ago we put out a press release about an entertainment (company). Their story was, 'We're going to build a new gaming environment.' Long story short, they said, 'Why not use the mainframe?' There are new clients coming to the mainframe.

IBD: Do mainframes help other IBM businesses?

Gelardi: Clearly. I have very broad coverage. We are the server vendor. We have the storage capacity; we have the operating environment; we have the software stack, (including) WebSphere, Tivoli, and DB2. We have the services capabilities. We have the consulting capability. You can sort of go on. It becomes an ecosystem that is really valuable to the company at large.

IBD: What mainframe customers were active in the second quarter?

Gelardi: Interesting enough (given the state of the industry), the financial services sector was very strong. That was particularly true in the Americas and in Europe. We have a pretty broad spread (of users), but there is no question that financial services is a core market."

IBM offers a lower total cost of ownership (TCO) than HP or Sun can offer. For more about the IBM System z10 EC, see my posts last month:

- [Seven Words #315]
- [Virtualization, Carpools and Marathons #316]
- [Summer Reading for the z10 EC #317]

And, of course, IBM is first-to-market on many mainframe enabling features in disk and tape storage systems. The combination of IBM servers with IBM storage systems is hard to beat!

⊘**technorati tags**: IBM, z10, EC, IBD, David Gelardi, HP, Sun

IBM has been in business since 1911, and is known for many "firsts" in the IT industry. I broke "radio silence" of IBM's "going dark" experiment to discuss IBM's breaking the 1 million Input/Output operations per second (IOPS) using SAN Volume Controller with Solid-State Drives.

2008 Aug 28 — IBM breaks 1 million IOPS barrier with Solid State Drive (336)

IBM once again delivers storage innovation!

(**Note:** The following paragraphs have been updated to clarify the performance tests involved.)

This time, IBM breaks the 1 million IOPS barrier, achieved by running a test workload consisting of a 70/30 mix of random 4K requests. That is 70 percent reads, 30 percent writes, with 4KB blocks. The throughput achieved was 3.5x times that obtained by running the identical workload on the fastest IBM storage system today (IBM System Storage SAN Volume Controller 4.3), and an estimated EIGHT* times the performance of EMC DMX. With an average response time under 1 millisecond, this solution would be ideal for online transaction processing (OLTP) such as financial recordings or airline reservations.

(*)**Note:** EMC has not yet published ANY benchmarks of their EMC DMX box with SSD enterprise flash drives (EFD). However, I believe that the performance bottleneck is in their controller and not the back-end SSD or FC HDD media, so I have given EMC the benefit of the doubt and estimated that their latest EMC DMX4 is as fast as an [IBM DS8300 Turbo] with Fibre Channel drives. If or when EMC publishes benchmarks, the marketplace can make more accurate comparisons. Your mileage may vary.

IBM used 4 TB of Solid State Drive (SSD) behind its IBM SAN Volume Controller (SVC) technology to achieve this amazing result. Not only does this represent a significantly smaller footprint, but it uses only 55 percent of the power and cooling.

The SSD drives are made by [Fusion IO] and are different than those used by EMC made by STEC.

The SVC addresses the one key problem clients face today with competitive disk systems that support SSD enterprise flash drives: choosing what data to park on those expensive drives? How do you decide which LUNs, which databases, or which files should be permanently resident on SSD? With SVC's industry-leading storage virtualization capability, you are not forced to decide. You can move data into SSD and back out again non-disruptively, as needed to meet performance requirements. This could be handy for quarter-end or year-end processing, for example.

For more on this, see the [IBM Press Release] or the articles in [Network World] by Jon Brodkin, and [CNET News] by Brooke Crothers.

Our clients have often told us at IBM that performance is one of their top purchase criteria. IBM once again has shown that it listens to the marketplace!

⊘technorati tags: IBM, SVC, million, IOPS, EMC, DMX, Network World, CNET, Jon Brodkin, Brooke Crothers, benchmark, leading, performance, SSD, EFD, FC, HDD, disk, systems, media

Comment from Chuck Hollis (EMC)

Hi Tony, nice to see you back and writing about storage again.

So, is this a pre-announcement of a product, or just a technology demonstration?

Funny -- IBM ships new products (XIV and DS5000) but doesn't announce them, and now announces something that isn't really a product...

I do have to agree with you, this enterprise flash is amazing stuff -- our customers are seeing spectacular results so far.

Comment from Jamon

When are the SPC-1 Results going to be published? It would be great to see the real results.

Response from Tony Pearson (IBM)

Chuck, IBM blogging guidelines prohibit me from pre-announcing products, I have to wait for the official IBM press release just like everyone else.

Six months ago, IBM and EMC were the only two major vendors selling Solid State Drive to the data center, and now everyone else seems to be jumping on the bandwagon.

I'll let my fellow IBM blogger, BarryW, discuss the product plans based on this technology demonstration. He's much closer to this than I am.
-- Tony

Comment from Barry Whyte (IBM)

As if by magic...

Jamon, as this is not a GA'd product we cannot provide official SPC-1 figures - although we have tested it - so what we did was run the same benchmark on the same SVC cluster config as we do have benchmarked, so that you could get a real-life comparison, it was this comparison that shows the flash system providing 3.5x IOPs at 1/20th response time (when compared like for like with the known SVC config) - so you can do the math and come up with a reasonable comparison.

For more details of what we did, what it is and so on, see the URL provided below.

Comment from Avra Hamn

Unlike PC where the user may replace not more than a dozen files per day, online transactions may write to certain DB rows every second, depending on applications.

Comment from Barry Burke (EMC), the Storage Anarchist

Tsk, tsk, Tony. Misrepresenting the facts once again...

As BarryW admits on his post, the SVC+FusionIO science experiment results were driven using a non-standard configuration of the SPC-1: 70/30 read/write instead of the official standard 60/40-ish.

And as BarryW points out, not only was the tested configuration not a GA configuration, it used a non-standard configuration of SVC with more than 8 nodes to aggregate the performance.

More significantly, I'm pretty sure that the SPC Bylaws prohibit EXACTLY the sort of extrapolated comparisons you've made here in this post. I believe the SPC rules also specifically prohibit modification of the test for any reason or purpose, and further prohibits publication of unaudited results under any circumstances.

Unless you've gotten a waiver from them (or used your influence to change the rules), this entire post appears to be in violation of SPC Bylaws and rules of membership.

And for what it's worth, I am pretty sure that the #1 customer purchase criterion is "Integrity."

Response from Tony Pearson (IBM)

BarryB, Yes, it was an internal test workload, 70/30 mix of 4K requests, and so I will update the post to reflect that. The press release was clearer on this, so I apologize to all that my post was vague and misleading.

-- Tony

Addition from Tony Pearson (IBM)

Chuck Hollis from EMC pokes fun at this here:

> http://chucksblog.typepad.com/chucks_blog/2008/09/hot-spots-and-f.html

-- Tony

 I don't know who coined the term "Blogoversary", but I thought this was fitting. I couldn't celebrate my first one since I had just been kicked out of marketing and was busy updating my resume looking for a job, but this one I could celebrate, in a job that was safe and secure.

2008 Aug 29 — Another Blogoversary Already? (337)

Next Monday, September 1, 2008, marks my two year "blogoversary" for this blog!

I won't be blogging on Monday, of course, because that is [Labor Day] holiday here in the United States.

> (From a Canadian colleague: "The US is not the only country that celebrates Labor Day on the first weekend in September. Canada also celebrates Labor Day on the first weekend in September. It's the only holiday (other than Christmas and New Year's) where we are in sync with US. Our Thanksgiving Days are different as is your July 4 vs. our July 1. But for Labor Day we are one with the Borg...")

> (From an Australian colleague: each province of Australia has its own day to celebrate Labor Day, see [Australia Public Holidays])

The rest of the world celebrates Labor Day on May 1, but the USA celebrates this on the first Monday of September, which this year lands on September 1. Originally, the day is intended to be a "day off for working citizens", IBM is kind enough to let managers and marketing personnel have the day off also. (Not that anyone is going to notice no press releases next Monday, right?)

I started this blog on September 1, 2006 as part of IBM's big ["50 Years of Disk Systems Innovation"] campaign. IBM introduced the first commercial disk system on September 13, 1956 and so the 50th anniversary was in 2006. Last year, IBM celebrated the 55th anniversary of tape systems.

Several readers have asked me why I haven't talked about recent current events, such as the Olympic Games in Beijing, or the U.S. National Conventions for the race for U.S. President. I have to remind them of one of the key precepts of IBM blogging guidelines:

> "8. Respect your audience. Don't use ethnic slurs, personal insults, obscenity, or engage in any conduct that would not be acceptable in IBM's workplace. You should also show proper consideration for others' privacy and for topics that may be considered objectionable or inflammatory - such as politics and religion."

I made subtle references to my senator from Arizona, John McCain, in my post [ILM for my iPod], and to Barack Obama in my post [Searching for matching information]. I don't think anyone would mind that I send a "Happy Birthday!" wish to both of them. Senator McCain turns 72 years old today, and Senator Obama turned 47 years old earlier this month.

And lastly, Tucson itself [celebrates this entire month] its 233rd birthday. That's right, Tucson, the 32nd largest city of the USA, and headquarters for IBM System Storage, is older than the USA itself. While the Tucson area has been continuously inhabited by humans for over 3500 years, it officially became Tucson on August 20, 1775.

Fellow blogger Justin Thorp has opined that [blogging is like jogging]. Some days, you are just too busy to do it, and other days, you make time for it, because you know it is important. For the record, it is not my job to blog for IBM; that ended last September 2007. I continue to blog anyways because I have benefited from it, both personally and professionally. I want to thank all of you readers out there for making this blog a great success! Being named one of the top 10 blogs of the IT storage industry by Network World, two back-to-back Brand Impact awards from Liquid Agency, and recently earning a "31" Technorati ranking, has really helped keep me going.

So, I look forward to next month, and beginning my third year on this blog. I am sure there will be lots of surprises and announcements you can all look forward to in the next coming weeks and months that I will have plenty to write about.

⚲technorati tags: IBM, blogoversary, anniversary, birthday, disk, tape, systems, Olympics, Olympic Games, Beijing, China, National Convention,

John McCain, Senator, Arizona, Barack Obama, Tucson, Justin Thorp, Network World, Technorati

Comment from Chris Mellor, the Register

Carry on blogging Tony. Your IBM evangelizing and IBM blogging culture rules are a contrasting tonic in the world of tech blogs!

Chris.

Comment from Barry Whyte (IBM)

Congrats on surviving another year, and enjoy your day off on Monday.

September

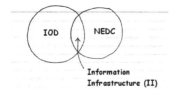

Information
Infrastructure (II)

IBM's Software Group was focused on its "Information On Demand" (IOD) initiative, and IBM Systems and Technology Group was focused on its "New Enterprise Data Center" (NEDC) initiative. The IBM System Storage marketing team wanted the new "Information Infrastructure" to take over the world, and supercede both IOD and NEDC. After months of heated conference calls, I solved the problem with a simple diagram, borrowing an idea from Jessica Hagy, author of the *Indexed* blog. Everyone in both the IOD and NEDC camps signed off on this, and we were able to launch on September 8 as scheduled.

2008 Sep 03 -- IBM Information on Demand 2008 Conference (338)

If you're not planning to attend next week's [IBM Storage Symposium in Montpellier] because the "South of France" is too far away, next month IBM will have the [Information on Demand 2008 conference] at the Mandalay Bay Hotel in Las Vegas, Nevada. Featured speakers include [Tom Davenport], [Dr. Irving Wladawsky-Berger], storage management guru [John R Foley], and comedian [Martin Short].

This conference is being hosted by IBM's Software Group, including [IBM Service Management] solutions from our Tivoli brand for managing your server and storage environment.

To learn more about the Information on Demand 2008 conference, check out the [Home Page] or go straight to the [Registration form].

⚙**technorati tags**: IBM, storage, symposium, Montpellier, Information on Demand, 2008, conference, Mandalay Bay, Las Vegas, Tom Davenport, Wladawsky-Berger, John Foley, Martin Short, Software Group, IT, service management, Tivoli, registration

Rather than talk about the products that were announced in July and August, I focused this series of blog posts on the new Information Infrastructure strategy itself.

2008 Sep 08 — IBM Information Infrastructure launches today (339)

Earlier this year, IBM launched its [New Enterprise Data Center vision]. The average data center was built 10-15 years ago, at a time when the World Wide Web was still in its infancy, some companies were deploying their first storage area network (SAN) and email system, and if you asked anyone what "Google" was, they might tell you it was ["a one followed by a hundred zeros"]!

> (**Full disclosure:** Google, the company, just celebrated its [10th anniversary] yesterday, and IBM has partnered with Google on a variety of exciting projects. I am employed by IBM, and own stock in both companies.)

In just the last five years, we saw a rapid growth in information, fueled by Web 2.0 social media, email, mobile hand-held devices, and the convergence of digital technologies that blurs the lines between communications, entertainment and business information. This explosion in information is not just "more of the same", but rather a dramatic shift from predominantly databases for online transaction processing to mostly unstructured content. IT departments are no longer just the "back office" recording financial transactions for accountants, but now also take on a more active "front office" role. For a growing number of industries, information technology plays a pivotal role in generating revenue, making smarter business decisions, and providing better customer service.

IBM felt a new IT model was needed to address this changing landscape, so IBM's New Enterprise Data Center vision has these five key strategic initiatives:

1. Highly virtualized resources
2. Business Resilience
3. Business-driven Service Management
4. Green, Efficient, Optimized facilities
5. Information Infrastructure

In February, IBM announced new products and features to support the first two initiatives, including the highly virtualized capability of the IBM z10 EC mainframe, and related business resiliency features of the [IBM System Storage DS8000 Turbo] disk system.

In May, IBM launched its Service Management strategic initiative at the Pulse 2008 conference. I was there in Orlando, Florida at the [Swan and Dolphin] resort to present to clients. You can read my three posts: [Day 1]; [Day 2 Main Tent]; [Day 2 Breakout sessions].

In June, IBM launched its fourth strategic initiative "Green, Efficient and Optimized Facilities" with [Project Big Green 2.0], which included the Space-Efficient Volume (SEV) and Space-Efficient FlashCopy (SEFC) capabilities of the IBM System Storage SAN Volume Controller (SVC) 4.3 release. Fellow blogger and IBM master inventor Barry Whyte (BarryW) has three posts on his blog about this: [SVC 4.3.0 Overview]; [SEV and SEFC detail]; [Virtual Disk Mirroring and More]

Some have speculated that the IBM System Storage team seemed to be on vacation the past two months, with few press releases and little or no fanfare about our July and August announcements, and not responding directly to critics and FUD in the blogosphere. It was because we were holding them all for today's launch, taking our cue from a famous perfume commercial:

"If you want to capture someone's attention -- whisper."

My team and I were actually quite busy at the [IBM Tucson Executive Briefing Center]. In between doing our regular job talking to excited prospects and clients, we trained sales reps and IBM Business Partners, wrote certification exams, and updated marketing collateral. Fortunately, competitors stopped promoting their own products to discuss and demonstrate why they are so scared of what IBM is planning. The fear was well justified. Even a few journalists helped raise the word-of-mouth buzz and excitement level. A big kiss to Beth Pariseau for her article in [SearchStorage.com]!

(Last week we broke radio silence to promote our technology demonstration of 1 million IOPS using Solid State Drive, just to get the huge IBM marketing machine oiled up and ready for today)

Today, IBM General Manager Andy Monshaw launched the fifth strategic initiative, [IBM Information Infrastructure], at the [IBM Storage and Storage Networking Symposium] in Montpellier, France. Montpellier is one of the six locations of our New Enterprise Data Center Leadership Centers launched today. The other five are Poughkeepsie, Gaithersburg, Dallas, Mainz and Boebligen, with more planned for 2009.

Although IBM has been using the term "information infrastructure" for more than 30 years, it might be helpful to define it for you readers:

"An information infrastructure comprises the storage, networks, software, and servers integrated and optimized to securely deliver information to the business."

In other words, it's all the "stuff" that delivers information from the magnetic surface recording of the disk or tape media to the eyes and ears of the end user. Everybody has an information infrastructure already, some are just more effective than others. For those of you not happy with yours, IBM has the products, services and expertise to help with your data center transformation.

IBM wants to help its clients deliver the right information to the right people at the right time, to get the most benefits of information, while controlling costs and mitigating risks. There might be more than a dozen ways to address the challenges involved, but IBM's Information Infrastructure strategic initiative focuses on four key solution areas:

- [Information Availability]
- [Information Security]
- [Information Retention]
- [Information Compliance]

Here is a short 2-minute video from IBM TV on this.

Over the next four days, I plan to cover each of these solution areas in more detail. More than 30 new or enhanced products and services were included with this launch, including the [IBM XIV Storage System], the [TS7650G ProtecTIER deduplication gateway], the new [DS5000] and[N series N6000] disk systems, enhanced[Scale-out File Services (SoFS)], and the new "deep archive" [S24 and S54 high-density HD frames] for the IBM 3584 and TS3500 tape libraries. It will probably take me the rest of this quarter to cover them all in this blog and to set the record straight on some of the more outrageous and factually inaccurate statements made by the competitors most threatened by today's announcements.

Last, but not least, I would like to welcome to the blogosphere IBM's newest blogger, Moshe Yanai, formerly the father of the EMC Symmetrix and now leading the IBM XIV team. Already from his first post on his new [ThinkStorage blog], I can tell he is not going to pull any punches either.

To learn more, here is the [IBM Press Release].

⊘**technorati tags**: IBM, New Enterprise Data Center, Google, z10, mainframe, DS8000, Turbo, disk, system, Web2.0, service management, green, Project Big Green, energy efficient, SVC, SEV, SEFC, BarryW, Beth Pariseau, Searchstorage.com, IOPS, SSD, Information Infrastructure, Andy Monshaw, storage, symposium, Montpellier, France, Leadership Centers, XIV, TS7650G, ProtecTIER, deduplication, DS5000, N6000, S24, S54, high-density, frame, 3584, TS3500, tape library, Moshe Yanai, ThinkStorage, EMC, Symmetrix

2008 Sep 09 — More Details about Information Availability (340)

In yesterday's post, [IBM Information Infrastructure launches today], I explained how this strategic initiative fit into IBM's New Enterprise Data Center vision. For those who prefer audio podcasts, here is Marissa Benekos interviewing Andy Monshaw, IBM General Manager of IBM System Storage.

This post will focus on Information Availability, the first of the four-part series this week.

Here's another short 2-minute video on Information Availability.

I am not in marketing department anymore, so have no idea how much IBM spent to get these videos made, but hate for the money to go wasted. I suspect the only way they will get viewed is if I include them in my blog. I hope you like them.

As with many IT terms, "availability" might conjure up different meanings for different people.

Some can focus on the pure mechanics of delivering information. An information infrastructure involves all of the software, servers, networks and storage to bring information to the application or end user, so all of the chains in the link must be highly available: software should not crash, servers should have "five nines" (99.999%) uptime, networks should be redundant, and storage should handle the I/O request with sufficient performance. For tape libraries, the tape cartridge must be available, robotics are needed to fetch the tape, and a drive must be available to read the cartridge. All of these factors represent the continuous operations and high availability features of business continuity.

In addition to the IT equipment, you need to make sure your facilities that support that equipment, such as power and cooling, are also available. Independent IT analyst Mark Peters from Enterprise Strategy Group (ESG) summarizes his shock about the findings in a recent [survey commissioned by Emerson Network Power] on his post [Backing Up Your Back Up]. Here is an excerpt:

> "The net take-away is that the majority of SMBs in the US do not have back-up power systems. As regional power supplies get more stretched in many areas, the possibility of power outages increases and obviously many SMBs would be vulnerable. Indeed, while the small business decision makers questioned for the survey ranked such power outages ahead of other threats (fires, government regulation, weather, theft and employee turnover) only 39% had a back-up power system. Yeah, you could say, but anything actually going wrong is unlikely; but apparently not, as 79% of those surveyed had experienced at least one power outage during 2007. Yeah, you might say, but maybe the effects were minor; again, apparently not, since 42% of those who'd had outages had to actually close their businesses during the longest outages. The DoE says power outages cost $80 billion a year and businesses bear 98% of those costs."

Others might be more concerned about outages resulting from planned and unplanned downtime. Storage virtualization can help reduce planned downtime, by allowing data to be migrated from one storage device to another without disrupting the application's ability to read and write data. The latest "Virtual Disk Mirroring" (VDM) feature of the IBM System Storage SAN Volume Controller takes it one step further, providing high-availability even for entry-level and midrange disk systems managed by the SVC. For unplanned downtime, IBM offers a complete range of support, from highly available clusters, two-site and three-site disaster recovery support, and application-aware data protection through IBM Tivoli Storage Manager.

Many outages are caused by human error, and in many cases it is the human factor that prevent quick resolution. Storage admins are unable to isolate the failing component, identify the configuration or provide the appropriate problem determination data to the technical team ready to offer support and assistance. For this, IBM TotalStorage Productivity Center software, and its hardware-version the IBM System Storage Productivity Center, can help reduce outage time and increase information availability. It can also provide automation to predict or provide early warning of impending conditions that could get worse if not taken care of.

But perhaps yet another take on information availability is the ability to find and communicate the right information to the right people at the right time. Recently, Google announced a historic milestone, their search engine now indexes over [One trillion Web pages]! Google and other search engines have changed the level of expectations for finding information. People ask why they can find information on the internet so quickly, yet it takes weeks for companies to respond to a judge for an e-discovery request.

Lastly, the team at IBM's [Eightbar blog] pointed me to Mozilla Lab's Ubiquity project for their popular Firefox browser. This project aims to help people communicate the information in a more natural way, rather than unfriendly URL links on an email. It is still beta, of course, but helps show what "information availability" might be possible in the near future. Here is a 7-minute demonstration:

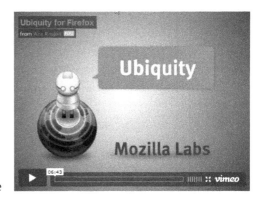

For those who only read the first and last paragraphs of each post, here is my recap: Information Availability includes Business Continuity and Data Protection to facilitate quick recovery, storage virtualization to maximize performance and minimize planned downtime, infrastructure management and automation to reduce human error, and the ability to find and communicate information to others.

technorati tags: IBM, Information Infrastructure, Information Availability, audio, podcast, Marissa Benekos, Andy Monshaw, Mark Peters, ESG, Emerson Network Power, SVC, VDM, SMB, Google, Mozilla, Ubiquity, Firefox, Business Continuity, Disaster Recovery, Continuous Operations, High Availability, Data Protection, storage, virtualization, infrastructure, management, automation

2008 Sep 10 — More Details about Information Security (341)

In Monday's post, [IBM Information Infrastructure launches today], I explained how this strategic initiative fit into IBM's New Enterprise Data Center vision. For you podcast fans, IBM Vice Presidents Bob Cancilla (Disk Systems), Craig Smelser (Storage and Security Software), and Mike Riegel (Information Protection Services), highlight some of the new products and offerings in this 12-minute recording.

This post will focus on Information Security, the second of the four-part series this week.

Here's another short 2-minute video, on Information [Security].

Security protects information against both internal and external threats.

For internal threats, most focus on whether person A has a "need-to-know" about information B. Most of the time, this is fairly straightforward.

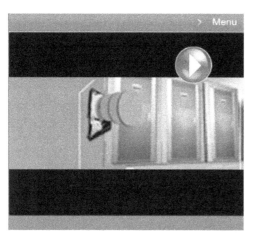

However, sometimes production data is copied to support test and development efforts. Here is the typical scenario: the storage admin copies production data that contains sensitive or personal information to a new copy and authorizes software engineers or testers full read/write access to this data. In some cases, the engineers or testers may be employees, other times they might be hired contractors from an outside firm. In any case, they may not be authorized to read this sensitive information. To solve this IBM announced the [IBM Optim Data Privacy Solution] for a variety of environments, including Siebel and SAP enterprise resource planning (ERP) applications.

I found this solution quite clever. The challenge is that production data is interrelated and typically live inside [relational databases]. For example, one record in one database might have a name and serial number, and then that serial number is used to reference a corresponding record in another database. The IBM Optim Data Privacy Solution applies a range of "masks" to transform complex data elements such as credit card numbers, email addresses and national identifiers, while retaining their contextual meaning. The masked results are fictitious, but consistent and realistic, creating a "safe sandbox" for application testing. This method can mask data from multiple interrelated applications to create a "production-like" test environment that accurately reflects end-to-end business processes. The testers get data they can use to validate their changes, and the storage admins can rest assured they have not exposed anyone's sensitive information.

Beyond just who has the "need-to-know", we might also be concerned with who is "qualified-to-act". Most systems today have both authentication and authorization support. Authentication determines that you are who you say you are, through the knowledge of unique userid/passwords combinations, or other credentials. Fingerprint, eye retinal scans or other biometrics look great in spy movies, but they are not yet widely used. Instead, storage admins have to worry about dozens of different passwords on different systems. One of the many preview announcements made by Andy Monshaw on Monday's launch was that IBM is going to integrate the features of [Tivoli Access Manager for Enterprise Single Sign-On] into IBM's Productivity Center software, and be renamed "IBM Tivoli Storage Productivity Center". You enter one userid/password, and you will not have to enter the individual userid/password of all the managed storage devices.

Once a storage admin is authenticated, they may or may not be authorized to read or act on certain information. Productivity Center offers role-based authorization, so that people can be identified by their roles (tape operator, storage administrator, DBA) and that would then determine what they are authorized to see, read, or act upon.

For external threats, you need to protect data both in-flight and at-rest. In-flight deals with data that travels over a wire, or wirelessly through the air, from source to destination. When companies have multiple buildings, the transmissions can be encrypted at the source, and decrypted on arrival. The bigger threat is data at-rest. Hackers and cyber-thieves looking to download specific content, like personal identifiable information, financial information, and other sensitive data.

IBM was the first to deliver an encrypting tape drive, the TS1120. The encryption process is handled right at the drive itself, eliminating the burden of encryption from the host processing cycles, and eliminating the need for specialized hardware sitting between server and storage system. Since then, we have delivered encryption on the LTO-4 and TS1130 drives as well.

When disk drives break or are decommissioned, the data on them may still be accessible. Customers have a tough decision to make when a disk drive module (DDM) stops working:

- Send it back to the vendor or manufacturer to have it replaced, repaired or investigated, potentially exposing sensitive information.
- Keep the broken drive, forfeit any refund or free replacement, and then physically destroy the drive. There are dozens of videos on [YouTube.com] on different ways to do this!

The launch previewed the [IBM partnership with LSI and Seagate] to deliver encryption technology for disk drives, known as "Full Disk Encryption" or FDE. Having all data encrypted on all drives, without impacting performance, eliminates having to decide which data gets encrypted and which doesn't. With data safely encrypted, companies can now send in their broken drives for problem determination and replacement. Anytime you can apply a consistent solution across everything, without human intervention and decision making, the less impact it will have. This was the driving motivation in both disk and tape drive encryption.

(Early in my IBM career, some lawyers decided we need to add a standard 'paragraph' to our copyright text in the upper comment section of our software modules, and so we had a team meeting on this. The lawyer that presented to us that perhaps only 20 to 35 percent of the modules needed to be updated with this paragraph, and taught us what to look for to decide whether or not the module needed to be changed. My team argued how tedious this was going to be, that this will take time to open up each module, evaluate it, and make the decision. With thousands of modules involved the process could take weeks. The fact that this was going to take us weeks did not seem to concern our lawyer one bit, it was just the cost of doing business. Finally, I asked if it would be legal to just add the standard paragraph to ALL the modules without any analysis whatsoever. The lawyer was stunned. There was no harm adding this paragraph to all the modules, he said, but that would be 3-5x more work and why would I even suggest that. Our team laughed, recognizing immediately that it was the fastest way to get it done. One quick program updated all modules that afternoon.)

To manage these keys, IBM previewed the Tivoli Key Lifecycle Manager (TKLM). This software helps automate the management of encryption keys throughout their lifecycle to help ensure that encrypted data on storage devices cannot be compromised if lost or stolen. It will apply to both disk and tape encryption, so that one system will manage all of the encryption keys in your data center.

For those who only read the first and last paragraphs of each post, here is my recap: Information Security is intended as an end-to-end capability to protect against both internal and external threats, restricting access only to those who have a "need-to-know" or are "qualified-to-act". Security approaches like "single sign-on" and encryption that applies to all tapes and all disks in the data center greatly simplify the deployment.

⊘technorati tags: IBM, Robert Cancilla, Craig Smelser, Mike Riegel, Optim, Data Privacy, Siebel, SAP, ERP, need-to-know, Andy Monshaw, credentials, biometrics, role-based, authorization, authentication, Tivoli, Access Manager, Enterprise, Single Sign-On, Productivity Center, encryption, in-flight, at-rest, TS1120, LTO-4, TS1130

Addition from Tony Pearson (IBM)

Article in ComputerWorld: "Data breaches spur hard-drive shredding boom - The customer pays about $10 for each hard drive destroyed"

> http://www.computerworld.com/action/article.do?command=vi ewArticleBasic&articleId=9114433&source=rss_topic12

-- Tony

2008 Sep 10 — More Details about Information Retention (342)

In Monday's post, [IBM Information Infrastructure launches today], I explained how this strategic initiative fit into IBM's New Enterprise Data Center vision. The launch was presented at the IBM Storage and Storage Networking Symposium to over 400 attendees in Montpelier, France, with corresponding standing-room-only crowds in New York and Tokyo.

This post will focus on Information Retention, the third of the four-part series this week.

Here's another short 2-minute video, on Information [Retention]

Let's start with some interesting statistics. Fellow blogger Robin Harris on his *StorageMojo* blog has an interesting post: [Our changing file workloads], which discusses the findings of study titled, "Measurement and Analysis of Large-Scale Network File System Workloads" [14-page PDF]. This paper was a collaboration between researchers from University of California Santa Cruz and our friends at NetApp. Here's an excerpt from the study:

Compared to Previous Studies:

- Both of our workloads are more write-oriented. Read to write byte ratios have significantly decreased.
- Read-write access patterns have increased 30-fold relative to read-only and write-only access patterns.
- Most bytes are transferred in longer sequential runs. These runs are an order of magnitude larger.

- Most bytes transferred are from larger files. File sizes are up to an order of magnitude larger.
- Files live an order of magnitude longer. Fewer than 50 percent are deleted within a day of creation.

New Observations:

- Files are rarely re-opened. Over 66 percent are re-opened once and 95% fewer than five times.
- Files re-opens are temporally related. Over 60 percent of re-opens occur within a minute of the first.
- A small fraction of clients account for a large fraction of file activity. Fewer than 1 percent of clients account for50 percent of file requests.
- Files are infrequently shared by more than one client. Over 76 percent of files are never opened by more than one client.
- File sharing is rarely concurrent and sharing is usually read-only. Only 5 percent of files opened by multiple clients are concurrent and 90 percent of sharing is read-only.
- Most file types do not have a common access pattern.

Why are files being kept *ten times longer* than before? Because the information still has value:

- Provide historical context
- Gain insight to specific situations, market segment demographics, or trends in the greater marketplace
- Help innovate new ideas for products and services
- Make better, smarter decisions

National Public Radio (NPR) had an interesting piece the other day. By analyzing old photos, a researcher for Cold War Analysis was able to identify an interesting [pattern for Russian presidents]. (Be sure to listen to the 3-minute audio to hear a hilarious song about the results!)

Which brings me to my own collection of "old photos". I bought my first digital camera in the year 2000, and have taken over 15,000 pictures since then. Before that, I used 35mm film camera, getting the negatives developed and prints made. Some of these date back to my years in High School and College. I have a mix of sizes, from 3x5, 4x6 and 5x7 inches, and sometimes I got double prints. Only a small portion are organized into scrapbooks. The rest are in envelopes, prints and negatives, in boxes taking up half of my linen closet in my house. Following the success of the [Library of Congress using Flickr], I decided the best way to organize these was to have them digitized first. There are several ways to do this.

Flat-bed scanner

This method is just too time consuming. Lift the lid place 1 or a few prints face down on the glass, close the lid, press the button, and then repeat. I estimate 70 percent of my photos are in [landscape orientation], and 30 percent in [portrait mode]. I can either spend extra time to orient each photo correctly on the glass, or rotate the digital image later.

Sheet-feed scanner

I was pleased to learn that my Fujitsu ScanSnap S510 sheet-feed scanner can take in a short stack (dozen or so) photos, and generate JPEG format files for each. I can select 150, 300 or 600dpi, and five levels of JPEG compression. All the photos feed in portrait mode, which I can then rotate later on the computer once digitized. A command line tool called [ImageMagick] can help automate the rotations. While I highly recommend the ScanSnap scanner, this is still a time-consuming process for thousands of photos.

Hire a professional service

Fellow blogger Matt on *Unclutterer* had a post [Have someone else digitize your old photos] that pointed me to this great service at [ScanMyPhotos.com]. From their website:

> "The best way to save your valuable photos may be by eliminating the paper altogether. Consider making digital images of all your photos."

Here's how it works: You ship your prints (or slides, or negatives) to their facility in Irvine, California. They have a huge machine that scans them all at 300dpi, no compression, and they send back your photos and a DVD containing digitized versions in JPEG format, all for only 50 US dollars plus shipping and handling, per thousand photos. I don't think I could even hire someone locally to run my scanner for that!

The deal got better when I contacted them. For people like me with accounts on Facebook, Flickr, MySpace or Blogger, they will [scan your first 1000 photos for free] (plus shipping and handling). I selected a thousand 4x6 inch photos from my vast collection, organized them into eight stacks with rubber bands, and sent them off in a shoe box. The photos get scanned in landscape mode, so I had spent about four hours in preparing what I sent them, making sure they were all face up, with the top of the picture oriented either to the top or left edge. For the envelopes that had double prints, I "deduplicated" them so that only one set got scanned.

The box weighed seven pounds, and cost about 10 US dollars to send from Tucson to Irvine via UPS on Tuesday. They came back the following Monday, all my photos plus the DVD, for 20 US dollars shipping and handling. Each digital image is about 1.5MB in size, roughly 1800x1200 pixels in size, so easily fit on a single DVD. The quality is the same as if I scanned them at 300dpi on my own scanner, and comparable to a 2-megapixel camera on most cell phones. Certainly not the high-res photos I take with my Canon PowerShot, but suitable enough for email or websites. So, for about 30 US dollars, I got my first batch of 1000 photos scanned.

ScanMyPhotos.com offers a variety of extra priced options, like rotating each file to the correct landscape or portrait orientation, color correction, exact sequence order, hosting them on their website online for 30 days to share with friends and family, and extra copies of the DVD. All of these represent a trade-off between having them do it for me for an additional fee, or me spending time doing it myself--either before in the preparation, or afterwards managing the digital files--so I can appreciate that.

Perhaps the weirdest option was to have your original box returned for an extra $9.95? If you don't have a huge collection of empty shoe boxes in your garage, you can buy a similarly sized cardboard box for only $3.49 at the local office supply store, so I don't understand this one. The box they return all your photos in can easily be used for the next batch.

I opted not to get any of these extras. The one option I think they should add would be to have them just discard the prints, and send back only the DVD itself. Or better yet, discard the prints, and email me an ISO file of the DVD that I can burn myself on my own computer. Why pay extra shipping to send back to me the entire box of prints, just so that I can dump the prints in the trash myself? I will keep the negatives, in case I ever need to re-print with high resolution.

Overall, I am thoroughly delighted with the service, and will now pursue sending the rest of my photos in for processing, and reclaim my linen closet for more important things. Now that I know that a thousand 4x6 prints weighs 7 pounds, I can now estimate how many photos I have left to do, and decide on which discount bulk option to choose from.

With my photos digitized, I will be able to do all the things that IBM talks about with Information Retention:

- Place them on an appropriate storage tier. I can keep them on disk, tape or optical media.
- Easily move them from one storage tier to another. Copying digital files in bulk is straightforward, and as new technologies develop, I

can refresh the bits onto new media, to avoid the "obsolescence of CDs and DVDs" as discussed in this article in [PC World].

- Share them with friends and family, either through email, on my TiVo (yes, my TiVo is networked to my Mac and PC and has the option to do this!), or upload them to a photo-oriented service like [Kodak Gallery] or [Flickr].
- Keep multiple copies in separate locations. I could easily burn another copy of the DVD myself and store in my safe deposit box or my desk at work. With all of the regional disasters like hurricanes, an alternative might be to backup all your files, including your digitized photos, with an online backup service like [IBM Information Protection Services] from last year's acquisition of Arsenal Digital.

If the prospect of preserving my high school and college memories for the next few decades seems extreme, consider the [Long Now Foundation] is focused on retaining information for centuries. They are even suggesting that we start representing years with five digits, e.g., 02008, to handle the deca-millennium bug which will come into effect 8,000 years from now. IBM researchers are also working on [long-term preservation technologies and open standards] to help in this area.

For those who only read the first and last paragraphs of each post, here is my recap: Information Retention is about managing [information throughout its lifecycle], using policy-based automation to help with the placement, movement and expiration. An "active archive" of information serves to help gain insight, innovate, and make better decisions. Disk, tape, and blended disk-and-tape solutions can all play a part in a tiered information infrastructure for long-term retention of information.

technorati tags: IBM, Information Infrastructure, Information Retention, ILM, Robin Harris, StorageMojo, UC Santa Cruz, NetApp, NPR, Russian, Presidents, digitize, scan, photos, photography, Library of Congress, Flickr, Facebook, Fujitsu ScanSnap, scanner, ScanMyPhotos.com, professional services, DVD, Arsenal Digital, Information Protection Services, Kodak Gallery, Long Now, Haifa, deduplication, long-term retention

Comment from Dave Tucker

What do you use to catalog and organize your photos? Something like Picasa from Google? May I also recommend Gallery:

http://gallery.menalto.com/

I find it very nice.

Regards
Dave

Response from Tony Pearson (IBM)

Dave, Looks like a great tool! Currently, I have a hosted website with thumbnails that point to albums on Kodak Gallery and Flickr. I will see if my Internet Service Provider that hosts my site will allow me to use this.
-- Tony

2008 Sep 12 — More Details about Information Compliance (343)

In Monday's post, [IBM Information Infrastructure launches today], I explained how this strategic initiative fit into IBM's New Enterprise Data Center vision. The launch has been reviewed in the press now all over the world.

This post will focus on Information Compliance, the fourth and final part of the four-part series this week. I have received a few queries on my choice of sequence for this series: Availability, Security, Retention and Compliance.

- Why not have them in alphabetical order? IBM avoids alphabetizing in one language, because then it may not be alphabetized when translated to other languages.
- Why not have them in a sequence that spells out an easy to remember mnemonic, like "CARS"? Again, when translated to other languages, those mnemonics no longer work.

Instead, I worked with our marketing team for a more appropriate sequence, based on psychology and the cognitive bias of [primacy and recency effects].

Here's another short 2-minute video, on Information [Compliance].

> **Full disclosure:** I am not a lawyer. The following will delve into areas related to government and industry regulations. Consult your risk officer or legal counsel to make sure any IT solution is appropriate for your country, your industry, or your specific situation.

IBM estimates there are over 20,000 regulations worldwide related to information storage and transmission.

For information availability, some industry regulations mandate a secondary copy a minimum distance away to protect against regional disasters like hurricanes or tsunamis. IBM offers Metro Mirror (up to 300km) and Global Mirror (unlimited distance) disk mirroring to support these requirements.

For information security, some regulations relate to privacy and prevention of unauthorized access. Two prominent ones in the United States are:

Health Insurance Portability and Accountability Act (HIPAA) of 1996

HIPAA regulates health care providers, health plans, and health care clearinghouses in how they handle the privacy of patient's medical records. These regulations apply whether the information is on film, paper, or stored electronically. Obviously, electronic medical records are easier to keep private. Here is an excerpt from an article from [WebMD]:

> "There are very good ways to protect data electronically. Although it sounds scary, it makes data more protected than current paper records. For example, think about someone looking at your medical chart in the hospital. It has a record of all that is happening -- lab results, doctor consultations, nursing notes, orders, prescriptions, etc. Anybody who opens it for whatever reason can see all of this information. But if the chart is an electronic record, it's easy to limit access to any of that. So a physical therapist writing physical therapy notes can only see information related to physical therapy. There is an opportunity with electronic records to limit information to those who really need to see it. It could in many ways allow more privacy than current paper records."

But according to AMI Partners Research 2008, only 4 percent of U.S. physicians in 2008 have a fully functional electronic health records system, and 13 percent have a basic one. For more information about the physical, technical and administrative safeguards required by HIPAA, see this [An Introductory Resource Guide for Implementing the Health Insurance Portability and Accountability Act (HIPAA) Security Rule] (137 pages) from the National Institute of Standards and Technology.

Gramm-Leach-Bliley Act (GLBA) of 1999

GLBA regulates the handling of sensitive customer information by banks, securities firms, insurance companies, and other financial service providers. Financial companies use tape encryption to comply with GLBA when sending tapes from one firm to another. IBM was the first to deliver tape drive encryption with the TS1120, and then later with LTO-4 and TS1130 tape drives.

For information retention, there are a lot of regulations that deal with how information is stored, in some cases immutable to protect against unethical tampering, and when it can be discarded. Two prominent regulations in the United States are:

U.S. Securities and Exchange Commission (SEC) 17a-4 of 1997

In the past, the IT industry used the acronym "WORM" which stands for the "Write Once, Read Many" nature of certain media, like CDs, DVDs, optical and tape cartridges. Unfortunately, WORM does not apply to disk-based solutions, so IBM adopted the language from SEC 17a-4 that calls for storage that is "Non-Erasable, Non-Rewriteable" or NENR. This new umbrella term applies to disk-based solutions, as well as tape and optical WORM media.

SEC 17a-4 indicates that broker/dealers and exchange members must preserve all electronic communications relating to the business of their firm from a specific period of time. During this time, the information must not be erased or re-written.

Sarbanes-Oxley (SOX) Act of 2002

SOX was born in the wake of [Enron and other corporate scandals]. It protects the way that financial information is stored, maintained and presented to investors, as well as disciplines those who break its rules. It applies only to public companies, i.e. those that offer their securities (stock shares, bonds, liabilities) to be sold to the public through a listing on a U.S. exchange, such as NASDAQ or NYSE.

SOX focuses on preventing CEOs and other executives from tampering the financial records. To meet compliance, companies are turning to the [IBM System Storage DR550] which provides on-erasable, Non-rewriteable (NENR) storage for financial records. Unlike competitive products like EMC Centera that function mostly as space-heaters on the data center floor once they filled up, the DR550 can be configured as a blended disk-and-tape storage system, so that the most recent, and most likely to be accessed data, remains on disk, but the older, least likely to be accessed data, is moved automatically to less expensive, more environment-friendly "green" tape media.

Did SOX hurt the United States' competitiveness? Critics feared that these new regulations would discourage new companies from going public. Ernst & Young found these fears did not come true, and published a study [U.S. Record IPO Activity from 2006 Continues in 2007]. In fact, the improved confidence that SOX has given investors has given rise to similar legislation in other parts of the world: Euro-Sox for the European Union Investor Protection Act, and J-SOX Financial Instruments and Exchange Law for Japan.

For those who only read the first and last paragraphs of each post, here is my recap: Information Compliance is ensuring that information is protected against regional disasters, unauthorized access, and unethical tampering, as required to meet industry and government regulations. Such regulations often apply if the information is stored on traditional paper or film media, but can often be handled more cost-effectively when stored electronically. Appropriate IT governance can help maintain investor confidence.

⊘**technorati tags**: IBM, Information Infrastructure, Compliance, cognitive bias, primacy, recency, WORM, tape, optical, TS1120, LTO-4, TS1130, NENR, HIPAA, GLBA, SEC, 17a-4, SOX, Euro-SOX, J-SOX, Ernst & Young

Since I was not allowed to blog or talk about that August 12th announcement of the XIV until September 8, many of our competitors took advantage of this by making up a lot of "bull" about the product and IBM's commitment to storage. I finally get around to setting the record straight and start to repair the damage that "going dark" had caused.

2008 Sep 15 — The Truth about XIV (344)

Last week, I presented IBM's strategic initiative, the IBM Information Infrastructure, which is part of IBM's New Enterprise Data Center vision. This week, I will try to get around to talking about some of the products that support those solutions.

There has been a lot of attention on XIV in the past few weeks, so I will start with that. Steve Duplessie, an IT industry analyst from Enterprise Strategy Group (ESG) had a post [Adaptec buys Aristos, Tom Cruise, XIV, and Logical Assumptions] with some interesting observations and some sage advice. Val Bercovici on his *NetApp Exposed* blog, has a post [Has Storage Swift-Blogging Finally Jumped the Shark?] which blasts EMC for their negativity.

(For those not in the USA, swift-blogging is a reference to false accusations and negative remarks made during the U.S. 2004 presidential election by the [Swift Boat Veterans], and ["jumping the shark"] is a reference to [a TV show that ran out of interesting and relevant topics]. For movie sequels, the comparable phrase is ["nuke the fridge"] in reference to the most recent Indiana Jones movie.)

I was going to set the record straight on a variety of misunderstandings, rumors or speculations, but I think most have been taken care of already. IBM blogger BarryW covered the fact that SVC now supports XIV storage systems, in his post [SVC and XIV], and addressed some of the FUD already. Here was my list:

Now that IBM has an IBM-branded model of XIV, IBM will discontinue (*insert another product here*)

I had seen speculation that XIV meant the demise of the N series, the DS8000 or IBM's partnership with LSI. However, the launch reminded people that IBM announced a new release of DS8000 features, new models of N series N6000,and the new DS5000 disk, so that squashes those rumors.

IBM XIV is a (*insert tier level here*) product

While there seems to be no industry-standard or agreement for what a tier-1, tier-2 or tier-3 disk system is, there seemed to be a lot of argument over what pigeon-hole category to put IBM XIV in. No question many people want tier-1 performance and functionality at tier-2 prices, and perhaps IBM XIV is a good step at giving them this. In some circles, tier-1 means support for System z mainframes. The XIV does not have traditional z/OS CKD volume support, but Linux on System z partitions or guests can attach to XIV via SAN Volume Controller (SVC), or through NFS protocol as part of the Scale-out File Services (SoFS) implementation.

Whenever any radical game-changing technology comes along, competitors with last century's products and architectures want to frame the discussion that it is just yet another storage system. IBM plans to update its Disk Magic and other planning/modeling tools to help people determine which workloads would be a good fit with XIV.

IBM XIV lacks (*insert missing feature here*) in the current release

I am glad to see that the accusations that XIV had unprotected, unmirrored cache were retracted. XIV mirrors all writes in the cache of two separate modules, with ECC protection. XIV allows concurrent code load for bug fixes to the software. XIV offers many of the features that people enjoy in other disk systems, such as thin provisioning, writeable snapshots, remote disk mirroring, and so on.

IBM XIV can be part of a bigger solution, either through SVC, SoFS or GMAS that provide the business value customers are looking for.

IBM XIV uses (*insert block mirroring here*) and is not as efficient for capacity utilization

It is interesting that this came from a competitor that still recommends RAID-1 or RAID-10 for its CLARiiON and DMX products. On the IBM XIV, each 1MB chunk is written on two different disks in different modules. When disks were expensive, how much usable space for a given set of HDD was worthy of argument. Today, we sell you a big black box, with 79TB usable, for (*insert dollar figure here*). For those who feel 79TB is too big to swallow all at once, IBM offers "capacity on demand" pricing, where you can pay initially for as little as 22TB, but get all the performance, usability, functionality and advanced availability of the full box.

IBM XIV consumes (*insert number of Watts here*) of energy

For every disk system, a portion of the energy is consumed by the number of hard disk drives (HDD) and the remainder to UPS, power conversion, processors and cache memory consumption. Again, the XIV is a big black box, and you can compare the 8.4 KW of this high-performance, low-cost storage one-frame system with the wattage consumed by competitive two-frame (sometimes called two-bay) systems, if you are willing to take some trade-offs. To get comparable performance and hot-spot avoidance, competitors may need to over-provision or use faster, energy-consuming FC drives, and offer additional software to monitor and re-balance workloads across RAID ranks. To get comparable availability, competitors may need to drop from RAID-5 down to either RAID-1 or RAID-6. To get comparable usability, competitors may need more storage infrastructure management software to hide the inherent complexity of their multi-RAID design.

Of course, if energy consumption is a major concern for you, XIV can be part of IBM's many blended disk-and-tape solutions. When it comes to being green, you can't get any greener storage than tape! Blended disk-and-tape solutions help get the best of both worlds.

Well, I am glad I could help set the record straight. Let me know what other products people you would like me to focus on next.

⊘**technorati tags**: IBM, XIV, disk, storage, system, Steve Duplessie, ESG, Val Bercovici, NetApp, BarryW, SVC, DS8000, N6000, DS5000, mainframe, z/OS, CKD, SoFS, NFS, ECC, HDD, RAID, UPS, availability, reliability, performance, usability, blended disk-and-tape, green

---

Comment from Barry Burke (EMC), the Storage Anarchist

Thanks for setting the record straight, Tony.

By omission, I think you have confirmed my assertion that an XIV dual-drive failure (before the 1st drive rebuild completes) WILL indeed cause irreparable damage to ALL of the data stored in the array, requiring every single LUN to be recovered from backup. The issue isn't one of probabilities; it is a matter of the scope of impact WHEN it occurs. And like I said, you do not have to believe me - ask your own XIV-trained service engineers.

You also neglected to mention that while the terms of PAYGO allow the customer to pay for only the first 25% of capacity in the array at time of acquisition, PAYGO also requires the customer to purchase the remaining capacity within 12 months of installation. More of a 12-month installment plan than pay-as-you-grow.

And of course, you are powering and cooling all 180 drives for the whole duration, whether you're using the capacity or not.

Which reminds me...you have done nothing to directly contradict the observation that the XIV array uses more power than a comparable CLARiiON or DMX, be they configured with the same usable capacity or with the identical number of 1TB SATA drives. When you are outright unable to get any more power into the data center, every excess watt is important.

Finally, and for the record, I am truly sorry that you mistook my factual observations as "negativity". While I'm obviously not going to sing the praises for you, I honestly tried to present a factual assessment, pointing out some things about XIV that others may have overlooked. One man's facts are another man's FUD, I guess.

But I will admit it came across pretty heavy-handed, especially when you and BarryW weren't able to respond until weeks later. Sorry about that...

Response from Tony Pearson (IBM)

BarryB,

Sorry, Barry, but you were misinformed.

Like most high-end, tier 1, enterprise-class storage systems, IBM XIV storage system is designed for no single point of failures. However, no disk system from any vendor is invulnerable to specific combinations of multi-component failure. These components could be drives, planar boards, power supplies, etc. In the case of XIV, some percentage of two-drive and three-drive failures are handled completely perfectly and automatically within the box, while others will require recover actions. Certainly, it is not irreparable since the recovery action in most cases is simply to switch with the disk mirror, or at worst case, recover from external tape or disk backup.

On typical disk systems, two-drive failures result in either (a) drive 1 fails, sending out errant electronic signals on the loop, and a second drive on the same loop gets a soft error from this signal; or (b) drive 1 fails, the "spare" disk is brought into play to perform rebuild, and either is already failed, or fails under load. Fortunately, the unique XIV architecture is not vulnerable to data loss from either of these two situations.

All major vendors, including IBM, EMC and others, recommend having a disk mirror, preferably several hundred kilometers away, to protect against these rare, unlikely multi-component failures and other regional disasters.

You are correct that most of IBM's Capacity-on-Demand pricing options have clauses to purchase the entire capacity installed within 12 months, but IBM Global Financing is available to minimize this as a financial concern. XIV storage is not intended for small and medium businesses whose workloads will not eventually fill the 79TB within the next 2-3 years. IBM offers other disk systems that are better positioned for the smaller customer segment.

According to EMC's own DMX4-950 Product Guide, you would need one system bay and one storage bay to have a comparable model against the XIV, for a maximum of 12.5 kW and steady-state operational of 10.9 kW. Compare that to IBM XIV with a maximum of 8.4 kW with steady-state at around 7.3 kW. IBM XIV consumes less energy, while providing consistent performance, hot-spot avoidance, faster rebuild times, and an easier to use GUI interface.

You were not the only blogger or journalist I was referring to in my post. I appreciate that you got most of your facts right on your original post, and retracted the one you got wrong. Others were not as thorough in their homework, and some had expressed strong negative opinions. I also appreciate that in most cases, the focus is on the product, the solution or the technology, and not attacks on the individual bloggers.

We'll just agree to disagree on some of those opinions. As for one man's facts are another man's FUD, not all FUD is false, but may be presented in a manner that puts fear and doubt in the mind of the listener. IBM is credited with being the inventor of FUD, using the statement, "Nobody every was fired buying from IBM," which while true, was enough to put fear, uncertainty and doubt from those clients considering the purchase of competitive mainframes.

Since then, IBM has adopted more ethical business conduct guidelines.
-- Tony

Comment from Stewey

I find it hilarious at how fascinated BarryB is with the XIV array. He's very excited, as a dog is to a pant leg, to point out the capabilities of the array. I think he has tremendous animosity towards Moshe and is really jealous of his success. There seems to be a serious personal vendetta going on here.

The problem with most of his arguments is that he's not doing an apples/apples comparison. You can't build a DMX or CLARiiON with similar performance or price to the XIV and have either the CLARiiON or DMX come out on top. It just ain't going to happen. I would bet that you could buy TWO XIV's and still be cheaper than a single CLARiiON or DMX and have the capability to replicate the data between two sites.

In fact, I challenge BarryB to provide a similar config of a DMX/CLARiiON, include usable capacity, Power (kWh), Cooling (KBTU/H), and footprint (SqFt). Let's pick a city in the US to determine the average $/KW:

(http://www.aps.org/policy/reports/popa-reports/energy/units.cfm)

And then do a combined footprint/power/cooling cost comparison. Then, let's pick a simple disk I/O benchmark tool to see how the configs compare against each other. From there, let's see who comes out on top.

Response from Tony Pearson (IBM)

Stewey, Thanks for the support. We'll see if BarryB or anyone from EMC takes you up on that challenge. We have several customers doing proof-of-concept projects at their own locations, with their own applications and data, making their own fair and balanced comparisons.
--Tony

Comment from Barry Burke (EMC), the Storage Anarchist

Tony, I will have to correct you on your DMX4 comparison - you are using ratings for the full complement of 240 drives in the drive bay, while my comparisons were for the actual number of drives used. Drives make up the vast majority of power, so there's a big difference between 240 and 180 drives.

As I'm sure you know, it is difficult to communicate the power requirements for all the various possible configurations, so, like IBM, EMC lists ratings for the maximum configurations. For the XIV, since there is no ability to remove drives, the maximum config is the same as the minimum; for the DMX4, the system can be configured with as few as 32 drives, and the power will be significantly lower than for the maximum 240 drive config.

Similar for the CLARiiON configs, by the way, which is a far more appropriate comparison to the all-SATA XIV array. At least some of those customers doing their own evals are finding that CLARiiON is not only faster, it's cheaper. Go Figure!

Oh, and UL rules require that you report the worst-case power draw, which in the case of the DMX includes the power required to recharge the integrated UPS's while operating under full load.

You really can't use spec sheets to compare power requirements, unless you take the time to understand what they really mean.

Of course, I probably should have used nominal operating power instead of maximum, although that would have shown even a bigger gap between the EMC arrays and the XIV.

But I would like to see you present documentation that shows that the damage is limited to a small subset of the LUNs in the event of a dual drive failure within, say, 5 minutes of each other. I will not betray my sources, but I am confident that I wasn't misinformed. As I have said, I am pretty sure that your own customer service people are advising customers that should two drives fail within a few minutes of each other, they should be prepared to restore every last byte of data stored in the array - there is no magical in-box recovery if the second drive that fails includes the only remaining copy of any of the blocks lost on the first failure. And worse, the loss cannot be tracked to the specific LUNs that were affected - there are no backwards pointers for the lost 1MB chunks. So you have to restore everything, or risk the effect of silently corrupted file systems and databases (a megabyte here and there can really be catastrophic!).

Go ahead - ask your XIV-trained CS engineers. I won't be surprised that you never admit it, but I'm pretty sure your CS engineers won't leave your customers in the dark, either.

As for Stewey - geez, lighten up a little... I am starting to feel like the boy who kept telling everyone the emperor had no clothes.

And you are sounding an awful lot like the emperor's tailor <grin>!

Response from Tony Pearson (IBM)

According to your own specs, the system bay of the DMX4-950 can hold only 120 drives, so a storage bay is required to have the full 180 drives. To get comparable performance, you would need 180 FC drives in the DMX4-950 versus the wide-striped performance of XIV storage using SATA. It would be an interesting comparison to actually see how much each would actually draw in terms of energy, as I agree it is uninteresting to argue over spec ratings (which you started, by the way, on your blog).

For each disk in the XIV, the 1MB chucks are only copied to 168 of the 180 drives. In other words, there are 11 other drives that do not contain mirrored data with any drive you pick. If your two drive failure occurred within 5 minutes on those two drives within this set, the system can handle this just fine, no LUNS are impacted, and no need to recover any data. In fact, XIV can lose an entire drawer of drives and still continue running without any loss of data and be able to recover from this situation just fine. I have confirmed this with our XIV team. I am sorry your sources have misinformed you again.

The same could be said about any other disk system from any major vendor. As most EMC systems are running either RAID1, RAID10 or RAID5, in some cases a two-drive failure would require major recovery, and in other cases, the two drives might not be part of the same RAID pair or rank to affect each other. Whether you are recovering 8TB or 80TB, the act of recovering from tape would take hours to days, depending on how much data you had actually written, and the act of recovering from a disk mirror would be substantially less time. All major vendors advise that disk mirroring is a smart thing to do for any data where time is of the essence for recovery. No vendor guarantees 100 percent uptime on any disk system, because there are always combinations of multiple component failure that cannot be recovered from internally.

In the case of XIV, when in disk mirroring mode, each 1MB chuck appears quadruple set, so you would need to have a four-drive failure to require recovery action. The system can perform regular rebuild process from any two-drive failure by using the third and fourth copies of each 1MB chunk, without having to switch over the entire system to the secondary site.

Having 3, 4 or more copies of data to ensure availability is what Google, Yahoo, and nearly every mainframe customer do for their most critical applications. The popularity of IBM Metro Mirror, EMC SRDF and HDS TrueCopy mirroring are used in these cases. XIV storage system is no different.
-- Tony

Comment from Barry Burke (EMC), the Storage Anarchist

Tony, Tony, Tony.

Although you say you are no longer in marketing, you still have the requisite mastery of the English language - you twist and turn every challenge back into a situation where you do not have to admit the limitations.

But the limitations are still there.

The power config I used was indeed 180 1TB SATA drives in a 950, including the separate bay. Apples to apples on drive count, or usable capacity, for both CX and DMX4 - whichever way you want to look at it.

Fact is that you have no proof for your assertion that the EMC arrays would have to use FC drives to match the performance of a XIV - that is nothing more than PowerPoint claims and Marketecture. Therefore, I will stand by my assertion that a CX4 or DMX4 with SATA drives will easily exceed the performance of an all-ATA XIV box.

And I have seen the customer tests that prove it.

Even your XIV poster child Leumi Bank admits that they cannot use the XIV for low-latency applications or with random-access applications or where bandwidth is the limitation.

That covers a lot of unstable territory, IMHO.

According to them, XIV is relegated instead to what Itzik Reuven calls the "fat middle" - sounds like the definition of SATA in a CX or DMX4...except that the EMC arrays can support BOTH tier 1 and "fat middle" in the same box - not to mention flash-based tier 0 as well.

Leumi even says that when performance starts to slow down on one of their XIV arrays, the management action is to stop adding new application data to that XIV array.

Translation: they aren't even able to use all of the (paltry) usable capacity of the array because of performance limitations! (I suspect they didn't pay full price for their Nextras if they can afford not to use all the capacity - especially when they claim that a backup clone would have been "cost prohibitive".)

In fact, that pretty much undermines Leumi's credibility right there - they wouldn't pay for a RAID 5 full-clone to protect their data, but they WILL buy MUCH MORE THAN TWICE the amount of physical storage required to meet their needs. Penny-wise, pound foolish, unless Moshe gave them the hardware for free…

In the interest of truthfulness and honest disclosure – let's just keep power comparisons apples-to-apples, SATA-SATA. OK?

As to disk loss...like a good marketing professional, you keep reforming the problem so it fits your architecture.

Let me keep it simple:

What happens when 2 drives in TWO DIFFERENT storage sets in the same XIV array fail within 5 minutes of each other?

Answer: Data Loss Scope: Unknown - 1 or more LUNs are missing 1 or more 1MB chunks of real data that cannot be recovered Solution: Rebuild/recover every single file system and database on every single LUN in the array

And no - the same is not true for the usual RAID implementations...if you lose 2 drives in a RAID 5 7+1 set, you lose all the LUNs on that RAID set -

but no more. And with advanced systems like CLARiiON and Symmetrix, you'll only lose the LUNs on the segments of the RAID set that hadn't yet completed rebuilding.

Most importantly, EMC customers can easily determine which LUNs were not totally recovered, and thus limit their restores to only the impacted LUNs.

This is the Achilles heel of XIV - there is no way for the customer (or IBM customer service, I've been told) to figure out which LUNs are missing 1 or more 1MB chunks.

You can keep wiggling, but my sources assure me my observation is accurate. And they should know...and I think you do too.

Why else would you wiggle so?

Comment from Barry Burke (EMC), the Storage Anarchist

Ahh... Your silence underscores the reality:

Some Factual Observations DON'T Mislead and Misrepresent.

Response from Tony Pearson (IBM)

BarryB, Since you do not have definitive, objective, third-party proof that XIV uses more or less power than comparable EMC models, and the "customer tests" you've seen are not public, it seems we are at a standstill. Arguing over the maximum kW specified in spec sheets does not accurately reflect the amount of energy used in typical workload situations, and diminishes the improved features of availability, performance and usability of the XIV.

As for the trade-off of recovery between recovering all the data on the box in rare cases when enough components fail on a DMX4, CX4 or XIV, or the more common recover of just a subset of LUNs contained to a single RAID rank on a DMX4 or CX4 that happens orders of magnitude more often, the situation is the same in that customers either (a) have a remote disk mirror and the recovery is quick and painless, or (b) perform recover on a list of LUNs from external tape or disk backup, and the recovery takes more time and effort.

I cannot speak about individual customers on this blog without permission. I will try to find other customer references to support the positive features of XIV.
--Tony

2008 Sep 16 — TS3500 Deep Archive High Density Frames (345)

Continuing this week's theme about new products that were mentioned in last week's launch, today I will cover the new [S24 and S54 frames].

Before these new frames, customers had two choices for their tape cartridges: keep them in an automated tape library, or on an external shelf. Most of the critics of tape focus almost entirely on the problems related to the latter. When tapes are placed outside of automation, you need human intervention

7ft.
10in.

to find and fetch the tapes, tapes can be misplaced or misfiled, tapes can be dropped, tapes can get liquids spilled on them, and so on. These problems just don't happen when stored in automated tape libraries.

Until now, the number of cartridges was limited to the surface area of the wall accessible by the robotic picker. Whether the robot rotates in a circle picking from dodecagon walls, or back and forth from long rectangular walls, the problem was the same.

But what about tapes that may not need to be readily accessible, but still automated? With the new high density frames, you can now stack tapes several cartridges deep, spring loaded deep shelves that push the tape cartridges up to the front one at a time. The high-density frame design might have been inspired by the famous [Pez] candy dispenser, but at 70.9 inches, does not beat the [World's Tallest Pez Dispenser].

(Note: PEZ® is a registered trademark of Pez Candy, Inc.)

In a regular cartridge-only frame, like the D23, you have slots for 200 cartridges on the left, and 200 cartridges on the right, and the robotic picker can pull out and push back cartridges into any of these slot positions. In the new S24, there are still 200 slots on the left, now referred to as "tier 0", but up to 800 cartridges on the right. In each slot there are up to four 3592 cartridges, the position immediately reachable to the picker is referred to as "tier 1", and the ones tucked behind are "tier 2", "tier 3" and "tier 4".

Tier 0	<- - S24 frame - >	Tier 1	Tier 2	Tier 3	Tier 4
Tape A	Robotic Picker	Tape B	Tape C	Tape D	Tape E

We have fun slow-motion videos we show customers on how these work. For example, in the diagram above, let's suppose you want to fetch Tape E in the "tier 4" position. The following sequence happens:

1. Robotic picker pulls "tier 1" tape cartridge B, and pushes it into another shelf slot. Tapes C, D and E get pushed up to be Tiers 1, 2 and 3 now.

2. Robotic picker pulls "tier 1" tape cartridge C, and puts it in another shelf slot. Tapes D and E get pushed up to be Tiers 1 and 2 now.

3. Robotic picker pulls "tier 1" tape cartridge D, and puts it in another shelf slot. Tape E gets pushed up to be Tier 1 now.

4. Robotic picker pulls "tier 1" tape cartridge E, this is the tape we wanted, and can move it to the drive.

5. The other three cartridges (B, C and D) are then pulled out of the temporary slot, and pushed back into their original order.

In this manner, the most recently referenced tape cartridges will be immediately accessible, and the ones least referenced will eventually migrate to the deeper tiers. The 3592 cartridges can be used with either TS1120 orTS1130 drives. Each cartridge can hold up to 3TB of data (1TB raw, at 3:1 compression), so the entire frame could hold 3PB in just 10 square feet of floor space. Five D23 frames could be consolidated down to two S24 frames. The S24 frame comes in "Capacity on Demand" pricing options. The base model of the S24 has just tiers 0, 1 and 2, for a total capacity of 600 cartridges. You can then later license tiers 3 and 4 when needed.

The S54 is basically similar in operation, but for LTO cartridges. It works with any mix of LTO-1, LTO-2, LTO-3 andLTO-4 cartridges. The left side holds tier 0 as before, but the right side has up to five LTO cartridges deep. For Capacity on Demand pricing, the base model supports 660 cartridges (tiers 0,1,2), with options to upgrade for the additional 660 cartridges. The total 1320 cartridges could hold up to 2.1 PB of data (at 2:1 compression). One S54 frame could replace three traditional S53 frames that held only 440 LTO cartridges each.

If you have both TS1100 series and LTO drives in your TS3500 tape library, then you can have both S24 and S54 frames side by side.

To learn more, here is the official[IBM Announcement Letter].

⊘technorati tags: IBM, TS3500, tape library, TS3500, S24, S54, deep archive, high density, tape, cartridge, storage, frame, TS1100, TS1120, TS1130, LTO, LTO-1, LTO-2, LTO-3, LTO-4

Comment from Harley (IBM)

Tony,

Sadly, I was not inspired by the Pez dispenser. I simply worked backwards from the end goal which was to more fully utilize the volume we store cartridges in. The real trick of course was to build it to maximize customer investment (add new frames to existing libraries) and keeping our focus on things such as speed and quality. It was quite a challenge in many ways to bring a product like this from concept to reality. I would gladly share my story with you later.

Now I'm working with NAND flash architectures (not SSDs specifically) so we'll see how successful I can be in pushing these revolutionary efforts forward. The bottom line is that there is no clear decision between either NAND Flash packages (commonly in SSDs) or HDD and the unique characteristics of each mean that solutions should contain a custom configuration with some ratio of each. Wish me luck and keep up the great work writing your blog.

Harley

2008 Sep 17 — TS7650G ProtecTIER Deduplication virtual tape gateway (346)

Continuing this week's theme about the products that were part of last week's IBM Information Infrastructure launch, I will cover today the IBM System Storage TS7650G ProtecTIER deduplication gateway.

Here is a [three minute video] about the TS7650G.

This product is based on the technology from the [IBM acquisition of Diligent], featuring in-line deduplication processing. To learn more about deduplication, see my post: [Eleven Answers about Deduplication from IBM #309].

So what did IBM change?

- Before acquisition, Diligent offered only software. The task of putting this software on an appropriate x86 server with sufficient memory and processor capability was left as an exercise for the storage admin. With the TS7650G, IBM installs the ProtecTIER software on the fastest servers in the industry, the IBM System x3850 M2 and x3950 M2. This eliminates having the storage admins pretend that they have hardware engineering degrees.
- Before acquisition, the software worked only on a single system. IBM was able to offer multiple configurations of the TS7650G, including a

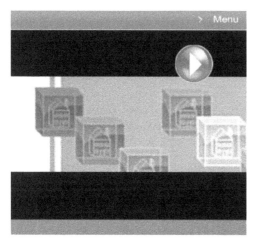

single-controller model as well as a clustered dual-controller model. The clustered dual-controller model can ingest data at an impressive 900 MB/sec, which is up to nine times faster than some of the competitive deduplication offerings.

- Before acquisition, ProtecTIER emulated DLT tape technology. This limited its viability, as the market share for DLT has dropped dramatically, and continues to dwindle. Most of the major backup software support DLT as an option, but going forward this may not be true much longer for new tape applications. IBM was able to extend support by adding LTO emulation on theTS7650G gateway, future-proofing this into the 21st Century.

At last week's launch, covering so many products with so few slides, this announcement was shrunken down to a single line "Store 25 TB of backups onto 1 TB of disk, in 8 hours" and perhaps a few people missed that this was actually covering two key features.

1. With deduplication, the TS7650G might get up to 25 times reduction on disk. If you back up a 1 TB data base that changes only slightly from one day to the next, once a day for 25 days, it might only take 1 TB, or so, of disk to hold all the unique versions, as most of the blocks would be identical, rather than 25 TB on traditional disk or tape storage systems. The TS7650G can manage up to 1 PB of disk, which could represent in theory up to 25 PB of backup data.

2. With an ingest rate of 900 MB/sec, the TS7650G could ingest 25 TB of backups during a typical 8 hour backup window.

The 25 TB of the first may not necessarily be the 25 TB of the second, but the wording was convenient for marketing purposes, and a comma was used to ensure no misunderstandings. Of course, depending on the type of application, the frequency of daily change, and the backup software employed, your mileage may vary.

⊘technorati tags: IBM, TS7650G, ProtecTIER, deduplication, gateway, Diligent, acquisition, DLT, LTO, cluster, ingest rate, x3850 M2, x3950 M2

2008 Sep 18 — IBM TS2900 Tape Autoloader (347)

Continuing this week's theme on products that were part of last week's IBM Information Infrastructure launch, today I'll cover the TS2900.

IBM System Storage TS2900 Tape Autoloader

This little baby is SWEET! At 1U high, it holds a single drive and up to 9 cartridges, up to a total of 14.4 TB at 2:1 compression. The drive can be a Half-Height (HH) LTO-3 or LTO-4 drive. (It is called an autoloader because there is only a single drive. Automation with multiple drives are called libraries).

This can be rack-mounted, or sit on your desktop. There is an I/O station for inserting or removing individual cartridges, as well as a removable tape magazine to populate or remove the tapes in a more efficient manner.

Both LTO3 and LTO-4 support a mix of regular and "Write Once, Read Many" (WORM) media to help comply with regulations demanding "Non-erasable, Non-rewriteable" storage. TheLTO-4 can also support on-drive encryption, managed by the IBM Encryption Key Manager (EKM).

To learn more, see the IBM System Storage[TS2900 page].

⊙**technorati tags**: IBM, TS2900, tape, autoloader, library, LTO-3, LTO-4, HH, WORM, NENR, encryption, EKM

The best way to sell products is to discuss solutions. I always try to show how an item in our portfolio is "part of a complete breakfast".

2008 Sep 19 — Talking about Solutions Not Products (348)

Well, this has been an interesting two weeks. On week 1, I focused on IBM's strategy and four key solutions areas: Information Availability, Information Security, Information Retention, and Information Compliance. On week 2, I focused on individual products, their attributes, features and functions.

Which week drew more blog traffic? You guessed it--week 1. Apparently, people want to know more about solutions to their challenges and problems, and not just see what piece part components are available.

While IBM had switched over to solution-selling a while ago, some of our competitors are still in product-selling mode, and try to frame all competitive comparisons on a product-by-product basis. In my post [Supermarkets and Specialty Shops], I drew the analogy that the IT supermarkets (IBM, HP, Sun and Dell) are focused on selling solutions, but the IT specialty shops (HDS, EMC, and others) are still focused on products.

Certainly, the transition from product-focused to solution-focused is not an easy one. As the IT industry matures, more and more clients are looking to buy solutions from their vendors. What does it take to change behavior of newly acquired employees, recently hired sales reps, and business partners, many of whom come from product-centric cultures, to match this dramatic shift in the marketplace? Let's take a look at change in other areas of the world.

On the [Freakonomics blog], Stephen Dubner discusses how clever people in Israel have figured out a way to get people to clean up after their pets in public places. This is a problem in many countries. Here we see an old idea, the [carrot-and-stick] approach, combined with new information technology. Here's an excerpt:

> "In order to keep a city's streets clean of dog poop, require dog owners to submit DNA samples from their pets when they get licenses; then use that DNA database to trace any left-behind poop and send the dogs' owners stiff fines.
>
> Well, it took three years but the Israeli city of Petah Tikva has actually put this plan to work:
>
> - The city will use the DNA database it is building to match feces to a registered dog and identify its owner.
>
> - Owners who scoop up their dogs' droppings and place them in specially marked bins on Petah Tikva's streets will be eligible for rewards of pet food coupons and dog toys.
>
> - But droppings found underfoot in the street and matched through the DNA database to a registered pet could earn its owner a municipal fine."

Sometimes, if enough people change, then changing behaviors of the few remaining becomes much easier. Dan Lockton on his *Architectures of Control* blog posts about the [London Design Festival - Greengaged]. This year, the festival focused on behavior changes for a greener environment, ecodesign and sustainable issues in design. Here's an excerpt and corresponding 5-minute YouTube video:

"Lea Simpson started with [this great Candid Camera clip] from 1960s demonstrating how easily social proof can be used to influence behavior.

Lea argued three important points relevant to behavior change:

1.   Behavior change requires behavior (i.e. the behavior of others: social effects are critical, as we respond to others' behavior which in turn affects our own; targeting the 'right' people allows behavior to spread)

2.   Behavior and motivation are two different things: To change behavior, you need to understand and work with people's motivations - which may be very different for different people.

3.   Desire is not enough: lots of people desire to behave differently, but it needs to be very easy for them to do it before it actually happens."

Of course, tax and government regulations can heavily influence behavior and decisions. Since today is [International Talk Like a Pirate Day], I thought I would finish this post off with this interesting piece on Google barges. Some companies, like IBM and Google, seem more adaptable to changing behavior and trying out fresh new ideas. Will Runyon over on the *Raised Floor* blog, has a post about Google's patent for [Data center barges on the sea]: "The idea is to use waves to power the data centers, ocean water to cool them, and a moored distance of seven miles or more to avoid paying taxes."

Arrr! Now that's what I call a new way of looking at things!

⊘**technorati tags**: IBM, strategy, Information Infrastructure, solution-selling, behavior, HP, Sun, Dell, EMC, HDS, DNA, database, Petah Tikva, Israel, Dan Lockton, Candid Camera, Lea Simpson, Will Runyon, Raised Floor, Google, patent, barges, taxes, regulations

---

2008 Sep 22 — When Factual Observations Mislead and Misrepresent (349)

Continuing my quest to "set the record straight" about [IBM XIV Storage System] and IBM's other products, I find myself amused at some of the FUD out there. Some are almost as absurd as the following analogy:

1. Humans share over 50 percent of DNA with bananas. [source]
2. If you peel a banana, and put the slippery skin down on the sidewalk outside your office building, it could pose a risk to your employees
3. If you peel a human, the human skin placed on the sidewalk in a similar manner might also pose similar risks.
4. Mr. Jones, who applied for the opening in your storage administration team, is a human being.
5. You wouldn't hire a banana to manage your storage, would you? This might be too risky!

The conclusion we are led to believe is that hiring Mr. Jones, a human being, is as risky as putting a banana peel down on the sidewalk. Some bloggers argue that they are merely making a series of factual observations, and letting their readers form their own conclusions. For example, the IBM XIV storage system has ECC-protected mirrored cache writes. Some false claims about this were [properly retracted] using ~~strike out~~ font to show the correction made, other times the same statement appears in another post from the same blogger that [have not yet been retracted] (**Update: has now been corrected**). Other bloggers borrow the false statement [for their own blog], perhaps not realizing the retractions were made elsewhere. Newspapers are unable to fix a previous edition, so are forced to publish retractions in future papers. With blogs, you can edit the original and post the changed version, annotated accordingly, so mistakes can be corrected quickly.

While it is possible to compare bananas and humans on a variety of metrics-- weight, height, and dare I say it, caloric value--it misses the finer differences of what makes them different. Humans might share 98 percent with chimpanzees, but having an opposable thumb allows humans to do things that ~~chimpanzees~~ **other animals** cannot.

> **Full Disclosure:** I am neither vegetarian nor cannibal, and harbor no ill will toward bananas nor chimpanzees. No bananas or chimpanzees were harmed in the writing of this blog post. Any similarity between the fictitious Mr. Jones in the above analogy and actual persons, living or dead, is purely coincidental.

So let's take a look at some of IBM XIV Storage System's "opposable thumbs".

- The IBM XIV system comes pre-formatted and ready to use. You don't have to spend weeks in meetings deciding between different RAID levels and then formatting different RAID ranks to match those decisions. Instead, you can start using the storage on the IBM XIV Storage System right away.

- The IBM XIV offers consistent performance, balancing I/O evenly across all disk drive modules, even when performing Snapshot processing, or recovering from component failure. You don't have to try to separate data to prevent one workload from stealing bandwidth from another. You don't have to purchase extra software to determine where the "hot spots" are on the disk. You don't have to buy other software to help re-locate and re-separate the data to re-balance the I/Os. Instead, you just enjoy consistent performance.

- The IBM XIV offers thin provisioning, allowing LUNs to grow as needed to accommodate business needs. You don't have to estimate or over-allocate space for planned future projects. You don't have to monitor if a LUN is reaching80 or 90 percent full. You don't have to carve larger and larger LUNs and schedule time on the weekends to move the data over to these new bigger spaces. Instead, you just write to the disk, monitoring the box as a whole, rather than individual LUNs.

- The IBM XIV Storage System's innovative RAID-X design allows drives to be replaced with drives of any larger or smaller capacity. You don't have to find the exact same 73GB 10K RPM drive to match the existing 73GB 10K RPM drive that failed. Some RAID systems allow "larger than original" substitutions, for example a 146GB drive to replace a 73GB drive, but the added capacity is wasted, because of the way most RAID levels work. The problem is that many failures happen 3-5 years out, and disk manufacturers move on to bigger capacities and different form factors, making it sometimes difficult to find an exact replacement or forcing customers to keep their own stock of spare drives. Instead, with the IBM XIV architecture, you sleep well at night, knowing it allows future drive capacities to act as replacements, and getting the full value and usage of that capacity.

Fellow blogger from EMC Mark Twomey on his *StorageZilla* blog, posted about [Steinhardt's Rule of Customer Beliefs] with his own *Twomey Corollary*. Here is an excerpt:

"In priority order, customers believe:

1. Their own experience

2. The experiences of other customers
3. Objective third-party sources
4. Everybody else
5. Vendors"

In the case of IBM XIV Storage System, it is not clear whether

- "Vendors" are those from IBM and IBM Business Partners, including bloggers like me employed by IBM, and "everybody else" includes IBM's immediate competitors, including bloggers employed by them.

  -- or --

- "Vendors" includes IBM and its competitors including any bloggers, so that "everybody else" refers instead to anyone not selling storage systems, but opinionated enough to not qualify as "objective third-party sources".

  -- or --

- "Vendors" includes official statements from IBM and its competitors, and "everybody else" refers to bloggers presenting their own personal or professional opinions, that may or may not correspond to their employers.

That said, feel free to comment below on which of these you think the last two points of Steinhardt's rule is trying to capture. Certainly, I can't argue with the top two: a customer's own experience and the experiences of other customers, which I mentioned previously in my post [Deceptively Delicious].

In that light, here is a 5-minute video on *IBM TV* with a customer testimonial from the good folks at [NaviSite], one of our many customer references for the IBM XIV Storage System.

For more about IBM XIV Storage System, check out IBM XIV team's *ThinkStorage* blog, with posts about [the Storage industry], and [Throttling up Performance].

⊘**technorati tags**: IBM, XIV, storage, system, banana, ECC, protected, mirrored, cache, writes, RAID, Snapshot, consistent performance, thin provisioning, Mark Twomey, StorageZilla, Steinhardt, NaviSite, customer reference

Comment from Barry Burke (EMC), the Storage Anarchist

My apologies. Post corrected.

If you had sent me an email about the earlier inaccuracy on my blog - I would have happily corrected it.

Comment from Rob Clare (IBM)

Tony, Bananas don't have opposable thumbs but I'm pretty sure chimps do. Peeling those bananas would be tough without them!

Keep up the good work!

Regards
Rob Clare, IBM UK

Comment from the Open Systems Guy (OSSG)

One question I did have relates to rebuild times. A single disk can be rebuilt in 30 minutes, but what if a node gets a bad memory stick or a motherboard failure? How long does it take to rebuild all the drives in that node? How much impact does this rebuild have on production? Also, I've heard two numbers regarding the usable and raw space. Could you clarify whether it's 80/120, or 80/160? Also, how many disks can be lost before there's a risk of data loss?

Thanks!

Response from Tony Pearson (IBM)

Robert, Good catch! Of all the animals I could have chosen for the analogy, I picked one that actually DOES have opposable thumbs like humans do. Mea culpa. I have corrected the post above.

-- Tony

Response from Tony Pearson (IBM)

OSSG, this sounds like more than one question! The worst case scenario for 1TB drives is 30 minutes, but typical times found by our clients is in the 3-10 minute range. That said, losing a drawer of 12 drives is theoretically 12x longer, so 1-6 hours, depending on the amount of data written, and the amount of activity for production I/O.

Whether you lose a single drive or all drives in a drawer, you are reading evenly across 168 drives. The impact has been measured to be about 1 percent performance degradation during the rebuild process.

If you do not have synchronous mirroring set, you can lose up to 12 drives on a single drawer before data loss. With synchronous mirroring, you can potentially lose more drives before data loss.

The usable TB in the IBM XIV Storage System is 79TB. This is a huge increase over the 51TB usable in the previous generation. Capacity on Demand pricing options allow you to get initially as little as 21TB with options to use more space as needed over time.
-- Tony

I love client success stories. Based in Thailand, Kantana Animation Studios make computer animations for television commercials, television series and featured films. This elephant is from their movie "Khan Kluay".

2008 Sep 23 — SoFS at Kantana Animation Studios (350)

Continuing this week's theme on customer references of IBM's solutions, today I will discuss the success at Kantana Animation Studios.

Here is a 3-minute video from the good folks at Kantana Animation Studios, part of the [Kantana Group]. They produced the animated movie [Khan Kluay] using IBM Scale-out File Services (SoFS), a product IBM announced last November 2007.

Of course, I have blogged about Scale-out File Services [SoFS] before, in my post [More details about IBM clustered scalable NAS]. SoFS is one of the many blended disk-and-tape storage solutions that IBM offers. In the case of Kantana, they used [IBM System Storage DS4800 disk] and [IBM System Storage TS3310 tape libraries].

As a film-maker myself (see this sample [Highlights clip]) and active member of the Tucson Film Society, I am pleased to see IBM so greatly involved in the film industry. I've had the pleasure to visit some of these animation studios myself and meet with other film-makers at various conferences.

For more details on Kantana's implementation, see the [Case Study].

⊘**technorati tags**: IBM, SoFS, DS4800, TS3310, Kantana Animation Studios, Tucson Film Society, Khan Kluay, computer animation

On the day after the tragedies of September 11, 2011, my team spent the day packing food at the Community Food Bank of Southern Arizona. This was part of an annual event that United Way calls "Days of Caring". I have participated in this event every year since.

2008 Sep 24 — Days of Caring 2008 (351)

No post today. I will be joining the majority of IBMers in Tucson for "Days of Caring" held annually byte [United Way of Tucson and Southern Arizona]. IBM has been doing this for years, and we are joined by volunteers from other local businesses, including HealthNet, Wells Fargo bank, Texas Instruments, KVOA local NBC affiliate, 94.9 MixFM radio, and others.

The "days" involve a kick-off last week (Sep 19) and two days of helping local charities (Sep 24 and 27). We are split into teams and are assigned out to help fix up old buildings, clean out gutters, re-paint walls. My team will be sorting canned goods at the local [Community Food Bank], and assembling boxes of items to be given out to needy families.

⊘**technorati tags**: IBM, Days of Caring, United Way, HealthNet, Wells Fargo, Texas Instruments, KVOA, MixFM, Community Food Bank

2008 Sep 25 — IBM helps Healthcare firms large and small (352)

Continuing this week's theme on customer references of IBM solutions, IBM helps companies large and small in the Healthcare and Life Sciences industry. I have two examples today.

First, we have [Northwest Radiology Network], a small firm with 180 employees, having to deal with ten thousand medical images per month. Here is an excerpt from the [IBM Press Release]:

> "IBM announced that Northwest Radiology Network has gone live with a new virtualized enterprise of IBM servers and storage to support its growing medical imaging needs, giving its four locations an enterprise-class infrastructure which enables its doctors to recover medical image reports faster for analysis and enables remote 24x7 access to its medical image report system.

> Founded in 1967, Northwest Radiology (NWR) is ranked as one of the largest physician groups in the Indianapolis, Indiana area. With 180 employees who offer the Central Indiana community comprehensive inpatient and outpatient imaging services such as mammography, ultrasonography, CT scans, PET-CT scans, bone density scans and MRIs, the Network had a dramatic need to develop a centralized infrastructure where large amounts of data could be stored and shared. A new data center would benefit the company's clientele; which includes area hospitals and doctor's offices serving thousands of patients each year.

> Storing more than ten thousand medical imaging reports and radiographic images each month for doctors to analyze, the Network realized it had single points of failure and at one point a critical report server failed. Northwest Radiology turned to IBM and IBM Business Partner Software Information Systems (SIS) for a more efficient solution to prevent any possible downtime in the future.

> SIS recommended and installed a virtualized infrastructure with IBM servers and storage as the heart of Northwest Radiology's Indianapolis data center. By April 2007, Northwest Radiology replaced eight servers and direct attached storage with just two IBM System x3650 servers connected to an IBM System Storage DS3400. Today, the new servers run 15 virtual servers to ensure the availability of their services 24x7. When the business needs it, a new server can be provisioned in just minutes. With a Fibre Channel on the SAN Disk, the DS3400 not only increased performance but also met NWR's requirement to not have one single point of failure. With three TB of storage capacity, they can

meet the demands of increased business well into the future. The systems are also now easily managed from a remote site.

'Uptime is paramount in our business. We selected IBM based on the reliability and flexibility of IBM System x servers and the IBM System Storage DS3400,' said Marty Buening, IT Director, Northwest Radiology Network. 'The virtualized infrastructure and the SAN storage array that SIS and IBM brought to the table is improving our service and giving our doctors and staff piece of mind knowing each patient's medical imaging reports are always available.'"

Second, we have [Iowa Health System], a large enterprise with over 19,000 employees, managing four million patients and hundreds of TBs of data.

Here is a 4-minute video on *IBM TV* from the good folks at Iowa Health System discussing the IBM Grid Medical Archive Solution (GMAS) as part of their information infrastructure for their Picture Archiving and Communication Systems (PACS) application.

For more details about Iowa Health System's deployment of GMAS, see Paul Shread's *GridComputing* article [Putting Medical Data on the Grid].

For more about GMAS, one of IBM's many blended disk-and-tape storage solutions, see the [IBM GMAS solution brief] and this 22-slide [GMAS presentation].

In both cases, IBM technology was able to provide remote access to medical information, making images and patient records available to more doctors, specialists and radiologists. Last January, in my post [Five in Five], IBM had predicted that remote access to healthcare would have an impact over the next five years.

Whether you are a small company or a large one, IBM probably has the right solution for you.

⌀**technorati tags**: IBM, Northwest Radiology Network, NWR, SIS, Iowa Health System, IHS, GMAS, PACS, remote, access, healthcare, life sciences, disk-and-tape

Before *"Big Data"* was a phrase used by everyone in the IT industry, IBM was providing decision support systems and Online Analytics Processing (OLAP).

2008 Sep 26 — Many Eyes and the Visualization of Data (353)

Wrapping up my week on successful uses of information, I thought I would discuss the visualization of data. Not just bar charts and pie charts, but how effective visual information can be on multi-variable plots.

IBM's [Many Eyes] recognizes that 70 percent of our sensory input neurons in our brain our focused on visual inputs, and so we might recognize patterns if only data was presented in more interesting and visual representations.

In addition to X/Y axis, variables can be presented by size of circle and color. Here's an example plot of the past US bailouts, with variables representing amount, year, company and industry. This plot does not include the current 700 Billion US Dollar bailout currently under discussion.

This is part of IBM's Collaborative User Experience (CUE) research lab. The software is available Web2.0style at no charge, just upload your data set, and choose one of 16 different presentation styles.

These plots get even more interesting when you animate them over time. In 2006, Hans Rosling presented data he gathered from the United Nations and other publicly funded sources and presented his findings at the TED conference. Here is the 20-minute video of that presentation (click on play at right), titled ["Debunking third-world myths with the best stats you've ever seen"], in which he debunks the myth that all countries fall into two distinct categories: Industrialized and Developing.

In 2007, Hans returned with another 19-minute presentation at TED, titled [New insights on poverty and life around the world].

Amazingly, the data--as well as the software to analyze it--is available at [GapMinder.org] website.

For more information on how you can deploy an information infrastructure that allows you to search, visualize and leverage the most value from your information, contact your local IBM representative or IBM Business Partner.

⌖**technorati tags**: IBM, Many Eyes, multi-variable plot, US bailout, CUE, TED, Hans Rosling, debunk, myths, poverty, global, health

2008 Sep 30 — IBM Tivoli Advanced Backup and Recovery for z/OS V2.1 (354)

Well, it's Tuesday again, which means IBM announcement day. With our [big launches] we had this year, there might be some confusion on IBM terminology on how announcements are handled. Basically, there are three levels:

Technology Demonstration

Technology demonstrations show IBM's leadership, innovation and investment direction, without having to detail a specific product offering. Last month's [Project Quicksilver], for example, demonstrated the ability to handle over 1 million IOPS with Solid State Drive. IBM is committed to develop solid state storage to create real-world uses across a broad range of applications, middleware, and systems offerings.

Preview Announcement

A preview announcement does entail a specific product offering, but may not necessarily include pricing, packaging or specific availability dates.

Announcement

An announcement also entails a specific product offering, and does include pricing, packaging and specific availability dates.

With our September 8 launch of the IBM Information Infrastructure strategic initiative, there were a mix of all three of these. Many of the preview announcements will be followed up with full announcements later this year.

Today, the IBM Tivoli Advanced Backup and Recovery for z/OS v2.1 was announced.

> **Note:** If you don't use z/OS on a System z mainframe, you can stop reading now.

As many of my loyal readers know, I was lead architect for DFSMS until 2001, and so functions related to DFSMS and z/OS are very near and dear to my heart. For Business Continuity, IBM created Aggregate Backup and Recovery Support (ABARS) as part of the DFSMShsm component. This feature created a self-contained backup image from data that could be either on disk or tape, including migrated data. In the event of a disaster, an ABARS backup image can be used to bring back just the exact programs and data needed for a specific application, speeding up the recovery process, and allowing BC/DR plans to prioritize what is most important.

To help manage ABARS, IBM has partnered with [Mainstar Software Corporation]to offer a product that helps before, during and after the ABARS processing.

Before

ABARS requires the storage admin to have a "selection list" of data sets to process as an aggregate. IBM Tivoli Advanced Backup and Recovery for z/OS includes Mainstar® ASAP™ to help identify the appropriate data sets for specific applications, using information from job schedulers, JCL, and SMF records.

During

ABARS has two simple commands: ABACKUP to produce the backup image, and ARECOVER to recover it. However, if you have hundreds of aggregates, and each aggregate has several backups, you may need some help identifying which image to recover from. IBM Tivoli Advanced Backup and Recovery for z/OS includes Mainstar® ABARS Manager™ to present a list of information, making it easy to choose from. To help prep the ICF Catalogs, there is a CATSCRUB feature for either "empty" or "full" catalog recovery at the recovery site.

After

The fact that storage admins may not be intimately familiar with the applications they are backing up is a common source of human error. IBM Tivoli Advanced Backup and Recovery for z/OS includes Mainstar® All/Star™ to help validate that the data sets processed by ABACKUP are complete, to support any regulatory audit or application team verification. This critical data tracking/inventory reporting not only identifies what isn't backed up, so you can ensure that you are not missing critical data, but also can identify which data sets are being backed up multiple times by more than one utility, so you can reduce the occurrence of redundant backups.

With v2.1 of Tivoli Advanced Backup and Recovery for z/OS, IBM has integrated Tivoli Enterprise Portal (TEP) support. This allows you to access these functions through IBM Tivoli Monitor v6 GUI on a Linux, UNIX or Windows workstation. IBM Tivoli Monitor has full support to integrate Web 2.0, multi-media and frames. This means that any other product that can be rendered in a browser can be embedded and supported with launch-in-context capability.

(If you have not separately purchased a license to IBM Tivoli Monitoring V6.2, don't worry, you can obtain the TEP-based function by acquiring a no-charge, limited use license to IBM Tivoli Monitoring Services on z/OS, V6.2.)

In addition to supporting IBM's many DFSMS backup methods, from ABARS to IDCAMS to IEBGENER, IBM Tivoli Advanced Backup and Recovery v2.1 can also support third-party products from Innovation Data Processing and Computer Associates.

As many people re-discover the mainframe as the cost-effective platform that it has always been, migrating applications back to the mainframe to reduce costs, they need solutions that work across both mainframe and distributed systems during this transition. IBM Tivoli Advanced Backup and Recovery for z/OS can help.

⊘technorati tags: IBM, Tivoli, ABARS, Advanced, Backup, Recovery, z/OS, DFSMS, DFSMShsm, Project Quicksilver, SSD, IOPS, launch, Information Infrastructure, Mainstar, GUI, Linux, UNIX, Windows, TEP

October

Every year, this is the busiest month at the Tucson EBC. IBM sellers and business partners bring clients to Tucson for golf and expertise on storage products.

2008 Oct 01 — New BladeCenter Chassis with Storage Inside (355)

Today, IBM announced its latest [BladeCenter S] with integrated redundant SAN fabric and disk storage inside the chassis. The tag line is "Data Center Capability, without the Data Center!"

I've gotten a few calls on this today, so I thought it would be good to blog about. To understand what is new, you need to understand what we had in other BladeCenter chassis. In those other chassis, there were up to 14 blade servers on the front, and switch modules for FCP and Ethernet on the back. The entire chassis was rack-mounted to be connected to external devices.

The BladeCenter S was announced a year ago. With the new "BladeCenter S" chassis, the storage can be included inside the chassis, as well as connecting tithe outside world. It is designed to be stand-alone, rather than rack-mounted, plugs into a standard 100v-240v office power outlet, and includes a dust filter in case you keep it close to the floor, under your desk for example.

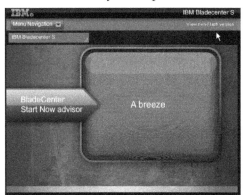

Click graphic at left for 4-minute video introduction.

(Here's also a more detailed [7-minute video] with fellow IBM colleague Alex Yost.)

Here's what you can get with the BladeCenter S:

- Up to six (6) server blades that can do the work of 25-45 traditional servers.
- Up to two (2) storage blades, each can have six (6) SAS or SATA disk drive modules (DDMs).
- Up to four (4) switch modules, with a variety to choose from.

- Shared KVM, DVD/CD burner, and USB port. You can designate which blade has access to these, useful for installing software, attaching external devices, and so on.

The blades use either Intel, AMD or POWER processors, so you can run Windows, Linux, AIX, and [IBM i] (the new name for i5/OS V6R1).

Back 20 years ago, I worked with people with System/36 and System/38 systems. They loved it. Everything in one package. This grew into the AS/400 server. Having everything in one package was such an advantage that IBM extended this to include a few "x86 blades" to run Windows applications but share the storage and network resources.

Now IBM has taken this one step further. The older models assumed the majority of applications run under IBM's OS/400 or i5/OS operating system, but this new BladeCenter S does not make that assumption. You can mix and match different blade servers as needed, and run the operating systems you need.

This is an ideal packaging for Small and Medium sized Business (SMB), remote branch offices, and retail stores. In fact, more than 4,000 retail stores plan to run their operations using BladeCenter S this holiday season! For more on this announcement, see the [IBM Press Release].

⊘**technorati tags**: IBM, BladeCenter S, SAN, fabric, disk, storage, FCP, Ethernet, SAS, SATA, KVM, USB, POWER, Windows, Linux, AIX, IBM i

I guess I am an "optimist" at heart, always looking on the bright side of life. Having read the book "America the Broke" which predicted this would happen, I was well-prepared to weather the storm financially. While others were selling off their stocks in a panic, I was able to pick up some shares at bargain prices!

2008 Oct 13 — A silver lining for the financial crisis (356)

As the popular idiom goes, ["Every cloud has a silver lining"], and perhaps there are some things that we gain from the recent financial collapse of the global world markets.

Let's examine some of these:

Consolidation and the [Economies of Scale]

As financial firms focus on costs, the IT departments will have an opportunity to consolidate their servers, networks and storage equipment. Consolidating disk and tape resources, implementing storage virtualization, and reducing energy costs might get a boost from this crisis. Consolidating disparate storage resources to a big SoFS, XIV, DS8000 disk system, or TS3500 tape library might greatly help reduce costs.

Establishing enterprise-wide Storage Resource Management (SRM)

Having mixed vendor environments that result from such mergers and acquisitions can be complicated to manage. Thankfully, IBM TotalStorage Productivity Center manages both IBM and non-IBM equipment, based on open industry standards like SMI-S and WBEM. Merged companies might let go IT people with limited vendor-specific knowledge, but keep the ones familiar with cross-vendor infrastructure management skills and ITIL certification.

Comparing different vendor equipment

It seems that often times when there is a merger or acquisition, the two companies were using different storage gear from different vendors. IBM has made some incredible improvements over the past three years, in both performance enhancements and energy efficiency, but many companies with non-IBM equipment may not be aware of them. If there was ever a time to perform a side-by-side comparison between IBM and non-IBM equipment, here is your chance.

For more on the impact of the financial meltdown on IT, see this InfoWorld [Special Report].

⚲**technorati tags**: IBM, cloud, silver lining, financial, collapse, crisis, meltdown, global, world, markets, consolidation, XIV, DS8000, SoFS, TS3500, performance, energy efficiency, SMI-S, WBEM, ITIL, TotalStorage Productivity Center, SRM, InfoWorld

Response from Tony Pearson (IBM)

Steve Duplessie from ESG weighs in as well on this:
http://esgblogs.typepad.com/steves_it_rants/2008/10/the-silver-lini.html

2008 Oct 14 — October 2008 SAN and Disk announcements (357)

Well, it's Tuesday, and more IBM announcements were made today. Many of my colleagues are in Dallas, Texas for the [Storage Networking World conference], and hopefully I will get some feedback from them before the week is over.

Today, IBM made announcements for Storage Area Networking (SAN) gear and disk systems.

8 Gbps Longwave transceivers

IBM now offers 8 Gbps Longwave SFP transceivers on the [IBM System Storage SAN256B and SAN768B] directors, as well as the IBM System Storage SAN24B-4 Express, SAN40B-4, and SAN80B-4 switches (orderable as [machine type models] or [part numbers]). These transceivers support single mode fiber up to 10km in distance, compared to the 50-75 meters supported by the Shortwave SFP transceivers.

Like the Shortwave SFP transceivers we already have available, these Longwave transceivers have "N-2" support, which means they can support two generations back: auto-negotiate down to 4 Gbps and 2 Gbps speeds. If you still have 1 Gbps equipment, now is a good time to consider upgrading those, or keep a few 4 Gbps ports available that can auto-negotiate down to 1 Gbps speed.

FICON Accelerator

Mainframe clients that sent data to a remote Business Continuity/Disaster Recovery (BC/DR) location often used "channel extenders", which were special boxes used to minimize performance delays when transmitting FICON across long distances. This was especially helpful for z/OS Global Mirror (what we used to call XRC) as well as electronic vaulting to tape.

Now, this functionality can be part of the directors and routers, eliminating the need for separate equipment. This is available for the SAN768B and SAN256B directors, as well as SAN18B-R and SAN04B-R routers.

Before the merger between Brocade and McDATA, IBM offered SAN18B-R routers from Brocade, and SAN04M-R routers from McDATA. The former had 16 Fibre Channel (FC) ports and two Ethernet ports, and the latter was less expensive with just four ports. Brocade came up with a clever replacement for both. The [IBM

System Storage SAN04B-R] router comes by default with two active FC ports and two Ethernet ports, but also with 14 additional FC ports inactive. A "High Performance Extension" feature activates these additional ports, bringing the SAN04B-R up to the SAN18B-R level, and allows it to support the FICON Accelerator feature above.

So, instead of having specialized channel extenders at both primary and secondary sites, you can have a director with FICON Accelerator at the primary site, sending FICON over Ethernet to a 1U-high router (also running the FICON Accelerator) at the secondary site, which can greatly reduce costs. The FICON Accelerator can in some cases double the amount of data transfer throughput, but of course, your mileage may vary.

DS3000 series

On the disk side, the [IBM System Storage DS3000 series] disk systems have been enhanced, with support for 450GB high-speed 15K RPM SAS drives, RAID-6 double-drive protection, more FlashCopy point-in-time copies, and more partitions. On the DS3000, "storage partitions" is what the rest of the industry calls "LUN masking". A storage partition allows you to isolate a set of LUNs to only be seen by a single host server, or host cluster that shares the same set of LUNs. Some clients felt that the default of four partitions was too low, so now up to 32 partitions can be configured.

(This is not to be confused with "Logical Partitions" that isolate processor and cache resources available on the IBM System Storage DS8000 and other high-end storage disk systems.)

IBM also extended the Operating System support. The DS3000 series now supports Solaris, either on x86 or SPARC-based servers. The DS3300 iSCSI support now supports Linux on POWER. The DS3400 allows support of IBM i (the new name for i5/OS V6R1) through the VIOS feature.

DCS9900

The [IBM System Storage DCS9900] is a bigger, faster version of the DCS9550. Like the DCS9550, the DCS9900 is designed for high performance computing (HPC) workloads. The DCS9550 supported up to 960TB in two frames, with 2.8 GB/sec throughput, and an optional disk spin-down capability. The new DCS9900 can support up to 1.2 PB in two frames, with 5.6 GB/sec throughput, but no spin-down capability.

So whether your data center is filled with System z mainframes, or other open systems, IBM has a solution for you.

⊘**technorati tags**: IBM, SNW, SAN, disk, storage, system, Shortwave, Longwave, SFP, transceiver, SAN256B, SAN768B, directors, SAN18B-R, SAN04B-R, routers, SAN24B-4, Express, SAN40B-4, SAN80B-4, switches, FICON Accelerator, Brocade, McDATA, Fibre Channel, FC, FCP, FICON, z/OS, XRC, channel extender, DS3000, DS3300, DS3400, Ethernet, iSCSI, SAS, RAID-6, Linux on POWER, Solaris, IBM i, i5/OS, VIOS, DCS9900, DCS9550, HPC

I was asked to blog about the new SVC "entry edition". I was inspired by a pink cross-bow 60 percent the weight of the standard model, but still powerful enough to kill a moose. The product manager at IBM in charge of SVC recognized that October was "Breast Cancer Awareness" month, and she quickly approved the RPQ to allow "Flamingo Pink" to be an official color. Since then, we have referred to the 2145-8A4 as the "pink" model!

2008 Oct 15 — Pink it and Shrink it (358)

Lakota Industries made news with the introduction of its [Sarah-Cuda Hunting Bow], named after moose-hunting U.S. Vice President nominee and Governor of Alaska [Sarah Palin]. This has all the same features as their other high-end hunting bows, but is lighter, smaller and available in Pink Camo. This "pink-it-and-shrink-it" move was designed to broaden the market share of hunting bows by reaching out to the needs of women hunters.

Not to be outdone, today, at the Storage Networking World Conference, IBM announced the new IBM System Storage SAN Volume Controller Entry Edition [SVC EE].

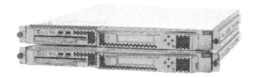

The new SVC Entry Edition, available in Flamingo Pink (RPQ) or traditional Raven Black (default color).

You might be thinking: "Wait! IBM SVC is already the leading storage virtualization product among SMB clients today, why introduce a less

---

expensive model?" With the global economy in the tank, IBM thought it would be nice to help out our smaller SMB clients with this new option.

This new offering is actually a combination of new software (SVC 4.3.1) and new hardware (2145-8A4). Here are the key differences:

	SVC Classic	SVC EE
Licensing	by usable capacity managed, up to 8 PB	by number of disk drives, up to 60 drives
Hardware	2145-4F2, 8F2, 8F4, 8G4, 8A4	2145-8A4
Cluster size	1, 2, 3 or 4 node-pairs, depending on performance requirements	only one node-pair needed
Copy Services	FlashCopy, Metro Mirror and Global Mirror, licensed by subset of capacity used	FlashCopy, Metro Mirror and Global Mirror, but with simplified licensing

The SVC EE is not a "dumbed-down" version of the SVC Classic. It has all the features and functions of the SVC Classic, including thin provisioning with "Space-efficient volumes", Quality of Service (QoS) performance prioritization for more important applications, point-in-time FlashCopy, and both synchronous and asynchronous disk mirroring (Metro and Global Mirror).

While IBM has not yet have SPC-1 benchmarks published, IBM is positioning the SVC EE as roughly 60 percent of the performance, at 60 percent of the list price, compared to a comparable SVC Classic 2145-8G4 configuration. The SVC Classic is already one of the fastest disk systems in the industry. By comparison, the SVC EE is twice as fast as the original SVC 2145-4F2 introduced five years ago. If you outgrow the SVC EE, no problem! The 2145-8A4 can be used in traditional SVC Classic mode, and the SVC EE software can be converted into the SVC Classic software license for upgrade purposes, protecting your original investment!

For those considering an HP EVA 4400 or EMC CX-4 disk system, you might want to look at combining an SVC EE with [IBM System Storage DS3400] disk. The combination offers more features and capabilities, and helps reduce your IT costs at the same time.

And if you are worried you can't afford it right now, IBM Global Financing is offering a ["Why Wait?" world-wide deferral of interest and payments] for 90 days, so you don't have to make your first payment until 2009, applicable to all IBM System Storage products, including the SVC EE, SVC Classic and DS3400 disk systems.

You can read more details on fellow blogger Barry Whyte's [Storage Virtualization] blog.

technorati tags: IBM, SVC, SVC EE, SVC Classic, Lakota Industries, Sarah-Cuda, Sarah Palin, Flamingo Pink, Raven Black, RPQ, SPC-1, 2145-8A4, DS4300, IBM Global Financing, Why Wait, FlashCopy, Metro Mirror, Global Mirror, Barry Whyte

Addition from Tony Pearson (IBM)

Chuck Hollis (EMC) pokes fun here:

> http://chucksblog.typepad.com/chucks_blog/2008/10/an-interesting.html

2008 Oct 16 — Four Steps to Enhance Competitiveness (359)

Continuing this week's theme on dealing with the global economic meltdown, recession and financial crisis, I found a great video that recaps

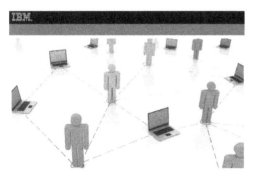

IBM CEO Sam Palmisano's recommendations to being more competitive in this environment.

In a recent speech to business leaders, Sam outlined what he sees as the four most important steps to thriving in the global economy. The highlights can be seen here in this [2-minute video] on IBM's "Forward View" eMagazine.

To learn more, here is the companion [PDF document].

technorati tags: IBM, CEO, Sam Palmisano, four steps, SMB, global economy, competitiveness

Comment from Donald

Today, business world is increasing rapidly by the time...

Years ago, our midrange disks were called Fibre Array Storage Technology (FAStT), pronounced "fast" to emphasize their speed. We dropped it because IBM executives could neither spell nor pronounce it correctly, with such variations as "FASTt" and "FAS-Tee".

2008 Oct 20 — First in its class - The DS5300 (360)

Over at *The Register*, Chris Mellor has an article titled [The IBM DS5000: Best in a field of one], discussing how the IBM System Storage DS5300 is in a class by itself.

IBM hired independent analyst Enterprise Strategy Group [ESG] to validate the box, and run workload-specific benchmarks. I agree with Chris, the results are impressive! The report includes results from Microsoft Exchange JetStress tool to provide insight into email performance, and another benchmark to simulate Web server IOPS.

Also, the published SPC-1 benchmark for the DS5300 puts it at about 29 percent improvement over the DS4800. Chris argues the DS5300 is similar in class to NetApp FAS3170, which IBM sells as the IBM System Storage N6070.

If you are interesting in either the DS5300 or N6070, contact your local IBM Business Partner or sales rep.

technorati tags: IBM, Chris Mellor, DS5000, DS5300, FAS3170, N6070, JetStress, SPC-1

2008 Oct 20 — Mainframe Disk and Tape Announcements (361)

Well, it's Tuesday again, and that means more announcements from IBM!

In conjunction with IBM's new [System z10 Business Class (BC)] mainframe designed for Small and Medium-sized Businesses (SMB), IBM also announced related storage product enhancements.

DS6000 series

Yes, it's alive! Contrary to the FUD you might have read from our competitors, IBM continues to sell thousands and thousands of IBM System Storage DS6800 disk systems, and now enhances them with the option for 450GB 15K RPM drives. What is nice about these 450GB drives is that they are as fast or faster* than 300GB drives, so the typical trade-off between performance and capacity do not apply.

(* I compared Seagate 15.6K (450GB) with 15.5K (300GB) models.

	450GB drives	300GB drives
Avg Seek time (Read)	3.4ms	3.5 ms
Avg Seek time (Write)	3.9ms	4.0 ms
Full Seek time (Read)	6.43ms	6.7 ms
Full Seek time (Write)	7.12ms	7.4 ms
Sustained Bandwidth	112-171 MB/sec	73-125 MB/sec

This may or may not result in application performance improvements, depending on workload pattern. Your mileage may vary.)

Our clients report back that these are incredibly stable systems that they don't have to worry about. This enhancement applies to both the [511/EX1 models] and [522/EX2 models].

DS8000 series

Understanding that clients want complete solutions from single vendors, IBM offers synergy between System z and the IBM System Storage DS8000 disk systems. The latest R4.1 microcode upgrade offers two key features on the various models [2107, 2421, 2422, 2423, and 2424].

- zHPF - High Performance FICON for System z. IBM was able to increase the throughput on 4 Gbps links. For OLTP workloads randomly accessing 4KB blocks, IBM internal tests showed zHPF doubled performance from 13,000 IOPS to 26,000 IOPS per channel. For sequential workloads, such as batch processing, zHPF increased performance 50 percent, from 350 MB/sec to 525 MB/sec.

- In February, IBM previewed [Incremental Resync] for z/OS Metro Global Mirror. However, some concepts are better explained with pictures.

One way to set up a 3-site disaster recovery protection is to have your production synchronously mirrored to a second site nearby, and at the same time asynchronously mirrored to a remote location. On the System z, you can have site "A" using synchronous IBM System Storage Metro Mirror over to nearby site "B", and also have site "A" sending data over to site "C" asynchronously using z/OS Global Mirror. This is called "z/OS Metro Global Mirror".

In the past, if the disk system in site A failed, you would switch over to site B, which would have to resend send all the data again to site C to be resynchronized. This is because site B was not tracking what the System Data Mover (SDM) reader had or had not yet processed.

With DS8000 4.1, the "incremental resync" function that, along with using IBM HyperSwap, requires site B to only send and resync the data that was in-flight when the outage occurred. When you compare the difference in sending this limited amount of in-flight data with the traditional complete volume of data, you can see how "Incremental Resync" can resynchronize the data 95% faster, and also greatly decrease your bandwidth requirements. This reduces the risk in case a subsequent outage occurs.

TS7700 series

Introduced originally in 1997 as the IBM Virtual Tape Server (VTS), the [IBM System Storage TS7700] series supports Grid capability to replicate tape image data across locations. Here's a quick recap of today's announcement:

- Existing TS7740 can be upgraded up to 9TB of disk cache. New models can have up to 13TB of disk cache.

- A new "tape-less" TS7720 that has up to 70TB of disk cache.
- Integrate Library Management support. I discussed [Integrated Removable Media Manager (IRMM)] before, and this is basically IRMM inside. For those with TS3500 tape libraries, this support eliminates the need for a separate IBM 3953 L05 Library Manager.
- TS1130 back-end tape drive support. These are the fastest 1TB drives in the industry, with support of built-in encryption, and now can be used as the physical tape back-end for the virtual tape TS7740 repository.

While our competitors might be boarding up their windows in preparation for the economic downturn in the USA economy, IBM remains generating solid results. San José Mercury News has an article that discusses this titled [IBM's 3Q profit strong on global sales]. There has never been a better time to buy from, or invest in, IBM!

⚲**technorati tags**: IBM, z10 BC, mainframe, SMB, DS6000, DS6800, 450GB, 15K, RPM, FUD, DS8100, DS8300, DS8000, zHPF, FICON, Incremental Resync, z/OS, MGM, HyperSwap, VTS, TS7700, TS7740, TS7720, tape-less, IRMM, TS1130, encryption, Mercury News, 3Q08, profit

Comment from Chuck

Tony –

How can you claim that the 450 GB drives are as fast or faster than the 300 GB drives and then conclude that capacity/performance trade-offs don't matter?? I checked HGST drive specs, the 300 and 450s have identical buffer sizes, latency and seek times. I think each drive can sustain just under 180 IOPS per drive (clear this up for me if I have missed something) and that the capacity/performance trade-off is alive and well. Is there some magic that happens inside a DS6800 or DS8000 that allow a 450 GB drive to handle more IOPS than a 300 GB drive?

Response from Tony Pearson (IBM)

Chuck, I compared Seagate models based on their DDM speeds, I had not looked at the HGST, but glad to hear that their 450GB are as fast as their 300GB also. The magic caching algorithms and design features in the DS6800 and DS8000 apply to both types of drive. Depending on the workload, these higher capacity drives could therefore help deliver the same or more IOPS and MB/sec throughput as the 300GB drives. I have updated to show the numbers I used for the comparison to clarify.

I have also clarified the Incremental Resync paragraph.

-- Tony

 In the blogosphere, sometimes I am in the middle of the brawl and other times I can enjoy the show from across the bar. This would be the start of many nasty public brawls between HP and Oracle.

2008 Oct 22 — HP and Oracle upset EMC (362)

Last month, HP and Oracle jointly announced their new "Exadata Storage Server". This solution involves HP server and storage paired up with Oracle software, designed for Data Warehouse and Business Intelligence workloads (DW/BI).

I immediately recognized the Exadata Storage Server as a "me too" product, copying the idea from IBM's [InfoSphere Balanced Warehouse] which combines IBM servers, IBM storage and IBM's DB2 database software to accomplish this, but from a single vendor, rather than a collaboration of two vendors. The Balanced Warehouse has been around for a while. I even blogged about this last year, in my post [IBM Combo trounces HP and Sun] when IBM announced its latest E7100 model. IBM offers three different sizes: C-class for smaller SMB workloads, D-class for moderate size workloads, and E-class for large enterprise workloads.

One would think that since IBM and Oracle are the top two database software vendors, and IBM and HP are the top two storage hardware vendors, that IBM would be upset or nervous on this announcement. We're not. I would gladly recommend comparing IBM offerings with anything HP and Oracle have to offer. And with IBM's acquisition of Cognos, IBM has made a bold statement that it is serious about competing in the DW/BI market space.

But apparently, it struck a nerve over at EMC.

Fellow blogger Chuck Hollis from EMC went on the attack, and Oracle blogger Kevin Closson went on the defensive. For those readers who do not follow either, here is the latest chain of events:

- Kevin: [Oracle Exadata Storage Server - Part I] , and [Part II]
- Chuck: [Oracle Does Hardware]
- Kevin: [A Black Box with No Statistics] , and
- Kevin: [Pessimistic Feelings about New Technology]
- Chuck: [I annoy Kevin Closson at Oracle]

When it comes to blog fights like these, there are no clear winners or losers, but hopefully, if done respectfully, can benefit everyone involved, giving readers insight to the products as well as the company cultures that produce them. Let's see how each side fared:

Chuck implies that HP doesn't understand databases and Oracle doesn't understand server and storage hardware, so cobbling together a solution based on this two-vendor collaboration doesn't make sense to him. The few I know who work at HP and Oracle are smart people, so I suspect this is more a claim against each company's "core strengths". Few would associate HP with database knowledge, or Oracle with hardware expertise, so I give Chuck a point on this one.

Of course, Chuck doesn't have deep, inside knowledge of this new offering, nor do I for that matter, and Kevin is patient enough to correct all of Chuck's mistaken assumptions and assertions. Kevin understands that EMC's "core strengths" isn't in servers or databases, so he explains things in simple enough terms that EMC employees can understand, so I give Kevin a point on this one.

So, what does Chuck propose as the preferred alternative: a three-way collaboration! EMC's counter-proposal is to cobble together [Dell servers, EMC storage, and Oracle software].

If two is bad, then three is worse! How much bubble gum and bailing wire do you need in your data center? The better option is to go to the one company that offers it all and brings it together into a single solution: IBM InfoSphere Balanced Warehouse.

⊘technorati tags: IBM, DW, BI, Oracle, HP, Exadata, InfoSphere, Balanced Warehouse, DB2, E7100, EMC, Chuck Hollis, Kevin Closson, database, storage, systems, Dell

Addition from Tony Pearson (IBM)

Updated: timeline fixed chronologically.

2008 Oct 23 — Enterprise Mashups for your Information Infrastructure (363)

Nicole Carrier over at IBM Lotus team has [posted a clever video] explaining enterprise mashups to promote IBM's work in this area.

A quick [4-minute video] explaining Enterprise Mashups.

While some might be familiar with mashups that combine public Web 2.0 sources of information, enterprise mashups go one step further, integrating with the "information infrastructure" of your data center. It's not just enough to deliver the right information to the right person at the right time, it has to being the right format, in a manner that can be readily understood and acted upon. Enterprise mashups can help.

Ready to start? Check out the [IBM Mashup Center eKit].

◯**technorati tags**: IBM, Nicole Carrier, enterprise, mashup, information infrastructure, eKit

2008 Oct 24 — Don't Hide from the Truth (364)

For a while now, IBM has been trying to explain to clients that focusing on just storage hardware acquisition costs is not enough. You need to consider the "Total Cost of Ownership" or TCO of a purchase decision. For active data, a 3-5 year TCO assessment can give you a better comparison of costs between IBM and competitive choices. For long-term archive retention, 7-10 year TCO assessment may be necessary.

Now, IBM has a cute [2-minute video] that brings an appropriate analogy to help IT and non-IT executives understand.

This is part of a video series called [Don't Hide from the Truth].

Enjoy the weekend!

◯**technorati tags**: IBM, TCO, iceberg, storage, hardware, acquisition, costs

2008 Oct 27 — IBM Launches Under the Microscope website (365)

In collaboration with [The Feminist Press] and the [National Science Foundation], IBM launched today a new website called ["Under the Microscope"] to encourage young women to pursue education and careers in science, technology, engineering and math (STEM).

The site is filled with information. One item I found particularly interesting was Science Debate 2008's [14 Questions about Science] where the top two U.S. presidential candidates answer questions about science. Barack Obama's answers in Democratic blue, and John McCain's answers in Republican red.

This is just one of the ways IBM is trying to reach out and help our next generation.

⚲**technorati tags**: IBM, Under The Microscope, Feminist Press, NSF, STEM, education, science, debate, Barack Obama, John McCain

2008 Oct 28 — More Announcements for October 2008 (366)

Well, it's Tuesday again, and that means more IBM announcements!

Storage Area Network (SAN)

IBM and Cisco announced [three new blades] for the Cisco MDS 9500 series directors: 24-port 8 Gbps, 48-port 8 Gbps, and 4/44 blended. The 4/44 blended has 4 of the faster 8 Gbps ports, and 44 of the 4 Gbps ports, so that you can auto-negotiate down to 1 Gbps for your older gear, and still take advantage of the faster 8 Gbps speeds during the transition.

On the Brocade side, IBM announced the new IBM System Storage Data Center Fabric Manager [DCFM] V10 software. This replaces the products formerly known as Brocade Fabric Manager and McDATA Enterprise Fabric Connection Manager (EFCM). This software can support up to 24 distinct fabrics, up to 9000 ports, including a mix of FCP, FICON, FCIP and iSCSI protocols.

And if you need help setting up your SAN, IBM has recently renamed its services, formerly known as "IBM Implementation Services for SAN fabric components" to ["IBM Storage and Data Product Services - IBM Implementation Services for storage software - SAN fabric components"]. There is no change to the services actually provided, which have been available since 2003, but IBM felt that renaming it would make good press coverage.

(On a related note, I heard that Microsoft is planning to rename "Windows Vista" to "Windows 7" next year! Like we say here in Tucson, if it ends in "-ista" it is going to fail in the marketplace! Perhaps EMC should rename their storage virtualization product to "In-7"?)

IBM System Storage DR550

IBM announced today that it now supports [RAID 6 on the DR550] compliance and retention storage system.

There are a few RAID-5 based EMC Centera customers out there who have not yet switched over to the IBM DR550, and now this might be just the little nudge they need. For long-term retention of regulatory compliance data, RAID-5 doesn't cut it, you need an advanced RAID scheme, such as RAID-6, RAID-DP or RAID-X.

The DR550 provides non-erasable, non-rewriteable (NENR) storage support to keep retention-managed data on disk and tape media. It supports 1TB SATA disk drives and 1TB tape cartridges to provide high capacity at low cost and "green" low energy consumption.

IBM System Storage N series

Several of our disk systems got improved and enhanced. Let's start with the IBM System Storage N series [hardware and software] enhancements. IBM now offers high-speed 450GB 15K RPM drives. These are Fibre Channel (FC) drives for the EXN4000 expansion drawers, and Serial Attached SCSI (SAS) drives for the entry-level N3300 and N3600 models.

The "gateway" models now support a variety of functions that were formerly only available on the appliance models. This includes Advanced Single Instance Storage (A-SIS), Disk Sanitization, and FlexScale.

A-SIS is IBM's "other" deduplication function, and I talked about this in my post [A-SIS Storage Savings Estimator Tool]. Disk

Sanitization will physically write ones and zeros over existing data to eliminate it, what IBM sometimes calls "Data Shredding".

The last feature, FlexScale, might be new for many. It is software to enable to use of the "Performance Accelerator Module" (PAM). The PAM is a PCI-Express card with 16GB on-board RAM that acts as a secondary cache behind main memory of the N series controller. Depending on the model, you can have one to five of these cards fit into the controller itself, boosting random read performance, metadata access, and write block destage.

IBM System Storage DS5000

IBM's latest entry into the DS family has been hugely successful. In addition to Linux, Windows and AIX, the DS5000 now supports [Novell Netware and Sun Solaris] operating systems.

For infrastructure management, IBM has enhanced the Remote Support Manager [RSM] that supports DS3000 and DS4000 has been extended to support DS5000 as well. This software can monitor up to 50 disk systems, will e-mail alerts to IBM when something goes wrong, and allow IBM to dial in via modem to get more diagnostic information to improve service to the client. Also, the IBM System Storage Productivity Center [SSPC] which now supports the DS8000 and SAN Volume Controller (SVC) has been extended to also support the DS5000.

IBM XIV Storage System

In addition to 1-year and 3-year maintenance agreements, IBM now offers [2-year, 4-year and 5-year] software maintenance agreements.

RFID labels for IBM tape media

IBM 3589 (20-pack of LTO cartridges) and IBM 3599 (20-pack of 3592 cartridges for TS1100 series) now offer [RFID labels]. These labels match the volume serial (VOLSER) with a 216-bit unique identifier and 256 bits of user-defined content. This can help with tape inventory, and to prevent people from walking out of the building with a tape cartridge stuffed in their jacket.

32GB memory stick

While not technically part of the IBM System Storage matrix of offerings, Lenovo announced their new [Essential Memory Key] which holds 32GB of memory and works with both USB 1.1 and USB 2.0 protocols.

I wish I could say this is it for the IBM announcements for October, given that this is the last Tuesday of the month, but there are three days left, so there might be just a few more!

⊘**technorati tags**: IBM, SAN, Cisco, MDS9500, DCFM, BFM, EFCM, FCP, FICON, FCIP, iSCSI, Windows Vista, Windows 7, EMC, Centera, DR550, RAID-6, RAID-DP, RAID-X, NENR, FC, EXN4000, SAS, N3300, N3600, A-SIS, Disk Sanitization, FlexScale, PAM, DS5000, Netware, Solaris, DS3000, DS4000, DS8000, SVC, XIV, RFID, 3589, 3599, LTO, 3592, tape, cartridges, VOLSER

2008 Oct 29 — Trends in Tech Spending 2008 (367)

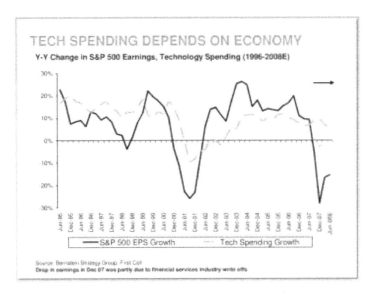

This is page 34 of Sequoia Capital's [56-slide presentation] about the current financial meltdown. In the past, IT spending tracked closely to the rest of the economy, but the latest downturn has not yet reflected in IT spend.

The rest of the deck is worth going through, with interesting stats presented in a clear manner.

⊘**technorati tags**: IBM, Sequoia Capital, tech spending, financial, crisis, meltdown, downturn

It's not hard to find contradictions at EMC, one of IBM's top competitors for disk systems. I caught them and spanked them for it, much like the manner television's Jon Stewart skewers politicians and pundits for their contradictions on "The Daily Show".

2008 Oct 30 — The Two Faces of EMC (368)

Perhaps the recent financial meltdown is making storage vendors nervous. Both IBM and EMC gained market share in 3Q08, but EMC is acting strangely at IBM's latest series of plays and announcements. Almost contradictory!

Benchmarks bad, rely on your own in-house evaluations instead

Let's start with fellow blogger Barry Burke from EMC, who offers his latest post [Benchmarketing Badly] with commentary about Enterprise Strategy Group's [DS5300 Lab Validation Report]. The IBM System Storage DS5300 is one of IBM's latest midrange disk systems recently announced. Take for example this excerpt from BarryB's blog post:

> "I was pleasantly surprised to learn that both IBM and ESG agree with me about the relevance and importance of the Storage Performance Council benchmarks.
>
> That is, SPC's are a meaningless tool by which to measure or compare enterprise storage arrays."

Nowhere does the ESG report say this, nor have I found any public statements from either IBM or ESG that make this claim. Instead, the ESG report explains that traditional benchmarks from the Storage Performance Council [SPC] focus on a single, specific workload, and ESG has chosen to complement this with a variety of other benchmarks to perform their product validation, including VMware's "VMmark", Oracle's Orion Utility, and Microsoft's JetStress.

Benchmarks provide prospective clients additional information to make purchase decisions. IBM understands this, ESG understands this, and other well-respected companies like VMware, Oracle and Microsoft understand this. EMC is afraid that benchmarks might encourage a client to "mistakenly" purchase a *faster* IBM product than a *slower* EMC product. Sunshine makes a great disinfectant, but EMC (and vampires) prefer their respective "prospects" remain in the dark.

Perhaps stranger still is BarryB's postscript. Here's an excerpt:

> "... a customer here asked me if EMC would be willing to participate in an initiative to get multiple storage vendors to collaborate on truly representative real-world 'enterprise-class' benchmarks, and I reassured him that I would personally sponsor active and objective participation in such an effort - IF he could get the others to join in with similar intent."

As I understand it, EMC was once part of the Storage Performance Council a long time ago, then chose to drop out of it. Why re-invent the wheel by creating yet another storage industry benchmark group? EMC is welcome to come back to SPC anytime! In addition to the SCP-1 and SPC-2 workloads, there is work underway for an SPC-3 benchmark. Each SPC workload provides additional insight for product comparisons to help with purchase decisions. If EMC can suggest an SPC-4 benchmark that it feels is more representative of real-world conditions, they are welcome to join the SPC party and make that a reality.

The old adage applies: ["It's better to light a candle than curse the darkness."] EMC has been cursing the lack of what it considers to be acceptable benchmarks but has yet to offer anything more realistic or representative than SPC. What does EMC suggest you do instead? Get an evaluation box and run your own workloads and see for yourself! EMC has in the past offered evaluation units specifically for this purpose.

In-house evaluations bad, it's a trap!

Certainly, if you have the time and staff to run your own evaluation, with your own applications in your own environment, then I agree with EMC that this can provide better insight for your particular situation than standardized benchmarks.

In fact, that is exactly what IBM is doing for IBM XIV storage units, which are designed for Web 2.0 and Digital Archive workloads that current SPC benchmarks don't focus on. Fellow blogger Chuck Hollis from EMC opines in his post [Get yer free XIV!]. Here's an excerpt:

> "Now that I think about it, this could get ugly. Imagine a customer who puts one on the floor to evaluate it, and -- in a moment of desperation or inattention -- puts production data on the device.
>
> Nobody was paying attention, and there you are. Now IBM comes calling for their box back, and you've got a

choice as to whether to go ahead and sign the P.O., or migrate all your data off the thing. Maybe they'll sell you an SVC to do this?

Yuck. I bet that happens more than once. And I can't believe that IBM (or the folks at XIV) aren't aware of this potentially happening."

Perhaps Chuck is speaking from experience here, as this may have happened with customers with EMC evaluation boxes, and is afraid this could happen with IBM XIV. I don't see anything unique about IBM XIV in the above concern. Typical evaluations involve copying test data onto the box, test it out with some particular application or workload, and then delete the data no longer required. Repeat as needed. Moving data off an IBM XIV is as easy as moving data off an EMC DMX, EMC CLARiiON or EMC Celerra, and I am sure IBM would gladly demonstrate this on any EMC gear you now have.

Thanks to its clever RAID-X implementation, losing data on an IBM XIV is less likely than losing data on any RAID-5 based disk array from any storage vendor. Of course, there will always be skeptics about new technology that will want to try the box out for themselves.

If EMC thought the IBM XIV had nothing unique to offer, that its performance was just "OK", and is not as easy to manage as IBM says it is, then you would think EMC would gladly encourage such evaluations and comparisons, right?

No, I think EMC is afraid that companies will discover what they already know, that IBM has quality products that would stand a fair chance of side-by-side comparisons with their own offerings. We have enough fear, uncertainty and doubt from our current meltdown of the global financial markets, don't let EMC add any more.

Have a safe and fun Halloween! If you need to add some light to your otherwise dark surroundings, consider some of these ideas for [Jack-O-Lanterns]!

⊘**technorati tags**: IBM, DS5300, ESG, benchmarks, SPC, SPC-1, SPC-2, SPC-3, VMware, VMmark, Oracle, Orion, Microsoft, JetStress, EMC, BarryB, RAID-X, RAID-5, DMX, CLARiiON, Celerra, XIV, financial, global markets, crisis, meltdown, Halloween, Jack-O-Lantern

Comment from Barry Burke (EMC), the Storage Anarchist

Fact Check - you wrote:

"Thanks to its clever RAID-X implementation, losing data on an IBM XIV is less likely than losing data on any RAID-5 based disk array from any storage vendor."

That is blatantly inaccurate and a total misrepresentation of facts, although you possibly don't understand the probability mathematics well enough to realize that.

Question: Would IBM actually make that guarantee in a legally-binding contract with a prospect or customer, with monetary penalties if proven wrong?

I seriously doubt it, but please - prove me wrong.

Also, if you truly are interested in honest and factual assessment, how about you guys shipping a fully loaded XIV array to my office at 176 South St., Hopkinton. Last we asked, we were told, "Sorry, we can't spare you one right now," - even when we offered to buy it outright (and become your second hard-cash-paying customer).

I promise we'll only run real-world benchmarks on it.

Oh - and one more thing. IBM and XIV people are out there bad mouthing me personally in front of customers... which probably explains why my readership continues to climb (and XIV sales continue to be flatlined at 0). Seems your folks still haven't come up with credible responses to my observations.

Thanks for the publicity, by the way. Just wish you'd all stay focused on what I said instead of attacking me personally.

TTFN – I'll be waiting for that RAID-X vs. RAID-5 guarantee - you know where to reach me...

Response from Tony Pearson (IBM)

So, BarryB, for you to convert this quote from ESG: "Traditional benchmarks running a single application workload can't help IT managers understand what happens when a mix of applications are deployed together in a virtual server environment," into your interpretation:

"SPC's are a meaningless tool by which to measure or compare enterprise storage arrays."

...would require that all IT departments run all workloads as a mix of applications in virtual server environments.

So, first, not every customer runs VMware or any other virtual server technology. Those that do don't do it for all of their workloads. Both IBM and VMware agree that some applications or workloads are better served on native machines instead of virtualized environments.

So, SPC benchmarks are helpful to decide which vendors to choose from, which models might best fit a particular amount of workload, which models have the sufficient scalability to handle anticipated growth, and which models might make the "short list" for further evaluation, including in-house proof-of-concept analysis in a mixed application / virtual server environment.

So, I dispute the term "meaningless", removing this makes the statement correct:

> "SPC's are a tool by which to measure or compare enterprise storage arrays."

-- Tony

Addition from Tony Pearson (IBM)

IBMer Barry Whyte weighs in here:

> http://www.ibm.com/developerworks/blogs/page/storagevirtualizat ion?entry=missing_the_point_misdirections_misinterpretations

Steve Duplessie from ESG talks about the ESG Lab here:

> http://esgblogs.typepad.com/steves_it_rants/2008/10/competitive-bus.html

Marc Farley from 3PAR

> http://www.storagerap.com/2008/10/anarchist-punches-out-ibm-and-tms-benchmarks---more.html

...posted his comment on BarryB's page. Here's an excerpt:

> "But I don't understand why EMC has it in for the SPC so badly. Sure there are imperfections in their system, but they do provide a vendor-independent workload to measure and 3rd party verification of the results. Those are two important steps towards objective, meaningful results. My personal complaint is that the information in Appendix C where the details of the configuration are listed is tough plowing and takes more effort than many customers can afford to give it. Heck, even you didn't have time to chase it down - somebody had to dig into it an email you what they found. That's obviously not working. My guess is that the SPC would like to figure out how to make this info more transparent and easier to digest, but that is very difficult considering the multiple configuration and tuning options used by all the various vendors.

> So, I understand your call for an overhaul, but I'm not sure that starting from scratch is the best way. From your perspective,

what's keeping the SPC from being more effective and useful for EMC?

Also, do you really think the problem of defining a "representative" workload will ever be resolved? I have a hard time believing vendors agreeing on something like this. That's the value of having an independent entity do it - warts and all."

Comment from Barry Burke (EMC), the Storage Anarchist

Tony - I see you haven't lost your skill in twisting words, even though it appears you are no longer in marketing.

But please, do explain to me how running a mix of applications on virtual servers against a single storage array differs from running a mix of applications on multiple physical servers? Or how about simply running a mix of applications on a single server, be it UNIX, Windows or Mainframe? From the storage perspective, are the I/O patterns any different between the three?

I think not, and thus by derivation, the SPCs can't help IT managers understand what happens when a mix of applications are deployed together in a server environment - the word "virtual" is an unnecessary qualifier!

And while you're at tell - tell me exactly how many customers you know who run a single application on a single server against a DMX-4 or a USP-V? Now, given the performance limitations of the mid-tier architecture DS8300 Turbo, you might actually have more than a few on that platform. But I can assure you, that would be the extremely rare exception for a REAL enterprise storage array.

And what - no update on that guarantee I asked about?

 If there is one thing that keeps CIOs up at night, it is dealing with the implication of uncontrolled storage capacity growth. I thought this was perfect for Halloween.

2008 Oct 31 — Exabyte Data Center for Archive (369)

There's some good discussion in the comments section over at Robin Harris' *StorageMojo* blog for his post [Building a 1.8 Exabyte Data Center]. To summarize, a student is working on a research archive and asked Robin

Harris for his opinion. The archive will consist of 20-40 million files averaging 90 GB in size each, for a total of 1800 PB or 1.8 EB. By comparison, an IBM DS8300 with five frames tops out at 512TB, so it would take nearly 3600 of these to hold 1.8 EB. While this might seem like a ridiculous amount of data, I think the discussion is valid as our world is certainly headed in that direction.

IBM works with a lot of research firms, and the solution is to put most of this data on tape, with just enough disk for specific analysis. Robin mentions a configuration with Sun Fire 4540 disk systems (aka Thumper). Despite Sun Microsystems' recent [$1.7 Billion dollar quarterly loss], I think even the experts at Sun would recommend a blended disk-and-tape solution for this situation.

Take for example IBM's Scale-out File Services [SoFS] which today handles 2-3 billion files in a single global file system, so 20-40 million would present no problem. SoFS supports a mix of disk and tape, with built-in movement, so that files that were referenced would automatically be moved to disk when needed, and moved back to tape when no longer required, based on policies set by the administrator. Depending on the analysis, you may only need 1 PB or less of disk to perform the work, which can easily be accomplished with a handful of disk systems, such as IBM DS8300 or IBM XIV, for example.

The rest would be on tape. Let's consider using the IBM TS3500 with [S24 High Density] frames. A singleTS3500 tape library with fifteen of these HD frames could hold 45PB of data, assuming 3:1 compression on 1TB-size 3592 cartridges. You would need 40 (forty) of these libraries to get to the full 1800 PB required, and these could hold even more as higher capacity cartridges are developed. IBM has customers with over 40 tape libraries today (not all with these HD frames, of course), but the dimensions and scale that IBM is capable lies within this scope.

> (For LTO fans, fifteen S54 frames would hold 32PB of data, assuming 2:1 compression on 800GB-size LTO-4 cartridges.so you would need 57 libraries instead of 40 in the above example.)

This blended disk-and-tape approach would drastically reduce the floorspace and electricity requirements when compared against all-disk configurations discussed in the post.

People are rediscovering tape in a whole new light. ComputerWorld recently came out with an 11-page Technology Brief titled [The Business Value of Tape Storage], sponsored by Dell. (Note: While Dell is a competitor to IBM for some aspects of their business, they OEM their tape storage systems from IBM, so in that respect, I can refer to them as a technology partner.) Here are some excerpts from the ComputerWorld brief:

> "For IT managers, the question is not whether to use tape, but where and how to best use tape as part of a comprehensive, tiered

storage architecture. In the modern storage architecture, tape plays a role not only in data backup, but also in long-term archiving and compliance.

'Long-term archiving is the primary reason any company should use tape these days,' says Mike Karp, senior analyst at Enterprise Management Associates in Boulder, Colo. Companies are increasingly likely to use disk in conjunction with tape for backup, but for long-term archiving needs, tape remains unbeatable.

After factoring in acquisition costs of equipment and media, as well as electricity and data center floor space, Clipper Group found that the total cost of archiving solutions based on SATA disk, the least expensive disk, was up to 23times more expensive than archiving solutions involving tape. Calculating energy costs for the competing approaches, the costs for disk jumped to 290 times that of tape.

'Tape is always the winner anywhere cost trumps anything else,' says Karp. No matter how the cost is figured, tape is less expensive.

Beyond IT familiarity with tape, analysts point to other reasons why organizations will likely keep tape in their IT storage infrastructures. Energy savings, for example, is the most recent reason to stick with tape. 'The economics of tape are pretty compelling, especially when you figure in the cost of power,' Schulz says."

So, whether you are planning for an Exabyte-scale data center, or merely questioning the logic of a disk-for-everything storage approach, you might want to consider tape. It's "green" for the environment, and less expensive on your budget.

⌐technorati tags: Robin Harris, StorageMojo, Exabyte, Data Center, IBM, blended, disk-and-tape, Sun, Huge Quarterly Loss, Thumper, SoFS, DS8300, XIV, N series, TS3500, S24, 3592, S54, LTO, LTO-4, ComputerWorld, Dell, Mike Karp, Greg Schulz

November

This month, I took a vacation to Bali and Singapore. This vacation was organized by my singles club, Tucson Fun and Adventures. We had about a dozen people in our group. The Bali hotel we first stayed in was the one associated with the terrorist bombing six years ago, and the three men who were responsible were executed that weekend. After a few days of being harassed by journalists for interviews, we moved to a hotel up in the mountains. We finished the trip with two days in Singapore.

2008 Nov 04 — IBM Tivoli Key Lifecycle Manager (370)

Well it's Tuesday, and ["election day"] here in the USA, and again IBM has more announcements.

IBM announced [IBM Tivoli Key Lifecycle Manager v1.0] (TKLM) to manage encryption keys. This provides a graphical interface to manage encryption keys, including retention criteria when sharing keys with other companies.

TKLM is supported on AIX, Solaris, Windows, Red Hat and SUSE Linux. IBM plans to offer TKLM for z/OS in 2009. TKLM can be used with Firefox or Internet Explorer web browser. This will include the Encryption Key Manager (EKM) that IBM offered initially to support encryption keys for the TS1120, TS1130, and LTO-4 drives.

While this is needed today for tape, IBM positions this software to also manage the encryption keys for "Full Disk Encryption" (FDE) disk drive modules (DDM) in IBM disk systems in 2009.

Tomorrow, I'll start my long-overdue vacation!

technorati tags: IBM, Tivoli, TLKM, AIX, Solaris, Windows, Linux, Firefox, IE, TS1120, TS1130, LTO-4, EKM, FDE, DDM

2008 Nov 21 — Data Center Conference in Las Vegas (371)

Well, I'm back from my vacation in Bali and Singapore, and am glad to see that my fellow blogger BarryB [aka *Storage Anarchist*] also had a chance to take a break to exotic locations.

Next Thursday, in the USA, is [Thanksgiving holiday], so this will give me a chance to catch up on my email and read everyone's blog posts and product announcements.

The following week, December 2-5, I'll be attending the 27th annual [Data Center Conference] at the MGM Grand hotel and casino in Las Vegas, Nevada. IBM is a Premier and Platinum sponsor for this event. Look for me in one of the many break-out sessions, one-on-one executive meetings, or IBM's "booth 20" at the solution center. Our team will be showing off IBM's XIV, SVC and TotalStorage Productivity Center offerings, as well as explaining IBM Information Infrastructure and the rest of the New Enterprise Data Center strategy.

⭕**technorati tags**: IBM, Bali, Singapore, Thanksgiving, LSC27, XIV, SVC, TotalStorage, Productivity Center, strategy, vision

Thanksgiving is one of my favorite holidays. Thanking EMC for their "failed" Atmos project seemed appropriate. EMC has its fair share of failures, and this was a great example. It allowed me to launch this week's theme of blog posts related to thankfulness.

2008 Nov 24 — Thankful for Atmos (372)

This week is Thanksgiving holiday in the USA, so I thought a good theme would be things I am thankful for.

I'll start with saying that I am thankful EMC has *finally* announced Atmos last week. This was the "Maui" part of the Hulk/Maui rumors we heard over a year ago. To quickly recap, Atmos is EMC's latest storage offering for global-scale storage intended for Web 2.0 and Digital Archive workloads. Atmos can be sold as just software, or combined with InfiniFlex, EMC's bulk, high-density commodity disk storage systems. Atmos supports traditional NFS/CIFS file-level access, as well as SOAP/REST object protocols.

I'm thankful for various reasons, here's a quick list:

It's hard to compete against "vaporware"

Back in the 1990s, IBM was trying to sell its actual disk systems against StorageTek's rumored "Iceberg" project. It took StorageTek some four years to get this project out, but in the meantime, we were comparing actual versus possibility. The main feature is what we now call "Thin Provisioning". Ironically, StorageTek's offering was not commercially successful until IBM agreed to resell this as the IBM RAMAC Virtual Array (RVA).

Until last week, nobody knew the full extent of what EMC was going to deliver on the many Hulk/Maui theories. Several hinted as to what it could have been, and I am glad to see that Atmos falls short of those rumored possibilities. This is not to say that Atmos can't reach its potential, and certainly some of the design is clever, such as offering native SOAP/REST access.

Instead, IBM now can compare Atmos/InfiniFlex directly to the features and capabilities of IBM's Scale-out File Services [SoFS], which offers a global-scale multi-site namespace with policy-based data movement, IBM System Storage Multilevel Grid Access Manager [GAM] that manages geographical distributed information, and IBM [XIV Storage System] that offers high-density bulk storage.

Web 2.0 and Digital Archive workloads justify new storage architectures

When I presented SoFS and XIV earlier this year, I mentioned they were designed for the fast-growing Web 2.0 and Digital Archive workloads that were unique enough to justify their own storage architectures. One criticism was that SoFS appeared to duplicate what could be achieved with dozens of IBM N series NAS boxes connected with Virtual File Manager (VFM). Why invent a new offering with a new architecture?

With the Atmos announcement, EMC now agrees with IBM that the Web 2.0 and Digital Archive workloads represent a unique enough "use case" to justify a new approach.

New offerings for new workloads will not impact existing offerings for existing workloads

I find it amusing that EMC is quickly defending that Atmos will not eat into its DMX business, which is exactly the FUD they threw out about IBM XIV versus DS8000 earlier this year. In reality, neither the DS8000 nor the DMX were used much for Web 2.0 and Digital Archive workloads in the past. Companies like Google, Amazon and others had to either build their own from piece parts, or use low-cost midrange disk systems.

Rather, the DS8000 and DMX can now focus on the workloads they were designed for, such as database applications on mainframe servers.

Cloud-Oriented Storage (COS)

Just when you thought we had enough terminology already, EMC introduces yet another three-letter acronym [TLA]. Kudos to EMC for coining phrases to help move new concepts forward.

Now, when an RFP asks for Cloud-oriented storage, I am thankful this phrase will help serve as a trigger for IBM to lead with SoFS and XIV storage offerings.

Digital archives are different than Compliance Archives

EMC was also quick to point out that object-storage Atmos was different from their object-storage EMC Centera. The former being for "digital archives" and the latter for "compliance archives". Different workloads, Different use cases, different offerings.

Ever since IBM introduced its [IBM System Storage DR550] several years ago, EMC Centera has been playing catch-up to match IBM's many features and capabilities. I am thankful the Centera team was probably too busy to incorporate Atmos capabilities, so it was easier to make Atmos a separate offering altogether. This allows the IBM DR550 to continue to compete against Centera's existing feature set.

Micro-RAID arrays, logical file and object-level replication

I am thankful that one of the Atmos policy-based feature is replicating individual objects, rather than LUN-based replication and protection. SoFS supports this for logical files regardless of their LUN placement, GAM supports replication of files and medical images across geographical sites in the grid, and the XIV supports this for 1MBchunks regardless of their hard disk drive placement. The 1MB chunk size was based on the average object size from established Web 2.0 and Digital Archive workloads.

I tried to explain the RAID-X capability of the XIV back in January, under much criticism that replication should only be done at the LUN level. I am thankful that Marc Farley on *StorageRap* coined the phrase [Micro-RAID array] to help move this new concept further. Now, file-level, object-level and chunk-level replication can be considered mainstream.

Much larger minimum capacity increments

The original XIV in January was 51TB capacity per rack, and this went up to 79TB per rack for the most recent IBM XIV Release 2 model. Several complained that nobody would purchase disk systems at such increments. Certainly, small and medium size businesses may not consider XIV for that reason.

I am thankful Atmos offers 120TB, 240TB and 360TB sizes. The companies that purchase disk for Web 2.0 and Digital Archive workloads do purchase disk capacity in these large sizes. Service providers add capacity to the "Cloud" to support many of their end-clients, and so purchasing disk capacity to rent back out represents revenue generating opportunity.

Renewed attention on SOAP and REST protocols

IBM and Microsoft have been pushing SOA and Web Services for quite some time now. REST, which stands for [Representational State Transfer] allows static and dynamic HTML message passing over standard HTTP. SOAP, which was originally [Simple Object Access Protocol], and then later renamed to "Service Oriented Architecture Protocol", takes this one step further, allowing different applications to send "envelopes" containing messages and data between applications using HTTP, RPC, SMTP and a variety of other underlying protocols. Typically, these messages are simple text surrounded by XML tags, easily stored as files, or rows in databases, and served up by SOAP nodes as needed.

It's hard to show leadership until there are followers

IBM's leadership sometimes goes unnoticed until followers create "me, too!" offerings or establish similar business strategies. IBM's leadership in Cloud and Grid computing is no exception. Atmos is the latest me-too product offering in this space, trying pretty much to address the same challenges that SoFS and XIV were designed for.

So, perhaps EMC is thankful that IBM has already paved the way, breaking through the ice on their behalf. I am thankful that perhaps I won't have to deal with as much FUD about SoFS, GAM and XIV anymore.

◯technorati tags: IBM, SoFS, XIV, GAM, DS8000, EMC, Atmos, Hulk, Maui, InfiniFlex, STK, StorageTek, Iceberg, RVA, thin provisioning, VFM, SOAP, REST, DMX, RAID-X, Micro-RAID

Addition from Tony Pearson (IBM)

Updated post to mention Grid Access Manager (GAM) also.

Mark Twomey of StorageZilla (EMC) pokes fun here:

http://storagezilla.typepad.com/storagezilla/2008/11/what-im-thankful-for.html

David Slik of Bycast, Inc. who make StorageGRID that IBM resells as Grid Archive Manager (GAM) mentioned in the post above, welcomes EMC to the party here:

http://intotheinfrastructure.blogspot.com/2008/11/welcome-emc.html

-- Tony

2008 Nov 25 — Thankful for a Smaller, Flatter, Smarter Planet (373)

Greg over at *IBM Eye* has a post [Leave Detroit Alone: It works for IBM] that points to Gaurav Sabnis' article [Detroit, Romney and IBM] commenting on Mitt Romney's Op-Ed piece in the New York Times ["Let Detroit Go Bankrupt"].

During the Republican primaries, Mitt Romney promised Michigan he would bring back all those jobs back to the Auto Industry, while his opponent, John McCain, told the audience that those jobs are gone forever, time to start learning new skills. Mitt won the state, but lost the nomination, and perhaps this snapped him back to reality. Mitt now has a new prescription for what ails the US Auto industry--straight talk that he should have been saying during his campaign, telling people what they should hear, rather than what they wanted to hear.

Gaurav takes this argument one step further, referring to IBM's amazing turn-around back in 1993. Whereas the US Auto Industry has pushed back against inevitable globalization, IBM has embraced it, re-inventing itself into a Globally Integrated Enterprise [GIE] and helping our clients do the same. I've been working for IBM since 1986, so I remember the pre-1993 IBM and how different it is now in the post-1993 era.

The marketplace has responded positively. Since 2004, more than 5,000 companies worldwide have replaced their HP, Sun, and EMC products with energy-efficient IBM Systems: Servers and Storage. Companies have invested in IBM's servers and storage to tackle their most challenging business objectives and to help reduce sprawling data center costs for labor, energy and real estate. This announcement was part of IBM's [Press Release] for its Migration Factory offering. The Migration Factory includes competitive server assessments, migration services, and other resources to help customers achieve energy and space savings and lower their cost of ownership.

Earlier this month, IBM's Chairman and CEO Sam Palmisano recently outlined the possibilities of a smarter planet to the Council on Foreign Relations. Steve Lohr of the *New York Times* weighs in with his article [I.B.M. Has Tech Answer for Woes of Economy], and Dr. Fern Halper of *Hurwitz & Associates* gives her take over at [IT-Director.com].

Transcontinental flights and the [Travel Channel] have made the world smaller. Thomas Friedman argued the world has also become "flatter", thanks to advances in computers and global communication, in his 2005 book [The World is Flat]. Now, IBM recognizes that Information Technology (I.T.) can help us solve the financial meltdown, global warming, and other major problems the world is now faced with.

How? First, our world is becoming *instrumented*. Sensors, RFID tags and other equipment are now inexpensive and readily available to be placed wherever they are needed. Second, our world is becoming more *interconnected*. We are closely approaching two billion internet users and four billion mobile subscribers, and these can connect to the trillions of RFID tags, sensors and other instrumentation. Third, our world needs to get more *intelligent*. Not just US auto workers learning new skills, but all these instruments providing information that can be acted on with intelligent algorithms. Algorithms can help with automobile traffic in large cities, enhance energy exploration, or improve healthcare.

I am thankful IBM is leading the effort to save the planet. To learn more about IBM's plans for a smarter planet, read [Sam's speech] and the [Ideas from IBM] page. See also fellow IBM blogger Bob Sutor's [Web 2.0 Summit presentation].

technorati tags: IBM, Detroit, Auto Industry, Mitt Romney, John McCain, Gaurav Sabnis, IBM Eye, GIE, HP, Sun, EMC, Migration Factory, Sam Palmisano, Smarter Planet, financial crisis, meltdown, global warming, climate change, traffic, energy, healthcare

 For my involvement with One Laptop Per Child (OLPC), I won the President's award for service.

2008 Nov 26 — Thanks for OLPC and G1G1 program (374)

Wrapping up this week's theme of thankfulness, I am thankful for the One Laptop Per Child [OLPC] and their Get-One-Give-One (G1G1) offer.

Last November, I was one of the first to [sign up for the G1G1], and when mine arrived December 24, I posted initial observations in this [OLPC series]. Over the past year, I have had the pleasure of helping out teams in Nepal and Uruguay, collaborating with developers in France, India and the United States. Giving back to others has been a richly rewarding experience for me. I made some new friends, built up new professional contacts, and learned some new tricks as well.

A quick 1-minute [YouTube video] featuring young Zimi.

Last year's G1G1 offer was limited to US and Canada, but this year, the OLPC have enlisted [Amazon.com] and made the offer available worldwide. You can choose either to give a single laptop for $199 USD, or get two laptops, get one for yourself or your family, and give the other to someone like Zimi, for $399 USD.

I'm thankful I did. Happy Thanksgiving to all my readers in the USA!

technorati tags: OLPC, G1G1, Zimi

Comment from Logan

Thank you, Tony, for the reminder about this program and the personal story. I was moved to send a note to several friends and colleagues to see how many laptops we can purchase as a group. I am overwhelmed by the generous response already.

Thanks much

December

IBM sellers and Business Partners don't bring clients to Tucson the last three weeks of the year, so my trip to Gartner's Data Center Conference was a nice way to end the year.

2008 Dec 02 — Day 1 - Red Badge of Courage (375)

Well, here I am in Las Vegas for the [Data Center Conference] at the MGM Grand Hotel and Casino.

I helped set up the IBM booth at the Solutions Center, third floor, where we will have various products on display, as well as subject matter experts to handle all the questions.

I also went ahead and got my conference badge. While most of my cohorts have purple badges, limiting them to the Solution Centers area, I have a red badge, so that I can attend the various keynote and break-out sessions this week.

In keeping with our "green" theme, we have all been given matching light green shirts, and these are 70 percent Bamboo cloth, and 30 percent cotton. They are very comfortable, and sustainable! If you see me, come up and just feel my shirt, go ahead, I won't mind!

Tomorrow, the fun begins with the keynote speakers!

⊘**technorati tags**: IBM, LSC27, Las Vegas, bamboo, green

2008 Dec 02 — Day2 - Data Center Conference Keynote Sessions (376)

Today is day 2 of my continuing coverage of the 27th annual [Data Center Conference], in Las Vegas.

I did not register soon enough to get into the MGM Grand itself, so I am staying at a Hilton at the other end of the Las Vegas strip, but am able to hop on the "Monorail" to get to the MGM, just in time for the breakfast and first welcome session.

This conference has a familiar set up: six keynote sessions, 62 break-out sessions, and four town hall meetings. Thanks to electronic survey devices on the seats, speakers were able to gather real-time demographics. A large portion of attendees, including myself, are attending this conference for their first time. Here's my recap of the first three keynote sessions:

The Future of Infrastructure and Operations: The Engine of Cloud Computing

How much do companies spend just to keep current? As much as 70 percent! The speaker noted that the best companies can get this down to 10 to 30 percent, leaving the rest of the IT budget to facilitate transformation. He predicts that companies are transforming their data centers from sprawled servers to virtualization, towards a fully automated, service-oriented, real-time infrastructure.

Whereas the original motivation for IT virtualization was to reduce costs, companies now recognize that they greatly improve agility, the ability to rapidly provision resources for new workloads, and that this will then lead to opportunities for alternative sourcing, such as cloud computing.

The operating system is becoming commoditized, focusing attention instead to a new concept: the "Meta OS". VMware's Virtual Data Center and Microsoft's Azure Fabric Controller are just two examples. Currently, analysts estimate only about 12 percent of x86 workloads are running virtualized, but that this could be over 50 percent by 2012. In this same time frame, year 2012, storage Terabytes is expected to increase 6.5x fold, and WAN bandwidth growing 35 percent per year.

Virtualization is not just for business applications. There are opportunities to eliminate the most costly part of any business: the Personal Computer, poster child of the skyrocketing costs of the client/server movement. Remote hosting of applications, streaming of applications, software as a service (SaaS) and virtual machines for the desktop can greatly reduce costs of customized PC images and help desk support.

Cloud computing not only reduces per costs per use, but provides a lower barrier of entry and some much needed elasticity. Draw a line anywhere along the application-to-hardware software/hardware stack, and you can define aloud computing platform/service. About 65 percent of the attendees surveyed indicated that they were already doing something with Cloud Computing, or were planning to in the next four years.

To help get there, the speaker felt that Value-added Resellers (VAR) and System Integrators (SI) would evolve into "service brokers", providing Small and Medium sized Businesses (SMB) "one throat to choke" in mixed multisourced operations. The term "multisource" caught me a bit off-guard, referring to having some workloads run internally (insourced) while other workloads run out on the Cloud (outsourced). Larger enterprises might have a "Dynamic Sourcing Team", a set of key employees serving as decision makers, employing both business and IT skills to determine the best sourcing for each application workload.

What are the biggest obstacles to getting there? The speaker felt it was the IT staff. People and culture are the most difficult to change. The second are lack of appropriate metrics. Here were the survey results of the attendees:

- 41 percent had metrics for infrastructure economic attributes
- 49 percent had metrics for qualities of service (QoS)
- 12 percent had metrics to measure agility, speed of resource provisioning

The Data Center Scenario: Planning for the Future

This second keynote had two analyst "co-presenters". The focus was on the importance of having a documented Data Center strategy and architecture. Unfortunately, most Data Centers "happen on their own", with a major overhaul every 5 to 10 years. The speakers presented some "best practices" for driving this effort.

The first issue was to identify tiers of criticality, similar to those by the [Uptime Institute]. In their example, the most critical workloads would have perhaps recovery point objectives (RPO) of zero, and recover time objectives of less than 15 minutes. This is achievable using synchronous mirroring with full automation to handle the failover.

The second issue was to recognize that many applications were designed for local area networks (LAN), but many companies have distributed processing over a wide area network (WAN). Latency over these longer distances can kill distributed performance of these applications.

The third issue was that different countries offer different levels of security, privacy and law enforcement. Canada and Ireland, for example, had the lowest risk, countries like India had medium risk, and countries like China and Russia had the highest risk, based on these factors.

The speakers suggested the following best practices:

- Get a better understanding of the costs involved in providing IT services

- Centralize applications that are not affected by latency, but regionalize those that are affected to remote locations to minimize distance delays.

- Work towards a "lights out" data center facility, with operations personnel physically separated from data center facilities.

For the unfortunate few that are trying to stretch out more life from their existing aging data centers, the speakers offered this advice:

- Build only what you need

- Decommission orphaned servers and storage, which can be 1 to 12 percent of your operations

- Target for replacement any hardware over five years old, not just to reduce maintenance costs, but also to get more energy-efficient equipment.

- Consider moving test workloads, and as much as half of your web servers, off UPS and onto the native electricity grid. In the event of an outage, this reduces UPS consumption.

- Implement power-capping and load-shedding, especially during peak times.

Enacting these changes can significantly improve the bottom line. Archaic data centers, those typically over 10 years old with power usage effectiveness (PUE) over 3.0 can cost over twice as much as a more efficient data center. To learn more about PUE as a metric, see the Green Grid's whitepaper [Data Center power efficiency metrics: PUE and DCiE].

While virtualization can help with these issues, it also introduces new problems, such as VM sprawl and dealing with antiquated licensing schemes of software companies.

The Four Traits of the World's Best-Performing Business Leaders

Best-selling author Jason Jennings presented his findings in researching his various books:

- It's Not the Big That Eat the Small... It's the Fast That Eat the Slow: How to Use Speed as a Competitive Tool in Business

- Less Is More : How Great Companies Use Productivity As a Competitive Tool in Business

- Think Big, Act Small

- Hit the Ground Running : A Manual for New Leaders

Jason identified the best companies and interviewed their leaders, including such companies as Koch Industries, Nucor Steel, and IKEA furniture. The leaders he interviewed felt a calling to serve as stewards of their companies, not just write mission and vision statements, and be willing to let go of projects or people that aren't working out.

Jason indicated a 2007 Gallup poll on the American workplace indicates that 70 percent of employees do not feel engaged in their jobs. The focus of these leaders is to hire people with the right *attitudes*, rather than the right *aptitudes*, and give those people with the knowledge and the right to make business decisions. If done well, employees will think and act as owners, and hold themselves accountable for their economic results. Jason found cases where 25-year-olds were given responsibility to make billion-dollar decisions!

I found his talk inspiring! The audience felt motivated to do their jobs better, and be more engaged in the success of their companies.

These keynote sessions set the mood for the rest of the week. I can tell already that the speakers will toss out a large salad of buzzwords and IT industry acronyms. I saw several people in the audience confused on some of the terminology, and hopefully they will come over to IBM booth 20 at the Solutions Expo for straight talk and explanation.

technorati tags: IBM, LSC27, Las Vegas, monorail, cloud computing, VAR, SI, VMware, Microsoft, Azure, QoS, RPO, RTO, PUE, Jason Jennings

2008 Dec 02 — Day2 - The Solution Showcase at IBM Booth 20 (377)

Continuing my ongoing coverage of the [Data Center Conference], tonight we open up the "Solution Showcase". IBM is at booth #20. Here are a few snapshots:

This is our banner with our tagline: Open. Virtual. Dynamic. Green.

This is our IBM XIV storage system on display.

This is a [KAON V-Osk] display to interactively show off products we don't have on the floor.

Of course we are not just featuring storage, but also our servers. Here is the IBM System z10 Business Class (BC) machine.

Lastly, here is more of the booth, with more cute animals, emphasizing how friendly IBM is to the environment.

If you are at this conference, stop by and see me and my colleagues at IBM Booth #20.

technorati tags: IBM, green, KAON, v-OSK, XIV, z10 BC, environmentally-friendly, LSC27

2008 Dec 02 — Day 2 - Quips, Quirks and Quotes at the Data Center Conference (378)

The title of this post is inspired by Baxter Black's [latest book]. Rather than give a recap of the break-out sessions, I thought I would comment on a few sentences, phrases or comments I heard in the afternoon and evening.

Stop buying storage from EMC or NetApp

The lunch was sponsored by Symantec. Rod Soderbery presented "Taking the cost out of cost savings", explaining some ideas to reduce IT costs immediately.

First, he suggested to "stop buying storage" from EMC or NetApp that charge a premium for tier-one products. Instead, Rod suggested that people should "think like a Web company" and buy only storage products based on commodity hardware to save money, and to use SRM software to identify areas of poor storage utilization. IBM's TotalStorage Productivity Center software is often used to help with this analysis.

His other suggestions were to adopt thin provisioning, data deduplication, and virtualization. The discussion at my table started with someone asking, "How do we adopt those functions without buying new storage capacity with those features already built-in?" I explained that IBM's SAN Volume Controller (SVC), N series gateways, and TS7650G ProtecTIER virtual tape gateway can all provide one or more of these features to your existing disk storage capacity.

IBM and HP are leaders in blade servers

In the session "Future of Server and OS: Disappearing Boundaries", the audience confirmed by electronic survey that IBM and HP are the leaders in blade servers, although blades represent only 8-10 percent of the overall server market.

Interestingly, 22 percent of the audience has deployed both x86 and non-x86 (POWER, SPARC, etc.) blade servers. The presenters considered this an interesting insight.

Another survey of the audience found that 3 percent considered Sun/STK as their primary storage vendor. One of the presenters was delighted that Sun is still hanging in there.

IBM Business Partners deliver the best of IBM and mask the worst

Elaine Lennox, IBM VP, and Mark Wyllie, CEO of Flagship Solutions Group, Inc. presented IBM-sponsored back to back sessions. Elaine presented IBM's vision, the New Enterprise Data Center, and the challenges that demand a smarter planet.

Mark focused on his company's experience working with IBM through Innovation Workshops. These are assessments that can help someone identify where you are now, where you want to be, and then action plans to address the gaps.

Cats and Dogs, Oil and Water, Microsoft Windows and Mission-critical applications: what do all of these have in common?

NEC Corporation of America sponsored some sessions on some x86-based solutions they have to offer. The first part, titled "Rats Nests, Snow Drifts and Trailers" focused on unified storage, and the second part, presented by Michael Nixon, focused on how to bring Microsoft Windows servers into the data center for mission-critical applications.

The Economy might be slowing, but storage is still growing

Two analysts co-presented "The Enterprise Storage Scenario". Unlike computing capacity, there is no on/off switch for storage, not from applications nor from end-users. The cost of power for storage is expected to be 3x by 2013. Virtual servers, including VMware and Microsoft's Hyper-V will drive the need for shared external disk storage. A survey of the audience found 20 percent were expecting to purchase additional storage capacity 4Q08.

When someone reaches age 52, they expect to coast the rest of their career

At dinner with analysts, the discussion of financial meltdown and bailouts is unavoidable, including everyone's views about the proposed bailout of the Big 3 automakers. I can't defend Ford, GM and Chrysler paying their people $70 US dollars per hour, when their US counterparts at Toyota or Honda are only paid $45 to $50 dollars per hour.

However, I have a close friend who retired after 20 years working for the fire department, and a cousin who retired after 20 years serving in the Navy (the US Navy, not the Bolivian Navy), and both are still in their forties in age. A long time ago, IT professionals retired after 30 years, in some cases with 50 to 60 percent of their base pay as their pension for the rest of their lives. A 52-year-old that has worked 30 years might expect to enjoy the rest of his old age playing golf and pursuing other hobbies. This is not "coasting", it is called "retirement". The few of my colleagues that I have seen who worked 35 to 40 years did so because they enjoyed the challenge of work at IBM. They enjoyed solving tough engineering problems and helping customers. As long as they were having fun on the job, IBM was glad to keep their wealth of experience on board and actively engaged.

Unfortunately, many people rely on their own investments in the stock market for retirement, rather than company pensions. With the current financial crisis, I suspect many people my age are reconsidering their previous retirement plans.

We're going to need more trains!

I took the monorail back to my hotel. The ride includes funny announcements and statistics, including this gem:

"Since 1940, Las Vegas has doubled in population every ten years, which means that by the year 2230, we will have over 1 trillion people calling Las Vegas home. We're going to need more trains!"

That wraps up Tuesday, Day 2 of my attendance here! Now for some sleep.

◔**technorati tags**: LSC27, Baxter Black, Symantec, IBM, TotalStorage, Productivity Center, EMC, NetApp, SVC, TS7650G, HP, blade server, x86, POWER, SPARC, Elaine Lennox, Mark Wyllie, NEC, Michael Nixon, VMware, Microsoft, Windows, Hyper-V, Big 3, Automakers, bailout, Bolivian Navy, population growth

2008 Dec 04 — Day3 - More Keynote Sessions at Data Center Conference (379)

Well, it's Wednesday, day three at the [Data Center Conference] here in Las Vegas, Nevada. Unlike other conferences that concentrate all of their keynote sessions at the front of the agenda, this conference spread them out over several days. They had three on Tuesday, two more Wednesday, and the last one on Thursday. Here are my thoughts on the two keynote sessions on Wednesday.

Top 10 Disruptive Technologies affecting the Data Center

The analyst presented his "top ten" technologies to watch:

1. Storage Virtualization - I was glad this made top of the list!

2. Cloud Computing - IBM was recognized for its leadership in this space. Cloud computing brings together new models of acquisition, billing, access, and deployment of new technology.

3. Servers: Beyond Blades - Currently, distributed servers have fixed CPU, memory and I/O capability, as manufactured at the factory, but what if you can re-assign these resources dynamically? New technologies might make this possible.

4. Virtualization for desktops - not just hosted virtual desktops, the speaker proposed having "portable personalities" that an employee might carry around on a CD-ROM or USB memory stick, and then use whatever computer equipment was nearby.

5. Enterprise Mashups - You know analysts have too much time on their hands when they come up with their own eight-layer reference architecture for enterprise adoption of Web 2.0 technologies.

6. Specialized Systems - These are sometimes called heterogeneous systems, hybrids, or application-specific appliances. Unlike general purposes servers, these are more difficult to re-purpose as your needs change. However, if done right, can provide better performance for specific workloads.

7. Social Software and Social Networking - A survey of the audience found 18 percent were already using Mashups in the enterprise, but 65 percent haven't looked at this at all. Because traditional hierarchically-organized companies can't re-structure their employees fast enough, the use of social software to develop "virtual teams" and "communities of interest" can be an effective way to get the "wisdom of crowds" from your employees. Rather than just installing this kind of software, the speaker felt it was better to just "plant seeds" and let social networks grow within the enterprise.

8. Unified Communications - Do you use different providers or software for cell phone, land line, Wi-Fi, internet, Instant Messaging (IM), audio conferencing, video conferencing, and email? The promise of Unified Communications is to bring this all together.

9. Zones and Pods - In the 1990s, traditional design for data centers tried to anticipate growth over the next 15-20 years, and build accordingly. These did not foresee all the changes in IT. The new best practice is a "pod approach" where you only build what you need for the next 5 to 7 years, with the architecture to expand as needed. A traditional 9000-square-foot data center that supports 150 "watts-per-square-foot" would cost over $20 million to build, and over $1 million in electricity every year. A pod alternative might cost less than $12 million to build, and nearly cut electricity costs in half.

10. Green IT - rapid "green" improvements are being demanded on IT operations, not just for political correctness, but also for cost savings. A survey of the audience found 7 percent willing to pay a premium price for green solutions, and another 26 percent willing to pay a slightly higher price for green features and attributes.

Don McMillan, Computer Engineer turned Stand Up Comic

Don gave a hilarious look at the IT industry. While most comics that are often hired to entertain the audience have only a layman's knowledge of what we do, Don has a master's degree in Electrical Engineering from Stanford and worked at a variety of IT companies, including AT&T Bell Labs and VLSI Technology. You can see more of his bio on his [Technically Funny] website.

Here's Don in a [four-minute video] demonstrating the kind of observational humor he performs.

It's good to see a bit of humor at IT conferences. With the pressures of IT staff and management to manage explosive growth with shrinking budgets, the attendees appreciated the mix of serious with the not-so-serious.

⊘**technorati tags**: LSC27, storage virtualization, IBM, cloud computing, desktop virtualization, enterprise mashups, Web2.0, social networking, unified communications, zones, pods, Green IT, Don McMillan

2008 Dec 04 — Day3 - Deploying Disruptive Storage Architectures (380)

Continuing this week's coverage of the 27th annual [Data Center Conference] I attended some break-out sessions on the "storage" track.

Effectively Deploying Disruptive Storage Architectures and Technologies

Two analysts co-presented this session. In this case, the speakers are using the term "disruptive" in the [positive sense] of the word, as originally used by Clayton Christensen in his book [The Innovator's Dilemma], and not in the negative sense of IT system outages. By a show of hands, they asked if anyone had more storage than they needed. No hands went up.

The session focused on the benefits versus risks of new storage architectures, and which vendors they felt would succeed in this new marketplace around the years 2012-2013.

By electronic survey, here were the numbers of storage vendors deployed by members of the audience:

- 14 percent - one vendor
- 33 percent - two vendors, often called a "dual vendor" strategy
- 24 percent - three vendors
- 29 percent - four or more storage vendors

For those who have deployed a storage area network (SAN), 84 percent also have NAS, 61 percent also have some form or archive storage such as IBM System Storage DR550, and 18 percent also have a virtual tape library (VTL).

The speaker credited IBM's leadership in the now popular "storage server" movement to the IBM Versatile Storage Server [VSS] from the 1990s, the predecessor to IBM's popular Enterprise Storage Server (ESS). A "storage server" is merely a disk or tape system built using off-the-shelf server technology, rather than customized [ASIC] chips, lowering the barriers of entry to a slew of small start-up firms entering the IT storage market, and leading to new innovation.

How can a system designed for no single point of failure (SPOF) actually then fail? The speaker conveniently ignored the two most obvious answers (multiple failures, microcode error) and focused instead on mis-configuration. She felt part of the blame falls on IT staff not having adequate skills to deal with the complexities of today's storage devices, and the other part of the blame falls on storage vendors for making such complicated devices in the first place.

Scale-out architectures, such as IBM XIV and EMC Atmos, represent a departure from traditional "Scale-up" monolithic equipment. Whereas scale-up machines are traditionally limited in scalability from their packaging, scale-out are limited only by the software architecture and back-end interconnect.

To go with cloud computing, the analyst categorized storage into four groups: Outsourced, Hosted, Cloud, and Sky Drive. The difference depended on where servers, storage and support personnel were located.

How long are you willing to wait for your preferred storage vendor to provide a new feature before switching to another vendor? A shocking 51 percent said at most 12 months! 34 percent would be willing to wait up to 24 months, and only 7 percent were unwilling to change vendors. The results indicate more confidence in being able to change vendors, rather than pressures from upper management to meet budget or functional requirements.

Beyond the seven major storage vendors, there are now dozens of smaller emerging or privately-held start-ups now offering new storage devices. How willing were the members of the audience to do business with these? 21 percent already have devices installed from them, 16 percent plan to in the next 12-24 months, and 63 percent have no plans at all.

The key value proposition from the new storage architectures were ease-of-use and lower total cost of ownership. The speaker recommended developing a strategy or "road map" for deploying new storage architectures, with focus on quantifying the benefits and savings. Ask the new vendor for references, local support, and an acceptance test or "proof-of-concept" to try out the new system. Also, consider the impact to existing Disaster Recovery or other IT processes that this new storage architecture may impact.

Tame the Information Explosion with IBM Information Infrastructure

The IBM VP of marketing for System Storage presented this vendor-sponsored session, covering the IBM Information Infrastructure part of IBM's New Enterprise Data Center vision. This was followed by Brad Heaton, Senior Systems Admin from ProQuest, who gave his "User Experience" of the IBM TS7650G ProtecTIER virtual tape library and its state-of-the-art inline data deduplication capability.

Best Practices for Managing Data Growth and Reducing Storage Costs

The analyst explained why everyone should be looking at deploying a formal "data archiving" scheme. Not just for "mandatory preservation" resulting from government or industry regulations, but also the benefits of "optional preservation" to help corporations and individual employees be more productive and effective.

Before there were only two tiers of storage, expensive disk and inexpensive tape. Now, with the advent of slower less-expensive SATA disks, including storage systems that emulate virtual tape libraries, and others that offer Non-Erasable, Non-Rewriteable (NENR) protection, IT administrators now have a middle ground to keep their archive data.

New software innovation supports better data management. The speaker recalled when "storage management" was equated to "backup" only, and now includes all aspects of management, including HSM migration, compliance archive, and long term data preservation. I had a smile on my face--IBM has used "storage management" to refer to these other aspects of storage since the 1980s!

The analyst felt the best tool to control growth is to "Delete" the data no longer needed, but felt that *nobody* uses Storage Resource Management (SRM) tools needed to make this viable. Until then, people will chose instead to archive emails and user files to less expensive media. The speaker also recommended looking into highly-scalable NAS offerings--such as IBM's Scale-out File Services (SoFS), Exanet, Permabit, IBRIX, Isilon, and others--when fast access to files is worth the premium price over tape media. The speaker also made the distinction between "stub-based" archiving--such as IBM TSM Space Manager, Sun's SAM-FS, and EMC DiskXtender--from "stub-less" archive accomplished through file virtualization that employs a global namespace--such as IBM Virtual File Manager (VFM), EMC Rainfinity or F5 ARX.

She made the distinction between archives and backups. If you are keeping backups longer than four weeks, they are not really backups, are they? These are really archives, but not as effective. Recent legal precedent no longer considers long-term backup tapes as valid archive tapes.

To deploy a new archive strategy, create a formal position of "e-archivist", chose the applications that will be archived and focus on requirements first, rather than going out and buying compliance storage devices. Try to get users to pool their project data into one location, to make archiving easier. Try to have the storage admins offer a "menu" of options to Line-of-Business/Legal/Compliance teams that may not be familiar with subtle differences in storage technologies.

While I am familiar with many of these best practices already, I found it useful to see which competitive products line up with those we have already within IBM, and which new storage architectures others find most promising.

⊘**technorati tags**: Clayton Christensen, SAN, NAS, DR550, VTL, SPOF, Scale-Up, Scale-Out, IBM, XIV, EMC, Atmos, Brad Heaton, ProQuest, TS7650G, ProtecTIER, deduplication, archive, SATA, NENR, HSM, SRM, VFM

Ever since my talk to the Institute of Management Accountants explaining "Cloud Computing" back in March, I have been considered an "expert" on the topic. Needless to say, Gartner's Data Center Conference would feature this topic prominently in their agenda.

2008 Dec 04 — Day3 - Its Partly Cloudy in Las Vegas (381)

Continuing my coverage of the 27th annual [Data Center Conference], the weather here in Las Vegas has been partly cloudy, which leads me to discuss some of the "Cloud Computing" sessions that I attended on Wednesday.

The x86 Server Virtualization Storm 2008-2012

Along with IBM, Microsoft is recognized as one of the "Big 5" of Cloud Computing. With their recent announcements of Hyper-V and Azure, the speaker presented pros-and-cons between these new technologies versus established offerings from VMware. For example, Microsoft's Hyper-V is about three times cheaper than VMware and offers better management tools. That could be enough to justify some pilot projects. By contrast, VMware is more lightweight, only 32MB, versus Microsoft Hyper-V that takes up to 1.5GB. VMware has a 2-3 year lead ahead of Microsoft, and offers some features that Microsoft does not yet offer.

Electronic surveys of the audience offered some insight. Today, 69 percent were using VMware only, 8 percent had VMware plus other, including Xen-based offerings from Citrix, Virtual Iron and others. However, by 2010, the audience estimated that 39 percent would be VMware plus Microsoft and another 23 percent VMware plus Xen, showing a shift away from VMware's current dominance. Today, there are 11 VMware implementations to Microsoft Hyper-V, and this is expected to drop to 3-to-1 by 2010.

Of the Xen-based offerings, Citrix was the most popular supplier. Others included Novell/PlateSpin, Red Hat, Oracle, Sun and Virtual Iron. Red Hat is also experimenting with kernel-based KVM. However, the analyst estimated that Xen-based virtualization schemes would never get past 8 percent marketshare. The analyst felt that VMware and Microsoft would be the two dominant players with the bulk of the marketshare.

For cloud computing deployments, the speaker suggested separating "static" VMs from "dynamic" ones. Centralize your external storage first, and implement data deduplication for the OS load images. Which x86 workloads are best for server virtualization? The speaker offered this guidance:

- The "good" are CPU-bound workloads, small/peaky in nature.
- The "bad" are IO-intensive, those that exploit the features of native hardware
- The "ugly" refers to workloads based on software with restrictive licenses and those not fully supported on VMs. If you have problems, the software vendor may not help resolve them.

Moving to the Cloud: Transforming the Traditional Data Center

IBM VP Willie Chiu presented the various levels of cloud computing.

- Software-as-a-Service (SaaS) provides the software application, operating system and hardware infrastructure, such as SalesForce.com or Google Apps. Either the software meets your needs or it doesn't, but has the advantage that the SaaS provider takes care of all the maintenance.

- Platform-as-a-Service (PaaS) provides operating system, perhaps some middleware like database or web application server, and the hardware infrastructure to run it on. The PaaS provider maintains the operating system patches, but you as the client must maintain your own applications. IBM has cloud computing centers deployed in nine different countries across the globe offering PaaS today.

- Infrastructure-as-a-Service (IaaS) provides the hardware infrastructure only. The client must maintain and patch the operating system, middleware and software applications. This can be very useful if you have unique requirements.

In one case study, Willie indicated that moving a workload from a traditional data center to the cloud lowered the costs from $3.9 million to $0.6 million, an 84 percent savings!

We've Got a New World in Our View

Robert Rosier, CEO of iTricity, presented their "IaaS" offering. "iTricity" was coined from the concept of "IT as electricity". iTricity is the largest Cloud Computing company in continental Europe, hosting 2500 servers with 500TB of disk storage across three locations in the Netherlands and Germany.

Those attendees I talked to that were at this conference before commented that this year's focus on virtualization and cloud computing is noticeably more than in previous years. For more on this, read this 12-page whitepaper: [IBM Perspective on Cloud Computing]

2008 Dec 04 — Day4 - The Future of the Data Center (382)

It's Thursday here at the [Data Center Conference] here in Las Vegas. Trying to keep up with all the sessions and activities has been quite challenging. As is often the case, there are more sessions that I want to attend than I physically am able to, so have to pick and choose.

Making the Green Data Center a Reality

The sixth and final keynote was an expert panel session, with Mark Bramfitt from Pacific Gas and Electric [PG&E], and Mark Thiele from VMware.

Mark explained PG&E's incentive program to help data centers be more energy efficient. They have spent $7 million US dollars so far on this, and he has requested another $50 million US dollars over the next three years. One idea was to put "shells" around each pod of 28 or so cabinets to funnel the hot air up to the ceiling, rather than having the hot air warm up the rest of the cold air supply.

The fundamental disconnect for a "green" data center is that the Facilities team pay for the electricity, but it is the IT department that makes decisions that impact its use. The PG&E rebates reward IT departments for making better decisions. The best metric available is "Power Usage Effectiveness" or [PUE], which is calculated by dividing total energy consumed in the data center, divided by energy consumed by the IT equipment itself. Typical PUE runs around 3.0 which means for every Watt used for servers, storage or network switches, another 2 Watts are used for power, cooling, and facilities. Companies are trying to reduce their PUE down to 1.6 or so. The lower the better, and 1.0 is the ideal. The problem is that changing the data center infrastructure is as difficult as replacing the phone system or your primary ERP application.

While California has [Title 24], stating energy efficiency standards for both residential and commercial buildings, it does not apply to data centers. PG&E is working to add data center standards into this legislation.

The two speakers also covered Data Center [bogeymen], unsubstantiated myths that prevent IT departments from doing the right thing. Here are a few examples:

- Power cycles - some people believe that x86 servers can typically only handle up to 3000 shutdowns, and so equipment is often left running 24 hours a day to minimize these. Most equipment is kept less than 5 years (1826 days), so turning off non-essential equipment at night, and powering it back on the next morning, is well below this 3000 limit and can greatly reduce kWh.

- Dust - many are so concerned about dust that they run extra air-filters which impacts the efficiency of cooling systems air flow. New IT equipment tolerates dust much better than older equipment.

- Humidity - Mark had a great story on this one. He said their "de-humidifier" broke, and they never got around to fixing it, and they went years without it, realizing they didn't need to de-humidify.

The session wrapped up with some "low hanging fruit", items that can provide immediate benefit with little effort:

- Cold-aisle containment--Why are so few data centers doing this?
- Colocation providers need to meter individual clients' energy usage -- IBM offers the instrumentation and software to make this possible
- Air flow management--Simply organizing cables under the floor tiles could help this.
- Virtualization and Consolidation.
- High-efficiency power supplies

Managing IT from a Business Service Perspective

The "other" future of the data center is to manage it as a set of integrated IT services, rather than a collection of servers, storage and switches. IT Infrastructure Library (ITIL) is widely-accepted as a set of best practices to accomplish this "service management" approach. The presenter from ASG Software Solutions presented their Configuration Management Data Base (CMDB) and application dependency dashboard. They have some customers with as many as 200,000 configuration items (CIs) in their CMDB.

The solution looked similar to the IBM Tivoli software stack presented earlier this year at the [Pulse conference]. Both ASG and

IBM "eat their own dog food," or perhaps more accurately "drink their own champagne," using these software products to run their own internal IT operations.

The next [IBM Pulse 2009 conference] will be held here at the MGM Grand Hotel and Casino, Las Vegas, February 8-12, 2009.

For many, the future of a "green" data center managed as a set of integrated service are years away, but the technologies and products are available today, and there is no reason to postpone these projects any longer than necessary. For more about IBM's approach to green data center, see [Energy Efficiency Solutions]. You can also take IBM's [IT Service Management self-assessment] to help determine which IBM tools you need for your situation.

✏**technorati tags**: LSC27, Green IT, data center, Mark Bramfitt, PG&E, Mark Thiele, VMware, PUE, ERP, ITIL, CMDB, IBM, Pulse08

Addition from Tony Pearson (IBM)

Mark Twomey (Zilla) from EMC uses the phrase "drink your own champagne" weeks later in this post:

http://storagezilla.typepad.com/storagezilla/2009/01/drink-your-own-champagne.html

 Few companies manage disaster recovery very well, so when I heard this success story, I recognized it as the best session of the week.

2008 Dec 04 — Day4 - Surviving Hurricane Katrina (383)

Marshall Lancaster from [United Stationers Technology Services] presented how their [Lagasse] subsidiary successfully survived [Hurricane Katrina in New Orleans] in 2005. I feel this was one of the best presentations of the week, here at the [Data Center Conference]!

Lagasse, Inc. sells janitorial supplies, such as mops, cleaning chemicals, waste receptacles, and garbage can liners. Of the 1000 employees of Lagasse nationwide, about 200 associates were located in New Orleans at their main Headquarters, primary customer care center, and primary IT computing center.

Amazingly, Lagasse did not have a formally documented BCP (Business Continuity Plan) but more of a BCI (Business Continuity Idea). They chose to take a ["donut tire"] approach, putting older previous-generation equipment at their DR site. They knew that in the event of a disaster, they would not be processing as many transactions per second. That was a business trade-off they could accept.

Evaluating all the different threat scenarios for impact and likelihood, and focused on hurricanes and floods. They had experienced previous hurricanes, learning from each, with the most recent being 2004 Hurricane Ivan and 2005 Hurricane Dennis. From this, they were able to categorize three levels of DR recovery:

- Tier 1 - The most mission-critical, which for them related to picking, packing and shipping products.
- Tier 2 - The next most important, focused on maintaining good customer service
- Tier 3 - Everything else, including reporting and administrative functions

The time-line of events went as follows:

August 25

> The US Government issues warning that a hurricane may hit New Orleans

August 27 - 7pm

> Lagasse declares a disaster, starts recovery procedures to an existing IT facility in Chicago, owned by their parent company. A temporary "Southeast" Headquarters were set up in Atlanta. Remote call centers were identified in Dallas, Atlanta, San Antonio, and Miami.

August 28 - just after midnight

> In just five hours, they recovered their "Tier 1" applications.

August 28 - 7:30pm

> In just over 24 hours, they recovered their "Tier 2" applications.

August 29 - 6am

> The Hurricane hits land. With 73 levees breached, the city of New Orleans was flooded.

The following week

> Lagasse was fully operational, and recorded their second and third best sales days ever.

I was quite impressed with their company's policy for how they treat their employees during a disaster. For many companies, people during a disaster prioritize on their families, not their jobs. If any associate was asked to work during a disaster, the company would take care of:

- The safety of their family
- The safety of their pets. (In the weeks following this hurricane, I sponsored people in Tucson to go to New Orleans to attend to lost and stray dogs and cats, many of which were left behind when rescuers picked up people from their rooftops.)
- Any emergency repairs to secure the home they leave behind

Marshall felt that if you don't know the names of the spouse and kids of your key employees, you are not emotionally-invested enough to be successful during a disaster.

For communications, cell phones were useless. They could call out on them, but anyone with a cell phone with 504 area code had difficulty receiving calls, as the calls had to be processed through New Orleans. Instead, they used Voice over IP (VoIP) to redirect calls to whichever remote call center each associate went to. Laptops, Citrix, VPN and email were considered powerful tools during this process. They did not have Instant Messaging (IM) at the time.

While the disk and tapes needed to recover Tiers 1 and 2 were already in Chicago, the tapes for Tier 3 were stored locally by a third-party provider. When Lagasse asked for their DR tapes back, the third-party refused, based on their [force majeure] clause. Force majeure is a common clause in many business contracts to free parties from liability during major disasters. Marshall advised everyone to strike out any *force majeure* clauses out of any future third-party DR protection contracts.

Hurricane Katrina hit the US hard, killing over 1400 people, and America still has not fully recovered. The recovery of the city of New Orleans has been slow. Massive relocations has caused a deficit of talent in the area, not just IT talent, but also in the areas of medicine, education and other professions. The result has been degraded social services, encouraging others to relocate as well. Some have called it the "liberation effect", a major event that causes people to move to a new location or take on a new career in a different field.

On a personal note, I was in New Orleans for a conference the week prior to landfall, and helped clients with their recoveries the weeks after. For more on how IBM Business Continuity Recovery Services (BCRS) helped clients during Hurricane Katrina, see the following [media coverage].

⌐**technorati tags**: Marshall Lancaster, United Stationers, Lagasse, BCP, Hurricane Katrina, Business Continuity, Disaster Recovery, donut tire, New Orleans, VoIP, Citrix, VPN, liberation effect, Chicago, force majeure, BCRS

I am famous for taking pictures with other people at conferences. Many attendees recognize me and ask to take

pictures with me to post on my blog. It is a nice break from the technical.

2008 Dec 04 — Day4 - Solution Showcase and Hospitality Suites (384)

The booths at a typical week-long tradeshow only go from day 2 to day 4, so that day 1 and day 5 can be used for unpacking and repacking all of the demo equipment and displays. This was the case here at the 27th annual [Data Center Conference] here in Las Vegas.

Solution Showcase

The solution showcase ended Thursday afternoon.

From left to right: George Lane, Ron Houston, Cris Espinosa, Patty Congdon, David Bricker, Paula Koziol, Steve Sams, Tony Pearson, Gary Fierko, Diane Hill, David Share, Nick Sardino, Carla Fleming, Bruce Otte.

Gary Fierko and I discuss IBM's vision and strategy, the TS7650G ProtecTIER gateway, and the differences between LTO-4 and IBM Enterprise tape, with attendees at the booth.

Behind the scenes were folks from the [George P. Johnson company] that run events. Deniese Dunavin here helped us be successful at this conference!

Here are just a portion of all the sponsors that made this event possible, printed on bags given to each attendee.

Hospitality Suites

After the booths closed down, we were invited to several different hospitality suites, sponsored by different vendors.

The Cisco hospitality suite had an Elvis impersonator and a beautiful bride. Her name was Trixie.

The bouncers at the Computer Associates (CA) hospitality suite wore the same shade of green and blue colors from their logo.

The APC hospitality suite went with an Island/Pirate theme.

The Brocade hospitality suite rocked the Casbah! Yes, that is a REAL snake she is holding.

Michael Nixon, a presenter from NEC Corporation of America.

By the time we got to the Data Domain hospitality suite, they were out of "dedupe-tinis", most of the attendees had left, but they were giving out these bumper stickers. For those considering Data Domain, you might want to look at the IBM TS7650G Virtual Tape gateway, which also provides inline data deduplication, but about six times faster ingest rate.

Needless to say, a good time was had by all.

⌐technorati tags: LSC27, IBM, solution showcase, hospitality suite, Deniese Dunavin, TS7650G, Cisco, CA, APC, Brocade, Data Domain

A lot of people leave conferences early, but since IBM spent so much for me to be at this conference, the least I could do is attend the last few sessions to get our money's worth.

2008 Dec 05 — Day5 - The Last Few Sessions for Data Center Conference 2008 (385)

This wraps up my week in Las Vegas for the 27th Annual [Data Center Conference]. This conference follows the common approach of ending at noon on Friday, so that attendees can get home to their families for the weekend, or start their weekend in Las Vegas early to watch the 50th annual Wrangler National Finals Rodeo.

I attended the last few sessions. Here is my recap:

Where, When and Why do I need a Solid-State Drive?

The internet provides transport of digital data between any devices. All other uses have evolved from this aim. Increasing data storage on any node on the Web therefore increases the possibilities at every other point. We are just now beginning to recognize the implications of this. The two speakers co-presented this session to cover how Solid State Drive (SSD) may participate.

Some electronic surveys of the audience provided some insight. Only 12 percent are deploying SSD now. 59 percent are evaluating the technology. A whopping 89 percent did not understand SSD technology, or how it would apply to their data center. Here is the expected time line for SSD adoption:

- 17 percent - within 1 year
- 60 percent - around 3 years from now
- 21 percent - 5 years or later

The main reasons cited for adopting SSD were increasing IOPS, reducing power and floorspace requirements, and expanding global networks. Here's a side-by-side comparison between HDD and SSD:

Disk array with 120 HDD, 73GB drives	Disk array with 120 SSD, 32GB drives
36,000 IOPS	4,200,000 IOPS
12 GB/sec	36 GB/sec
1,452 Watts	288 Watts
8.8 TB	3.8 TB
Per 73GB drive	Per 32GB drive
100MB/sec per drive	Read 250 MB/sec per drive Write 170 MB/sec per drive
300 IOPS per drive	35,000 IOPS per drive
12 Watts per drive	2.4 Watts per drive

However, the cost-per-GB for SSD is still 25x over traditional spinning disk, and the analysts expected SSD to continue to be 10-20x for a while. For now, they estimate that SSD will be mostly found in blade servers, enterprise-class disk systems, and high-end network directors.

The speakers gave examples such as Sun's ZFS Hybrid, and other products from NetApp, Compellent, Rackable, Violin, and Verari Systems.

Taking fear out of IT Disaster Recovery Exercises

The analyst presented best practices for disaster recovery testing with a "Pay Now or Pay Later" pre-emptive approach. Here were some of the suggestions:

- Schedule adequate time for DR exercises
- Build DR considerations into change control procedures and project lifecycle planning
- Cross-train personnel
- Document interdependencies between applications and business processes
- Bring in the "crisis team" on even the smallest incidents to keep skill sharp
- Present the "State of Disaster Recovery" to Senior Management annually

The speaker gave examples of different "tiers" for recovery, with appropriate RPO and RTO levels, and how often these should be tested per year. A survey of the audience found that 70 percent already have a tiered recovery approach.

In addition to IT staff, you might want to consider inviting others to the DR exercise as reviewers for oversight, including: Line of Business folks, Facilities/Operations, Human Resources, Legal/Compliance officers, even members of government agencies.

DR exercises can be performed at a variety of scope and objectives:

- Tabletop Test - IBM calls these "walk-throughs", where people merely sit around the table and discuss what actions they would take in the event of a hypothetical scenario. This is a good way to explore all kinds of scenarios from power outages, denial of service attacks, or pandemic diseases.

- Checklist Review - Here a physical inventory is taken of all the equipment needed at the DR site.

- Stand-alone Test - Sometimes called a "component test" or "unit test", a single application is recovered and tested.

- End-to-End simulation - All applications for a business process are recovered for a full simulation.

- Full Rehearsal - Business is suspended to perform this over a weekend.

- Production Cut-Over - If you are moving data center locations, this is a good time to consider testing some procedures. Other times, production is cut-over for a week over to the DR site and then returned back to the primary site.

- Mock Disaster - Management calls this unexpectedly to the IT staff, certain IT staff are told to participate, and others are told not to. This helps to identify critical resources, how well procedures are documented, and members of the team are adequately cross-trained.

For exercise, set the appropriate scope and objectives, score the results, and then identify action plans to address the gaps uncovered. Scoring can be as simple as "Not addressed", "Needs Improvement" and "Met Criteria".

Full Speed Ahead for iSCSI

The analyst presented this final session of the conference. He recognized IBM's early leadership in this area back in 1999, with the IP200i disk system. Today, there are many storage vendors that provide iSCSI solutions, the top three being:

- 23 percent - Dell/EqualLogic
- 15 percent - EMC
- 14 percent - HP/LeftHand Networks

This protocol has been mostly adopted for Windows, Linux and VMware, but has been largely ignored by the UNIX community. The primary value proposition is to offer SAN-like functionality at lower cost. When using the existing NICs that come built-in on most servers, iSCSI can be 30-50 percent less expensive than FC-based SANs. Even if you install TCP-Offload-Engine (TOE) cards into the servers, iSCSI can still represent a 16-19 percent cost savings. Many IBM servers now have TOE functionality built-in.

Since lower costs are the primary motivator, most iSCSI deployments are on 1GbE. The new 10Gbps Ethernet is still too expensive for most iSCSI configurations. For servers running a single application, two 1GbE NICs is sufficient. For servers running virtualization with multiple workloads might need four or five NICs (1GbE), or consider two 10GbE NICs if 10Gbps is available.

The iSCSI protocol has been most successful for small and medium sized businesses (SMB) looking for one-stop shopping. Buying iSCSI storage from the same vendor as your servers makes a lot of sense: EqualLogic with Dell servers, LeftHand software with HP servers, and IBM's DS3300 or N series with IBM System x servers. The average iSCSI unit was 10TB for about $24,000 US dollars.

Security and Management software for iSCSI is not as fully developed as for FC-based SANs. For this reason, most network vendors suggest having IP SANs isolated from your regular LAN. If that is not possible, consider VPN or encryption to provide added security. Issues of security and management imply that iSCSI won't dominate the large enterprise data center. Instead, many are watching closely the adoption of Fibre Channel over Ethernet (FCoE), based on revised standards for 10Gbps Ethernet. FCoE standards probably won't be finalized till mid-2009, with products from major vendors by 2010, and perhaps taking as much as 10 percent marketshare by 2011.

I hope you have enjoyed this series of posts. In addition to the sessions I attended, the conference has provided me with 67 presentations for me to review. Those who attended could purchase all the audio recordings and proceedings of every session for $295 US dollars, and those who missed the event can purchase these for $595 US dollars. These are reasonable prices, when you realize that the average Las Vegas visitor spends 13.9 hours gambling, losing an average of $626 US dollars per visit. The audio recordings and proceedings can provide more than 13.9 hours of excitement for less money!

⊙**technorati tags**: LSC27, Las Vegas, Rodeo, SSD, IOPS, HDD, Sun, ZFS, Disaster Recovery, RPO, RTO, iSCSI, IBM, IP200i, Dell, EqualLogic, EMC, HP, LeftHand Networks, NetApp, Compellent, Rackable, Violin, Verari Systems, DS3300, N series, System x, FCoE

2008 Dec 08 — An Exercise in Utility (386)

Well, I am exhausted from last week's trip to Las Vegas, so I will take it easy on my readers and let them enjoy this short [IBM 2-minute video]:

⊙**technorati tags**: IBM, green, smart grid, pizza delivery

2008 Dec 09 — Appeal for a Smarter Food System (387)

Continuing this week's theme on becoming a smarter planet, here is another [IBM 2-minute video]:

Special thanks for [Eightbar] for pointing me to this!

⊙**technorati tags**: IBM, frozen chicken, carrots

2008 Dec 10 — Happy Holidays from the TEBC staff (388)

Continuing this week's theme, my team here at the Tucson Executive Briefing Center (EBC) have made these two videos for me, using cloud-computing facilities from OfficeMax and the folks at JibJab. Only five people were allowed per video, so we had to make two to get everyone in.

(From left to right: Shelly Jost, Lee Olguin, Tony Pearson, Kristy Knight, Bill Terry)

If you have been to the Tucson Executive Briefing Center, perhaps you can recognize some of our faces!

(From left to right: Kris Keller, Jack Arnold, Vaughn Johnson, Harley Puckett, Mysti Wood)

⚲**technorati tags**: IBM, cloud computing, TEBC, OfficeMax, JibJab, Elf yourself

Scott Adams is my hero. His engineering background shows through in his wry wit on his blog and in his comic strip.

2008 Dec 11 — Is Storage the Next Confusopoly? (389)

Ten years ago, Scott Adams, of *Dilbert* fame, coined the phrase ["confusopolies"] in his 1998prediction:

> "In the future, all barriers to entry will go away and companies will be forced to form what I call 'confusopolies'.
>
> Confusopoly: A group of companies with similar products who intentionally confuse customers instead of competing on price."

John Quarterman brought this up in his post [Confusopoly, Scott Adams, Prophet of Finance], and Joshua Gans comments on related predictions in his post [10 Years Ago for Scott Adams]. Here's an excerpt from John Quarterman:

> "...But look at the list of industries he identified as already being confusopolies:
>
> - Telephone service.
> - Insurance.
> - Mortgage loans.
> - Banking.
> - Financial services.
>
> Telephone companies of course since then have gone to great lengths to try to nuke net neutrality.
>
> And the other four are the source of the current economic meltdown, precisely because they sold products that customers couldn't understand. Worse, they didn't even understand them!"

I wonder if the IT storage industry is not becoming its own confusopoly itself. Take for example a recent tiff between fellow bloggers [Chuck Hollis from EMC] and [Kostadis Roussos from NetApp].

Let's start with this little gem from Chuck:

> "If you've spent any time in the storage biz, you probably realize that the server vendors sell more storage than they have any right to."

This is the old [Supermarkets-vs.-Specialty Shops] debate I discussed over a year ago. The debate goes along the lines that some people prefer to buy their entire information infrastructure (servers, storage, software and services) from a single vendor, one-stop shopping, while others might prefer to buy their pieces as components from different vendors that specialize in each technology. Because of this, Specialty shops tend to focus on other Specialty shops as their primary competitors (EMC vs. NetApp), while Supermarkets tend to focus on other Supermarkets (IBM vs. HP).

The apparent contradiction is that Chuck feels the Supermarkets (IBM, HP, Sun and Dell) should not have any right to sell storage, in the same manner that butchers, bakers and candlestick makers do not believe that Supermarkets should have any right to sell meat, bread or candles? If servers and storage are so different, how can self-proclaimed storage-only specialist EMC have the right to sell their non-storage offerings, from server virtualization (VMware) to cloud-computing services? With EMC's latest announcement of DW/BI centers, I think we can safely take EMC off the list of storage-only specialists. We will need to come up with a third category for those caught in limbo between being one-stop shopping Supermarkets like IBM and being a pure storage-only Specialists like NetApp. Perhaps EMC has become the IT equivalent of Wal-Mart's [Neighborhood Market].(*No offense intended to my friends at Wal-Mart!*)

Then Chuck continues with these statements:

> "It is rarely is it the case that a server vendor can offer you a better storage product, or better service, or better functionality than what a storage specialist can do.

> ...Interestingly enough, Dell appears to do a sizable amount of storage business 'off base' with EMC products -- outside the context of a specific server transaction."

This second contradiction relates to products that are manufactured by specialty shops, but sold through supermarket channels. Chuck would like to imply that the only storage products anyone should consider is gear made by specialty shops, whether you get it directly from them, or through Supermarket's with appropriate OEM agreements. Storage made by Supermarkets, either organically developed or through acquisitions, should not be considered? What happens when a Supermarket acquires a specialty shop? We've already seen how negative EMC has been against IBM's acquisitions of XIV and Diligent, which allowed a Supermarket like IBM to provide better products in both cases than what is available from any specialty shop. Kind of pokes a big hole in that argument!

But Dell also acquired EqualLogic, which Chuck admits might have a "fit in the marketplace". As it turns out, companies would rather buy EMC equipment from Dell sales people, than from EMC directly, and perhaps this is because Dell, like IBM, sees the big picture. Dell, IBM and the rest of the IT Supermarkets understand the entire information infrastructure, not just the storage components of a data center. With HP and Sun selling HDS gear, and IBM selling NetApp gear, it becomes obvious that EMC needs Dell more than Dell needs EMC.

Chuck then pokes fun at NetApp in comparing the EMC NX4 to NetApp's FAS2020, comparable to IBM System Storage N series N3300. Here's an excerpt:

> "Like other Celerras, it does the full unified storage thing: iSCSI, NAS and 'real deal' FC that isn't emulated."

The irony, of course, is that the NX4 does not actually use "real" Fibre Channel drives, but rather SAS and SATA drives. I guess Chuck's concern is that the NetApp, which <u>does</u> use "real" Fibre Channel drives, provides FC-attached LUNs to the host through its WAFL mapping, rather than through EMC's traditional RAID-rank mapping approach. How Chuck can imply that anything in the IT industry that is "emulated" is somehow seriously worse than "real", but then spend 40 percent of his posts devoted to the benefits of VMware, which offers "emulated" virtual machines, seems to be yet another contradiction.

The confusion continues in the battle over cloud-oriented storage. On *Enterprise Storage Forum*, Marty Foltyn has an article titled [The Cloud Offers Promise for Storage Users], cites a Gartner press release [Gartner Says Cloud Computing Will Be As Influential As E-business]. Here's an excerpt from Marty Foltyn's article:

> "'Cloud computing' has been ill-defined and over-hyped, yet storage vendors have been quick to trot out their own 'cloud storage' offerings and end users are wondering whether there's significant cost savings in these services for them, particularly in tough economic times.

> 'Cloud-speak' can be downright confusing....

> Surprisingly, Gartner considers the amorphous nature of the term to be good news: 'The very confusion and contradiction that surrounds the term *cloud computing* signifies its potential to change the status quo in the IT market,' the IT research firm said earlier this year."

Consistent with Scott Adams's original prediction, the barriers of entry have lowered for storage vendors as well. Rather than competing on function and price through valued relationships and trusted expertise, some vendors would rather confuse instead. EMC tries to paint the NX4 as being "just as good as" a NetApp or IBM N series for unified storage, and EMC tries to create new categories, like Cloud-Oriented Storage (COS), to give their me-too products the impression they are in a league of their own. All of this to discourage customers from making their own comparisons and doing their own research.

IBM doesn't play that way. If you want straight talk about IBM's products, contact your local IBM Business Partner or sales rep.

⊘**technorati tags**: Scott Adams, Dilbert, prediction, confusopoly, economic meltdown, Chuck Hollis, EMC, Kostadis Roussos, NetApp, Supermarkets,

---

Specialty Shops, IBM, HP, Sun, Dell, HDS, VMware, Wal-Mart, EqualLogic, OEM, N3300, Fibre Channel, FC, iSCSI, NX4, COS

2008 Dec 12 — IBM's Third Annual Five in Five (390)

Wrapping up this week's theme on ways to make the planet smarter, and less confusing, I present IBM's third annual [five in five]. These are five IBM innovations to watch over the next five years, all of which have implications on information storage. Here is a quick [3-minute video] that provides the highlights:

◌technorati tags: IBM, five-in-five, innovations, solar, health, talking Web, shopping assistants, forgetting

Comment from Amy

Just a quick note on the "Forgetting will become like a distant memory" in particular the phrase – "improve their short-term memory". Seeing as I've come from a psychology background and have studied the brain I don't see how this could be true. Surely by relying on technology and not trying to remember/exercising our own brain... Our memory will in fact become unused and worse. This will not help our memory at all in fact quite the contrary. It is well known that when we don't use areas of our brain the neurons actually become inactive, and when we do frequently use areas of our brain they become more wired and sharp -- neuro-plasticity. In particular the part of the brain that deals with memory changes very easily, so by not exercising it and relying on technology to recall memories it will only make our memory and ability to retrieve memories WORSE and create a growing independence on the technology! So this seems crazy and completely contradictory!

Response from Tony Pearson (IBM)

Amy, The point is not to improve the mind, but to minimize the impact of the mind's physical limitations. Whether it's a deck of index cards kept together with a binder clip, or more sophisticated electronic technology, people have relied on external memory aids. For example, I have hundreds of telephone numbers programmed into my cell phone, so that I don't have to memorize any in my head.

-- Tony

 For the longest time, I could not understand Twitter. My blog posts average 700 words, and you want me to make statements limited to 140 characters? But the marketing team was persistent in asking me to join. Now I love using it!

2008 Dec 18 — IBM Storage Now On Twitter (391)

Well, I am here in New York City visiting clients, and was hoping to return to Tucson tomorrow morning, but now the weather folks are predicting a terrible snow storm that could delay my return.

I will be on vacation the rest of the year, so until then, you can follow the latest about IBM storage on [Twitter].

technorati tags: IBM, New York City, Twitter

2009

The year 2009 would prove tough for many people. Personally, one of the local companies that I invested in was not doing well, forcing me to take over as president, working evenings and weekends to manage nine employees, re-negotiate contracts, and restructure operations in time to sell it off by the end of the year. All of this was good real-life learning experience for me as a "Business Consultant" at IBM.

January

January is always tough as I have to be careful what I write during blackout period, typically the two weeks prior to each quarterly or year-end financial results announcement. I am not provided exact dates when each blackout period starts, only that I know it is over when IBM makes an official press release of its results. This is always a good time for some light-hearted posts while I wait for the 2008 year-end results of IBM to be announced.

2009 Jan 06 — The New Year in Six Words (392)

Happy New Year, everyone!

I hope everyone had some time these past few weeks of the Winter Solstice to enjoy some time off with friends and family. I had a great trip to New York City, got to visit my brother and his friends, went to see my friends in Michigan to celebrate New Year's Eve, and saw the world premiere of [LexiBaby], an independent film from fellow filmmaker Jonathan Petro.

Talking to people in New York, Michigan, and Arizona gave me some perspective on what 2008 was like for them, and what they anticipate for the new 2009 year. Borrowing the meme from last month's Freakonomics contest [Got Six Words to Inspire America] and the book [Not Quite What I Was Planning: Six-Word Memoirs by Writers Famous and Obscure], I can summarize the responses I heard into three groups:

- Sadly, life is full of disappointment
- In holding pattern, checking fuel level
- Am I dreaming? Someone pinch me!

The latter of course from fellow IBMers, corporate executives receiving bailout money, attorneys that specialize in foreclosures, and the lucky few who will be in Washington DC for the US Presidential Inauguration. In addition to all the bailout money from banks, insurance companies and automakers that will be spent on IBM equipment and services, there might be additional funds from the US Government to improve our country's information infrastructure. In a recent *Forbes* article titled [The Tech Solution to the Recession], Andy Greenberg writes about US president-elect Barack Obama's ideas about a stimulus to the economy. Here's an excerpt:

> "IBM, for starters, believes that a massive infusion of cash should go toward cutting-edge technology. Last month, IBM CEO Sam Palmisano presented a report to Obama's transition team from the Information Technology and Innovation Foundation ([ITIF]) that argues that a $30 billion investment in universal broadband, health information technology and a smarter power grid could create 950,000 jobs.

> Those disparities, and IBM's argument for focusing a stimulus plan on technology in general, come from what economists have dubbed 'network multipliers'. The computing giant, and ITIF, argue that technology creates more jobs than other types of infrastructure by enabling new types of businesses.

> 'If you build more roads, people don't buy more tires or GPS systems, but if you build better networks, you create entirely new business applications,' says Rob Atkinson, president of ITIF and an author of the think tank's report. 'Something like YouTube could never have existed without broadband.'

> Regardless of precisely how tech stimulus money gets spent, IBM will likely sweep up a significant chunk of those taxpayer funds, given the computing giant's diverse hardware, software and services businesses. Other IT infrastructure giants like Microsoft, Hewlett Packard, Oracle and SAP are also likely to vie for pieces of Obama's stimulus package aimed at technology.

> But among those tech companies, IBM has been especially active in driving home the need for national investment in tech systems. In a November speech to the Council on Foreign Relations, Palmisano argued that that the U.S. needs to invest in innovation not just as a solution to our current recession but as a competitive measure in an increasingly integrated and technologically advanced world."

The concept and advantages of network multipliers are not new. For more on this, read the whitepapers [Segmentation, Network Multipliers and Spillovers: A Theory of Rural Urban Migration for a Traditional Economy] by Vegard Iversen, and [Network multipliers and the optimality of indirect communication] by Andrea Galeotti and Sanjeev Goyal.

Every year, I make New Year's resolutions. Some people think the practice is silly, but I think there is always room for improvement for everyone, including myself. Inside IBM, all employees must agree to a set of "Personal Business Commitments" that we will then serve as the basis for our year-end appraisal.

2009 Jan 12 — New Year's Resolutions for 2009 (393)

This is our so-called blackout period that prevents me from talking about how well IBM is doing or making predictions about our industry that might affect stock prices, so instead I will talk about my New Year's Resolutions.

First, let's see how well I did against last year's [Resolutions for 2008]:

Improve my writing skills

> For this, I purchased the [Associated Press (AP) Stylebook] which some consider to be the *Journalist's Bible* for how to spell, write and phrase things correctly. I also followed various blogs about writing, including John E. McIntyre's [You Don't Say], Dan Santow's [Word Wise], and the Quotation's Page [Quotes of the Day].

Improve my HTML and Web design skills

> I helped out several local organizations with their websites, and learned some of the latest HTML features, Common Style Sheets (CSS), JavaScript, and Active Service Pages (ASP).

Contribute to the OLPC Foundation

> Last year, I resolved to contribute my time and effort to the One Laptop Per Child [OLPC] project led by Nicholas Negroponte. It didn't take long for them to contact me, and I had wonderful experiences helping the folks in Nepal and Uruguay. Despite building and delivering half a million laptops to deserving kids, the OLPC team has been impacted by the recent economic meltdown. From their [announcement], the OLPC team is making some shifts in their direction and priorities. Here's an excerpt:

"This restructuring is also the result of an exciting new direction for OLPC. Our technology initiatives will focus on:

1) Development of Generation 2.0
2) A no-cost connectivity program
3) A million digital books
4) Passing on the development of the Sugar Operating System to the community.

With regard to deployments:

- Latin America will be spun off into a separate support unit
- Sub-Saharan Africa will become a major learning hub
- The Middle East, Afghanistan and Northwestern Pakistan will become a major focus"

It's not clear how involved I will be with OLPC in 2009, and I will probably wait for the dust to settle on this one.

Eat Healthier and Drink more

I hired a nutritionist and improved my diet. I also drank more. (That was an easy one to keep!) Unfortunately, there is still room for improvement on this one.

Attend more movies and film-making events

I've renewed my membership with the Tucson Film Society, and attended several of their events in 2008. I also met with Will Conroy, screenwriter for the Action/Suspense thriller [*Transsiberian*] starring Woody Harrelson and Ben Kingsley.

Get Better Organized

Well, I carried my [Hipster PDA] in my back pocket most of 2008, but it just did not catch on. I did get somewhat better organized, with three-ring binders and a scanner that converts paper documents into searchable PDF files.

While some might find the concept of New Year's resolutions silly or pointless, I find them useful. Here's some interesting research on Wikipedia:

"Recent research shows that while 52 percent of participants in a resolution study were confident of success with their goals, only 12 percent actually achieved their goals. Men achieved their goal 22 percent more often when they engaged in goal setting, a system where small measurable goals are used (lose a pound a week, instead of saying 'lose weight'), while women succeeded 10 percent more when they made their goals public and got support from their friends."

Here are mine for 2009:

Spend More Time with Friends and Family

According to this [article by Albrecht Powell], reconnecting with friends and family is the number one on the Top 10 list. I think the economic meltdown served as a great wake-up call for people to focus what is most important in your life and adjust your priorities accordingly.

Enjoy Life More

Back in 2007, I vowed to laugh more. While the current economic crisis might not seem like an appropriate time for this one, I think there is hope, a new US President, and some much-needed enthusiasm for change.

Learn Something New

At a dinner with clients, one of the IBMers had brought his 20-something daughter and her similarly-aged friend. Their college was closed for the week after a student shooting, and he felt it best to give them a change of scenery. They couldn't wait until they were "done with school" so they could get on with their lives. I had to break the bad news to them that in today's world, they should expect life-long learning. Gone are the days where you could learn a specific skill or trade, and do that the rest of your life. Hopefully I didn't frighten both into giving up a career in favor of marriage with such advice!

With the world getting smaller, flatter, and, yes, "smarter" also, I resolve to learn something new. I don't necessarily know what that is yet, but I will keep it in the back of my mind.

Make Tucson a better place, and enrich the lives of its residents

I've actually gotten complaints that I was helping people in other countries, through OLPC and [Kiva], and that I should do more for people right here in Tucson. That's fair. This year I resolve to investigate that further.

Get Better Organized

Last year was a good start, but I can certainly do better in 2009, both at home and at the office. Perhaps I need to dust off my old copy of [*Getting Things Done*] by David Allen and read it again!

Hopefully, this list might inspire you to come up with your own resolutions. Not surprisingly, writing them in a public forum helped me keep most of them, and stick to my resolutions throughout the year. Here are [other hints to help you], and some [expert advice on maintaining resolutions].

⊘technorati tags: IBM, New Year's Resolutions, AP, Stylebook, HTML, CSS, ASP, OLPC, Transsiberian, Will Conroy, Woody Harrelson, Ben Kingsley, PDA, PDF, Kiva, GTD, David Allen

Addition from Tony Pearson (IBM)

Those not familiar with Kiva can see their video here:

> http://vimeo.com/2769845

-- Tony

 This is one of my infamous "mailbag" posts, in which I take three letters and answer them publicly. The first referred to IBM's decision to "ground" me as an outbound traveling presenter, limiting me to speaking to clients in Tucson. The second came from my personal trainer, hoping that mentioning her services would drive new clients for her, and the third came from an IBMer who wanted me to poke fun at an EMC blogger's reading selection.

2009 Jan 14 — "Dear Tony" letters for 2009 (394)

I've gotten some strange emails lately, so I thought I would address them here.

Dear Tony,
In your last post about [New Year's Resolutions for 2009], you mention spending more time with friends and family, which is typically a phrase used by people leaving a company.

Are you announcing your retirement?

> No, I don't plan to retire anytime soon. Like most companies, IBM had [changed its retirement plans]. Those lucky enough to be on the

old plan could retire after 30 years of service to IBM, and get 12 percent of their last five years' salary as an annual pension the rest of their lives. If you averaged $100K per year the last five years, then you could retire on $60K per year. Many IBMers in Tucson took their pension and moved to Mexico, and lived like kings!

To qualify for the old plan, you had to be a certain age, have a minimum number of years working for IBM, or be an executive of Italian-American descent. I missed it by a few months, so I am on the *new plan* instead. This involves employer contribution matches to a 401(k) plan and reflects the trend from working for a single company all your life, to changing careers or companies every 5 to 10 years. Many of my colleagues on the *old plan* had announced early last year their plans to retire by the end of 2008, but then changed their minds after the economic downturn.

For both personal and professional reasons, I plan to travel less in 2009, so that will give me more time to reconnect with friends and family, especially my friends over at [Tucson Fun and Adventures], the premiere singles activities club in Southern Arizona; the [Tucson Laughter Club], recognized as one of the oldest laughter clubs in the United States; and the Tucson Film Society at the [Loft Cinema].

Dear Tony,
Why not make a New Year's Resolution for an "exercise regime"?

I made that lifestyle change back in 2003, joining [Performance at McMahon's] fitness training facility, and have been lifting weights there, several times per week, ever since.

This is my personal trainer Christine. Our gym had their annual *Elite Performer* athletic contest running August to November last year, and I came in fifth place. If you are looking for a personal trainer in the Tucson area to jump-start your own fitness goals, I recommend Performance at McMahon's.

Normally, I consider New Year's Resolutions for starting new things, changing bad behaviors, or revisiting things I have long forgotten, not really intended for continuing to do the same as the year before. However, if it makes you happy, I resolve to continue my exercise regime of lifting weights three times a week, and will try to do more [cardio] as well.

Dear Tony,
What's up with your fellow blogger Chuck Hollis from EMC and his post [Timely Reading], suggesting we should read Ayn Rand's hefty novel *Atlas Shrugged*?

What's your take on this?

I don't talk with Chuck personally about his posts, so I can only guess that he is under the same blackout period rules, which typically commences the day following the end of the fiscal quarter and ends after the issuance of a news release disclosing the quarterly financial results.

That said, Chuck is an avid reader, and often recommends books he likes. For example, based on his recommendation, I read Tim Harford's [The Undercover Economist] and found it an excellent choice. In the book *Atlas Shrugged*, Ayn Rand renounces religion, socialism and a variety of other ills facing society in 1950s America. Since [93 percent] of scientists and engineers are Atheist, Agnostic or other form of non-believer, I suspect most readers of the Storage blogosphere are at least somewhat familiar with Ayn Rand's works. Personally, I prefer the works of fellow atheist authors [Douglas Adams], [Sir Isaac Asimov], [Richard Dawkins], and [George Orwell].

Chuck mentions he saw Stephen Moore's article [*Atlas Shrugged*: From Fiction to Fact in 52 Years] in the *Wall Street Journal*, which considers this tome to be the second most influential book, second only to the Bible. No doubt many of the bailout plans proposed today sound similar to the government acts covered in the novel. One warning rings true for me:

> "When profits and wealth and creativity are denigrated in society, they start to disappear -- leaving everyone the poorer."

However, I suspect his post might also be partly motivated by Josh Bernoff's report [Time to Rethink Your Corporate Blogging Ideas] from Forrester Research. I've read the full report, and it has some interesting results. Only 16 percent of those surveyed who use company blogs say they trust them. The situation improves slightly if you look at people who are active in the blogosphere. Among those who read blogs regularly, only 24 percent trust company blogs. And only 39 percent of bloggers, who actually write their own blogs, trust company blogs. This ranks lower than every other form of content Forrester asked about, including broadcast and print media, direct mail, and email from companies.

This would mean company blogs are just slightly more trustworthy than self-proclaimed UFO alien abductees, tabloids at the grocery store checkout lane, and perhaps politicians like Vice President Dick Cheney or former Secretary of Defense Donald Rumsfeld. Josh insists that this report is not meant as a plea for existing corporate bloggers to give up blogging, but rather to be more thoughtful on how and why they blog.

Perhaps Chuck is suggesting that bloggers are like the creative types in *Atlas Shrugged* who felt under-appreciated, and that perhaps all IT Storage bloggers should go on strike?

Well, I'm not retiring, not quitting my exercise routine, and not planning to stop blogging. Last year, thanks to you my dear readers, I was ranked the third most influential blog on IBM DeveloperWorks. Congratulations to my fellow IBM bloggers [Bobby Wolf] and ["Turbo" Todd Watson], who ranked first and second!

technorati tags: New Year's Resolutions, IBM, retirement, TFA, TLC, Loft Cinema, exercise, Performance, personal trainer, bad behavior, EMC, Chuck Hollis, Tim Harford, Undercover Economist, Ayn Rand, Atlas Shrugged, Douglas Adams, Sir Isaac Asimov, Richard Dawkins, George Orwell, Stephen Moore, WSJ, Josh Bernoff, Forrester Research, UFO

 When I first joined IBM, you could retire after twenty-five years of service. This was known as joining the Quarter Century Club (QCC). Today, you can still retire after 25 years, but won't have the "defined benefit" based on your last five year's salary as your annual pension. I hope you contributed to your 401-K plan!

2009 Jan 15 — Congratulations Ken on your QCC milestone! (395)

Today, fellow IBMer Ken Hannigan celebrated his 25th year anniversary with IBM, which inducts him into the IBM Quarter Century Club [QCC]. I was surprised to hear that there are over 900 QCC members currently residing in Arizona. In the past, QCC was shortly followed by retirement, but in these economic times, it marks a mid-point in one's career.

I met Ken back in 1988, I was working on DFHSM and he was part of the DFDSS team that moved from San José, California to Tucson, Arizona. Later, Ken and I would work in the same department as *architects* for the DFSMS product that included DFSMShsm and DFSMSdss components.

Ken was then offered a chance to lead the effort to launch a new product from an internal project called Workstation Data Save Facility (WDSF) that was changed to Data Facility Distributed Storage Manager (DFDSM), then renamed to ADSTAR Distributed Storage Manager (ADSM), and finally to the name it has today: [IBM Tivoli Storage Manager].

Over the years, Ken's had some interesting experiences. Two examples:

Saving the Democracy of Peru

During a hotly contested election in the Latin American country of Peru, there were technical problems with the ballot records. Management needed someone from Tucson to go, and my name was floated around, since I spoke Spanish fluently. My schedule did not permit, so they sent Ken instead. Ken was able to recover the lost ballot information and avoid a revolution.

Assisted with the Technical team for a Major Motion Picture

Ken was part of the IBM technical team that helped [DreamWorks SKG] produce the movie [The Prince of Egypt], a major animated motion picture. IBM is heavily involved in the digital media community, and was instrumental in helping film-makers set up their information infrastructure.

Ken has been one of my best friends over the past twenty years. I introduced him to his wife, and was the *best man* at his wedding. It is quality people like Ken that make working at IBM so special.

⊙**technorati tags**: IBM, QCC, Ken Hannigan, DFHSM, DFDSS, TSM, Tivoli, Peru, election, DreamWorks, The Prince of Egypt, Information Infrastructure

I have helped many others start their own blogs. I make a point of introducing them to drive some traffic.

2009 Jan 19 — A New Blog about Smarter Planet (396)

IBM has launched a new blog, focused on making [a smarter planet]. In my post, [The New Year in Six Words], I discussed the part of Sam Palmisano's speech that mentioned a small $30 Billion investment could result in 950,000 new jobs. For those who wondered how IBM arrived to that figure, here are two posts:

- [Investing in Smarter Infrastructure]
- [More on the Proposed Stimulus Package]

Can this week get any better? We have the Arizona Cardinals going to the Super Bowl, and tomorrow we inaugurate Barack Obama as the 44th US President.

technorati tags: IBM, smarter planet, Sam Palmisano, information infrastructure, new jobs, Barack Obama, Super Bowl, Arizona Cardinals, Stimulus Package

2009 Jan 20 — Power and Strength through Diversity (397)

Today we watched Barack Obama get inaugurated as the 44th President of the United States, and he reminded all Americans that the power and strength of this country comes through its diversity. To some extent, this is also what gives IBM its power and strength as well. While not quite the orator of President Obama, IBM's own CFO, Mark Loughridge, gave a rousing speech about IBM's 4Q08 and year-end financial results.

In 2008, IBM was not just successful because it had a wide diversity of servers and storage hardware products, but also a diversity of software, and a diversity of service offerings. And lastly, IBM sells to a diversity of clients in different industries, throughout a diversity of markets. While the current economic meltdown might have affected businesses focused on the US and other major markets, IBM did particularly well last year in growth markets, including the so-called BRIC countries (Brazil, Russia, India and China).

IBM's approach to invest in R&D and its nearly 400,000 employees for long-term success continues to pay off. Where "Cash is King," IBM can also afford all those acquisitions and strategic initiatives, positioning the company for a brighter future.

Where there are challenges, IBM finds opportunity.

Addition from Tony Pearson (IBM)

BusinessWeek comments on this here:

> http://www.businessweek.com/globalbiz/blog/globespotting/archives/2009/01/ibm_the_non_com.html?campaign_id=rss_daily

2009 Jan 22 — Instant Messaging in 3D with IBM Sametime (398)

In the post [Flowing Workflow], the folks over at *Eightbar* point to the latest 3D work being done with IBM Lotus Sametime.

IBM Sametime is IBM's instant messaging facility, which has been extended to include Voice over IP (VOIP) capability similar to Skype, and now is being developed as a launch point for 3D impromptu meetings "in-world", similar to [Second Life].

Enjoy this quick [3-minute video].

With many companies facing hard times and considering travel restrictions for face-to-face internal meetings, an information infrastructure that adopts this technology might be a reasonable alternative.

⊙**technorati tags**: IBM, Lotus, Sametime, IM, chat, Eightbar, Skype, SecondLife, travel restrictions

Comment from Barry Everett

OK, I'm ready, and I've been preaching Virtual Collaboration for about 2 years, I network with IBMers on 3 continents. How do I participate in the Sametime 3D pilot project? Let's Roll.

Response from Tony Pearson (IBM)

Barry,

The pilot appears to be limited to those who have access inside IBM's "W3" firewall. If you have this, then go to

> https://w3.tap.ibm.com/myTAP/innovation/viewInnovation.wss?ass etId=1025#support

for instructions.
-- Tony

 A client asked me whether they should buy SVC or XIV. Rather than explain that this was apples-and-oranges, I chose spaghetti and sauce. This analogy has served me well over the past few years for a variety of other situations to compare IBM's various virtualization offerings, and how they can be combined with physical disk and tape to optimize for particular workloads.

2009 Jan 28 — Foundations and Flavorings for Storage (399)

We've been quite busy here at the Tucson Executive Briefing Center. I am often asked to explain the relationship between IBM's various storage products. While automakers don't have to explain why they sell sports coupes, pickup trucks and minivans, this analogy does not adequately cover IT storage products. So, I have come up with a new analogy that seems to be a better fit: foundations and flavorings.

 All over the world, meals are often comprised of a foundation, perhaps rice, potatoes or pasta, covered with some form of flavoring, sauces, pieces of meat or fish, grated cheese and spices. In Puerto Rico, I had dishes where the foundation was mashed bananas called [plantains]. Sandwich shops often let you pick your choice of bread, the foundation, and then your meats and cheeses, the *flavorings*. At our local steakhouse, [McMahon's], the menu lists a set of steaks, the *foundation* such as Rib Eye, Filet Mignon, Prime Rib or New York Strip, and various

flavorings, such as sauces and rubs to cover the steak. Last night, I had the Delmonico steak with the Cristiani sauce consisting of Portobello mushrooms, garlic and aged Romano cheese.

This serves as a useful analogy for IBM's storage strategy. Allowing the foundations and flavorings to be separately orderable greatly simplifies the selection menu and provides a nearly any-to-any approach to meeting a variety of client needs. Let's take a look at both.

- **Foundations**

  IBM's foundation products are the DS family [DS3000, DS4000, DS5000, DS6000 and DS8000 series], [DS9900 series], and [XIV] for disk, and the TS family [TS1000, TS2000, TS3000] series for tape drives and libraries. In much the same way you might prefer brown rice instead of white rice, or *linguine* instead of *penne* pasta, you might find the attributes of one storage foundation more attractive based on its performance, scalability and availability features for your particular application workloads.

- **Flavorings**

  IBM System Storage SAN Volume Controller [SVC]

  Fellow IBM blogger Barry Whyte discusses SVC at great length on his [Storage Virtualization] blog. Flavoring disk foundation storage with SAN Volume Controller can provide you additional features and functions, and help improve the scalability, performance or availability characteristics. For example, if you have DS4000, DS8000 and XIV, you might use SVC to provide a consistent methodology for asynchronous replication, a form of consistent "flavoring" if you will.

  N series Gateways

  The [N series gateways] offer flavoring to disk foundation, including unified NAS, iSCSI and FCP protocol host attachment, and application aware capabilities. (As for our IBM N series appliances or "filers", these could be foundational storage behind an SVC, but that's perhaps a topic for another post.)

  Scale-out File Services [SoFS]

  SoFS provides a global namespace with clustered NAS access to files. This is a blended disk-and-tape solution with built-in backup and Information Lifecycle Management [ILM]. Policies can be used to place different files onto different tiers of storage, automate the movement from tier to tier, including migration to tape, and even expiration when the data is no longer needed.

DR550

The [IBM System Storage DR550] provides Non-erasable, Non-rewriteable (NENR) flavoring to storage. While the DR550 comes with internal disk storage, it can front end a tape library filled with WORM cartridges. The DR550 has been paired up with small libraries (TS3200 or TS3310) as well as larger libraries like the TS3500.

Grid Access

The IBM Grid Medical Archive Solution [GMAS] provides a variety of capabilities for storing and accessing medical images, using a blended disk-and-tape approach. This allows hospital and clinic networks to provide access for doctors and radiologists from multiple locations.

The underlying technology is [IBM System Storage Multilevel Grid Access Manager] which can be used to provide grid access across multiple locations for any industry or application.

IBM TS7650G ProtecTIER deduplication gateway

Many of the flavorings are called "gateways". The IBM TS7650G flavors disk that provides a virtual tape library [VTL] with inline data deduplication capability. Recent performance tests pairing the TS7650G flavoring with XIV foundation storage found this combination to be an excellent match.

Let me know what you think. Does this help you understand IBM's storage strategy and acquisitions? Enter your comments below.

⊘technorati tags: IBM, TEBC, foundation, flavoring, plantains, McMahon, DS3000, DS4000, DS5000, DS6000, DS8000, DCS9900, XIV, TS1000, TS2000, TS3000, NAS, iSCSI, FCP, NENR, WORM, ILM, GAM, GMAS, TS7650G, ProtecTIER

2009 Jan 28 — IBM Meets with President Obama (400)

In an effort to deal with "Great Depression 2.0", US President Barack Obama invited IBM Chairman Sam Palmisano and dozen other CEOs to the White House yesterday to talk about the economic stimulus package.

Here is a [quick clip] of Sam's speech.

Barack's response was insightful on his thoughts on this. Here are some excerpts:

> "A few moments ago, I met with some of the leading business executives in the country. And it was a sober meeting because these companies and the workers they employ are going through times more trying than any we've seen in a long, long while.
>
> ...
>
> And yet, even as we discussed the seriousness of this challenge, we left our meeting confident that we can turn our economy around.
>
> ...
>
> But these executives also understand that without wise leadership in Washington, even the best-run businesses can't do as well as they might.
>
> ...
>
> And that is why I hope to sign an American Recovery and Reinvestment Plan into law in the next few weeks. And most of the money we're investing as part of this plan will get out the door immediately and go directly to job creation, generating or saving 3 (million) to 4 million new jobs. And the vast majority of these jobs will be created in the private sector because, as these CEOs well know, business, not government, is the engine of growth in this country.
>
> ...
>
> But even as this plan puts Americans back to work, it will also make the critical investments in alternative energy, in safer roads, better health care and modern schools that will lay the foundation for long-term growth and prosperity, and will invest in broadband and emerging technologies, like the ones imagined and introduced to the world by people like Sam and so many of the CEOs here today, because that's how America will retain and regain its competitive edge in the 21st century.

...

We will invest in what works. Instead of politicians doling out money behind a veil of secrecy, decisions about where we invest will be made public on the Internet and will be informed by independent experts whenever possible. And we will launch a sweeping effort to root out waste, inefficiency and unnecessary spending in our government. And every American will be able to see how and where we spend taxpayer dollars, by going to a new website to [recovery.gov], because I firmly believe what Justice Louis Brandeis once said, that sunlight is the best disinfectant.

...

In the end, the answer to our economic troubles rests less in my hands or in the hands of our legislators than it does with America's workers and the businesses that employ them. They are the ones whose efforts and ideas will determine our economic destiny, just as they always have. For in the end, it's businesses, large and small, that generate the jobs, provide the salaries and serve as the foundation on which the American people's lives and dreams depend. All we can do, those of us here in Washington, is to help create a favorable climate in which workers can prosper, businesses can thrive and our economy can grow."

I certainly find Sam's efforts and Barack's responsiveness encouraging.

technorati tags: IBM, Sam Palmisano, Barack Obama, The American Recovery and Reinvestment Act, Washington, sunlight, disinfectant, recovery.gov

February

The month of February has given birth to George Washington, Abe Lincoln, Charles Dickens, Jules Verne, Thomas Edison and Charles Darwin, along with traditions like Groundhog Day and the troubles that leap years cause with computers. The enormity of the US recession became more clear, with Arizona being one of the hardest hit areas in the country, along with Florida, Michigan, Nevada and California.

2009 Feb 05 -- A Brief History of Intelligence (401)

Here's a cute 2-minute video that explains a brief history of using information intelligently to help get things done.

IBM's emphasis on "Information Infrastructure" is to help organizations get the right information, to the right people at the right time. This helps them to have the right insights, make the right decisions, and develop the right innovations needed for the challenges at hand.

As the planet got smaller and flatter, IBM led the way. Now, as the planet needs to get smarter-- with more efficient health care,

energy distribution, financial institutions, and IT infrastructures--IBM will once again take the lead.

This is going to be an interesting year!

⊘**technorati tags**: IBM, IBM TV, Information Infrastructure, Intelligence

I love "spy" movies like the James Bond franchise from Ian Fleming. In many films, the use of microfiche to store photos or sensitive documents was often the way spies passed their information along. When I first started at IBM, we used microfiche to hold the compiled output for our software programs.

2009 Feb 06 — Storage on a Postage Stamp (402)

When I was a kid, I used to love old spy movies where they would hide a small microchip or microfiche behind the stamp on a letter or postcard. "Yeah, right," I would think to myself, "How much information could that little thing possibly hold?" On their post [Bringing the "New Intelligence" Down to Earth: Intro to Semantic Web, Internet-of-Things], my fellow IBM bloggers Jack Mason and Adam Christensen pointed me to a crazy new product called "Mir:ror" that connects to your PC or laptop.

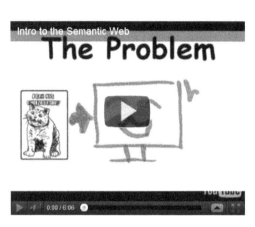

A four-minute [video] about Mir:ror:

At first, I thought it was another product spoof, like Onion News Network's video of the [Apple MacBook Wheel] that eliminates the need for a keyboard. But no, this product is real, from a company called [Violet]. The mir:ror, the internet-connected rabbits, and the tiny postage stamps called "ztamps" with embedded RFID chips that allow everything to be interconnected. I can see a lot of interesting uses for the ztamps. Squishing CD-ROMs or memory sticks inside presentation folders was always awkward. But these are small, flat and discrete. I don't know how many GBs of storage each ztamp holds, but they look cool, don't they?

Just another example of becoming a smarter planet!

◎**technorati tags**: IBM, Jack Mason, Adam Christensen, Apple, Macbook Wheel, Onion News Network, RFID, Violet

In the game of Golf, when your drive off the tee is just awful, you can call a "Mulligan", a do-over of sorts, for a second chance to hit another ball. The NEDC did not do well with customer focus groups, so IBM renamed it Dynamic Infrastructure.

2009 Feb 09 — IBM Launches Dynamic Infrastructure Initiative (403)

It seems like [only yesterday] I was talking about IBM's strategic initiatives for the New Enterprise Data Center, including the launch of asset and service management at [Pulse 2008] in Orlando, Florida.

This week, my colleagues are at [Pulse 2009] in Las Vegas, Nevada. (I'm not there this time, so stop asking all my colleagues where I am!) Obviously, a lot has change in the last 12 months: the world's financial economy has collapsed, our delicate environment continues to unravel, and a new US President was elected to fix all that was broken by the former occupant. As a result, IBM's strategy has evolved beyond just data centers for large enterprises.

Dynamic Infrastructure

I can't think of a better time to emphasize the need for a more dynamic infrastructure. And this is not just focused on IT operations, but smarter *business* infrastructure as well, as the two now are very much intertwined. Everything from smarter healthcare, smarter telecom, smarter retail, smarter distribution, smarter transportation, and smarter financial services. IBM's [Dynamic Infrastructure] is one of four strategic initiatives to help build a smarter planet.

Let's take a quick look at the key benefits:

Improve Service

Do you remember back to the days that the IT department was like the accounting department in the back office, merely recording what happened in a series of transactions? Not anymore! Today, IT is front and center of most businesses, helping to generate revenue, drive innovation, and provide better customer service. We are finding a convergence between the physical world of running business with the digital world of IT. Intelligence is everywhere, embedded in systems and operations throughout, not just in a data center.

Reduce Costs

Imagine only 10-15 years ago the primary concern for IT operations was the cost of hardware. Now, thanks to [Moore's law], hardware is cheaper, but other IT budget costs like labor, management software, power and cooling costs are growing faster and becoming more predominant factors. IBM recognizes that you must consider the total cost of ownership, not just the acquisition cost of new hardware. But again, this isn't just reducing the costs of IT, but making more effective use of IT resources to reduce costs everywhere else, in scheduling transportation, in managing manufacturing assets, and so on.

Manage Risks

While the world feels much safer now that Barack Obama has taken over, there are still risks and threats out there, and businesses large and small have to manage them. Economic swings like we have experienced lately help weed out those companies that had fixed costs and static infrastructures, in favor of those with more variable costs and dynamic infrastructures. When the marketplace slows down, can your business "dial down" its operations to match? And when the recession is over and business is booming again, can your business "ramp up" fast enough to take on new opportunity? With IBM's Cloud Computing, companies can minimize their fixed investments and use a variable amount of computing as business needs change dynamically.

To learn more about Dynamic Infrastructure, read the IBM [Press Release].

⊙**technorati tags**: IBM, NEDC, Pulse 2009, Dynamic Infrastructure, strategy, strategic initiative, improve service, reduce costs, manage risks, Barack Obama

2009 Feb 10 -- Dynamic Infrastructure - Disk Announcements 1Q09 (404)

Well, it's Tuesday, so that means IBM announcements!

We had so much announced, that I will just cover the disk systems today, and deal with tape systems and software tomorrow.

IBM System Storage DS8000 series

IBM continues to invest heavily in its strategic [DS8000 series]. For [existing 2107 machines], IBM's new DS8000 microcode supports:

- 1 TB 7200 rpm Serial ATA (SATA) Disk Drives

  Now that IBM XIV has proven that 1TB SATA are safe for high-end tier-1 enterprise class use, we extended DS8000 support to include SATA support also. DS8000 supports RAID-6 and RAID-10 for these.

- Intelligent Write Caching

IBM Research conducts extensive investigations into improved algorithms for cache management. Intelligent Write Caching boosts performance for both temporal and spatial locality.

- Remote Pair FlashCopy®

  This allows you to FlashCopy volume A to volume B, with Volume B remotely mirrored to Volume C at a secondary location, via Metro Mirror. This allows you to have a consistent copy of your data at both locations.

For [newly ordered 242x models], you get all the features above, plus the following additional support:

- Full Disk Encryption (FDE)

  IBM was the first in the industry to deliver tape-drive encryption, so it makes sense that IBM is also the first in the industry to deliver disk-drive encryption. These are 15K rpm drives in standard 146GB, 300GB and 450GB capacities. As with tape, encrypting at the disk device eliminates the huge overhead from server-based encryption methods.

- Solid State Drive (SSD)

  You can also have Solid State Drives in your DS8000, in 73GB and 146GB capacities, protected by RAID-5. If you are wondering what data to put on these much-faster drives, IBM has taken the work and worry out by having intelligence in DB2 to optimize what gets placed on SSD to get the most performance improvement.

IBM System Storage XIV

Continuing the incredible marketplace excitement over its Cloud-Optimized Storage [XIV series], IBM now has announced [new capacity options]. The IBM XIV R2 that we announced last August 2008 was a fixed 15 module configuration. In the new configurations, you can start with as little as six modules, representing a 40% partial rack of the original full model. Here is a table that shows the details:

Total Modules	6	9	10	11	12	13	14	15
Useable Capacity (TB)	27	43	50	54	61	66	73	79
Interface Modules	3	6	6	6	6	6	6	6
Data Modules	3	3	4	5	6	7	8	9
Disk Drives	72	108	120	132	144	156	168	180
Fibre Channel Ports	8	16	16	20	20	24	24	24
iSCSI Ports	0	4	4	6	6	6	6	6
Cache Memory (GB)	48	72	80	88	96	104	112	120

IBM System Storage N series

And last, but not least, we have two new models in IBM's [N6000 series]. The [N6060] has model A12 (single controller) and model A22 (dual controller). These are disk-less controllers that you can configure in either *appliance* mode or *gateway* mode. In appliance mode, you can attach disk drawers such as the EXN1000, EXN2000 or EXN4000. In gateway mode, you attach external disk systems, such as the IBM DS8000 or XIV above.

Also, IBM introduces the new [2101 model N42 rack], which has the following features:

- It's *ruggedized* to handle earthquakes. IBM brings a feature that we've had for a while on other disk systems to the N series with a collection of bolts and anchors to secure the rack from physical tremors.
- It's *instrumented* for IBM Active Energy Manager, a component of IBM Systems Director. New iPDUs are designed to help measure and monitor energy management components. As companies get more concerned about the fate of the planet, monitoring energy consumption can help reduce carbon footprint.

I'll cover the rest of the announcements tomorrow!

⚲technorati tags: IBM, DS8000, SATA, SSD, Encryption, SATA, RAID-5, RAID-6, RAID-10, FlashCopy, FDE, COS, XIV, N6060, EXN1000, EXN2000, EXN4000, N42, earthquakes, ruggedized, instrumented, iPDU, carbon footprint

Comment from Barry Burke (EMC), the Storage Anarchist

Clarifying questions:

1) The DS8K can only FDE on new systems, using the specific drives mentioned, and the entire array must be encrypted - all or nothing - correct?

   a) Can you later choose to un-encrypt the entire array?

   b) Is the encryption one key per system, one key per drive, or multiple keys per drive?

   c) Can you re-key the drives non-disruptively?

2) The DS8K cannot encrypt either Flash or SATA drives, under any configuration – correct?

3) The minimum purchase of Flash drives for the DS8K is 16, of which 14 are usable (RAID 5 protection required), and 2 are hot spares - correct?

4) You do not support RAID 5 on SATA drives in the DS8K - correct?

Thanks...

Response from Tony Pearson (IBM)

Hi BarryB, happy new year!

Here are the answers to your questions. Most of this is in the announcement letters, but for the benefit of everyone who may not pick up on some of the subtleties, I will spell it out.

1) The DS8K can only FDE on new systems, using the specific drives mentioned, and the entire array must be encrypted - all or nothing - correct?

Correct, for now. From the press release:

"The Full Disk Encryption support feature is available only as plant order. Plant configured encryption supporting systems will be allowed to increase the number of drive sets installed at the installed location. Intermixing of drives is not supported, thus the entire subsystem is either encrypted drives (#5xxx features) or intermixed devices of Fibre Channel, SATA, and SSD devices (#2xxx and #6xxx features)."

a) Can you later choose to un-encrypt the entire array?

Yes, IBM offers this as a simple means to securely erase all the data for decommissioning the array. (Normally, clients hire someone to erase all the data securely, to protect sensitive information for compliance reasons, for example, and now they can do it themselves to save money)

b) Is the encryption one key per system, one key per drive, or multiple keys per drive?

Not exactly. One key per "Storage Facility Image". If you have a DS8100 or DS8300 in non-LPAR mode, then this is the same as one key per system. If you split your DS8300 into separate LPARs, then each LPAR can have its own key.

   c) Can you re-key the drives non-disruptively?

Currently, no, the FDE drives do not yet support that.

   2) The DS8K cannot encrypt either Flash or SATA drives, under any configuration - correct?

The encryption is done at the HDD level, not in the array itself. However, you can continue to encrypt data using the application or operating system as you have today, onto data that is stored on Flash SSD or SATA disks. If sometime in the future Flash SSD or SATA drives are manufactured with FDE capability, then IBM can offer this as well, but currently FDE drives currently only come in 15K rpm drive speeds.

   3) The minimum purchase of Flash drives for the DS8K is 16, of which 14 are usable (RAID 5 protection required), and 2 are hot spares - correct?

Two hot spares are required per storage facility instance, not per drive set, so the first drive set will have two RAID-5 ranks of 6+P+S and the rest of the drive sets can be 7+P. Only RAID-5 is supported for now at this time under standard terms and conditions. Clients can submit an RPQ if they want RAID-6 or RAID-10 support.

   4) You do not support RAID 5 on SATA drives in the DS8K - correct?

Some industry experts consider RAID-5 on large SATA drives to be the equivalent of "professional malpractice" because it takes a long time to rebuild from an HDD failure and there is risk during those hours that a second drive might fail, resulting in tape recovery. Based on these concerns, IBM decided not to support this at this time under standard terms and conditions for the DS8000. However, if clients are willing to accept the risks, perhaps the data is temporary or easily re-creatable, they can submit an RPQ requesting RAID-5 support on their DS8000 SATA drives. IBM also offers plenty of other disk arrays that support RAID-5 SATA, including our DS4000 and DS5000 series, where mainframe attachment is not required.

Hope that answers everything, Barry!

2009 Feb 10 — Dynamic Infrastructure - 1Q09 Tape and Software Announcements (405)

Continuing my two-part series on this week's announcements, I present IBM's latest for tape and storage software.

IBM TS7650 and TS7650G ProtecTIER deduplication

In addition to the [TS7650G gateway model] new [Enterprise Edition V2 software], IBM announced four new [TS7650 appliance models] for a complete, integrated solution. The four configurations include the controller and disk:

- 7TB, single controller
- 18TB, single controller
- 36TB, single controller
- 36TB, dual controller in clustered configuration

These disk capacities can have up to 25x times their effective capacity with IBM's HyperFactor in-line deduplication capability. So the smallest 7TB model could be as effective as 175TB of traditional disk storage.

IBM Tivoli Storage Manager (TSM) v6

After years and years in development, IBM announces [TSM v6]. Here's a quick summary of the key features:

- DB2 instead of an internal database

  For years, people have complained that IBM used its own internal relational database. This was because when TSM was first launched back in 1993, the DB2 did not have all the features on all of the various server platforms that TSM needed. Today, DB2is the leading relational database on all the key platforms that TSM server runs on, and therefore good enough for use within Tivoli Storage Manager. If you don't already have DB2, it is included for use with TSM v6.1 at no additional charge. Do you have to become a DB2 expert to use TSM? No! The TSM administration commands have been updated to hide all the complexity of DB2 away, behind the scenes. You now just use TSM commands to administer the database, as you did before. IBM will provide conversion utilities to help existing TSM customers migrate to this new database environment.

- Better Operational Reporting

  Another big complaint was that TSM had fixed reporting, and administrators that wanted customized reports often had to resort to purchasing third party products. With the change over to DB2, TSM now enables you to create your own reports using Eclipse's Business Intelligence and Reporting Tools [BIRT]! If you haven't used BIRT, you can download a free open source copy and start playing around with its capabilities. This is combined with a revamped GUI that provides a customizable dashboard using IBM's Integrated Solutions Console (ISC) infrastructure.

- Software-based Deduplication

Lastly, IBM has incorporated deduplication capability within the TSM v6.1 software for its own disk storage pools. This is done in a post-process manner so as to dedupe all of your legacy backup data as well, not just the new stuff, without impacting the current TSM server performance.

At this point, you might be thinking "Wait, what about IBM TS7650 ProtecTIER deduplication?" which is really two questions.

1. **Can I use TSM v6.1 with IBM TS7650 ProtecTIER?**

   Yes, however since TSM *progressive incremental* method is vastly more efficient than other backup products like Veritas NetBackup or EMC Legato NetWorker, the TS7650 may only get 10x reduction of TSM backups, versus up to 25x with full-backups-every-night backup schemes. TSM only dedupes its disk storage pools, so it won't dedupe data directed at tape systems like the TS7650 or other tape libraries. This avoids the "double dedupe" concern.

2. **When should I use TSM's software version versus TS7650's hardware deduplication?**

   This is a positioning question. For now, the cut-over point is about 10TB per night backup processing. If you backup more than 10TB per night, TS7650 hardware may be the better approach. If you are a smaller customer nowhere near that volume of data, then using TSM v6.1 software deduplication may be a more cost-effective solution. If you start small, and grow beyond 10TB per night, it is easy to bring in a TS7650 into an existing TSM environment and migrate the data over.

- Sub-capacity Licensing

If you run TSM server on a logical partition (LPAR) or virtual guest OS under VMware ESX, Xen or Microsoft's Hyper-V environment, why should you have to license it for the whole box? With TSM v6.1, you now can pay for only the amount of processors you use, down to a single core even. If you currently run TSM v5 on z/OS, you can migrate over to TSM v6.1 server for Linux on System z to take advantage of cost savings using IFL engines.

IBM Tivoli Key Lifecycle Manager (TKLM) v1.0

Don't let the "v1.0" scare you, this is the successor to IBM's Encryption Key Manager (EKM) that has thousands of clients using today with IBM encrypting tape drives. The new TKLM adds support for full disk encryption (FDE) drives--like those for the DS8000 I mentioned in [yesterday's post]--as well as new features to support key rotation for compliance and business controls.

IBM Tivoli Storage Productivity Center

Last, but not least, we have IBM Tivoli Storage Productivity Center [TSPC]. No, that is not a typo. IBM is renaming IBM TotalStorage Productivity Center to Tivoli Storage Productivity Center to avoid trademark conflicts with the [Professional Golfers' Association].

This is not just renaming existing product. Here some key improvements:

- TSPC brings back together Productivity Center Standard Edition (Disk, Tape, SAN and Data) with Productivity Center for Replication, which were separate at birth a few years ago.
- TSPC adds support for IBM's Storage Enterprise Resource Planner [SERP] from the NovusCG acquisition.
- End-to-end view for EMC storage devices connected to supported servers via EMC PowerPath multipathing driver. As customers switch away from EMC Control Center over to IBM's Productivity Center, IBM can continue to provide support for existing EMC gear.

Of course, IBM will still offer IBM System Storage Productivity Center [SSPC] which is a piece of hardware pre-installed with Productivity Center software.

Hopefully, you can now see why I had to split up all these announcements into separate posts across multiple days!

⊘**technorati tags**: IBM, TS7650, TS7650G, gateway, appliance, ProtecTIER, HyperFactor, TSM, DB2, BIRT, deduplication, Veritas, NetBackup, EMC,

Legato Networker, LPAR, VMware, Xen, Hyper-V, z/OS, Linux, TKLM, TSPC, SSPC, Productivity Center

FUD refers to the "Fear, Uncertainty and Doubt" that aggressive salespeople at established companies use to dissuade customers against competitive solutions. The acronym was coined by ex-IBMer Gene Amdahl in 1975 to refer to statements like, "Nobody ever got fired buying IBM equipment." Today, FUD is used to refer to any fact, rumor or misinformation used as a competitive weapon.

2009 Feb 12 — Frankenstein - The icon of FUD (406)

Fellow blogger Chuck Hollis from EMC has a post titled [Whither Frankenstorage] causing quite a stir in the [*Stor-o-Sphere*]. He is not the first EMC blogger to use this phrase, I credit [BarryB] for coining the term back in September 2008. Frankenstein serves as the ideal icon for EMC's FUD machine. In the novel, Dr. Frankenstein was attempting to do something nobody else had ever attempted, to create human life from various dead body parts, a process full of uncertainty and doubt, with frightful results.

Perhaps it was a coincidence that I discussed IBM's storage strategy in my post [Foundations and Flavorings] on January 28, shortly followed by NetApp's announcing V-series gateway [support of Texas Memory Systems' RamSan-500] on February 3. These two events might have been the trigger that pushed ChuckH over the edge to put ~~pen to paper~~... finger to keyboard.

Flinging FUD in all directions was ChuckH's not-so-subtle way to remind the world that EMC is the only major storage vendor to not offer a successful storage virtualization product. Without first-hand experience with well-designed storage virtualization, ChuckH conjectures that a configuration matching intelligent front-ends to reliable back-ends *might* be more expensive, *might* be more difficult to manage, or *might* be harder to support.

> (**Note:** Rest assured, IBM can demonstrate that a modular approach, combining intelligent front-ends to reliable back-ends can help reduce costs, be easier to manage, and be fully supported. Contact your local IBM Business Partner or storage sales rep for details.)

The reaction was not as much a *blogfight* and more of a [dog pile]. Defending NetApp were [Alex McDonald], [Kostadis Roussos], and [Stephen Foskett, Pack Rat]. On the HDS front, we have [Tony Asaro]. My fellow blogger from IBM took his swing with [How Quickly We Forget]. And finally, pointing out EMC's hypocrisy, overall, was [James Or] from Storage Monkeys.

My favorite was from Nigel Poulton's post on [Ruptured Monkey]. Here's an excerpt:

> "In fact, I'm fairly certain that EMC don't back away from customers who run HP or IBM servers and say, 'Sorry we can't help you here, an end to end HP or IBM solution would be much better for you when it comes to troubleshooting…' Putting our storage in would only add extra layers of complexity and make things messy."

On most other days, ChuckH has well-written, insightful blog posts that show that EMC brings some value to the industry. I could have made a snarky reference to [Dr Jekyll and Mr. Hyde], or indicate this post proves that nobody at EMC is editing or reviewing Chuck's thoughts before they get posted. But it's too late, Chuck already got the message, and added the following to bring the discussion back to civility:

> "When considering the broad range of storage media service levels available today (flash, FC, SATA, spin-down, etc.) what's the best way to offer these media choices in an array? Is the answer (a) combine smaller arrays from different vendors together behind a virtualization head, or (b) invest the time and effort to build arrays that can directly support all of these media types?

> Would anyone like to try a cogent response to the question posed, please?"

To address ChuckH's question, Nigel's post gave me the idea to use today's 200th year celebration of [Charles Darwin].

Over millions of years, Charles Darwin argued, evolution results in change in the inherited traits of a population of organisms from one generation to the next. A key component of this is a biological process called [mitosis] that allows a single cell to split and become two cells. In some cases, these individual daughter cells can then specialize to specific functions, such as nerve cells, muscle cells or bone cells. Over time, adaptations that work well carry forward, and those that don't get left behind.

I find it interesting that before [On the Origin of Species] was published in 1859, works of fiction like Mary Shelley's [Frankenstein] had monsters being "created", and afterward, monsters were the result of mutation or selective adaptation.

Nigel compares EMC's monolithic approach to placing an intelligent front-end with a reliable back-end as, "One man band, where one guy is trying playing all the instruments himself," versus the "Philharmonic Orchestra". I would take it one step further, comparing single-cell organisms to multi-cell life forms.

Innovative companies like Google and Amazon can't wait for a completely integrated solution from a major IT vendor to meet their needs. Why should they? There are open standards, and ways to interconnect the best intelligence into a [dynamic infrastructure]. You don't need to wait another million years to see which way the IT marketplace considers the better approach. Just look at the last 60 years. Back then, computer systems were all integrated, server, storage, and the wires that connected them were all inside a huge container. Then, mitosis happened, and IBM created external tape storage in 1952, and external disk storage in 1956. Open standards for interfaces allowed third party manufacturers like HDS, StorageTek and EMC to offer plug-compatible storage devices.

On the server side, it didn't take long for functionality in mainframes to split off. Mitosis happened again, with front-end UNIX systems processing incoming data, and mainframes handling the back-end data bases and printing. The client-server era replaced dumb terminals with more intelligent desktops and workstations, and these could handle the front-end processing to display information, with the back-end storage and number-crunching being handled by the UNIX and mainframe systems they connected to. Connections between desktops and servers, and from servers to storage, have also evolved. From thousands of direct-attach cables to networks of switches and directors.

Charles Darwin was particularly interested in cases where evolution happened faster or slower than in other cases. While IBM and Microsoft encouraged third-party innovations on the PC side, Apple resisted mitosis, trying to keep its machines pure single-cell, integrated solutions. For the same reasons that you can't fight the laws of nature, Apple ended up having to support I/O ports to external devices. Thanks to open standards like USB and FireWire, you can connect third-party storage to Apple computers. My little Mac Mini at home has more devices hanging off it than any of my Windows or Linux boxes! And Apple's iPod is successful because its iTunes software runs on both Windows and Mac OS operating systems.

Every time mitosis happens in the IT industry, it opens up opportunities to specialize, to innovate, to adapt to a dynamically changing world. When mitosis is suppressed, you get limiting products and frustrated engineers leaving to form their own start-up companies. But when mitosis is encouraged, you get successful products, solutions and partnerships positioned for a smarter planet.

Happy Valentine's Day, Chuck!

🗩**technorati tags**: EMC, Chuck Hollis, frankenstorage, Frankenstein, FUD, IBM, NetApp, TMS, V-series, RamSan-500, storage virtualization, FC, SATA, Charles Darwin, HDS, StorageTek, Microsoft, Apple, UNIX, Linux, Windows, iPod, iTunes, mitosis, Invista, EDL, NX4, Centera, Valentine's Day, dynamic infrastructure, smarter planet

Comment from Barry Burke (EMC), the Storage Anarchist

Geez, Tony - did you feel slighted because Chuck didn't include you in his Valentine's list, or something?

Or did you actually miss his comment where he acknowledged that maybe he had been a bit myopic, and backed down. You've already won - no need to pig-pile on the topic a week later...

> (And yes, I cut him some slack for stealing my word - plagiary is the sincerest form of flattery, you know :)

Or perhaps you and the new management team of IBM storage still haven't gotten over the fact you lost your soup-to-nuts vertically-integrated proprietary vendor lock-in on servers and storage back in the 1980s to a little upstart company with mainframe compatible storage offered at a fraction of your previously sole-source offerings. A company who then went on to earn and maintain #1 market share in almost every storage market segment they engage in - even to this day.

I guess the bitterness is understandable.

Why else would IBM be today trying to reverse the server/storage mitosis with repeated rounds of server storage lock-in tactics like DB2 integration with DS8K flash drives (or EAVs and HyperPAVs for that matter)?

I mean seriously, is that really in the best interests of our customers?

I think not.

Here's an idea - how about you get IBM to immediately publish the DB2/Flash interface specs so that anybody's storage can participate in that little piece of proprietary vendor lock-in? You know, level the playing field, open competition, let the products compete on their merits rather than restricting competition, and all that...

I should think that many of your server and DB2 customers would prefer to get those same benefits from Flash without having to switch storage vendors... Don't you agree?

Comment from Ruptured Monkey

Actually, I think it's a good thing that you posted this despite Chuck clearly already having lost the argument...

How often to do we see the press (usually the gutter press - any comparisons with the EMC blog machine purely coincidental) make front page articles dragging somebody or something through the mud, only to issue a tiny apology in microscopic print on page 23 where nobody sees it? Quite clever of them actually.

I think it's good to put this on your front page, Barry. Well done.

And TSA (the Storage Anarchist), this is not a cheap attempt at mutual back slapping between myself and Tony.

Response from Tony Pearson (IBM)

Hi BarryB, As you know, some of my posts take several days to research and write. I had actually started this post the week before ChuckH had made his update, and then spent a few days figuring out how to answer his new question, which is why I then posted cogent response to address that instead.

I guess it is fair for EMC to ask IBM for help to make its DMX as good as IBM's DS8000. IBM DS8000 is the recognized leader for mainframe attachment disk arrays.

Synergy is one area that the IT supermarkets (IBM, Sun, HP and Dell) offers added value over the storage specialty shops. That IBM and HP, both IT supermarkets, hold the #1 and #2 market share for storage solutions overall should not surprise anyone.

Offering great products that work well together is not "fighting mitosis" but embracing the benefits of having exerts in each area collaborating to make the world a better place. No, an example of "fighting mitosis" would be to keep the AS/400 with internal disk. Instead, IBM now has POWER systems that run the new "IBM i" operating system that allows for standard external disk attachment such as IBM DS4000 disk via open standard Fibre Channel interfaces.

Of course, IBM would be happy to help any mainframe customer migrate from DMX to IBM DS8000 to improve their performance.
-- Tony

Comment from Barry Burke (EMC), the Storage Anarchist

So, are you saying that IBM is NOT willing to share information that would allow DB2 to take better advantage of flash drives on non-IBM storage platforms?

Response from Tony Pearson (IBM)

BarryB, Not at all. Perhaps you have been out of development too long. Here's the process.

Step 1. IBM spends months and millions of dollars in research to come up with something truly exciting.

Step 2. Third party company requests to license the technology to help their products be as good as IBM's products. In the past, EMC has licensed a variety of IBM's technologies, for example FlashCopy.

Step 3. IBM and third party bring their patent and Intellectual Property lawyers to work out a suitable agreement and license fee.

Step 4. Third party either decides to pay the millions of dollars to compensate IBM's investment, or decides not to.

Step 5. Even if third party decides to license the interface, their engineers have to update their product to actually make use of it. This includes any hardware, software or microcode changes to implement the interface. Sometimes this can take quite a while. Other times, third party licenses the technology, but then decides not to actually implement the function.

The process can also work in the other direction, where IBM requests to license interface from a third party. However, with IBM having the most US Patents now 15 years in a row, the general direction is the one listed above.

IBM Blogging Guidelines prevent me from disclosing the status of any such negotiations, so you may want to contact your local EMC Legal rep to find out which stage, if any, EMC is in. Whether they tell you or not is purely on a need-to-know basis.

Clients can either hope and wait for EMC to go through the above steps, or switch over to IBM. For those that aren't willing to wait 18-24 months to make great use out of expensive SSD Flash disks, IBM will be happy to help them migrate over to IBM DS8000.

Comment from Barry Burke (EMC), the Storage Anarchist

Gee, somewhere along the line it seems that the intent of those Open Standards you so proudly trumpet in your post seems to have gotten lost.

Fortunately, the REST of the industry is working to forge standard methods for storage to advertise its capabilities to hosts and applications so that they can in turn can optimize themselves to any storage platform.

It's interesting that rather than help to accelerate such standards, IBM more often than not chooses to create proprietary approaches intended to lock customers into vertically-integrated IBM solutions.

Thanks for documenting the process, though – I'm sure several audiences will find it quite revealing!

Comment from Barry Burke (EMC), the Storage Anarchist

A couple more questions, if I may:

- What's the expected GA date of the DB2 code update which supports DS8K Flash integration?

- What's the expected GA date of the DS8K code update which supports DB2 integration for Flash?

- Is this feature for the mainframe implementation of DB2 only, or for all DB2 platforms?

Thanks!

Response from Tony Pearson (IBM)

BarryB, let's take a quick look at open standards. Are you suggesting that EMC and others are participating in a standards organization that IBM is not aware about? I can't think of a single one that IBM is not actively involved with, so please enlighten me on what you are referring to.

On the database side, Oracle, Sybase and IBM DB2 all support the open SQL language standard, but each competes heavily with their own Intellectual Property (IP) to support those standards with better performance, smaller footprint, better tools and instrumentation for monitoring and reporting, etc.

On the operating system side, Solaris, AIX, and z/OS are all UNIX that meet the Open Group's standards for certification, but each has their own IP to support those standards with better performance, etc.

On the disk side, HDS USP-V, EMC DMX and IBM DS8000 all support open ESCON and FICON interfaces that allow interoperability. However, each has IP to support those standards with better performance, advanced features and so on.

Even if IBM posted its IP publicly, it might still take 18-24 months for EMC or HDS to actually come out with a product that exploits the capability.

As to your question on planned availability dates. The planned date for DS8000 SSD including supporting microcode is listed in the announcement letter as April 24, 2009.

http://www-01.ibm.com/common/ssi/cgi-
bin/ssialias?subtype=ca&infotype=an&appname=iSource&supplier=89
7&letternum=ENUS109-120&open&cm_mmc=4546-_-n-_-
vrm_newsletter-_-10207_103678&cmibm_em=dm:0:16661896

Changes to optimize the support for SSD were made in z/OS v1.8
component called Media Manager. DB2 for z/OS uses Media Manager
already. Other third party software that run on z/OS have also licensed the
Media Manager interface.

DB2 for other platforms is actually a separate product on separate schedules,
and I have not yet seen any announcements related to that yet. That does not
mean they are not going to support SSD, just that do not use z/OS Media
Manager, and therefore would have to come up with an alternative method
of implementation.
-- Tony

2009 Feb 16 — Vegas in Blue and Green (407)

Jim Frey over at *NetworkWorld* has a nice summary of Pulse 2009 titled
[Vegas in Blue (& Green)]. Here's an excerpt:

> "I've just returned from the IBM Tivoli Pulse conference in Las
> Vegas, a meeting of over 4000 customers, partners, and IBM
> employees…
>
> There was a lot to digest, but three of the major themes caught my
> attention, and my imagination…
>
> First, IBM put a huge push behind their Dynamic Infrastructure
> initiative. Sounds like so many other automation and autonomic
> initiatives of the past, right? Well, things are getting better, and
> 'dynamic' is becoming more of a realistic possibility, especially
> with the emergence of cloud computing and cloud services
> models…
>
> Second, a lot of time was spent on IBM's Service Management
> Industry Solutions. When I first heard of this, my thought was that
> IBM was creating solutions for the Service Management industry
> (i.e. food services, janitorial services, hospitality services). But this
> is much larger than that-- much, much larger. IBM is taking their
> unique ability to pair business (non-IT) expertise with IT
> consulting, planning, and technology delivery, and constructing
> (careful-- here comes the 'f' word) frameworks for several vertical
> industry segments…

IBM is perhaps the only organization in the world that can take this on fully and hope to deliver a meaningful result. But beyond that, this represents a huge opportunity for IT professionals to become the transformation agents within their own organizations, contributing at a whole new level...

Lastly, I was really impressed by IBM's Smarter Planet initiative. The primary thought here was that the key to a greener planet is to take inefficiencies out of just about every form of business through the intelligent application and deployment of technology. At first I was thinking this was just another marketing initiative, but in the course of this event, listening to the keynotes and talking to a number of IBM execs, it became apparent that this is a substantial cultural shift within IBM itself. Just think about that for a moment-- when 400,000 employees all change their direction and focus, their sheer mass is going to make a noticeable difference...

Magic (Johnson) gave an excellent talk, and reminded the audience that you should do two things no matter what your job or role. First, service starts with knowing your customers not just who they are, but what they do and what is important to them. And second, always over-deliver. Go that extra step. Exceed expectations. The boost in loyalty, goodwill, and improved customer relationships will be well worth the effort. Good thoughts to keep with us."

If you missed Pulse 2009, perhaps because your company has put a clamp down on travel expenses, you are in luck! IBM is hosting the "Dynamic Infrastructure Forum" March 3-4, 2009, on your computer. This is an IBM Virtual event, no travel required! [Register Today!]

technorati tags: Jim Frey, NetworkWorld, IBM, ibmpulse, pulse2009, service management, dynamic infrastructure, smarter planet, Magic Johnson, Las Vegas

2009 Feb 16 — Enhanced DS3200 for Boot and Data storage (408)

Well, it's Tuesday again, and that means more IBM announcements!

Today, IBM announced the enhanced IBM System Storage DS3200 disk system. It is in our DS3000 series, the DS3200 is SAS-attach, DS3300 is iSCSI-attach, and DS3400 is FC-attach. All of them support up to 48 drives, which can be a mix of SAS and SATA drives.

The DS3200 supports the following operating environments (see IBM's [Interop Matrix] for details):

- Microsoft Windows
- Linux (both Linux-x86 and Linux on POWER)
- AIX
- Sun Solaris
- VMware
- Novell NetWare

With today's announcements, the DS3200 can be used to boot from, as well as contain data. This is ideal to combine with IBM BladeCenter. With the IBM BladeCenter you can have 14 blades, either x86 or POWER based processors, attached to a DS3200 via SAS switch modules in the back of the chassis.

Let's take an example of how this can be used for a Scale-out File Services [SoFS] deployment.

Servers

First, we start with servers. We can have either three [IBM System x3650] servers, but this would use up all six of the direct-attach ports. Instead, we'll choose the [BladeCenter H chassis], with three HS21 blades for SoFS, and that leaves us with eleven empty blade slots we could put in a management node, or other blades to run applications.

SAS connectivity modules

The IBM BladeCenter [SAS Connectivity Module] allows the blade servers to connect to a DS3200. Two of them fit right in the back of the BladeCenter chassis, providing full redundancy without consuming additional rack space.

DS3200 and EXP3000 expansion drawers

We'll have one DS3200 controller with twelve internal drives, and three expansion EXP3000 drawers with twelve drives each, for a total of 48 drives. Using 1TB SATA, this would be 48 TB raw capacity.

The end result? You get a 48TB NAS scalable storage solution, supporting up to 7500 concurrent CIFS and NFS users, with up to 700 MB/sec with large block transfers. By using BladeCenter, you can expand performance by adding more blades to the Chassis, or have some blades running SAP or Oracle RAC have direct read/write access to the SoFS data.

Just another example on how IBM can bring together all the components of a solution to provide customer value!

◌**technorati tags**: IBM, DS3200, BladeCenter, Linux, AIX, Windows, Solaris, VMware, NetWare, POWER, SAS, EXP3000, SATA, CIFS, NFS, SoFS

Comment from Brad

So if an AS/400 (System I) customer wants to use 10 GBE and our LaserVault Backup software to backup to an IBM storage server at 400 MB/second and up, should they be looking at IBM System Storage DS3200, or the IBM XIV?

Response from Tony Pearson (IBM)

Brad, The DS3200 is supported on IBM i operating system, but the XIV does not yet support this, so I recommend going with the supported one. You will need multiple backup threads, as each SAS cable handles only 300 MB/sec.

With the IBM i operating system (new name for i5/OS), you can use the DS3200 via SAS, or DS3400 via FCP. The DS3300 that offers iSCSI attachment is not yet supported on IBM i operating system. See the DS3000 Interoperability Matrix for details:

> http://www-03.ibm.com/systems/resources/
> systems_storage_disk_ds3000_pdf_interop.pdf

For XIV interoperability matrix, check here:

> http://www-03.ibm.com/systems/support/storage/config/ssic/
> displayesssearchwithoutjs.wss?start_over=yes

Thanks,
Tony

Comment from Dangel

Hi! Tony,

Based on your post I can have 3 x3650 booting from the DS3200 but the Interop Matrix indicates otherwise "Boot from DS3200 is supported when attached to BladeCenter SAS switch, not for direct attached DS3200".

Kindly confirm if this setup is possible and if so what the requirements are (HBA, BIOS/firmware upgrade...).

Also since there are 6 ports on the DS3200 (dual controller with 2-port daughter cards), can it accommodate 6 x3650 M2?

Thanks!

Response from Tony Pearson (IBM)

Hi Dangel, Thanks for the questions. The Boot-from-SAS capability currently is only supported for blade servers through the BladeCenter SAS switch, not for rack-optimized servers through direct SAS attachment. Despite having six ports, the maximum supported for direct-attach is only three x3650 M2.
-- Tony

Comment from Drew

Is this supported while running the SAS Raid controller modules in a BladeCenter "S" model.

Response from Tony Pearson (IBM)

Drew, Sorry, but it is not supported for the SAS RAID controller on BladeCenter S chassis. I wish this were just a testing issue, but it there are more issues involved, so no plans in 2009 to address this. Sorry
-- Tony

 Ron Korngiebel, the Sun/STK executive mentioned in the post below, called me at my home shortly after this was posted. We had a lovely chat. I thought he was going to ask for a retraction or re-write, but instead he just asked for me to correct the spelling of his name. He had a great sense of humor and seemed like a nice guy on the phone.

2009 Feb 18 — Jon Peake awarded Project Bulldog jacket (409)

 With mixed emotions, Jon Peake announced he will retire from IBM next week. Jon is known as the father of IBM Virtual Tape Server (VTS), the industry's first virtual tape system, announced in 1996and generally available in 1997. One of my 19 patents was for the VTS pre-migration capability, and as lead architect for DFSMS, I worked closely with Jon and his tape systems team to ensure its success.

From left to right:

- Chris Telford, IBM Development manager for Enterprise Tape Integration
- Jon Peake, IBM Distinguished Engineer and Master Inventor
- Annette Estelle, Jon's global admin assistant

At his retirement celebration, Jon was awarded the coveted "Project Bulldog" jacket, which has an interesting history.

In response to IBM's 1996 VTS announcement, the top StorageTek (STK) tape sales teams and most of the dedicated tape technicians were invited to a global assembly at a fancy resort in Winter Park, CO (about 90 miles west of STK's Louisville headquarters) in early 1997. The gathering was named *Project Bulldog*, after Ron Korngiebel, STK's director of competitive marketing, who I am told had voice and facial resemblance to justify the project moniker. Ron had recruited Fred Moore, Steve Blenderman, and other prized engineers as speakers. I have seen both Fred and Steve speak at various conferences such as SHARE and GUIDE, and agree they are high quality speakers.

The goal was to have STK's brightest in Louisville go down in the trenches, work the field guys into a frenzy, defend STK Tape at any cost, and send IBM packing. At the end of the two day fest, many participants received the coveted *Project Bulldog* jacket.

Former STKers who now work at IBM can remember this meeting involved:

- Bashing of the [IBM Seascape] architecture approach. The use of commodity servers and components to build storage systems continues today in the IBM System Storage DS8000, SAN Volume Controller, XIV, and TS7650 Deduplication solutions.

- Explanations how and why IBM's VTS would never work, and how only STK virtual tape would make it in the market. Today, IBM is the leader in storage virtualization, both for disk and tape.

- Mock interview videos with claims that IBM could never figure out how to attach IBM drives to the STK Silo. I was a big proponent of this, having visited customers who specifically asked for IBM to sell its better, faster IBM drives into their existing STK silos. At first, upper management was hesitant to do this, but the IBM engineers worked out what changes were needed, and today many STK tape automation libraries run with IBM tape drives.

While some analysts frowned on Sun's [2005 acquisition of StorageTek], IBM was delighted, given Sun's previous track record in storage company acquisitions. I joke that we are still picking up confetti in the hallways of IBM's Tucson lab. I was in New York City when I heard Sun's announcement, and it didn't take long for STK employees offering me their resumes. Since then, many STK engineers, technicians and sales team have left Sun, many coming over to IBM. Back then, there were many intelligent and talented people working for StorageTek, and IBM is glad to have hired them.

With the resurgence of interest in tape systems, from dealing with new legislation for long term retention of electronic data to a focus on energy efficiency, Jon leaves much like a champion retiring at the top of his game.

Jon, I am going to miss you! Enjoy your retirement!

⌖**technorati tags**: IBM, Tucson, Jon Peake, VTS, DFSMS, StorageTek, Project Bulldog, Sun, virtual tape, tape systems

2009 Feb 19 — Dynamic Infrastructure and Pulse 2009 videos (410)

Wrapping up this week's theme on IBM's Dynamic Infrastructure® strategic initiative, we have a few more goodies in the goody bag.

First item: Dave Bricker shows off the XIV cloud-optimized storage at Pulse 2009

Second item: Rodney Dukes discusses the latest features of the DS8000 disk system at Pulse 2009

Third item: IBM launches the [Dynamic Infrastructure Journal]. You can read the February 2009 edition online, and if you find it useful and interesting, subscribe to learn from IBM's transformation experts how to reduce cost, manage risk and improve service.

Whether or not you attended the IBM Pulse 2009 conference, you might enjoy looking at the rest of the series of videos on [YouTube] and photographs on [Flickr].

⌖**technorati tags**: IBM, Dynamic Infrastructure, Dave Bricker, XIV, COS, DS8000, disk system, Rodney Dukes, Journal, ibmpulse, Pulse2009, YouTube, Flickr

When the client told me she was from Flin Flon, I asked her to spell that because I could not understand what she said. She told me that it was spelled like the "Flip Flop" sandal, but spelled with N instead of P. My readers have told me they like that I break up the monotony of technical discussion with light-hearted posts like this one.

2009 Feb 25 — The Kingpin of Flin Flon (411)

While the rest of Americans were glued to their televisions watching President Obama explain his plan for recovery, my colleagues and I had dinner with clients from Canada.

One in particular claimed her father was known as the kingpin of [Flin Flon]. She lives in Ontario now, but she grew up in this small mining town in Manitoba made famous for winning a government contract to grow crops for *medicinal purposes*.

Shown at left is the town's mascot, Flinty. Yes, apparently the town was named after a fictional character of a paperback novel.

Of course, in conversations with clients, it is best to avoid topics like politics or drugs, but the intersection of government health care and implications on IT can't be disregarded. Since Canada has a more efficient healthcare process, the government enjoys a lower cost per citizen. President Obama has suggested that the United States should adopt reforms to make the American system more efficient, including electronic medical records.

Not surprisingly, [smarter healthcare] is part of IBM's latest set of strategic initiatives. Digitizing medical information has a variety of benefits:

- **Information isn't stranded on islands**

    If there is any situation that needs to deliver the right information, to the right people, at the right time, healthcare is certainly one of them. Having the right information can help reduce medical mistakes.

- **Physicians spend time with their patients, not paperwork**

I personally know some doctors here in Tucson, and they are the first to admit that they would prefer to focus on their core strengths, which they spent many years in medical school, and leave the administrative details to someone else. Focusing on core strengths is a common theme for successful businesses, and this is no different.

- **Expertise needs no passport**

  Medical emergencies do not always happen near the hospital or clinic that your medical records are stored at. An exciting feature of digital information is that it is easy to transport to where it is needed, unlike paper records or X-ray film.

To learn more about IBM's strategy and vision, see IBM's [Smarter Planet] website.

⦿**technorati tags**: IBM, Barack Obama, smarter planet, smarter healthcare, Flin Flon, Canada, electronic medical records

Response from Tony Pearson (IBM)

IBM blogger Adam Christensen also mentions Smarter Healthcare here:

> http://www.asmarterplanet.com/blog/2009/02/smarter-healthcare---the-most-personal-issue-of-all.html

-- Tony

 Here is another one of my famous "mailbag" posts. Of course, I asked permission to use his name, and he agreed to let me publish his questions, and my responses, publicly on my blog.

2009 Feb 25 — Three Answers for Gowri Ananthan (412)

An avid reader of this blog pointed me to a blog post [A Small Tec DIGG on IBM XIV], by Gowri Ananthan, a System Engineer in Singapore. Basically, she covers past ~~battles~~ er... discussions between me and fellow blogger BarryB from EMC, and [blegs] for answers to three questions.

Gowri, here are your answers:

Q1. Does IBM offer a Pay-as-you-Go [PAYGO] upgrade path for its IBM XIV disk storage system?

The concern was expressed as:

"PAYGO also requires the customer to purchase the remaining capacity within 12 months of installation. So it is more of a 12-month installment plan than pay-as-you-grow."

A1. Actually, IBM offers several methods for your convenience:

- With IBM's Capacity on Demand (CoD) plan, you get the full frame with 15 modules installed on your data center floor, but only pay for the first four modules 21 TB, then pay for 5.3TB module increments as you need them over the next 12 months. This is ideal for companies that don't know how fast they will grow, but do not want to wait for new modules to be delivered and installed when needed.

- With IBM's Partial Rack offering, you can get a system with as little as six modules (27TB), and then over time, add more modules as you need. This does not have to be done within 12 months, you can stay at six modules for as long as you like, and you can take as long as you want to add more modules. When you are ready for more capacity, the drawer or drawers can be delivered, and installed non-disruptively.

Neither of these are "payment installment plans", but certainly if you want to spread your costs into regularly-scheduled monthly payments across multiple years, IBM Global Financing can probably work something out.

Q2. Does IBM consider the XIV as *green* storage?

The concern was expressed as:

"You are powering (8.4KW) and cooling all 180 drives for the whole duration, whether you're using the capacity or not. Is it what you called *greener* power usage…?"

A2. Yes. IBM considers the IBM XIV as *green storage*. The 8.4KW per frame is less than the 10-plus KW that a comparable 2-frame EMC DMX-950 system would consume. The energy savings in IBM XIV comes from delivering FC-like speeds using slower SATA disks that rotate slower, and therefore take less energy to spin.

In the fully-populated or *Capacity on Demand* configuration, you would spin all 180 disks. However, using the partial rack configuration, the 6-module has only 40 percent of the disks, and therefore consumes only 40 percent of the energy. If you don't plan to store at least 20-30 TB, you might consider the DS3000, DS4000, DS5000, or DS8000 disk system instead.

Q3. How do you connect more than 24 host ports to an IBM XIV?

The concern was expressed as:

> "And finally do not forget my question on 24-FC Ports...
> Up to 24 Fibre Channel ports offering 4 Gbps, 2Gbps or 1
> Gbps multi-mode and single-mode support. Stop... Stop...
> How you gonna squeeze an existing bunch of FC cables in
> 24 ports?"

A3. Best practices suggest that if you have ten or more physical servers, each with two separate FC ports, then you should use a SAN switch or director in between. If you require four ports per server, then you would need a SAN switch beyond six servers to connect to the IBM XIV. If you consider that 24 FC ports, at 4Gbps, represents nearly 10 GB/sec of bandwidth, you will recognize that this is not a performance bottleneck for the system.

Gowri, I hope this answers your questions!

⚲**technorati tags**: IBM, XIV, Gowri Ananthan, EMC, BarryB, CoD, partial rack, full rack, FC, SATA, DMX-950, green, disk system, multi-mode, single-mode, best practices

Comment from Gowri

Hi Tony,

Thanks for answering my questions. I'm happy to share with you that we finally planned to go with IBM XIV.

But I still have some concerns about my last question because if you assume that we fully populate the XIV, then there will be no space to put the additional FC switches. Need another rack to mount them, which will increase our rack foot print. BTW most of our servers will be connected to XIV.
Thanks.
- Gowri

March

Despite the great success I had at last year's Pulse conference, I was not invited to the one this month, nor to the ones in 2010 nor 2011. Perhaps this was retaliation from my fall-out with my former boss, the VP of Marketing for System Storage, that had connections with the folks from IBM Tivoli that ran this event.

Engineers have to deal with numbers that are very small and very large. In 1968, IBM sponsored a short American Documentary called "Powers of 10" written and directed by Ray and Charlie Earnes. It was selected for preservation in the United States National Film Registry by the Library of Congress as being "culturally, historically, or aesthetically significant".

2009 Mar 03 — Millions, Billions and Trillions for Healthcare (413)

People are confused over various orders of magnitude. News of the economic meltdown often blurs the distinction between millions (10^6), billions (10^9), and trillions (10^{12}). To show how different these three numbers are, consider the following:

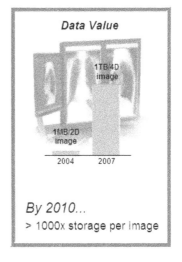

- A million seconds ago - you might have received your last paycheck (12 days)

- A billion seconds ago - you were born or just hired on your current job (31 years)

- A trillion seconds ago - cavemen were walking around in Asia (31,000 years)

That these numbers confuse the average person is no surprise, but that it confuses marketing people in the storage industry is even more hilarious. I am often correcting people who misunderstand MB (million bytes), GB (billion bytes) and TB (trillion bytes) of information. Take this graph as an example from a recent presentation.

At first, it looks reasonable, back in 2004, black-and-white 2D X-Ray images were only 1MB in size when digitized, but by 2010 there will be fancy 4D images that now take 1TB, representing a 1000x increase. What? When I pointed out this discrepancy, the person who put this chart together didn't know what to fix. Were 4D images only 1GB in size, or was it really a 1000000x increase?

If a 2D image was 1000 by 1000 pixels, each pixel was a byte of information, then a 3D image might either be 1000 by 1000 by 1000 [voxels], or 1000 by 1000 at 1000 frames per second (fps). The first being 3D volumetric space, and the latter called 2D+time in the medical field, the rest of us just say "video". 4D images are 3D+time, volumetric scans over time, so conceivably these could be quite large in size.

The key point is that advances in medical equipment result in capturing more data, which can help provide better healthcare. This would be the place I normally plug an IBM product, like the Grid Medical Archive Solution [GMAS], a blended disk and tape storage solution designed specifically for this purpose.

So, as government agencies look to spend billions of dollars to provide millions of people with proper healthcare, choosing to spend some of this money on a smarter infrastructure can result in creating thousands of jobs and save everyone a lot of money, but more importantly, save lives.

Short 2-minute [video] argues the case for Smarter Healthcare

For more on this, check out Adam Christensen's blog post on [Smarter Planet], which points to a podcast by Dr. Russ Robertson, chairman of the Counsel of Medical Education at Northwestern University's Feinberg School of Medicine, and Dan Pelino, general manager of IBM's Healthcare and Life Sciences Industry.

technorati tags: IBM, smarter healthcare, 2D+time, 3D+time, 4D, medical images, Adam Christensen, Russ Robertson, Dan Pelino

Comment from Jeff Cerny

10 Questions for the Healthcare IT Executive

Healthcare and its intrinsic need for timely, accurate information often puts the CIO in a prime position to be the champion or the goat.

Increasingly, healthcare CIOs are being made responsible for more than just managing information. They are called on to be change agents and organizational drivers that make or break the numbers.

Patrick Moroney is a CIO with a knack for being a professional change agent as well as a world-class networker, which is a winning combination by any measure.

Check out the new 10Q interview in TechRepublic for the whole story:

> http://blogs.techrepublic.com.com/10things/?p=549

(If you like this article, be sure to click on the "Worthwhile?" icon.)

Comment from Harley

What I have been wondering for many years now is: What comes after a Yottabyte?

kilobyte, megabyte, gigabyte, terabyte, petabyte, exabyte, zettabyte, yottabyte

Response from Tony Pearson (IBM)

Xonabyte, Wekabyte, Yundabyte, Udabyte, Tredabyte, Sortabyte, Rintabyte, Quexabyte, Peptabyte, Ochabyte, Nenabyte, Mingabyte, Lumabyte.

A frequent adage, when someone is asked what they want to be called, they respond with "You can call me anything, but don't call me late for dinner". I have received many nicknames throughout the years, so when I was assigned the nickname Tony *"Late-for-Dinner"* Pearson, I had a great laugh!

2009 Mar 05 — Late for Dinner, Really? (414)

 I nearly fell out of my chair laughing.

Nigel Poulton over at Ruptured Monkey suggests a variety of nick names for the various storage bloggers, in his post [Storage Blogwars and the Vendor Fight Club].

Of these, fellow blogger Marc Farley suggested for me "Tony Late for Dinner Pearson", which is fair, I guess, given that I often work late to make sure my blog posts are well written, and sometimes that means I am the last to leave the building.

Full Disclosure: I've known Marc for a while now; we have attended events together and even were co-speakers on a conference call for customers.

Perhaps more disturbing is that, for the most part, the storage blogosphere is entirely dominated by men. Where are the women bloggers for storage?

✐technorati tags: IBM, Late For Dinner, Marc Farley, Nigel Poulton, RupturedMonkey

Comment from Nigel Poulton

So Tony... What is the real reason Marc has christened you "Late for Dinner"?

Response from Tony Pearson (IBM)

Nigel, Back in April 2007, I had mentioned that I was attending the SNW 2007 in San Diego. Fellow blogger Anil Gupta from Quantum organized a "bloggers dinner" for Monday night, and I did respond that I would be there, but I got stuck in my flights in Phoenix due to sand storms. I missed the dinner, but made it in time for the reception afterwards.

Later in the week, I was able to take photo with two other storage bloggers:

http://www.ibm.com/developerworks/blogs/page/InsideSystemStorage?entry=snw_spring_2007_part_3

-- Tony

Comment from Marc Farley (3PAR)

Tony, the sole reason for the nickname is because I know you are such a hard working guy. After that, there is only subliminal stuff running around my brain. It just seemed like a fit to me.

2009 Mar 09 — IBM releases its 2008 Annual Report (415)

IBM released its [2008 Annual Report]. IBM has improved in revenues, profits and earnings per share compared to recent past years. Part of the success comes from IBM's focus on [generating higher value]. Here are some excerpts:

1. "Several years ago, we saw change coming.

Value was shifting in the IT industry, driven by the rising tide of global integration, a new computing paradigm and new client needs. These shifts meant the world was becoming not just smaller and 'flatter,' but also smarter.

2. **We remixed our businesses in order to move to the emerging higher-value spaces.**

    IBM has divested commoditizing businesses like personal computers, and strengthened its position through strategic investments and acquisitions in higher-value segments like business intelligence and analytics, virtualization and green solutions.

    From 2000 to 2008 we acquired more than 100 companies to complement and scale our portfolio of products and offerings. This has changed our business mix toward higher-value, more profitable segments of the industry.

3. **We became a globally integrated enterprise in order to capture the best growth opportunities and improve IBM's profitability.**

    IBM operates in more than 170 countries and enjoys an increasingly broad-based geographic reach. Our non-U.S. operations generated approximately 65 percent of IBM's revenue in 2008. IBM's Growth Markets unit, which was established in 2008, grew 10 percent last year, and made up 18 percent of our revenues. Revenue increased 18 percent (15 percent in local currency) in Brazil, Russia, India and China.

4. **As a result, IBM is a higher-performing enterprise today than it was a decade ago.**

    Our business model is more aligned with our clients' needs and generates better financial results.

5. **We have therefore been able to invest in future sources of growth and provide record return to investors...**

    ...while continuing to invest in R&D — more than $50 billion from 2000 to 2008.

6. **This gives us confidence that we are entering the current economic environment from a position of strength...**

    In 2008 we made progress toward our 2010 objectives by growing earnings per share 24 percent. And with this strong 2008 performance, we are clearly ahead of pace on our road map to $10–$11 of earnings per share.

7. **...and that we will emerge from it even stronger, thanks to our long-term fundamentals and our agenda for a smarter planet.**

All around the world, businesses, governments and institutions are investing to reduce costs, drive innovation and transform their infrastructure. The economic downturn has intensified this trend, as leaders seek not simply to repair what is broken, but to prepare for a 21st Century economy.

Many of their key priorities are in areas where IBM has leading solutions — such as smarter utility grids, traffic, healthcare, financial systems, telecommunications and cities. We are aggressively pursuing this transformational, global opportunity."

It is good to see that IBM continues to proceed with long-term investments during these tough times!

⟳technorati tags: IBM, annual report, smarter planet, smarter utility, smarter traffic, smarter healthcare, smarter telecom, BRIC

 IBM is a leader in Solid-State technology, and was one of the first vendors to include non-volatile storage in servers and storage devices. However, the timing could not have been worse. These Solid-State Drives (SSD) were 15 to 25 times more expensive than regular spinning disk, and the world was in the middle of a global economic meltdown.

2009 Mar 10 — IBM Announces another SSD Disk offering! (416)

Well, it's Tuesday, which means IBM makes its announcements!

This week, IBM announces that it now supports 50GB Solid State Drive (SSD) in its [IBM System Storage EXP3000] disk systems. IBM has already made announcements about SSD enablement in the DS8000 and SAN Volume Controller (SVC), but now the EXP3000 brings SSD technology down to smaller System x server deployments.

Adoption of this new exciting technology is still in the early stages, despite the fact that IBM and other vendors have been touting this technology for a while.

(For a quick blast to the past, here was my first post on the subject back from December 20, 2006: [Hybrid, Solid State and the future of RAID])

Recently, fellow blogger BarryB admitted that EMC have only sold SSD to [hundreds of their customers], and to be fair, I suspect IBM's sales of SSD in its BladeCenter servers [available since July 2007] have been in similar single-digit percentage territory as well.

The advantage of today's announcement is that you can mix and match SSD drives with SAS and SATA drives in the EXP3000. You won't have to buy the entire drawer of SSD, you can start with just a few, depending on your business needs. On the other extreme, you can have up to two drawers, with 12 SSD drives each, for a total of 24 drives directly attached to System x servers via the ServeRAID MR10M SAS/SATA controller adapter.

⊘technorati tags: IBM, System x, ServeRAID MR10M, SAS, SATA, 50GB, SSD, EMC, BladeCenter

Comment from Sandeep

 The SSD fever seems to keep rising and rightly so. I had done some crude GPFS performance testing with the SSD enabled IBM Blades against the HDD and the outcome was obvious -- higher performance. I can share the result if someone is interested. Well I had to force an hybrid storage setup for it, but I am glad that the mix-n-match is available with the new offerings. That is a smarter and more pragmatic way -- it will keep the cost under control and will enable different sizes for different people (customers) -- enable SMBs. Thanks Tony for the timely update. What most data centers (and eventually data clouds) are going to see in near future is hybrid storage -- SATA solid state drive intermixed with other conventional SATA and SAS drives. What will follow is the smart usage of the two by the application stack above it.

 Cheers,
Sandeep

Comment from Carlos Pratt (IBM)

 Tony, As always great update! I fully agree with Sandeep's remark on the hybrid storage to be viewed on the near future. Adding to his remark, let's not forget that the cost of the SSDs will go down. Maybe not dramatically but I am thinking that in the next 3 to 4 years its price will be near to the traditional spinning disks. What will happen then? Only the market can tell.

 Regards!
Carlos

Comment from Sandeep

I believe the nature of hybrid will stay for a time. Could be in next 5 years SSD may eat up HDD (like what USB flash drives have done to Floppy and little bit of CD). But then there will possibly be newer storage like "Racetrack Memory" which might make sure that storage with hybrid characteristics will continue. Now with HDD and SSD... in the future with SSD and Racetrack Memory (or similar)...

Racetrack Memory

 http://www.almaden.ibm.com/spinaps/research/sd/?racetrack

Laters,
Sandeep

Response from Tony Pearson (IBM)

Sandeep, can you please share the results? I am very interested but can't find a way to contact you directly.

Thanks!

2009 Mar 19 — IBM Presents April 2009 at upcoming SNW in Orlando (417)

If you are looking for a reason to travel to Florida next month, IBM will be presenting at the [Storage Networking World conference], April 6-9, 2009 in Orlando. This conference is organized by ComputerWorld and the Storage Networking Industry Association [SNIA]. IBM is a platinum sponsor for this event, and will have various executives presenting IBM's leadership in storage:

- Barry Rudolph, VP, Strategy and Stack Integration, Storage Platform
- Kelly Beavers, Director, IBM Storage Software
- Clod Barrera, Distinguished Engineer & Chief Technical Strategist, Storage Platform

IBM will be demonstrating solutions throughout the conference, including eight SNIA tutorial and breakout speaking sessions, a panel discussion, two new Summits (Cloud Computing, and Solid-State Storage), and four Hands-on-Labs:

- Virtualization
- Data Deduplication
- Storage Management
- Storage Security

Plus, IBM will have a huge 10 foot by 20 foot booth located in the Expo hall and a kiosk in the Platinum Galleria. The demonstrations highlighted in the IBM booth will showcase Information Infrastructure solutions, which will help simplify, reduce risk, increase efficiency and lower costs. I won't be there myself, but you can ask my IBM colleagues about:

- The Next Generation of Storage: IBM XIV Storage System
- Storage Virtualization with SAN Volume Controller (SVC)
- Infrastructure Management with IBM Tivoli Storage Productivity Center
- Data Deduplication using the IBM ProtecTIER solution
- Storage and Data Services

As sponsor of this event, IBM has received a limited number of free conference passes. We will be assigning these upon request to IBM clients and prospective clients. If you would like to go, contact your IBM Business Partner or local storage rep. Act fast! First come, first served.

technorati tags: IBM, SNW, SNWUSA, SNW09, SNIA, ComputerWorld, Barry Rudolph, Kelly Beavers, Clod Barrera, Cloud Computing, Solid State, Solid-State, SSD, storage, virtualization, deduplication, security, XIV, SVC, TSPC, Tivoli, Productivity Center, ProtecTIER

I sometimes think the marketing team regrets asking me to blog about certain topics. In this case, I was asked to put my spin on "Smarter Water", one of the 20 or so initiatives of IBM's Smarter Planet campaign. As it turned out, I had found this graphic of Darth Vader filtering sea water, and used this for my blog post.

2009 Mar 20 — Water Water Everywhere (418)

..., nor any drop to drink."
From *Rime of the Ancient Mariner* (1798), by Samuel Taylor Coleridge

Actually, I've been so busy this week that I am just now getting to this week's theme of Smarter Water. Since it was St. Patrick's Day this week, I thought of discussing IBM's project to help Ireland. Working with the Marine Institute Ireland, IBM has created a system to monitor wave conditions, marine life and pollution levels in and around Galway Bay. Here is quick excerpt from IBM [Press Release]:

> "This real-time advanced analytics pilot is turning mountains of data into intelligence, paving the way for smarter environmental management and development of the bay.

> The vision for SmartBay is a marine research infrastructure of sensors and computational technology interconnected across Galway Bay collecting and distributing information on coastal conditions, pollution levels and marine life. The monitoring services, delivered via the web and other devices, benefits tourism, fishing, aquaculture and the environment.

> The pilot, which includes a move from manual to instrumented data gathering, will allow researchers to deploy quicker reactions to the critical challenges of the bay such as pollution, flooding, fishing stock levels, green energy generation and the threats from climate change."

Or... I could have used water as a metaphor for the "tidal wave" of information. For many, we have a lot of raw data, but not suitably digestible information in the form we need it.

But then I found this photo.

Source: [Picture is Unrelated Blog]

Ok, I admit it is a silly photo, Darth Vader standing in the middle of the ocean filtering sea water into a plastic jug, but it helps focus on the problem. Long before we are done fighting over the last few drops of oil, we will be fighting over water.

This Sunday, March 22, is "World Water Day". Over the past 100 years, water consumption has increased six fold, twice the growth of human population. Today, one in five people on this planet lack access to suitable drinking water. I have been to countries where people not just lack water filters, and in some cases didn't have closeable plastic jugs to carry the water in.

By 2015, the World Health Organization [WHO] estimates that water problems will impact over half the world's population. Here is their [Top 10 Facts File] on water scarcity.

At this point, you might be asking what any of this has to do with IBM.

The smart folks at IBM Research lab, the same location where we do storage research, were able to take some of their knowledge of chemistry, solid state memory, and nanotubes to help the planet with the water situation. Here is a quick [2-minute video].

☉technorati tags: IBM, Smarter Water, Marine Institute, Ireland, Galway Bay, SmartBay, Star Wars, Darth Vader, World Water Day, World Health Organization, WHO

2009 Mar 25 — Barbara Sewell explains IBM N series (419)

I just got a series of videos made at last month's IBM Pulse 2009 conference. Rather than flood you with all of them all at once, I will post them all separately.

Barbara Sewell presents the IBM N series in this[6-minute video]

technorati tags: IBM, N series, Barbara Sewell, NetApp, N6060, disk storage, appliance, gateway

2009 Mar 26 — Pulse 2009: IBM Disk with Tivoli FastBack (420)

Continuing this week's series on Pulse 2009 video, we have a double header.

Bob Dalton discusses our entry-level IBM System Storage [DS3000] and midrange IBM System Storage [DS4000] disk systems, followed by Dan Thompson discussing [IBM Tivoli Storage Manager FastBack] software.

Here is Bob Dalton and Dan Thompson in a quick [4-minute video]

IBM Tivoli Storage Manager FastBack is the result of IBM's [acquisition of FilesX], a company in Israel that developed software to backup servers at remote branch offices running Microsoft Windows operating system.

technorati tags: IBM, DS3000, DS4000, disk system, Tivoli Storage Manager, TSM, FastBack, FilesX, Israel, Microsoft Windows

2009 Mar 27 — Pulse 2009: IBM ProtecTIER data deduplication (421)

Finishing off this week's series of Pulse 2009 videos, I wrap up with a video on IBM's exciting data deduplication appliance.

Victor Namechek presents IBM TS7650 ProtecTIER in this [3-minute video]

technorati tags: IBM, virtual tape, ibmpulse, Pulse2009, TS7650, TS7650G, ProtecTIER, deduplication

2009 Mar 30 — SNW 2009 Best Practices Award Finalists (422)

Next week is the Spring 2009 Storage Networking World [SNW]. In the category of "Innovation and Promise", there are three finalists for the "Best Practices Award":

- Activision Publishing, Inc., Santa Monica, California
- Argus Information & Advisory Systems, White Plains, New York
- CIGNA - Health Insurance, Windsor, Connecticut

The awards will be announced on Tuesday, April 7th at the event during the General Session:

10:00-10:15 am "Best Practices in Storage" Awards Program

Of course, I'll be rooting for the one above that used IBM's XIV disk storage system to reduce their energy consumption, improve their utilization, and simplify their management.

technorati tags: IBM, SNW, SNW2009, Innovation Promise, Best Practices, Activision, Argus, CIGNA

Reference

Blog Roll

The following are some of the blogs and RSS feeds that I have found useful or interesting. I have included my own blog that this book is based on for completeness. The listings are not in any obvious order. Where possible, I have tried to identify them by vendor, category and job role.

IBM Blogs

Inside System Storage, by Tony Pearson, IBM

> https://www.ibm.com/developerworks/mydeveloperworks/blogs/InsideSystemStorage/

The Raised Floor, hosted by IBM, Eaton, Forrester and others

> theraisedfloor.typepad.com/blog/

Storage Virtualization, by Barry Whyte, IBM

> https://www.ibm.com/developerworks/mydeveloperworks/blogs/storagevirtualization/

Eightbar, by Ian Hughes and Roo Reynolds, IBM

> eightbar.co.uk/

Bob Sutor's Open Blog, by Bob Sutor, IBM

> http://www.sutor.com/c/

Benchmarking and systems performance, by Elisabeth Stahl, IBM

> https://www.ibm.com/developerworks/mydeveloperworks/blogs/benchmarking

Freakonomics Blog, by Steven D. Levitt, Steven J. Dubner, et al.

> http://www.freakonomics.com/blog/

Other Blogs

Taylor's Take on Storage by Taylor Allis

> http://blogs.oracle.com/TA/

Ask the Open Systems Storage Guy! by Open Systems Guy

> opensystemsguy.wordpress.com/

Grove's Green IT, by Deborah Grove

      grovesgreenit.typepad.com/green_it_is_sustainable/

Rough Type, by Nicholas Carr

      www.roughtype.com/

The Bigger Truth by Steve Duplessie, Enterprise Strategy Group (ESG)

      http://www.thebiggertruth.com/

Ruptured Monkey by Ron Singler, Nigel Poulton, C2olen, stephen2615

      blogs.rupturedmonkey.com/

The Storage Architect by Chris Evans

      http://www.thestoragearchitect.com/

DrunkenData by Jon W Toigo

      www.drunkendata.com/

The Tech Lounge, by Brian Kristensen, Kurtis Kronk, and staff

      www.thetechlounge.com/

StorageMojo, by Robin Harris

      storagemojo.com/

Storage Sanity by Kirby Wadsworth, F5 Networks

      storagesanity.blogspot.com/

Storage Rap by Marc Farley, 3PAR

      http://www.storagerap.com/

Claus Mikkelsen's Blog by Claus Mikkelsen, Hitachi Data Systems

      blogs.hds.com/claus/

Chuck's Blog by Chuck Hollis, EMC

      chucksblog.typepad.com/chucks_blog/

The Storage Anarchist by Barry A. Burke, EMC

      thestorageanarchist.typepad.com/weblog/

Hu Yoshida, by Hu Yoshida, Hitachi Data Systems

      blogs.hds.com/hu/

StorageZilla, by Mark Twomey, EMC

      storagezilla.typepad.com/storagezilla/

DaveBlog, by Dave Hitz, Network Appliance (NetApp)

      blogs.netapp.com/dave/

Social Media, Marketing and Public Relations Blogs

Social Media and the Open Enterprise, by Paul Gillen

www.paulgillin.com/

The YouBlog, by John Windsor

youblog.typepad.com/the_youblog/

Creative Think by Roger von Oech

blog.creativethink.com/

Word Wise, by Dan Santow

wordwise.typepad.com/blog/

How to Change the World, by Guy Kawasaki

blog.guykawasaki.com/

Seth Godin's Blog, by Seth Godin

sethgodin.typepad.com/seths_blog/

Indexed, by Jessica Hagy

indexed.blogspot.com/

Productivity, Time Management and Career Advice Blogs

Four Hour Work Week, by Tim Ferriss

fourhourworkweek.com/blog/

Dilbert, by Scott Adams

www.dilbert.com/

Web Worker Daily, by Jackson West

webworkerdaily.com/

Life Hacker, by Gina Trapani

Lifehacker.com/

Results-Oriented Work Environment (ROWE) by Cali and Jody

http://gorowe.com/blog/

The Happiness Project, by Gretchen Rubin

www.happiness-project.com/happiness_project/

IBM Social Computing Guidelines

Blogs, wikis, social networks, virtual worlds and social media

In the spring of 2005, IBMers used a wiki to create a set of guidelines for all IBMers who wanted to blog. These guidelines aimed to provide helpful, practical advice to protect both IBM bloggers and IBM. In 2008 , IBM turned to employees to re-examine our guidelines in light of ever-evolving technologies and online social tools to ensure they remain current to the needs of employees and the company. These efforts have broadened the scope of the existing guidelines to include all forms of social computing.

Below are the current and official "IBM Social Computing Guidelines," which we review periodically so that they may evolve to reflect emerging technologies and online social tools.

These guidelines are publicly available at:

> http://www.ibm.com/blogs/zz/en/guidelines.html

Introduction
Responsible engagement in innovation and dialogue

Online collaboration platforms are fundamentally changing the way IBMers work and engage with each other, clients and partners.

IBM is increasingly exploring how online discourse through social computing can empower IBMers as global professionals, innovators and citizens. These individual interactions represent a new model: not mass communications, but masses of communicators. Through these interactions, IBM's greatest asset--the expertise of its employees--can be shared with clients, shareholders, and the communities in which it operates.

Therefore, it is very much in IBM's interest — and, we believe, in each IBMer's own — to be aware of and participate in this sphere of information, interaction and idea exchange:

To learn: As an innovation-based company, we believe in the importance of open exchange — between IBM and its clients, and among the many constituents of the emerging business and societal ecosystem--for learning. Social computing is an important arena for organizational and individual development.

To contribute: IBM — as a business, as an innovator and as a corporate citizen — makes important contributions to the world, to the future of business and technology, and to public dialogue on a broad range of societal issues. Because our business activities provide transformational insight and high-value innovation for business, government, education, healthcare and nongovernmental organizations, it is important for IBM and IBMers to share with the world the exciting things we're learning and doing.

In 1997, IBM actively recommended that its employees use the Internet — at a time when many companies were seeking to restrict their employees' Internet access. In 2003, the company made a strategic decision to embrace the blogosphere and to encourage IBMers to participate. We continue to advocate IBMers' responsible involvement today in this rapidly growing environment of relationship, learning and collaboration.

IBM Social Computing Guidelines

1. *Know and follow IBM's Business Conduct Guidelines.*

2. IBMers are personally responsible for the content they publish on-line, whether in a blog, social computing site or any other form of user-generated media. Be mindful that what you publish will be public for a long time — protect your privacy and take care to understand a site's terms of service.

3. Identify yourself — name and, when relevant, role at IBM — when you discuss IBM or IBM-related matters, such as IBM products or services. You must make it clear that you are speaking for yourself and not on behalf of IBM.

4. If you publish content online relevant to IBM in your personal capacity use a disclaimer such as this: "The postings on this site are my own and don't necessarily represent IBM's positions, strategies or opinions."

5. Respect copyright, fair use and financial disclosure laws.

6. Don't provide IBM's or another's confidential or other proprietary information and never discuss IBM business performance or other sensitive matters publicly.

7. Don't cite or reference clients, partners or suppliers without their approval. When you do make a reference, link back to the source. Don't publish anything that might allow inferences to be drawn which could embarrass or damage a client.

8. Respect your audience. Don't use ethnic slurs, personal insults, obscenity, or engage in any conduct that would not be acceptable in IBM's workplace. You should also show proper consideration for

others' privacy and for topics that may be considered objectionable or inflammatory — such as politics and religion.

9. Be aware of your association with IBM in online social networks. If you identify yourself as an IBMer, ensure your profile and related content is consistent with how you wish to present yourself with colleagues and clients.

10. Don't pick fights, be the first to correct your own mistakes.

11. Try to add value. Provide worthwhile information and perspective. IBM's brand is best represented by its people and what you publish may reflect on IBM's brand.

12. Don't use IBM logos or trademarks unless approved to do so.

Detailed Discussion

The IBM Business Conduct Guidelines and laws provide the foundation for IBM's policies and guidelines for blogs and social computing.
The same principles and guidelines that apply to IBMers' activities in general, as found in the IBM Business Conduct Guidelines, apply to IBMers' activities online. This includes forms of online publishing and discussion, including blogs, wikis, file-sharing, user-generated video and audio, virtual worlds* and social networks.

As outlined in the Business Conduct Guidelines, IBM fully respects the legal rights of our employees in all countries in which we operate. In general, what you do on your own time is your affair. However, activities in or outside of work that affect your IBM job performance, the performance of others, or IBM's business interests are a proper focus for company policy.

IBM supports open dialogue and the exchange of ideas.
IBM regards blogs and other forms of online discourse as primarily a form of communication and relationship among individuals. When the company wishes to communicate publicly as a company — whether to the marketplace or to the general public — it has well established means to do so. Only those officially designated by IBM have the authorization to speak on behalf of the company.

However, IBM believes in dialogue among IBMers and with our partners, clients, members of the many communities in which we participate and the general public. Such dialogue is inherent in our business model of innovation, and in our commitment to the development of open standards.

We believe that IBMers can both derive and provide important benefits from exchanges of perspective.

One of IBMers' core values is "trust and personal responsibility in all relationships." As a company, IBM trusts — and expects — IBMers to exercise personal responsibility whenever they participate in social media. This includes not violating the trust of those with whom they are engaging. *IBMers should not use these media for covert marketing or public relations.* If and when members of IBM's Communications, Marketing, Sales or other functions engaged in advocacy for the company have the authorization to participate in social media, they should identify themselves as such.

Know the IBM Business Conduct Guidelines. If you have any confusion about whether you ought to publish something online, chances are the BCGs will resolve it. Pay particular attention to what the BCGs have to say about proprietary information, about avoiding misrepresentation and about competing in the field. If, after checking the BCG's, you are still unclear as to the propriety of a post, it is best to refrain and seek the advice of management.

Be who you are. We believe in transparency and honesty; anonymity is not an option. When discussing topics relevant to IBM, you must use your real name, be clear who you are, and identify that you work for IBM. If you have a vested interest in something you are discussing, be the first to point it out. But also be smart about protecting yourself and your privacy. What you publish will be around for a long time, so consider the content carefully and also be judicious in disclosing personal details.

Be thoughtful about how you present yourself in online social networks. The lines between public and private, personal and professional are blurred in online social networks. By virtue of identifying yourself as an IBMer within a social network, you are now connected to your colleagues, managers and even IBM's clients. You should ensure that content associated with you is consistent with your work at IBM. If you have joined IBM recently, be sure to update your social profiles to reflect IBM's guidelines. You may not use IBM logos or trademarks as a part of your postings, including in your identity on a site, unless you are approved to do so.

Speak in the first person. Use your own voice; bring your own personality to the forefront.

Use a disclaimer. Whenever you publish content to any form of digital media, make it clear that what you say there is representative of your views and opinions and not necessarily the views and opinions of IBM. For instance, in your own blog, the following standard disclaimer should be prominently displayed: "The postings on this site are my own and don't necessarily represent IBM's positions, strategies or opinions." If a site does not afford you enough space to include this full disclaimer, you should use your best judgment to position your comments appropriately.

Managers and executives take note: This standard disclaimer does not by itself exempt IBM managers and executives from a special responsibility when participating in online environments. By virtue of their position, they must consider whether personal thoughts they publish may be misunderstood as expressing IBM positions. And a manager should assume that his or her team will read what is written. Public forums are not the place to communicate IBM policies to IBM employees.

Respect copyright and fair use laws. For IBM's protection and well as your own, it is critical that you show proper respect for the laws governing copyright and fair use of copyrighted material owned by others, including IBM's own copyrights and brands. You should never quote more than short excerpts of someone else's work. And it is good general blogging practice to link to others' work. Keep in mind that laws will be different depending on where you live and work.

Protecting confidential and proprietary information. Social computing blurs many of the traditional boundaries between internal and external communications. Be thoughtful about what you publish — particularly on external platforms. You must make sure you do not disclose or use IBM confidential or proprietary information or that of any other person or company in any online social computing platform. For example, ask permission before posting someone's picture in a social network or publishing in a blog a conversation that was meant to be private.

IBM's business performance and other sensitive subjects. Some topics relating to IBM are sensitive and should never be discussed, even if you're expressing your own opinion and using a disclaimer. For example, you must not comment on, or speculate about, IBM's future business performance (including upcoming quarters or future periods), IBM's business plans, unannounced strategies or prospects (including information about alliances), potential acquisitions or divestitures, similar matters involving IBM's competitors, legal or regulatory matters affecting IBM and other similar subjects that could negatively affect IBM. This applies to anyone including conversations with financial analysts, the press or other third parties (including friends). If you're unsure of the sensitivity of a particular subject, seek advice from your manager or legal team before talking about it or simply refrain from the conversation. IBM policy is not to comment on rumors in any way. You should merely say, "no comment" to rumors. Do not deny or affirm them (or suggest the same in subtle ways), speculate about them or propagate them by participating in "what if"-type conversations.

Protect IBM's clients, business partners and suppliers. Clients, partners or suppliers should not be cited or obviously referenced without their approval. Externally, never identify a client, partner or supplier by name without permission and never discuss confidential details of a client engagement. Internal social computing platforms permit suppliers and business partners to participate so be sensitive to who will see your content. If a client hasn't given explicit permission for their name to be used, think carefully about the content you're going to publish on any internal social media and get the appropriate permission where necessary.

It is acceptable to discuss general details about kinds of projects and to use non-identifying pseudonyms for a client (e.g., Client 123) so long as the information provided does not make it easy for someone to identify the client or violate any non-disclosure or intellectual property agreements that may be in place with the client. Be thoughtful about the types of information that you share, which may inadvertently lead others to deduce which clients, partners and suppliers that you are working with. This might include travel plans or publishing details about your current location or where you are working on a given day. Furthermore, your blog or online social network is not the place to conduct confidential business with a client, partner or supplier.

Respect your audience and your coworkers. Remember that IBM is a global organization whose employees and clients reflect a diverse set of customs, values and points of view. Don't be afraid to be yourself, but do so respectfully. This includes not only the obvious (no ethnic slurs, personal insults, obscenity, etc.) but also proper consideration of privacy and of topics that may be considered objectionable or inflammatory — such as politics and religion. For example, if your blog is hosted on an IBM-owned property, avoid these topics and focus on subjects that are business-related. If your blog is self-hosted, use your best judgment and be sure to make it clear that the views and opinions expressed are yours alone and do not represent the official views of IBM. Further, be thoughtful when using tools hosted outside of IBM's protected Intranet environment to communicate among fellow employees about IBM or IBM related matters. Also, while it is fine for IBMers to disagree, but please don't use your external blog or other online social media to air your differences in an inappropriate manner.

Add value. IBM's brand is best represented by its people and everything you publish online reflects upon it. Blogs and social networks that are hosted on IBM-owned domains should be used in a way that adds value to IBM's business. If it helps you, your coworkers, our clients or our partners to do their jobs and solve problems; if it helps to improve knowledge or skills; if it contributes directly or indirectly to the improvement of IBM's products, processes and policies; if it builds a sense of community; or if it helps to promote IBM's Values, then it is adding value. It is best to stay within your sphere of expertise, and whenever you are presenting something as fact, make sure it is a fact. Though not directly business-related, background information you choose to share about yourself, such as information about your family or personal interests, may be useful in helping establish a relationship between you and your readers, but it is entirely your choice whether to share this information.

Don't pick fights. When you see misrepresentations made about IBM by media, analysts or by other bloggers, you may certainly use your blog — or add comments on the original discussion — to point that out. Always do so with respect, stick to the facts and identify your appropriate affiliation to IBM. Also, if you speak about a competitor, you must make sure that what you say is factual and that it does not disparage the competitor. Avoid unnecessary or unproductive arguments. Brawls may earn traffic, but nobody wins in the end and you may negatively affect your own, and IBM's, reputation in the process. Don't try to settle scores or goad competitors or others into inflammatory debates. Here and in other areas of public discussion, make sure that what you are saying is factually correct.

Be the first to respond to your own mistakes. If you make an error, be up front about your mistake and correct it quickly, as this can help to restore trust. If you choose to modify content that was previously posted, such as editing a blog post, make it clear that you have done so.

Adopt a warm, open and approachable tone. Remember that much of IBM's image is developed by the public's interaction with real IBMers. We all want that image to be a positive one. Your tone, your openness and your approachability can help with that, just as they can with your own personal "brand".

Use your best judgment. Remember that there are always consequences to what you publish. If you're about to publish something that makes you even the slightest bit uncomfortable, review the suggestions above and think about why that is. If you're still unsure, and it is related to IBM business, feel free to discuss it with your manager. Ultimately, however, you have sole responsibility for what you post to your blog or publish in any form of online social media.

Don't forget your day job. You should make sure that your online activities do not interfere with your job or commitments to customers.

> *Virtual worlds present a number of unique circumstances, not all of which are covered in these guidelines. Please refer to the companion, "Virtual worlds Guidelines" for additional guidelines around identity, behavior, appearance and intellectual property.

Glossary of Acronyms and Terms (GOAT)

This glossary is intended to help understand the various acronyms and industry-specific terms used in this book and elsewhere. Rather than page number, I will list the blog post, or list of posts, where used or explained. Not all entries have post numbers, but are included to help support other definitions.

Terms are sorted alphanumerically, letters before digits. Where possible, I have tried to use the correct upper/lower case. Websites of companies and organizations are enclosed in [brackets]. Additional information can be obtained at the following websites:

- http://www.acronymfinder.com/
- http://www.ibm.com/storage
- http://searchstorage.com
- http://wikipedia.org

A —

AaaS   Archive as a Service

ABARS   Aggregate Backup and Recovery Support

ACL   Access Control List

Adaptec   Storage hardware manufacturer [adaptec.com]

ADSM   ADSTAR Distrubuted Storage Manager

Advanced Single Instance Storage (A-SIS)

De-duplication feature on IBM System Storage N series

AEM   IBM Active Energy Manager software

AES   Advanced Encryption Standard

AIX   IBM UNIX operating system for POWER-based servers

AFS   IBM's Andrew File System

Amazon   Online store [amazon.com]

AMD   Advanced Micro Devices [amd.com]

Apache

Open source organization for developing software [apache.org]

APC   American Power Conversion Corporation

API   Application Programming Interface

appliance   Purpose-built modular hardware

application-aware

Having intelligence about relevant or specific applications, utilization patterns, and usage conditions

Approach   IBM Lotus relational database software

archive

An intelligent process for managing inactive or infrequently accessed data, that still has value, while providing the ability to preserve, search and retrieve the information during a specified retention period

ARC

DS8000 Adaptive Replacement Cache algorithm, or also used to refer to IBM Almaden Research Center

Arsenal Digital   Backup service provider acquired by IBM

ARX   F5 Acopia's intelligent file virtualization devices

ASC Purple

A partnership between the DOE/NNSA Advanced Simulation and Computing Program (ASC) and IBM Corporation with Lawrence Livermore National Laboratory as the lead laboratory. The ASC Purple contract scheduled the demonstration of 100-teraFLOPS peak performance in June 2005

ASIC   Application-Specific Integrated Unit

A-SIS   See "Advanced Single Instance Storage"

ASP   Active Service Page

asymmetric key

Part of a key pair. One key is used for encryption, the other for decryption. The first is often called a "public key" and can be given out to all senders of data. The second is often called "private key" as only the authorized recipient of the data has this

at-risk

Data that does not have backup or other method of recovery

AT&T   American Telephone and Telegraph [att.com]

ATM   Automatic Teller Machine

Atmos   EMC cloud-optimized storage, code-named Maui

at-rest

> Data as it resides on disk or tape storage media, as opposed to data "in-flight"

ATS   Advanced Technical Support

Avamar

> Client-side deduplication software company acquired by EMC

Azure   Microsoft public cloud computing offering

B —

BaaS   Backup as a Service

backbone

> A larger transmission line that carries data gathered from smaller lines that interconnect with it

BackPack   Online to-do list and calendar [packpackit.com]

Bake-off

> A side-by-side performance or comparison test, typically done by a client to compare the wares of two vendors

Balanced Warehouse

> IBM InfoSphere Balanced Warehouse, an integrated stack of servers, storage and software for database processing

Barney

> Press release where two companies profess their love for each other, based on theme song of TV show "Barney and Friends"

battery backup

> A battery-based system to provide electrical power in the event that main power source is interrupted. See also "UPS"

BC   See "Business Continuity"-- do not use for "BladeCenter"

BC/DR Business Continuity/Disaster Recovery

BCP   Business Continuity Plan

BCRS   IBM Business Continuity Recovery Service

benchmark

> The result of running a set of standard tests in order to assess the relative performance of a storage device

best practice

> Most recent set of guidelines based on experience that provides best results given current technologies and techniques available

best-of-breed   Best in a particular class of products

BFD   Bigger, Faster, Denser

BI   See "Business Intelligence"

Big Data

> The analysis of information to identify trends, patterns and insights to make better business decisions, from a collection of structured and unstructured data sources, including real-time input streams, resulting in sets of data so large they are awkward to work with using traditional database technologies

Big Green   See "Project Big Green"

big iron   High-end hardware, such as servers or storage

BIND   A domain name server (DNS) for UNIX and Linux systems

biometrics

> methods for uniquely recognizing humans based upon one or more intrinsic physical traits, such as fingerprint or retinal scan

BIRT   Business Intelligence and Reporting Tools

Black Hat   A conference

blackout period

> The days or weeks before IBM announces quarterly or year-end financial results that bloggers cannot discuss certain topics

blade   A server or SAN component that slides into a larger chassis

BladeCenter   IBM blade servers and chassis systems

bleg

> the process of publically begging for information or assistance in a blog

block

> A fixed or variable-length contiguous set of bytes, typically a multiple a power of 2, such as 512 or 4096 bytes

---

block-oriented Storage that is accessed by block, rather than by file

blog short for "web log"

blogfight

>A public disagreement between two or more bloggers, often serving as a useful debate to explore differences in corporate culture or product designs

Blogger a blogging website

blogketing

>short for "blog marketing", when a blogger expresses an opinion that competition does not agree with

Bloglines A popular feed reader [www.bloglines.com]

blogosphere

>The connected community of bloggers, their blogs, their readers, and their interconnections

blogoversary An anniversary of the inception of a blog

Bluetooth

>A standard and communications protocol primarily designed for low power consumption, typically with a short range

BMW Bayerische Motoren Werke AG

bogeyman

>An amorphous imaginary being used by adults to frighten children into behaving

Bolivares Monetary unit in Venezuela

Bolivian Navy

>The unofficial name for the Bolivan Naval Force, a separate branch of the armed forces for the landlocked country, needed to patrol the large tributaries of the Amazon river as well as Lake Titicaca that borders with the country of Peru

BRICK Brazil, Russia, India, China and Korea, also known as BRIC

Brocade Brocade Communications Systems, Inc. [brocade.com]

BTW Abbreviation for "by the way"

bubble gum and bailing wire

>The predecessors to "duct tape" as the American farmer's tools of choice for ad-hoc repairs

---

Business Continuity (BC)

The combination of continuous operations through non-disruptive upgrades, high availability through redundant designs, and disaster recovery planning

Business Intelligence (BI)

Technologies, applications, and practices for the collection, integration, analysis, and presentation of business information

Business Partner (BP)

IBM Business Partners are authorized resellers or distributors of IBM offerings. Since this is a formal IBM program, both "B" and "P" are capitalized. Use lower case if you are discussing business partners of other companies in general

C —

CA   Computer Associates [ca.com]

cache

Storage, either in the server or storage device, to hold recently accessed information to improve I/O performance

campus   A set of buildings within 10km Fibre Channel distance

Capacity-on-Demand

The option to install additional compute or storage capacity but not pay for it until it is actually used

CARS

mnemonic for IBM's Information Infrastructure themes: Compliance, Availability, Retention and Security

CAS   See "Content-Addressable Storage"

Cat5   Twisted pair copper cable designed for high signal integrity

CBT tape

A collection of freeware for mainframe users [cbttape.org]

CCMDB   Tivoli Change and Configuration Database

CCW   Channel Command Word, used on mainframes to send data

CD   Compact Disc, short for CD-ROM

CDC   Change Data Capture

CDL

> CLARiiON Disk Library, an EMC VTL or Linux on System z Compatible Disk Layout

CDP   Continuous Data Protection

CD-ROM   Compact Disc Read Only Memory

CDU   Cooler Distribution Unit

Celerra   A family of EMC storage devices

Centera   An EMC storage device for fixed content data

CERN

> Originally *Conseil Européen pour la Recherche Nucléaire* (European Council for Nuclear Research) changed to *Organisation Européenne pour la Recherche Nucléaire* (European Organization for Nuclear Research) in 1954, but kept acronym as CERN [cern.ch]

CFO   Central Financial Officer

channel

> Name for various business routes to market, such as OEMs, ISVs, VARs, resellers and system integrators, or to refer to communications channel, see also "Fibre Channel"

Chassis   BladeCenter container, 7U high holds 14 blades

CIFS   Common Internet File System, a NAS protocol

CIM   Common Information Model

CIMOM   CIM Object Manager

Cinco de Mayo

> Spanish for Fifth of May; the day on which the Mexican Army defeated the French at the Battle of Puebla in 1862

CI   Confuguration Items

Cisco   Cisco Systems, Inc. [cisco.com]

CKD   Count-Key-Data, a disk layout for mainframe disk systems

CLARiiON   EMC midrange disk

Clipper Group   Industry analyst [clipper.com]

cloud computing

> A pay-per-use model for enabling network access to a pool of computing resources that can be provisioned and released rapidly with minimal management effort or service provider interaction

---

CloudScape

>   IBM relational database management system, a commercial release of the Apache Software Foundation's (ASF) open source project called *Derby*

cluster   A group of servers or nodes that work together

CMDB Configuration Management Database

CMU   Carnegie Mellon University

CNET Technology news publisher [cnet.com]

CNN   Cable News Network

CoD   Capacity on Demand

Cognos Business Analytics Software company acquired by IBM.

Coke-vs-Pepsi A marketplace dominated by two major players.

cold-aisle containment

>   Often referred to as hot-aisle/cold-aisle, a set of best practices to align the fronts and backs of servers, storage and switches in a row of racks such that all fans blow from front to back, so that cold air can be introduced through holes in the floor tiles in the front, and hot air can be removed through ceiling vents near the back

colocation

>   The provisioning of floor space, power and cooling so that several entities can place their computer equipment into a single location

comfort zone   Situations or locations that a person is comfortable in

commodity servers

>   Low cost/mass produced hardware based on industry standards

CommonStore IBM archive software

Compression

>   Scheme to store data in fewer bytes than traditional encoding

ComputerWorld IT industry publisher [www.computerworld.com]

confusopoly

>   A group of companies with similar products who intentionally confuse customers instead of competing on price

Content Manager   IBM Content Manager software

---

content-adressable storage (CAS)

> Storage where data is addressed based on characteristics of the data itself, rather than some external handle such as block number or file name

controller   IT storage hardware that interfaces with host servers

convergence   When two distinct technologies come together

CoolBlue   IBM portfolio of energy efficiency products

Copan MAID disk storage company acquired by SGI

Copy Export   A feature to export virtual tapes onto physical tape

copy services   Point-in-time copy and disk mirroring features

core   CPU processing engine, see dual-core or quad-core

core-edge architecture

> A SAN configuration with larger directors (core) surrounded by smaller less-expensive (edge) switches

COS   Cloud-Oriented Storage

CPU   Central Processing Unit

CRAC Computer Room Air Conditioning

crash   System hardware failure, see "head crash"

CRM   Client Relationship Management software

CRN   Technology news publisher [crn.com]

CSS   Common Style Sheet

CTO   Chief Technology Officer

CU   Control Unit

CUPS Common Unix Printing System

CWDM   Coarse Wave Division Multiplexing

CX-4   EMC CLARiiON midrange disk system model

cylinder   A region on disk, typically 15 tracks

C06   IBM Tape 3592 Control Unit model

D —

Dark fiber

> Dedicated optical cabling that has been put into place but does not yet carry any signal

DARPA Defense Advanced Research Projects Agency

Darth Vader

> The chief antagonist in the popular *Star Wars* film series (post #418)

DAS

> Direct Attached Storage, an internal or external storage not connected via network gear

DASD

> Direct Access Storage Device, a set of storage devices that allowed random access to data, comprised of tapes, drums and disk drives. Today, used to refer to mainframe-attached disk systems that support CKD disk layout

Data at-rest See "at-rest"

Data center Facility used to house servers, storage and networking gear

Data General A mini-computer company, acquired by EMC in 1999

Data Mobility Services IBM services to migrate data

Data Shredding

> the act of physically writing zeros and ones over existing data to eliminate it

data set Data on z/OS or z/VM mainframe operating system

DataCore Storage virtualization software vendor [datacore.com]

day job Official job responsibilities

DB abbreviation for "database"

DBA Database Administrator

DB2 IBM relational database management system

DC Direct Current

DCE Data Center Ethernet

DCFM Data Center Fabric Manager, IBM software (post #366)

DCiE

> Data Center Infrastructure Efficiency, a rating calculated by dividing the amount of energy consumed by IT equipment compared to all the energy consumed by the data center. Typically 40 to 60%, but some facilities have achieved ratings over 80 percent

DCS See "Deep Computing Storage"

DDS-6 The 6th Generation of DAT, often referred to as DAT-160 for 160GB.

DCS990

> IBM System Storage disk system for HPC workloads, replacing the DCS9550

DCS9550 IBM System Storage disk system for HPC workloads

DDM Hard Disk Drive Module, same as HDD

Debug Identifying and troubleshooting defects

DEC Computer company acquired by Hewlett-Packard

decision support system

> an interactive computer-based information system intended to help decision makers compile useful information from a combination of raw data, documents, and business models to identify problems and make decisions related to management, operations and planning

decryption

> The process of transforming encrypted information back to readable clear text

dedupe See "deduplication"

deduplication

> Software or storage feature that recognizes duplicate pieces of data, and stores only one copy

"Deep Blue"

> A computer created by IBM in 1997 to beat Grand Master Champion Gary Kasparov in chess

Deep Computing Storage

> Storage systems intended for HPC environments

Dell Dell Corporation [dell.com], an IT systems vendor

Derby   Apache open source database

destination volumes

> The receiving end of a point-in-time copy or other volume operation, sometimes referred to as "target volumes," but "destination volumes" is the politically-correct preferred term

DeveloperWorks

> IBM's resource website for developers [ibm.com/developerworks]

DFDSS   Data Facility Data Set Services, now DFSMSdss

DFHSM   Data Facility Hierarcical Storage Manager, now DFSMShsm

DFS   IBM's Distributed File System

DFSMS

> Data Facility Storage Management Subsystem, the storage management element of the IBM z/OS operating system

DFSMS   Hierarchical Storage Manager component of DFSMS

Dharma Initiative

> Department of Heuristics and Research on Material Applications (DHARMA) was a fictional research project featured in the television series *Lost*

DHCPd   Daemon for Dynamic Host Configuration Protocol

"diff" comparison   a byte-for-byte file comparison

Digital Projection

> Technology to project movies from a digital source, such as DVD, onto a large movie screen

Digital Video Surveillance (DVS)

> Surveillance using digital video cameras and analytics

Diligent   Deduplication software company acquired by IBM

dinosaur

> A set of extinct animals that inspire by their immense size, considered the mascot of the mainframe. The primary z/OS DFSMS module is called IGDZILLA, named after the monster that appeared in Godzilla movies

direct-access

> To access data without having to read past other data first, also referred to as "random access". Opposite of sequential access typical of tape storage

---

DirectIO

A driver on various operating systems that provides enhanced performance reading blocks from a file system

director

A SAN switch, typically highly available 99.999% with over 100 ports, designed for non-disruptive upgrades via removable blades

Director

IBM Systems Director, software to manage servers. Also used to refer to IT Director, the lead manager of an IT department

disk farm   A large collection of disk systems

disk shelf   A horizontal row of disks, typically in 19 inch rack

diskless

Without internal disk. RAM-only servers can boot their Operating System over iSCSI or FC SAN instead

DiskXtender

Software to migrate data from Windows servers to tape, acquired by EMC

distance extension

Technology to extend protocol distances. For example, CWDM, DWDM and FCIP

distributed system

Can refer to servers that run Linux, UNIX or Windows; or any of these operating systems themselves

DLL   Windows "Data Link Library" file extension

DMX

EMC high-end disk system, such as DMX3 or DMX4

DNA

Deoxyribonucleic acid, the material in which most genetic information is coded, reproduced and stored

Domino   IBM Lotus email server software

do not try this at home

A list of activities to avoid based on risks or past experience

---

Dollar-per-GB cost of storage per GB capacity

"donut tire" approach

>   The approach to have less powerful equipment at a second Disaster Recovery location to reduce expenses

DR Disaster Recovery. Sometimes used for "Data Retention"

DRAM Dynamic Random Access Memory

drinking from a firehose

>   To be overwhelmed with information or work

drink one's own champagne

>   To use one's own solutions, nicer to say than "eat our own dog food"

DRS Distrubuted Resource Scheduler

DR site A secondary location for the purposes of Disaster Recovery

DrunkenData see Blog Roll

DR1/DR2 Models of Data Retention DR550 storage

DR550

>   An IBM archive storage system that can store archive objects on disk and optionally move them to tape

DS Disk System, IBM prefix for disk system family of products

DS3000 series IBM's set of entry-level block-based disk systems

DS3200 An IBM entry-level SAS-attach disk system

DS3300 An IBM entry-level iSCSI-attach disk system

DS3400 An IBM entry-level FC-attach disk system

DS4000 series IBM midrange disk systems

DS4200 Smallest model of DS4000 series

DS4700 Medium model of the DS4000 series

DS4800 Fastest model of the DS4000 series

DS5000 series IBM's set of midrange block-based disk systems

DS5300 The high-end model of IBM's DS5000 midrange disk systems

DS6800 IBM modular high-end storage for the IBM System z mainframe

DS8000 series IBM high-end disk systems

DS8100 2-way POWER5 model of DS8000 series

DS8300 4-way POWER5 model of DS8000 series

dual-controller

> Storage system models that have two controllers, typically set up as an active/active redundant node cluster

dual-core   A CPU chip that contains two processing engine cores

dual vendor strategy

> A strategy whereby a customer purchases equipment from two (or more) independent vendors, as a means to negotiate lower prices

dumb terminal

> A keyboard/display device driven by a central computer

dump

> To copy the entire contents of one storage onto another media, such as memory is dumped to disk, or disk is dumped to tape

DVD   Digital Versatile Disc

DVE   Dynamic Volume Expansion

DVR   Digital Video Recorder

DVS   See "Digital Video Surveillance"

DWDM   Dense Wave Division Multiplexing

Dynamic Infrastructure

> An IBM strategic initiatives with the goal to create a "smarter planet"

D2D2T

> Disk-to-Disk-to-Tape, a backup scheme were backup copies of disk data is initially sent to another disk, such as an N series or VTL, and then later moved to tape

E —

Earth Day

> a day that is intended to inspire awareness and appreciation for the Earth's natural environment

eat one's own dog food   See "drink one's own champagne"

EAV   Extended Addressability Volume for IBM z/OS

EB   Exabyte, see the Reference Section "Units of Storage"

eBay   Online auction service [ebay.com]

ECC-protection

> To protect stored information with an Error Correction Code that can detect and in some cases correct errors

ECKD Enhanced CKD disk layout for mainframe servers

Eclipse Foundation

> An open source community whose projects are focused on building an open development platform comprised of extensible frameworks, tools and runtimes for building, deploying and managing software across the lifecycle [eclipse.org]

ECM Enterprise Content Manager

edge switches Switches connected to servers or storage devices

eDiscovery

> Electronic search for records requested by courts or government agencies, as it relates to a case, investigation or litigation

EDL EMC Disk Library, a virtual tape library

EFCM McDATA Enterprise Fabric Connection Manager

Eightbar

> Second Life group of IBM employees, based on the 8 bar IBM logo [eightbar.com]

EKM See "Encryption Key Manager"

eMag Solutions Tape services company [emaglink.com]

embedded Designed inside, such as OS or other technology

EMC Egan Marino Corporation [emc.com]

EMC World An EMC conference (post #308)

encryption

> The process of transforming information (referred to as clear text) to make it unreadable to anyone except those possessing special knowledge, usually referred to as a key

Encryption Key Manager (EKM)

> IBM's Java-based software to generate and transmit encryption/decryption keys

Energy efficiency

> Percentage of total energy input consumed for useful work

enterprise

> A corporation, non-profit or government agency

enterprise-wide

> Reporting or Policy-enforcement across all sites or data centers of an enterprise

enterprise class

> Large-- for Small, Medium, Large designations, often used to refer to five nines (99.999%) availability, superior functionality and performance.

Enterprise Resource Planning (ERP)

> Generic term for software that manages payroll, general ledger, accounts payable, inventory management, and other financial operations

entry level

> Small-- for Small, Medium, Large designations, often used to refer to low-cost models intended for SMB clients

EOS   Earth Observing System

EqualLogic

> Storage vendor acquired by Dell [equallogic.com]

ERP   See "Enterprise Resource Planning"

ESCON   Enterprise Serial Connection, cabling for mainframes

ESG   Enterprise Strategy Group [esg.com], an industry analyst

ESS   Enterprise Storage Server, predecessor of DS8000 series

EST   Eastern Standard Time, GMT-5:00 hours.

ESX   VMware hypervisor

Ethernet   A network cabling protocol

ETL   Extract, Transfer, Load

ETSI   European Telecommunications Standards Institute, see "NEBS"

EVA   HP Enterprise Virtual Array, disk system

Evangelist

> A person who attempts to build a critical mass of support for a given technology

Exadata

Oracle's integrated stack of servers, storage and software for database processing

Exanet Scale-out NAS competitor, acquired by Dell

Exchange Microsoft Exchange email server software

EXITE Exploring Interests in Technology and Engineering

EXN1000

Expansion drawer for N series holding 7200 RPM SATA drives

EXN2000

Expansion drawer for N series holding 10K and 15K RPM FC drives

EXN4000

Expansion drawer for N series holding 10K and 15K RPM FC drives

expansion drawer

A physical unit of additional disk capacity, often 2U to 4U in height

Express / Express Portfolio

The set of IBM Express offerings designed for SMB customers to be easy to purchase, deploy and use

EXP3000 An IBM entry-level expansion disk drawer

EXP420 SATA disk Expansion drawer for DS4000

EXP810 FC and SATA disk expansion drawer for DS4000

EXT3 Extended File System three, a journaled file system for Linux

E7100 model of the IBM InfoSphere Balanced Warehouse

F —

fabric Used to refer to Storage Area Networks

Face-to-Face

In-person meetings, as well as a direct sales force people that calls on prospective clients in person

FalconStor Storage software company [falconstor.com]

FAQ Frequently Asked Questions document or webpage

FAS3040 NetApp version of IBM Nseries N5300 disk system

FAS3170   NetApp's version of IBM's N6070 disk system

FAST

Fully Automated Storage Tiering, EMC's automated tiering algorithm in response to IBM's "Easy Tier" capability

FAStT

IBM's Fibre Array Storage Technology, renamed to the DS3000, DS4000 and DS5000 series

FATA

Fibre ATA disk, designed to better resist vibrational shock than SATA, used in DS8000 disk systems

FBA   Fixed Block Addressing, disk layout format for most systems

FC   see Fibre Channel, refers to the cabling and the storage devices

FC-AL Fibre Channel Arbitrated Loop

FCIP   Fibre Channel over IP, sending FC packets over an IP network

FCoCEE   Fibre Channel over Converged Enhanced Ethernet

FCoE   Fibre Channel over Ethernet [fcoe.com]

FCP   Fibre Channel Protocol, sending SCSI commands over FC

feed reader

RSS content such as my blog can be read using software called an "RSS reader," "feed reader" or an "aggregator"

FH   full-height tape drive

Fiber   Optical cabling

Fibre   short for Fibre Channel, used to refer to both FICON and FCP

Fibre Channel

An interface standard that supports multiple protocols, can use either copper or optical cabling

FICON

Fibre Connection, CCW over Fibre Channel for mainframes

File System Gateway (FSG)

An IBM NAS gateway for the DR550 family of products

filer

A NAS disk system appliance that contains internal disk, such as the IBM N3000 series

---

FileNet   An ECM company acquired by IBM

Firefox   Mozilla's open source web-browser software

Flagship   Primary, strategic, or most popular product

flash memory Solid-state drives

Flash video   Adobe video format

FlashCopy®   IBM Point-in-Time disk copy capability

"flexnode" server

> A server that can be partitioned into individual server nodes and back again as needed

FlexScale

> Software to manage the N series Performance Accelerator Module (PAM)

Flickr   Internet-based photo storage and sharing service

Flin Flon

> A small mining town in Manitoba, Canada, made famous for winning a government contract to grow crops for "medicinal purposes"

FOS   Brocade's Fabric Operating System

FOSS Free Open Source Software

FRA   Federal Record Act

FRCP US Federal Rules for Civil Procedures

free space   Space on disk available to ingest more data

fsck An OS command to perform "file system checking"

FSG   See "File System Gateway"

FTF   See "Face-to-Face"

FUD   Fear, Uncertainty and Doubt [#406]

Fusion IO   An IBM supplier of Solid-State Drives

Fuji Film   Tape cartridge manufacturer [fujifilm.com]

Fujitsu ScanSnap S510   A document scanner for home or office use

FWIW Internet abbreviation "For what it's worth…"

F2F   See "Face-to-Face"

F5   File virtualization and management company [f5.com]

G ▬

GA

> General Availability, the date at which a product can be purchased by anyone

GAM See "Grid Access Manager"

game console

> A computer system purpose-built to play video games, such as the Microsoft Xbox 360, Nintendo Wii, and Sony Play Station 3

GAO Government Accountability Office

Garry Kasparov

> World Chess Champion, defeated by IBM's Deep Blue computer (post #343)

Gartner Industry analysts [gartner.com]

gateway

> IT equipment that performs protocol translation or controls data traffic, see "NAS gateway" and "File System gateway"

GbE Gigabit per second Ethernet, typically optical cabling

Gbps

> Gigabit per second transmission rate, see "Units of Storage" section of this book

GB 1 billion bytes, see "Units of Storage" section of this book

GDDR EMC's Geographically Dispersed Disaster Restart

GDPS

> Formerly the "Geographically Dispersed Parallel Sysplex", but now just GDPS, an IBM service offering that provides mainframe and distributed operating system fail-over capability

GDPS/DCM Distributed Cluster Manager (post #308)

geo-thermal energy

> thermal energy generated and stored in the Earth, such as used in hot springs

Giant Magnetoresistance (GMR)

> A quantum mechanical effect, observed in thin film structures composed of alternating ferromagnetic and nonmagnetic metal layers, used in disk read/write heads

---

GIE   Globally Integrated Enterprise

GigE   See "GbE"

GIMP   Graphics manipulation program

GLBA   Gramm-Leach-Bliley Act of 1999

Global Mirror   IBM's asynchronous disk mirroring capability

Global Warming

> The climate change and increase in the average temperature of the Earth's surface and oceans in recent decades

GMAS   See "Grid Medical Archive Solution"

GMR   See "Giant Magnetoresistance"

"going dark"

> To intentionally not make any public statements, based on the tradition by Broadway shows to be "dark" one night a week to give the cast a day of rest

Google   Google, Inc. [google.com]

Google Apps

> Google's Software-as-a-Service offering for email and office documents, comparable to IBM's LotusLive offering

governance

> A process or part of management system that makes decisions that define expectations, grant power, or verify performance

GPFS   IBM's General Parallel File System

GPS

> A space-based navigation satellite system that provides reliable location anywhere on or near the Earth

Grand Challenge

> An IBM project that aim to push the boundaries of and demonstrate the capabilities of technology; e.g. the "Deep Blue" and "Watson" computers (post #434)

green

> To be sensitive of the earth's environment includes reducing energy consumption, expelling less carbon dioxide and other "greenhouse" gases, and disposing fewer toxic chemicals into landfills

grid   A collection of nodes that work together

Grid Access Manager (GAM)

IBM System Storage software to support a storage grid with CIFS and NFS protocol, such as the IBM System Storage Grid Medical Archive Solution

Grid Medical Archive Solution (GMAS)

IBM System Storage solution to store PACS application data

GSA   IBM's internal Global Storage Architecture.

GTD   *Getting Things Done*, book by David Allen

GTS   IBM Global Technology Services group

GUI   Graphical User Interface

GUIDE

A user group for IBM's Mainframe systems, ceased operations in 1999. Many members moved over to SHARE, and often referred to as GUIDE/SHARE or SHARE/GUIDE in various parts of the world

G1G1   "Give 1 Get 1" promotion of One Laptop per Child

H —

HACMP

IBM High Availability Cluster Multiprocessing, later renamed PowerHA

HAL9000

The fictional supercomputer featured in Arthur C. Clarke's novel *2001: A Space Odyssey* and the 1968 film of the same name

half-Barney

A press release where one company professes its love for another company, see "Barney"

hard quota

In IT storage, a strictly-enforced upper maximum of space allowed to a user, department or application. Once reached, all further requests for additional storage result in rejection

hash code   A number generated from a sequence of bytes

HBA   Host Bus Adaptor

HCLS   Healthcare and Life Sciences

HDD   Hard Disk Drive Module, same as DDM

HDS   Hitachi Data Systems, subsidiary of Hitachi [hds.com]

HDS Math

> Also known as Hitachi Math, outrageous claims, typically by HDS bloggers, exaggerating the capabilities of their offerings

head crash   A disk drive module failure

Hercules   An IBM mainframe emulator

heterogeneous From different systems or platforms

Hewlett-Packard   IT systems vendor [hp.com]

HFS Hierarchical File System

HGST see "Hitachi Global Storage Technologies"

HH   Half-height tape drives

HHSNBN

> "He Hu Shall Not Be Named", EMC Barry Burke's nickname for Hu Yoshida, an HDS blogger

high-end   See also "Enterprise Class"

High Performance Computing (HPC)

> Computing performance by supercomputers, typically made up of grid cluster of processing nodes that work together to perform mathematical computations for scientific, technical or financial applications

HIPAA   Health Insurance Portability and Accountability Act

Hipersockets System z Virtual Local Area Network

Hipster PDA

> A low-tech alternative to a Personal Digital Assitant, composed of a stack of 3x5 index cards held together by a binder clip

Hitachi Global Storage Technologies (HGST)

> Formerly a joint venture between IBM and Hitachi to manufacture disk drive modules (DDM), now an IBM supplier and wholly-owned subsidiary of Hitachi [hitachigst.com]

HL7

> Standards for the exchange, management and integration of electronic healthcare information [hl7.org]

Hot/Cold Aisle

> Best practice for data center design, in which racks of IT equipment are aligned so that an aisle is either for cold air that comes up from perforated floor tiles, or for hot air exhaust to the ceilings

hot spots

> A section of disk that is accessed more frequently than other parts of the disk system, or a section of the datacenter floor that generates more heat

HP   See "Hewlett-Packard"

HPC   See "High Performance Computing"

HPQ   See "Hewlett-Packard"

HSM

> Hierarchical Storage Manager, used colloquially to either DFSMShsm or Tivoli Storage Manager HSM for Windows

HS21   Particular model of IBM BladeCenter blade server

HTML   Hypertext Markup Language, formatting for web pages

HTTP   Hypertext Transfer Protocol, used for web-serving

HTTPd   HTTP daemon

Hulk   EMC InfiniFlex 12000, later renamed EMC Atmos

HW   colloquial abbreviation for Hardware

Hybrid

> A storage device with a mix of media, for example a disk drive module with a solid state chip, or a disk and tape blended solution

hydro-electric energy

> The production of electrical power through the use of the gravitational force of falling or flowing water

HyperPAV   PAV feature between System z and DS8000 disk

HyperSwap   z/OS fail-over method from a failed disk system

Hyper-V

> Microsoft's x86 server virtualization hypervisor, based on the open source Xen

I —

I/O   Input/Output, a request to read or write data

I/O density IOPS per TB. Rule of thumb: 600-700 IOPS per TB

IaaS Infrastructure-as-a-Service, a Cloud Computing deployment model

IBM International Business Machines Corporation [ibm.com]

IBM i IBM's new name for i5/OS operating system, replacing the OS/400

IBM Systems The new brand for server and storage product lines

IBM Systems Director Software to manage IBM servers

IBRIX HP's competitive offering to IBM Scale-Out NAS system

"Iceberg" project

>A project to offer thin-provisioned disk storage for the mainframe, resold by IBM as the RAMAC Virtual Array (RVA)

ICL Inner-Chassis Link, a link that connects two SAN directors together

iDataPlex IBM internet-scale data center

IDC IDC Corporation [idc.com], industry analyst

IDCAMS

>Mainframe software utility for manipulating VSAM data sets

IEBGENER Mainframe software utility for copying flat text data

IEEE Institute of Electrical and Electronics Engineers, Inc. [ieee.org]

IFL

>Integrated Facility for Linux, a specialty CPU engine for IBM System z mainframes

iKeyMan

>The GUI associated by EKM and IBM Tivoli Key Lifecycle Manager

ILM see "Information Lifecycle Management"

ILMT IBM License Metric Tool

IM Instant Messaging

image

>An instance of application, disk system, or LUN, stored in memory, on disk or tape. Also used to refer to graphics files or scans

image mode

>On IBM SAN Volume Controller, one-for-one mapping

IMHO Internet abbreviation "In my humble opinion…"

IMS   Information Management System

incumbent

> The existing vendor that is already installed at a customer

Independent Software Vendor (ISV)

> A company that sells software that is not owned or controlled by the hardware vendor. Some ISVs are also IBM Business Partners, in that they can sell IBM hardware to go with their software. Others are certified under the IBM System Storage Proven™ program that their software works properly with IBM hardware

InfiniFlex   EMC's entry-level disk system, code-named Hulk

in-flight

> Data that is in transmission between servers and/or storage devices

Information Infrastructure

> The "stuff" that delivers information from the magnetic surface recording of the disk or tape media to the eyes and ears of the end user

Information Lifecycle Management (ILM)

> Policies, processes, practices, and tools used to align the business value of information with the most appropriate and cost effective IT infrastructure from the time information is conceived through its final disposition. Information is aligned with business requirements through management policies and service levels associated with applications, metadata, and data

inmates running the asylum

> Development process driven by engineers, based on Alan Cooper's book: *The Inmates Are Running the Asylum: Why High Tech Products Drive Us Crazy*

Innovator's Dilemma   A book by Clayton Christensen

Intel   x86 microprocessor manufacturer [intel.com]

Invista EMC disk virtualization system

IOD   Information on Demand

IOPS   I/O requests Per Second, a measurement of disk performance

IOstat UNIX and Linux performance measurement command

IP   Internet Protocol, also used for "Intellectual Property"

IP SAN

A dedicated network using Ethernet or other IP technology via iSCSI protocol, rather than a traditional Fibre Channel

iPDU   Intelligent Power Distribution Unit

iPhone Apple's smartphone

iPod   MP3 music player from Apple, Inc.

ISC   Integrated Solutions Console

iSCSI Internet SCSI protocol

ISE   Xiotech's Intelligent Storage Element

Isilon Competitor to IBM Scale-Out NAS

ISL   Inter-switch Link

island Used for "SAN Island" or a region in Second Life

ISO   International Organization for Standardization (ISO) [iso.org]

ISP   Internet Service Provider

ISV   see "Independent Software Vendor"

IT   Information Technology

IT environment

The set of IT equipment in a data center, including servers, networks and storage

ITIF   Information Technology and Innovation Foundation

ITIL   IT Infrastructure Library

ITSM   IT Service Management

IT Specialty Shops

Vendors that provide only a subset of IT equipment, such as EMC, NetApp, Quantum, Symantec and HDS

IT Supermarkets

Vendors that provide one-stop shopping for servers, storage, software, switches and services, such as IBM, HP, Dell and Oracle

iTunes   Apple software to manage music files

i5/OS New name for IBM OS/400 on System i servers

i515   IBM System i server model

J —

Jag3   Code name for TS1130 drive

Java

    Sun's programming language and binary execution platform

Jack-O-Lantern   A lantern made up of a carved pumpkin and candle

JBOD   Just a Bunch of Disks, used for non-RAID configurations

JCL   IBM Mainframe Job Control Language

JDBC   Java Data Base Connectivity API

JetStress   Microsoft performance benchmark for Exchange

JFS2   IBM's Journal File System (v2) for AIX operating system

journaling   To keep a log of updates to help with recovery

JPEG   Joint Photographic Experts Group, picture encoding format

JS22   IBM's POWER-based blade server for the IBM BladeCenter

K —

KAON V-Osk

    An interactive touch-screen used in briefing centers and at conference events

katazukeru   Japanese for "Space Management"

KB   1000 bytes, see "Units of Storage" section of this book

Kevin Bacon, six degrees of

    A trivia game based on the idea that, due to his prolific screen career, any Hollywood actor can be "linked" to another in a handful of "steps" based to actor Kevin Bacon

Keynote

    Apple's presentation software, similar to Microsoft Powerpoint

killer app

    Any software that is unexpectedly useful, necessary or desirable that it provides the core value of some larger technology

Kodak   [kodak.com] Photographic equipment manufacturer

KPI   Key Performance Indicators

kVA   Kilovolt-ampere, a unit for measuring electricity

KVM Keyboard, Video, Monitor. Also used for Kernel Virtual Machine

KVOA NBC affiliate local to Tucson, Arizona

kW

> 1000 watts, roughly equivalent to the electrical consumption of the average American household

L —

LAMP Linux, Apache, MySQL and PHP software stack

LAN see "Local Area Network"

laptop Portable computer, sometimes called "notebook"

laptop mentality Inability for humans to think in large scale

Large Hadron Collider

> World's largest and highest-energy particle accelerator

Laser Light Amplification by Stimulated Emission of Radiation

latency Time delay experienced in a system

LCRB Low cost RAID brick

Leader Quadrant Upper right corner of Gartner Magic Quadrant

LeftHand Maker of iSCSI-only disk systems, acquired by HP in 2008

Legato NetWorker Backup software, acquired by EMC

Lenovo IBM sold off its Personal Computer division to Lenovo

library

> A tape automation system, typically involving shelves containing tape cartridges, several tape drives and robotics to move cartridges between shelves and drives, or a disk-based system that emulates such a tape environment. Also used on mainframes to refer to a data set that contains programs or JCL jobs

Linux

> An open source operating system developed by Linux Torvalds

Linux on System z

> Distributions of Linux packaged for the S/390 instruction set

Liquid Agency Agency that recognizes brand recognition

LiveCD

A bootable CD that contains an entire operating system

Local Area Network (LAN)

A computer network covering a small geographic area, typically based on IP technology such as Ethernet or Wi-Fi

Logical Partition (LPAR)

A subset of a physical system's resources, virtualized to appear as its own separate system, applies to servers and storage

Long Tail

The infrequent items that can represent a majority, based on the article and book by Chris Anderson

Longwave

Light transmission at 1310 to 1550 nanometers, for distances up to 50km over single-mode fiber optic

LOST Popular American TV show

Lotus

Software company acquired by IBM, now an IBM brand for collaboration software, including Lotus Domino (email server), Lotus Notes (email client), and other software

LotusSphere IBM confernece for users of Lotus software

low hanging fruit

Items that can provide immediate benefit with little effort (post #382)

LPAR See Logical Partition

LPI

Linux Professional Institute, a non-profit organization for certification exams

lpr spooling daemon to print files

LSI

IBM supplier of DS3000, DS4000 and DS5000 disk systems, partially acquired by NetApp

LTO Linear Tape Open, a consortium of IBM, HP and Quantum [lto.org]

LTO-3 LTO generation 3. Used for both drives and cartridges

LTO-4

LTO generation 4. Used for both drives and cartridges

LUN

Logical unit number for an individual disk presented to a host, and often refers to the disk itself. For example, a LUN can be the "D:" drive of a Windows server, or raw logical volume (pdisk) on a UNIX system

Lustre   A clustered file system, acquired by Sun Microsystems

LUW   Linux, UNIX, and Windows operating systems

LZH   File format compressed with the Lempel-Zip-Huffman algorithms

M —

Mac Mini   Personal computer from Apple, Inc.

Mac OS   Apple's operating system

Magic Quadrant   Gartner's 2x2 grid to evaluate vendors

MAID

Massive Array of Idle Disk, sometimes referred to as Spin-Down or Sleep-Mode

mapping

The process of connecting virtual resources to physical resources

Mainstar®   Mainstar Software Corporation [mainstar.com]

mashup

A creative combination of media, such as music and other sounds, created by other artists (post #363)

Maui   EMC Atmos software

Maximo   A technology conference

MB   1,000,000 bytes, see "Units of Storage" section of this book

Mbps   Million bits per second transmission

McDATA   SAN equipment manufacturer acquired by Brocade

MCF   Management Complexity Factor

MDS   Cisco SAN "Multilayer Director Switch" family of products

---

media

>The actual physical recording structure, either solid state chip, magnetic coated disk or tape, or optical disc

megawatt   one million Watts

metadata

>Information about other data, to provide additional context, such as a caption under a photograph

metrics

>A system of parameters or ways of quantitative and periodic assessment of a process that is to be measured

Metro Mirror   IBM's synchronous disk mirroring capability

microcode

>lowest-level instructions that directly control a microprocessor inside storage device

microfiche

>Flat sheets of photographic film containing documents reduced to about twenty-fifth of original size

Microsoft

>Software company which creates Windows and many other products [Microsoft.com]

mid-sized companies   Companies with 100-999 employees

middleware   Software that acts as a platform for other applications

midrange   Medium-- for Small, Medium, Large designations

MIPS

>Million Instructions per Second, used to compare CPU processor cycles capability between different mainframe server models

mission-critical   The most important applications of a business

MIT   Massachusetts Institute of Technology

MMORPG   Massively multiplayer online role-playing game

model T

>an automobile produced by the Ford motor company that is generally considered to have been the first affordable car, thanks in part to Ford's process of assembly line production

Mohave experiment

> An experiment conducted by Microsoft in an attempt to understand negative reactions to their Vista operating system (post #332)

monolithic

> A scale-up system containing all components in one or more connected frames

mount

> The process to put a tape cartridge into a tape drive, also the process of connecting one files system to another file system

MPG Miles Per Gallon

MPIO Multipathing IO driver, typically native to OS

MP3 MPEG-1 Audio Layer 3, an audio recording format

MRO Software Maximo Software maker, acquired by IBM

MSFT See "Microsoft"

MTBF Mean Time Between Failures, measured in unit-hours

Multipathing driver

> A host-based driver that manages multiple FC paths to storage devices, such as for load balancing or fail over

multisource

> The approach to have multiple suppliers, either for parts or for outsourced computer services, or to blend internal with external sources

Myers-Briggs

> A system of categorizing personalities into types based on the work of Isabel Myers-Briggs and Carl Jung

Myrinet

> A high-speed local area networking system designed by Myricom to be used as an interconnect between multiple machines to form computer clusters, such as for high performance computing (HPC)

MySpace Social interaction website [myspace.com]

MySQL

> Open source database management system [mysql.com] acquired by Sun Microsystems and subsequently by Oracle

MzGM   Metro Mirror with z/OS Global Mirror

N —

N series

> IBM's unified storage disk systems

NAND

> "Not AND", often refers to Solid-State flash memory that uses a series of floating gate transistors

Nanotechnology

> The study of the controlling of matter on an atomic and molecular scale, with structures sized between 1 to 100 nanometer in at least one dimension

NAS   see "Network Attached Storage"

NAS gateway

> A disk system that offers NAS interfaces to host servers, and attaches to external storage systems to store data

NAS head   See "NAS gateway"

NDMP

> Network Data Management Protocol, an open standard protocol for enterprise-wide backup of network-attached storage (NAS)

NEBS

> Network Equipment-Building System, Telecommunication standards for IT hardware

NEDC New Enterprise Data Center

NENR   see "Non-erasable, Non-rewriteable"

NetApp

> Network Appliance, Inc. [netapp.com]

NetBackup   Backup software from Symantec

Network Attached Storage (NAS)

> Storage accessed via IP connectivity, typically through a file-level protocol such as CIFS, NFS, HTTP or FTP

Network File System (NFS)

A protocol originally developed by Sun Microsystems in 1984 for Network-Attached Storage (NAS) devices

Network Interface Card (NIC)

An interface card inside a server to connect to IP network, such as Ethernet or Token Ring

NetworkWorld   News publisher [networkworld.com]

Nextra   Original name of IBM XIV system

NFS   See "Network File System"

NGO   Non-governmental organization

NIC

Network Interface Card, a computer card that connects a computer's bus to an external Local Area Network, such as Ethernet

NOAO   National Optical Astronomy Observatory

Non-disruptive migration

Moving data from one storage device to another without impacting access to read and write data

Non-disruptive update

To update the microcode or other software on a server or storage device without impacting access to data

Non-disruptive upgrade

To add or update hardware on a server or storage device without impacting access to data

Non-erasable, Non-rewriteable (NENR)

A generic term that refers to disk-based compliance storage solutions, as well as WORM tape and optical, which enforce that data, once written, is not deleted or modified for a specific time period, after which the data can be deleted or destroyed. Based on language in US SEC 17a-4 legislation

non-repudiation

A state of affairs where the purported maker of a statement will not be able to successfully challenge the validity of the statement, such as with a notarized or digital signature

Non-volatile Storage (NVS)

> Storage that does not lose its information when primary power is lost, such as computer memory protected by battery backup

Notebook   A laptop computer

Notepad   Microsoft built-in text editor

NovusCG   Novus Consulting Group, acquired by IBM

NPIV   N-post ID Virtualization

NPML   Noise-predictive Maximum Likelihood

NPR   National Public Radio [npr.org]

NT   New Technology, Microsoft Windows operating system, see OS/2

NTFS   Windows NT File System

NTFS-3G   NTFS read/write driver for Linux [ntfs-3g.org]

NVS   See "non-volatile storage"

NYT   New York Times [nytimes.com]

NYSE   New York Stock Exchange [nyse.com]

N3000 series   Entry-level N series disk systems

N5000 series   Midrange IBM System Storage N series

N6000 series

> IBM's midrange disk systems for unified block and file level access

N6070   A model of IBM's midrange unified disk system

N7000 series   Enterprise-class IBM System Storage N series

O —

Octagon Global Recruiting   See "Dharma Initiative"

ODF   Open Document Format

OEM

> The company that originally manufactured the product or component. Also used as a verb for re-branding, namely where one company uses a component of another company within its product, or sells the product of another company under its own brand

Office 2007   Microsoft office productivity software suite

offline   Disconnected from network or computing facility

offload   To transfer responsibility to peripheral device

off-topic   Blog postings that do not relate to blog topic

OLAP Online Analytics Process

OLAP cube

A multi-dimensional data structure that allows for fast access for Online Analytics Processing (OLAP)

OLPC One Laptop Per Child organization [laptop.org]

OLTP Online Transaction Processing

one-for-one mapping

A mapping in which the entire physical resource is mapped to a virtual resource

one throat to choke

A benefit of working with a single supplier or one-stop shopping "IT Supermarket". If something goes wrong with your servers, storage, or switches, you can make a single phone call to IBM and it will be all taken care of for you

ONTAP

NetApp's proprietary operating system which includes code borrowed from Berkeley Net/2 BSD Unix and other operating systems

open source

Source code of software that is available to the general public with relaxed intellectual property restrictions

open source community

The users and developers of a particular piece of open source software

open storage

The concept of building your own storage systems from commodity servers and open source file systems promoted by Sun Microsystems

open systems

All IBM servers are open systems, indicating that they can run one or more Linux, Unix and Windows operating systems that meet the Open Group's Single UNIX specification. Sometimes used within storage to refer to "distributed systems" that use standard 512-byte block SCSI commands to access data to disk or tape devices

OpenOffice

A multiplatform and multilingual office suite and an open-source project, based on Sun's StarOffice [openoffice.org]

OpenSolaris

Open source computer operating system based on Solaris created by Sun Microsystems

OPEX   Operational Expenditures

Optim   Archive software from Princeton Softech, acquired by IBM

Optim Data Privacy Solution

IBM software to identify potential privacy issues relating to database schema

Oracle   Oracle Corporation [oracle.com], database and applications

Orion Utility   Oracle I/O Calibration Tool

organization

A business enterprise, government agency or non-profit entity

OS   Operating System

OSX   Apple Macintosh Operating System version 10

OS/390   Operating System/390, renamed to z/OS

OS/400   Operating System/400, renamed to i5/OS

P —

PaaS   Platform-as-a-Service

packet   a contiguous set of bytes that serve as unit of transmission

PACS   Picture Archiving and Communication System

Paleolithic diet

A modern dieting regimen that excludes food products which did not exsit prior to the advent of agriculture (post #294)

PAM   Performance Accelerator Module

PA-RISC

Hewlett Packard's "Precision Architecture, Reduced Instruction Set Computing" CPU chipset

Passport Advantage

IBM ordering system for some of its software and hardware products

PAV   On IBM System z, Parallel Access Volume

PAYGO   A Pay-as-you-go plan for XIV (#344)

PB   1000 Terabytes, see "Units of Storage" section of this book

PC   Personal Computer

PCFE   Power, Cooling, Floorspace Environments

PDA   Personal Digital Assistant

PDF   Portable Document Format

PDT

Pacific Daylight Time, also used within IBM for "Product Development Team"

PDU   Power Distribution Unit

PERCS   Productive, Easy-to-use, Reliable Computing System

Permalink

A URL that points to a specific blogging entry even after the entry has passed from the front page into the blog archives

Persistent Data

Existing or continuing for a long time, typically across system reboots, shutdowns or other outages

PetaFLOP   A quadrillion floating point operations per second

PEZ   A popular candy (post #345)

PHP   PHP Hypertext Preprocessor

pi   3.14159265358979323846264338327950288419716939937511...

pink slip

An American term that refers to being fired or laid off from one's job

PlateSpin

A subsidiary of Novell that produces tools to help manage server virtualization environments

P.O. Purchase Order

PoC Proof of Concept, a trial to show fit for purpose

pods modular sections of a data center

poke fun

To tease, mock, or disparage another blogger, their employer, or their products and offerings

policy-based

Software design principal to enforce broad policies for automated decision making

PolyServe a clustered file system, acquired by HP

portability The ability to transfer a solution to a new platform

POSIX

Portable Operating System Interface, an IEEE standard for file systems

PostgreSQL

Open source database management system [postgresql.org]

POWER

IBM's Power Architecture microprocessor family, including POWER4, POWER5 and POWER6, used in System i and System p server product lines as well as various storage products.

PowerExecutive IBM software to monitor energy consumed

PowerVM IBM's hypervisor for POWER Systems servers

PPRC Peer-to-Peer Remote Copy

presence awareness

Technologies that are able to take physical presence of end user into account, such as GPS, BlueTooth, or RFID

PRA Presidential Records Act

press release

A written or recorded communication directed at members of the news media for the purpose of announcing something claimed as having news value

---

Prime Directive

Concept in TV show "Star Trek" to honor the sovereignty of other cultures, on other worlds, and play by their rules when you are on their planet

Princeton Softech

Archive software company acquired by IBM

private key   See Asymmetric key

processor

In software, an individual CPU core. In hardware, the CPU chip that fits into a single socket that contains one or more cores

PROFS   Professional Office System

Project Big Green

IBM's bold initiative to help both clients and internal departments within IBM to use less energy in the data center

Project Quicksilver

IBM's research project to support Solid-State Drives in IBM SAN Volume Controller

provisioning   The process to deploy resources into usage

public key   See Asymmetric key

PUE   Power Usage Effectiveness

Pulse   A technology conference

PVU   Processor Value Unit

Q —

Q&A   Question and Answer, discussion with a panel of experts

QA system

Question Answering system, such as the one Watson uses (post #434)

QCC   IBM Quarter Century Club

Qlogic Semiconductor manufacturer [qlogic.com]

QoS   Quality of Service

qualifier   one to eight characters, part of z/OS data set name

quad-core   A CPU chip that contains four processing engine cores

Quantum   Quantum Corp. [quantum.com]

Quota

In sales, the minimum amount of revenue, profit or units to be sold to reach a desired incentive level.. In IT storage, see "hard quota" and "soft quota"

Quicken   Financial software ISV [quicken.com]

R —

R&D   Research and development

R/3

SAP's ERP software application, now called the SAP ERP module of the SAP Business Suite

RAC   Oracle Real Application Cluster

Racetrack Memory   A form of Storage Class Memory

RACF   IBM z/OS Resource Access Control Facility element

RAID   Redundant Array of Independent Disks

RAID-DP

Diagonal parity, performance-enhanced RAID-6 on IBM System Storage N series that protects against multiple disk failure

RAID-X   IBM's version of RAID-10 for the IBM XIV Storage System

RAID-0   Striping data across two or more disk drive modules

RAID-1   Disk mirroring between two disk drive modules

RAID-10   Data that is striped and mirrored, RAID-1 with RAID-0

RAID-5

Striping data, with an added parity that is spread across three or more disk drive modules

RAID-6   Parity schemes that protect against multiple disk failures

RAID rank   Two or more disks that are the complete RAID set

RAINfinity   A file virtualization company acquired by EMC

raised floor

> In a typical data center, a structure holding tiles 12-18 inches above ground level, used to direct cooled air and to store cables

RAM   Random Access Memory, including SRAM, DRAM and SDRAM

RAM drive   disk system emulated in RAM memory

RAMAC

> Random Access Memory Accounting System, IBM's first IBM mainframe server to use external disk systems. Later, the name RAMAC was re-used for IBM disk systems

RAMAC Virtual Array (RVA)

> IBM's first thin-provisioning disk system for mainframe servers

RAMsan   SSD disk system from Texas Memory Systems

RAMsan-500   A model of RAMsan Disk System

random access

> Storage access that does not require starting at the beginning of the storage media and positioning forward. Often used for disk and memory type storage

RAS   Reliability, Availability and Serviceability

Rational   Software company acquired by IBM, now an IBM brand

Rationalization

> In ILM, the process of associating business value to the information represented by particular data, often used as a first step of a deployment to find unnecessary or low-value data

Raven Black   Official color of IBM Systems server and storage hardware

RDBMS   Relational Database Management System

RDHX Rear Door Heat Exchanger

RDM   Raw Device Mapping, VMware

RDMA   Remote Direct Memory Access protocol

Really Simple Syndication (RSS)

> A family of Web feed formats used to publish frequently updated content such as blog entries, news headlines or podcasts

Rear Door Heat Exchanger

> IBM's water-cooled back door for 42U enterprise racks to help remove as much as 55% of the heat generated by equipment in the rack

reboot The process of restarting a server or other system

rebuild

> After a DDM failure in a RAID rank, the process to take a new blank DDM, and reconstruct the data based on parity or disk mirror

reclamation

> Moving valid data from existing tape to fewer number of new tapes. This is the TSM and VTS version equivalent of similar RECYCLE function.

Recovery Point Objective (RPO)

> The amount of time prior to disaster outage that you are willing to lose in the event of a disaster

Recovery Time Objective (RTO)

> The amount of time after a disaster outage that you desire to be back in operational mode

RECYCLE

> An IBM z/OS DFSMS command to consolidate valid data from a set of tapes onto a fewer number of tapes

recycle

> To restart or reboot a system or application, see also "reclamation"

Redbook   IBM how-to manual [www.redbooks.ibm.com]

re-driving

> The process of replacing existing disk drive modules with new ones that are faster, higher capacity or use less energy

redundant

> Exceeding what is necessary, either using duplicate components, or one or more extra components, to increase availability

render To display or present data into human-understandable form

replication

> Copy services that involve making a second copy, such as disk mirroring, or tape clusters

resilience

> Ability to recover from, or to resist being affected by, some spike in workload, outage, or disturbance

resolution

> The level of granularity for pictures and video, typically based on number of pixels, or dots per square inch

REST

> Representational State Transfer, a style of software architecture for distributed hypermedia systems such as the World Wide Web

restore

> To copy the dumped contents back to original media, often as a first step in data recovery

rewriteable   storage that can be erased and/or re-written

RFID   Radio Frequency Identification

RFP   Request for Proposal

RHEL   Red Hat Enterprise Linux

rich media   Audio, Graphic or Video data

rip   To capture digital music files from an Audio CD

rip-and-replace

> To remove all elements of an existing infrastructure entirely and replace with all brand new infrastructure. For example, to remove all EMC disk and replace with all IBM disk at a data center

RoHS   European Union (EU) Restriction of Hazardous Substances Directive

ROI   Return on Investment percentage, a financial term

Roller

> Open source Java blog server that drives blogs.sun.com, IBM Developer Works blogs and numerous other sites [rollerweblogger.org/project/]

root cause analysis (RCA)

> In debugging, to find the initial cause of a symptom

router

> A specialized switch that has the added ability to connect different SAN networks, either through Fibre Channel directly, or conversion to IP network such as FCIP protocol

---

ROWE Results Oriented Work Environment

RPO see "Recovery Point Objective"

RPM Revolutions Per Minute

RPQ

> Request for Product Quote, typically a one-off request to test and support a specific platform, operating system, or feature (#182)

RSA

> Remote Service Adapter, also can refer to "Rivest, Shamir, & Adleman, security" ISV company acquired by EMC

RSS see "Really Simple Syndication"

RTO see "Recovery Time Objective"

RVA see "RAMAC Virtual Array"

S —

SaaS Software as a Service, cloud computing delivery model

Safari Apple web browser, from the Kiswahili word "journey"

SalesForce

> Software-as-a-Service company focused on CRM [salesforce.com]

SAM-FS

> Open source file system developed by Sun Microsystems, also known as SAM-QFS or just QFS

SAN Storage Area Network

SAN Integration Server (SIS)

> A disk system containing SAN Volume Controller and DS4000 disk

SAN island A SAN isolated from the rest of the data center

SAN Volume Controller IBM's leading disk virtualization product

sandbox

> Term for "test systems" to train new storage administrators

SANSymphony DataCore storage virtualization software

SAN04B-R IBM Fibre Channel Router, with 2 FC and 2 IP ports

SAN18B-R IBM Fibre Channel Router, with 16 FC and 2 IP ports

SAN256B   IBM SAN director, manufactured by Brocade

SAN24B-4   IBM entry-level SAN switch with maximum 24 ports

SAN40B-4   IBM midrange SAN switch with maximum 40 ports

SAN768B

> IBM high-end SAN director with maximum 384 ports, with option to connect two together

SAN80B-4   IBM midrange SAN switch with maximum 80 ports

SAP

> Originally, Systemanalyse und Programmentwicklung AG. In 2005, renamed to Systeme, Anwendungen, Produkte in der Datenverarbeitung AG, which is German for "Systems, Applications, and Products in Data Processing, Inc.", an Enterprise Application software ISV [sap.com]

Sara-Cuda

> A crossbow from Lakota Industries, clad in pink-toned camouflage, weighs in at 3.4 pounds, with a draw length of 25 to 31 inches, especially designed to accommodate women hunters and archers

Sarbanes-Oxley (SOX)

> Also known as the US Public Company Accounting Reform and Investor Protection Act of 2002 and commonly called SOX or Sarbox, named after sponsors Senator Paul Sarbanes (D-MD) and Representative Michael G. Oxley (R-OH)

SAS   Serial Attached SCSI, also used for SAS Institute Inc. [sas.com]

SATA

> Serial ATA, a mass-produced disk drive module that spins slower, and consumes less energy that faster drives

Scale-out

> Adding more capacity by adding individual nodes to a cluster, such as server nodes to a grid or supercomputer deployment

Scale-up

> Increasing the capacity and performance of a single system

Scale-within

> To add workloads through virtual/logical partitioning

ScanMyPhotos A photo-scanning service company [scanmyphotos.com]

SCON Server Consolidation (do not confuse with ESCON).

scratch tape   A tape that is empty, or can be over-written

SCSI   Small Computer System Interface

SDD

   IBM Subsystem Device Driver, a multipathing driver for IBM
   DS8000 and SAN Volume Controller, the acronym also used for the
   OASIS Solution Deployment Descriptor interface

SDH   Synchronous Digital Hierarchy standard

SDM   System Data Mover, component of z/OS

SDRAM   Synchronous Dynamic Random Access Memory

SDRF/EDP   Extended Data Protection (post #426)

SE   Space Efficient, also used for Systems Engineer

Sea-Land Co.   A transportation company, sold to Maersk in 1999

Seagate   Disk drive module supplier [Seagate.com]

SEC   US Securities and Exchange Commission

SEC 17a-4   Legislation by the U.S. Securities and Exchange Commission

Second Life   A virtual world with 3D animation [secondlife.com]

second tier   Typically slower disk, see "tier"

SEFC   Space-Efficient FlashCopy

semi-structured

   Systems like email that are not completely structured databases, but
   offer some structure to find records

SERP   Storage Enterprise Resource Planner

ServeRAID   IBM RAID adapater for IBM System x servers

service offering

   Software sold with services and billed as a service, rather than as a
   product

serviceability

   Ability of technical support personnel to debug or perform root
   cause analysis in pursuit of solving a problem with a product

SEV   Space-Efficient Volume

SFP

Small form-factor pluggable (SFP), a compact, hot-pluggable transceiver used for both telecommunication and data communications applications. It interfaces a network device mother board to a fiber optic or copper networking cable, to support SONET, Gigabit Ethernet, and Fibre Channel

ShadowImage HDS point-in-time disk copy

SHARE SHARE, Inc., an IBM user group [share.org]

shelf-resident

Removable media, such as tape or optical cartridges, that are not housed in an automated library

shell

For laptops, the outer casing minus hard disk and CD/DVD drive. Also used to refer to run-time interactive command line environment on LUW platforms

shimau Japanese for "Data Retention"

Shortwave 850nm light used for fiber optic transmission of data

shred To overwrite storage media with random patterns of data

SI System Integrators

single-controller Storage system models that have a single controller

single point of failure (SPOF)

A component in a system that if failed would cause system outage failed. Most IBM products are designed to have no single point of failure

single pane of glass

Having all parts of a management or monitoring system on a single computer screen

single point of repair (SPOR)

A component in a system that to repair or replace would require system outage. Most IBM products are designed to have no single point of repair

Single Sign-On

Identity management software that allows a single userid/password to be used for multiple systems

Singularity, the

> The hypothetical future emergence of greater-than-human intelligence through technological means, proposed initially by Raymond Kurtzweil

six degrees   see "Kevin Bacon"

Skype   Online phone and video communication service [skype.com]

SL   See Second Life

SLA   Service Level Agreement

SLES   SUSE Linux Enterprise Server

SLURL   Second Life URL [slurl.com]

SMART   Self-Monitoring, Analysis, and Reporting Technology

SmartSuite   IBM Lotus SmartSuite collaboration software

sMash

> WebSphere sMash, a development and execution platform for quickly building agile, web-based applications

SMB   Small and Medium sized Business, typically 1-999 employees

SME

> Subject Matter Expert.   Sometimes used to refer to "Small and Medium sized Enterprises", an extension to SMB that also includes non-profit organizations and government agencies

SMF

> IBM System Management Facility for the z/OS mainframe operating system

SMI

> Storage Management Initiative. The SNIA task force of vendors including IBM that wrote the SMI-S specification

SMI-S   Storage Management Initiative Specification

SnapLock™

> NENR protection on IBM System Storage N series

SNIA   Storage Networking Industry Association [snia.org]

SNW   Storage Networking World conference [snwonline.com]

SOA   Service Oriented Architecture, previously Simple Object Access

SOAP   SOA protocol for applications to exchange data

Social bookmarking

> Facility to bookmark web pages with tags so that others can see them, such as Del.icio.us

Social networking

> Using Web 2.0 websites to meet and collaborate

SoFS   Scale-out File Services

Soft quota

> In IT storage, a loosely-enforced upper maximum of space allowed to a user, department or application. Once reached, all further requests for additional will be permitted, but will notify storage administrators that such limit had been reached

Softek   Data migration company acquired by IBM

Softech   See "Princeton Softech"

SOHO   Small Office/Home Office, a market segment for entry-level

Solaris   Sun Microsystems operating system

sole-sourced   To have a single supplier for a particular component

SONET   Synchronous Optical NETwork standard

Sony   Electronics manufacturer, including tape [sony.com]

SOX   See Sarbanes-Oxley

SPAM   Unwanted email, derived from the 1970 Monty Python sketch

SPAM filter   Policies to automate the handling of SPAM

SPARC

> Scalable Processor Architecture, a RISC instruction set architecture developed by Sun Microsystems

spare disk

> Extra unused disk drive modules that are available in case of disk failure, typically used for rebuild

sparse file

> A file that may have long sequences of zeros that are not physically stored on the device

SPC   Storage Performance Council [storageperformance.org]

Specialty Shop   Analogy for some vendors

spin-lock

> A lock where the thread is simply busy waiting in a loop repeatedly checking until the lock becomes available

spinning disk

> Disk system based on rotational platters, as opposed to memory-based disk systems that do not have any rotating parts

SPOF   See "Single Point of Failure"

SPOR   See "Single Point of Repair"

SQL   See "Structured Query Language" or "SQL Server"

SQL Server   Microsoft's database management system

SRDF   Symmetrix Remote Data Facility, EMC's disk mirroring

SRM   Storage Resource Management

SSA

> Serial Storage Architecture, an IO protocol. Sometimes also used for "Storage Sales Academy"

SSAM   System Storage Archive Manager

SSD   Solid-State Device, memory-based storage system

SSH

> Secure Shell, a network protocol that allows data to be exchanged using a secure channel between two networked devices

SSP   Storage Service Provider

SSPC   IBM System Storage Productivity Center

stack

> A set of software, and sometimes hardware, that depend on each other and offered in workload-optimized systems

stand-alone   Not part of a tape library or rack environment

STEC   (post #336)

stewardship

> Personal responsibility for taking care of another person's property, information, or financial affairs

STG   See "Systems and Technology Group"

STK   StorageTek, now a subsidiary of Sun Microsystems

storage admin

> An IT administrator responsible for storage-related tasks, such as deploying and maintaining storage, configuring devices, monitoring performance, and performing backups

Storage Anarchist   see Blog Roll

StorageMojo   see Blog Roll

StorageZilla   see Blog Roll

Storage Tank   An IBM research project, now called SONAS

StorageTek   Storage manufacturer acquired by Sun Microsystems

StoreAge   A disk virtualization company acquired by LSI Logic

Stor-o-Sphere

> Unofficial name for the subset of the Blogosphere related to IT storage topics

STP   Server time Protocol

structured data   Data stored in databases

Structured Query Language (SQL)

> Computer language designed for the retrieval and management of data in relational database management systems (RDBMS).

"sub-capacity" licensing   (post #423)

subsystem

> A portion of a total system, appropriate for DFSMS or SDD software, or internal storage, but not appropriate to refer to external disk or tape systems.

Sun   Sun Microsystems [sun.com]

Sun Fire X2100 (post #312)

sunshine makes a great disinfectant   (post #368)

supercomputer

> A cluster of computer nodes, typically Linux on x86 hardware, designed to run mathematically-intense computations, such as animated graphics, fluid dynamic calculations, nuclear energy research, and petroleum exploration. [www.top500.org/]

supermarket   Analogy for some vendors

survival phrases

> A handful of important useful phrases in a foreign language

SVC   see SAN Volume Controller

SVC "entry edition"

The 2145-8A4 model of the IBM SAN Volume Controller

SVC for Cisco MDS 9000 blade

An implementation of SVC on a Cisco MDS 9000 blade form factor

SW

Abbreviation for Software, also used internally for the Southwest IOT in EMEA.

Sybase   Sybase Inc. [Sybase.com]

Symantec   Symantec Corp, storage software ISV [Symantec.com] (#252)

symmetric key

A single key that can be used for both encryption and decryption

symposium

In ancient Greece, the symposium was a drinking party (from Greek *sympotein*, "to drink together"). Today, used as a term for a conference for researchers and others to present and discuss their work, providing an important channel for exchange of information

Sysplex

Short for System Complex: two or more System z that share a common timer, known as a "Sysplex timer"

SysRescCD   System Rescue CD [sysresccd.org]

System i   IBM "integrated" server product line

System p   IBM's POWER-based UNIX server product line

System Storage Archive Manager (SSAM)

IBM's software for managing archives, formerly called "Tivoli Storage Manager for Data Retention"

System x   IBM's x86 server product line

System z   IBM's near-zero downtime mainframe server product line

Systems and Technology Group (STG)

One of the primary groups within IBM, responsible for servers, storage, retail point-of-sale cash registers, and microprocessors

S24

IBM High-Density TS3500 frame that can hold up to 1,000 Enterprise tape cartridges

IBM High-Density TS3500 frame that can hold up to 1,320 LTO tape cartridges

T —

TADDM   Tivoli Application Dependence Discover Manager

tag   Keyword to help find blog post or web site

Tagmastore   See USP

Tape Volume Cache   The disk portion of a disk-and-tape VTL

target volumes   See "destination volumes"

TB   1000 Gigabytes (see "Units of Storage" section of this book)

TCA   Total Cost of Acquisition

TCM   Turner Classic Movies

TCO   Total Cost of Ownership

TCP   Transport Communication Protocol

TDMF   See "Transparent Data Mover Facility"

Technorati   A search engine for blogs [www.technorati.com]

TED

Technology, Entertainment, Design -- a conference held in Monterey, California

temporary files   Files that can be deleted when system is restarted

TEP   Tivoli Enterprise Portal

"Test Plan Charlie"

A test of running 98,000 Linux guest images on a single mainframe by David Boyes of Sine Nomine Associates

TEU   Twenty-foot equivalent unit

Texas Memory Systems   storage vendor [texmemsys.com]

TFA   Tucson Fun and Adventures

thermophiles   algae and bacteria that thrive in extreme heat

ThinkPad   laptop computers made by Lenovo

Tipping Point   Start of an epidemic or trend

tier

A level of storage with particular cost point or other characteristics. Typically "tier 1" refers to fastest (10K or 15K RPM) disk, and "tier 2" for slower 7200 RPM disk. Tiers can also be used with tape and optical devices

TiVo Developer of digital video record software [tivo.com]

Tivoli A software company acquired by IBM

TKLM IBM Tivoli Key Lifecycle Manager v1.0

TOE TCP-Offload-Engine (post #385)

Top Gun IBM sales training classes

topology A diagram showing IT equipment connections

Toshiba Laptop and electronics manufacturer [toshiba.com]

TotalStorage Former IBM brand for storage offerings

TotalStorage Productivity Center

IBM storage infrastructure management software, later renamed to IBM Tivoli Storage Productivity Center

TOE TCP Offload Engine, an enhanced NIC

TPC

Tournament Players Club [tpc.com], a registered trademark of the Professional Golfers' Association. Sometimes used for IBM "Tivoli Storage Productivity Center", or that IBM is one of the three "technology provider companies" of the LTO consortium, or that IBM servers participate in Transaction Processing Performance Council [tpc.org] benchmarks

TPC-C Server performance benchmark

TPC-H Decision Support Performance benchmark

TPF Transaction Processing Facility, operating system for System z

Transparent Data Mover Facility (TDMF)

Host-based software to move data non-disruptively from one storage device to another, part of IBM's acquisition of Softek

TrueCopy HDS long-distance disk replication feature

TS Tape System. IBM prefix for tape system family of products

TSA The Storage Anarchist (Barry Burke)

TSM See Tivoli Storage Manager, backup and archive software

TS1120	An IBM Enterprise tape drive
TS2230	An IBM LTO tape drive
TS2900	An IBM tape auto-loader, holds LTO drives
TS3100	An IBM tape library, holds LTO drives
TS3200	An IBM tape library, holds LTO drives
TS3400	An IBM tape library, holds TS1120 drives

TS3500

IBM's flagship tape library, can house both LTO and TS1120 drive technology

TS650G	IBM ProtecTIER data de-duplication VTL
TS7520	IBM VTL for Linux, UNIX, and Windows
TS7530	IBM VTL for Linux, UNIX, and Windows
TS7650G	(post #339)
TS7700	Family of IBM VTL for System z mainframe servers
TS7720	Disk-only model of TS7700 virtual tape library
TS7740	Disk-and-tape model of TS7700 virtual tape library
TTFN	Ta-Ta For Now (internet slang)
TUAM	Tivoli Usage and Accounting Manager

Turbo

Often used to designate "second generation" such as DS8300 Turbo is the follow-on to the original DS8300 disk system

Turing, Alan

English mathematician, logician, cryptanalyst and computer scientist, influential in the development of computer, concept of the algorithm, and computation with the Turing machine

| **Twitter** | A social microblogging service [twitter.com] |
| **T60** | IBM/Lenovo ThinkPad laptop model |

U —

U	A unit of height for computer equipment, 1.75 inches
Ubiquity project	A simple Linux installer for Ubuntu
Ubuntu	A distribution of Linux [ubuntu.com]

UCB   Unit Control Block, used for I/O on z/OS servers

UDP   User Datagram Protocol

uncheck   To remove a checkmark from a computer screen

unified communications

> the integration of real-time communication services such as instant messaging, telephony and video conferencing with non-real-time services like email, SMS text messages and fax

unified storage

> Storage such as the IBM System Storage N series that offers multiple protocols, such as file-level CIFS and NFS as well as block-level iSCSI and FCP protocols

Universal Database   IBM DB2 database

unstructured data

> Data that is not in a database or email repository, such as individual text files, music files, images, and so on

uptime Time when system is operational and accessible.

UPS   Uninterruptible power source, such as battery backup

URL   Universal Record Locator

USB   Universal Serial Bus

USB key   A memory-based disk system that connects via USB

USD   United States Dollar

User-Centered Design (UCD)

> Process in which the needs, wants, and limitations of the end user are factored into the design the human-machine interface

USP

> HDS TagmaStore Universal Storage Platform family of disk systems

USP-V   Particular model of HDS USP disk system family

utilization

> The percentage of actual data stored divided by total capacity available

V —

v-business   Doing business through 3D internet virtual worlds

---

VAC

> Volts Alternating Current, may also be used to refer to Vác, Hungary, an IBM Manufacturing location

VAR Value-added Resellers

vdisk Virtual Disk, such as those from IBM SVC

VEF Venezuelan monetary currency, Bolívares Fuertes

vendor lock-in

> Attributes or features that prevent customers from choosing alternative vendors, forcing clients to continue with the incumbent vendor

Veritas   A software company acquired by Symantec

vertically-integrated

> The degree to which a firm owns its upstream suppliers and its downstream buyers.

VFM IBM Virtual File Manager

VHS Video Home System, video cartridge format

VIOS Virtual I/O Server

VIPA Virtual IP Addressing

Virtual Iron

> Server virtualization management software acquired by Oracle

Virtual Tape Library (VTL)

> Generic term for a disk-based tape system that emulates a physical tape library

Virtual Tape Server (VTS)

> IBM's VTL for mainframe environments, replaced by TS7700 series

virtualization

> Technology that makes one set of resources look and feel like a different set of resources. Virtualization can be used for servers, storage, and networks

Virtualization Engine   IBM designator for virtualization offerings

virus Software that copies itself to other computers

Vista Microsoft Windows operating system

VLSI Technology   Very Large Scale Integration

VM Virtual Machine, also used to refer to IBM's z/VM operating system

V-Max An EMC storage platform

VMDK Virtual Machine Disk file format

VMfs VMware File System

Vmotion

> VMware feature to allow live migration of VM guest from one host machine to another with zero downtime

VMmark Performance benchmark test for VMware workloads

VMware

> Server virtualization software company [vmware.com], majority-owned by EMC

VoIP Voice Over IP

VOLSER Six-character volume serial number

VP Vice President

VPN Virtual Private Network

VSAM

> Virtual Storage Access Method, can also refer to databases and other data sets that are accessed using this interface

VSM

> Virtual Storage Manager, a virtual tape library developed by StorageTek, then acquired by Sun Microsystems

VSS Microsoft Volume Shadow Copy Services

VTL See "Virtual Tape Library"

VTS See "Virtual Tape Server"

W —

walk out the door each evening

> Famous quote: "Our assets walk out of the door each evening. We have to make sure that they come back the next morning." -- N.R. Narayana Murthy, InfoSys

walk-through

> A method to test Disaster Recovery plans by discussing potential scenarios

---

WAN Wide Area Network

WAS IBM WebSphere Application Server

Watson

Codename for an IBM computer designed to defeat human contestants on the show *Jeopardy!*

Watt SI unit of power, equal to one joule of energy per second

WAVV World Alliance VSE VM and Linux

WBEM Web-based Enterprise Management

web server

A system that provides information via HTTP or FTP protocol

Web 2.0

Originally a conference on the resurgence of the Internet after the dot-com crash of 2001, but now refers to the new uses of the Web as a platform, harnessing collective intelligence via Wikis, Blogs, Search Engines, and other social media

webinar A "web seminar," on-line conference

WebSphere An IBM software brand

Western Digital Disk drive module manufacturer [wdc.com]

whiteboard

A white dry-erase board, used instead of chalkboard to communicate information. Also, verb "to use a whiteboard to communicate"

whitepaper An authoritative report

WHO World Health Organization

Wi-Fi Wireless Fidelity technology by Wi-Fi Alliance [wi-fi.org]

wiki

Hawaiian word for "quick'. Today, a "wiki" is a web-page which can be edited by anyone with access to it, allowing for group collaboration

Wikipedia An on-line wiki-based encyclopedia

Windows PE Windows Preinstalled Environment

Wired News publisher [wired.com]

WORD Microsoft Office word processing software

WORM

> Write Once Read Many, indelible recording on tape or optical media

write cycle

> For Flash memory, a write involves a complete erasure of a block of data, followed by writing the new data

WSJ   Wall Street Journal, a newspaper publisher

WWPN   World Wide Port Name

X ━

XAM   eXtensible Access Method (XAM) specification

XCAT   Extreme Cluster Administration Toolkit

Xen   Open-source server virtualization software

XenSource   Open-source distributor for Xen [xensource.com]

Xeon   Intel x86 processor model

Xiotech   Former name of XIO Storage company

XIV

> Storage hardware company founded in 2002 by five graduates from the 14th class (hence the XIV) of the Israeli Army's elite "Talpiot" program

XO

> The XO model of the OLPC laptop, the "X" represents arms and legs of a child, and the "O" represents the head of the child

XOR   Exclusive Or, a binary operation between two bit inputs

XRC   eXtended Remote Copy, now called z/OS Global Mirror

XS   The XS school server for the OLPC laptops

x3650 M2   IBM x86 rack-mounted server (post #408)

x3850 M2   IBM x86 rack-mounted server (post #346)

x3950 M2   IBM x86 rack-mounted server (post #346)

x86

> AMD and Intel processors that support an instruction set architecture based on the Intel 8086 CPU

x86-64   64-bit version of x86 instruction set

Y —

YAC   Yet Another Configurator

Yogi Berra   Baseball player known for his humorous quotations

YouTube   Online video sharing subsidiary of Google, Inc. [youtube.com]

Y2K

> Year 2000 problem, specifically defects with computer programs that caused some date-related processing to operate incorrectly for dates and times on and after January 1, 2000

Z —

z/OS   Primary OS for System z mainframe servers

z/TPF   Transaction Processing Facility, operating system for System z

z/VM   Virtual Machine operating system for System z

z/VSE   Virtual Storage Extended, operating system for System z

zAAP   IBM System z Application Assist Processor

ZDnet   Technology news publisher [zdnet.com]

zFS   IBM z/OS File System

ZFS   Sun Microsystem's Zettabyte File System

zHPF   High Performance FICON for System z

zIIP   IBM System z Application Assist Processor

zone

> In SAN design, a zone limits which servers talk to which ports, which talk to which storage devices

zone membership

> Servers and storage devices that belong to a SAN zone

z10   IBM System z10 mainframe server

z10 Business Class (BC)   Lower-capacity System z mainframe model

1 —

1GbE   1 Gbps Ethernet over optical cabling

1U   A unit of height for computer equipment, 1.75 inches

1:1 mapping   See "one-for-one mapping"

10/100/1000   Mbps for Ethernet, indicates copper cabling

10GbE 10Gbps Ethernet using optical cabling, see Units of Storage

10K   10,000, typically for disk Revolutions per Minute (RPM)

15K   15,000, typically for disk Revolutions per Minute (RPM)

2 —

2-site

Disaster Recovery planning involving two locations. Typically, the first location is the production site, and second location is disaster site

2U   A unit of height for computer equipment, 3.5 inches

3 —

3-site

Disaster Recovery planning involving three locations. Typically, the first location is the production site, second location is nearby "bunker" site, and third location is remote distant "disaster" site

3D   Three-dimensional, such as animation in Second Life

3D Internet   Virtual words accessed over the Internet

3PAR   3PAR Company, a start-up storage vendor [3par.com]

3U   A unit of height for computer equipment, 5.25 inches

305   The first IBM server (RAMAC) to connect to a 350 disk system

3330   An IBM disk system (DASD) circa 1970s

3350   An IBM disk system (DASD) circa 1970s

3380   An IBM disk system (DASD) circa 1980s

3380K   A particular model of the 3380 DASD

3420   IBM tape reels

3480   IBM tape cartridges

350   The industry's first commercial disk system (1956)

3592   The cartridges used in the TS1120 enterprise tape drive

3831   An IBM disk controller circa 1970s

3850

    IBM Mass Storage System (MSS), the industry's first disk virtualization system, introduced in 1974

3995   Optical library, with option to emulate disk for mainframes

3996   Optical library for System p and System i servers

4 ▬

4-digit area codes   Potentially the next Y2K problem

4Gbps   4 Gigabits per second, see Units of storage

42U   Standard computer rack height, 73.5 inches

5 ▬

50 years of disk systems innovation

    IBM introduced the first disk system September 1956

6 ▬

6+P+S

    An 8 disk RAID-5 rank, containing 6 disk volumes' worth of data, parity spanning across 7 volumes, and an empty spare disk

7 ▬

7+P

    An 8 disk RAID-5 rank, containing 7 disk volumes' worth of data, and parity spread across all 8 drives

7U   A unit of height for computer equipment, 12.25 inches

70/30   A workload involving 70% reads and 30% writes

70/30 rule   70 percent truth, 30 percent embellishment

70/30/50

    A 70/30 workload, where 50% of the reads are cache hits

8 —

8-bit byte   Standard byte size, can represent a letter or digit

8-node cluster   The maximum SVC disk system configuration

8F4   8GB cache/4 Gbps model of SAN Volume Controller

8G4   8GB cache/4 Gbps model of SAN Volume Controller

80-characters   The standard size for punched card

800   IBM Enterprise Storage Server (ESS) 800 model

802.1g   Wi-Fi standard, runs up to 54Mbps

9 —

9124   Cisco entry-level switch with 8 to 24 ports

9216A   Cisco midrange switch, with 16 FCP ports

9216i   Cisco midrange switch, with 14 FCP port, two 1GbE ports

99.9%   "Three Nines" availability, no more than 9 hours downtime per year

99.99%

          "Four Nines" availability, no more than 53 minutes downtime per year

99.999%

          "Five Nines" availability, no more than 5 minutes downtime per year

Units of Storage

A bit is a "0" or "1". Data was originally stored as 7-bit characters, but is now in 8-bit "bytes". Multiples of bytes are shown in Table 1.1 below.

Table 1.1: How Big is an Exabyte?	
Kilobyte (KB)	*1,000 bytes OR 10^3bytes* 2 Kilobytes: A Typewritten page. 100 Kilobytes: A low-resolution photograph.
Megabyte (MB)	*1,000,000 bytes OR 10^6 bytes* 1 Megabyte: A small novel OR a 3.5 inch floppy disk. 2 Megabytes: A high-resolution photograph. 5 Megabytes: The complete works of Shakespeare. 10 Megabytes: A minute of high-fidelity sound. 100 Megabytes: 1 meter of shelved books. 500 Megabytes: A CD-ROM.
Gigabyte (GB)	*1,000,000,000 bytes OR 10^9 bytes* 1 Gigabyte: a pickup truck filled with books. 20 Gigabytes: A good collection of the works of Beethoven. 100 Gigabytes: A library floor of academic journals.
Terabyte (TB)	*1,000,000,000,000 bytes OR 10^{12} bytes* 1 Terabyte: 50000 trees made into paper and printed. 2 Terabytes: An academic research library. 10 Terabytes: The print collections of the U.S. Library of Congress. 400 Terabytes: National Climactic Data Center (NOAA) database.
Petabyte (PB)	*1,000,000,000,000,000 bytes OR 10^{15} bytes* 1 Petabyte: 3 years of Earth Observing System (EOS) data (2001). 2 Petabytes: All U.S. academic research libraries. 20 Petabytes: Production of hard-disk drives in 1995. 200 Petabytes: All printed material.
Exabyte (EB)	*1,000,000,000,000,000,000 bytes OR 10^{18} bytes* 2 Exabytes: Total volume of information generated in 1999. 5 Exabytes: All words ever spoken by human beings.

Source: University of Berkeley's 2003 "How Much Information?" study.

The University of Berkeley's 2003 "How Much Information" is an excellent study in the sources, patterns and trends of storage. You can find it at:

http://www2.sims.berkeley.edu/research/projects/how-much-info-2003/execsum.htm

The study indicates many of the examples above were taken from Roy Williams "Data Powers of Ten" web page at Caltech.

Two more units have been defined.

Zettabyte   *1,000,000,000,000,000,000,000 bytes OR 10^{21} bytes*

Yottabyte   *1,000,000,000,000,000,000,000,000 bytes OR 10^{24} bytes*

Note that all units have been standardized as powers of ten. Historical use of powers of 2 have been renamed to avoid confusion; they are now KiB, MiB, GiB, etc.

Quantities of bytes					v·d·e
SI prefixes		**Historical use**		**Binary prefixes**	
Symbol (name)	**Value**	**Symbol**	**Value**	**Symbol (name)**	**Value**
kB (kilobyte)	$1000^1 = 10^3$	KB	$1024^1 = 2^{10}$	KiB (kibibyte)	2^{10}
MB (megabyte)	$1000^2 = 10^6$	MB	$1024^2 = 2^{20}$	MiB (mebibyte)	2^{20}
GB (gigabyte)	$1000^3 = 10^9$	GB	$1024^3 = 2^{30}$	GiB (gibibyte)	2^{30}
TB (terabyte)	$1000^4 = 10^{12}$	TB	$1024^4 = 2^{40}$	TiB (tebibyte)	2^{40}
PB (petabyte)	$1000^5 = 10^{15}$	PB	$1024^5 = 2^{50}$	PiB (pebibyte)	2^{50}
EB (**exabyte**)	$1000^6 = 10^{18}$	EB	$1024^6 = 2^{60}$	EiB (exbibyte)	2^{60}
ZB (zettabyte)	$1000^7 = 10^{21}$	ZB	$1024^7 = 2^{70}$	ZiB (zebibyte)	2^{70}
YB (yottabyte)	$1000^8 = 10^{24}$	YB	$1024^8 = 2^{80}$	YiB (yobibyte)	2^{80}

Source: http://en.wikipedia.org/wiki/Exabyte

Mb and Gb refer to transmission rates. IBM prefers to use Mbps and Gbps to avoid confusion. Each 8-bit byte is transmitted as 10 bits, so 1 Gbps = 100 MB/sec. Some protocols introduce overhead, so the actual data rate is reduced. Typically, NAS runs 40% of rated speed, and iSCSI runs 80% of rated speed. So, for 1 Gbps link, NAS would be 40 MB/sec, iSCSI would be 80 MB/sec, and Fibre Channel would be 100 MB/sec.

Other Books by Tony Pearson

Inside System Storage:
Volume I

Inside System Storage:
Volume II

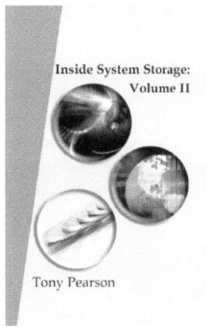

Order Online:
http://www.lulu.com/spotlight/990_tony

Inside System Storage - hosted by Tony Pearson

This blog is for the open exchange of ideas relating to storage and storage networking hardware, software and services. **Tony Pearson** has been working in IBM storage for over 25 years, and helped launch the IBM System Storage™ product line.

This blog-based book, or "blook", comprises nearly a year of posts from *Inside System Storage*, a blog discussing computer storage concepts in general, and IBM System Storage™ products in particular.

And thus, the adventure continues. Tony Pearson, IBM Master Inventor and Senior Managing Consultant, shares his thoughts and experiences about:

- IT storage and storage networking concepts
- IBM strategy, hardware, software and services
- Big Data, Business Analytics, and Cloud Computing
- Disk systems, Tape systems, and storage networking
- Storage and infrastructure management software
- Twitter, Facebook, and other Web 2.0 platforms
- IBM's many alliances, partners and competitors
- How IT storage impacts society and industry

www.ingramcontent.com/pod-product-compliance
Lightning Source LLC
Chambersburg PA
CBHW051221050326
40689CB00007B/749